Women of Science Fiction
and Fantasy Television

ALSO BY KAREN A. ROMANKO

*Television's Female Spies and Crimefighters:
600 Characters and Shows, 1950s to the Present*
(McFarland, 2016)

# Women of Science Fiction and Fantasy Television

*An Encyclopedia of 400 Characters and 200 Shows, 1950–2016*

Karen A. Romanko

McFarland & Company, Inc., Publishers
*Jefferson, North Carolina*

LIBRARY OF CONGRESS CATALOGUING-IN-PUBLICATION DATA

Names: Romanko, Karen A., 1953– author.
Title: Women of science fiction and fantasy television : an encyclopedia of 400 characters and 200 shows, 1950–2016 / Karen A. Romanko.
Description: Jefferson, North Carolina : McFarland & Company, Inc., Publishers, 2019 | Includes index.
Identifiers: LCCN 2019035918 | ISBN 9781476668048 (paperback) ∞ | ISBN 9781476638485 (ebook)
Subjects: LCSH: Women on television. | Women heroes on television. | Science fiction television programs. | Fantasy television programs.
Classification: LCC PN1992.8.W65 R67 2019 | DDC 791.45/6522—dc23
LC record available at https://lccn.loc.gov/2019035918

BRITISH LIBRARY CATALOGUING DATA ARE AVAILABLE

ISBN (print) 978-1-4766-6804-8
ISBN (ebook) 978-1-4766-3848-5

© 2019 Karen A. Romanko. All rights reserved

*No part of this book may be reproduced or transmitted in any form or by any means, electronic or mechanical, including photocopying or recording, or by any information storage and retrieval system, without permission in writing from the publisher.*

Front cover: Katie Saylor as Liana in the 1977 television series *The Fantastic Journey* (National Broadcasting Company)

Printed in the United States of America

*McFarland & Company, Inc., Publishers*
  *Box 611, Jefferson, North Carolina 28640*
  *www.mcfarlandpub.com*

For television's queens
of sf/fantasy
and
for Bob,
my own mad scientist

# Table of Contents

Preface:
What's in This Book
1

Introduction:
A Woman's Place Is in the Home—
Or on a Spaceship
3

**Television's Women
of Science Fiction and Fantasy
by Character Last Name
and by Series Title**
15

Appendix:
Honorable Mentions
219

A Note on Sources
231

Index
233

# Preface: What's in This Book

From Samantha Stephens with her twitchy nose to Buffy Summers and "Mr. Pointy," from Lt. Uhura with her "hailing frequencies" to Wonder Woman and her Lasso of Truth, television's women of science fiction and fantasy are iconic and unforgettable, yet there hasn't been a reference work devoted to them until now.

*Women of Science Fiction and Fantasy Television* shines a light on female television characters who run the gamut from superheroes, extraterrestrials, and time travelers, to witches, vampires, and even mere mortals who deal with the fantastic in their lives every day. The focus is on live-action shows produced in the United States from television's inception through August 2016. Coverage is selective, emphasizing lead and/or groundbreaking characters, with some latitude, since "lead" has become a muddier concept in the ensemble cast era and "groundbreaking" can be in the eye of the beholder. For series considered for the main body of the book, but ultimately excluded, please see the Appendix of honorable mentions.

Every show in the main body of the book receives at least one entry under series title, filed alphabetically, and the listing includes the range of years in production, number of episodes, and the country of origin. Under the title is a listing of series credits, including creator, production company, original U.S. network, and main cast. A synopsis of the series follows, covering notable plot points, important or fun facts, and sometimes critical commentary. Among those plot points, facts, and critical comments, the occasional spoiler creeps in, so readers using the book as a viewer's guide should consider this a universal spoiler alert.

Female characters whose names are highlighted in bold within the series entry also have entries under their own names (last name first) to provide more in-depth coverage, while female characters not receiving separate entries are listed with a cross-reference back to the series title. Thus, readers are able to reference characters by either series title or the character's name.

For the fantasy series *Bewitched*, for example, the main entry is under:

**Bewitched (1964–1972, 254 episodes, USA)**

---

The lead character on *Bewitched*, **Samantha Stephens**, a popular fixture on 60s television, receives her own entry, including observations about her background and personality, under:

**Stephens, Samantha (*Bewitched*)**

---

Samantha's mother Endora, although not the lead character, is a well-known and distinctive supporting character, so she receives a brief description with a cross-reference:

**Endora (*Bewitched*)**

Sartorially resplendent witch, none too happy about her daughter's marriage to a mortal.

See: **Bewitched (1964–1972, 254 episodes, USA)**

---

Cross-references are also provided for alternate series titles, such as:

***The New Adventures of Wonder Woman***

See: **Wonder Woman (1975–1979, 59 episodes, USA)**

---

Entries which begin with numbers are filed as though the numbers are spelled out. The following entry for ***The 4400***, for example, is found under "F," as though it were "Forty-four hundred":

***The 4400* (2004–2007, 44 episodes, USA)**

---

Covering 400 female characters who have appeared in 200 science fiction and fantasy series since the 1950s, this book celebrates the essential contributions of women to SF/fantasy television.

# Introduction: A Woman's Place Is in the Home— Or on a Spaceship

In 1964, NBC commissioned a pilot episode for a new science fiction adventure series called *Star Trek*. In the episode, known as "The Cage," the second-in-command of the USS *Enterprise* was not a certain pointy-eared Vulcan, but rather a pants-wearing, logical woman known simply as Number One (Majel Barrett). NBC rejected this pilot as well as the female command officer, and when the *Star Trek* we know whooshed across our TV screens in 1966, the new woman on the bridge was Lieutenant Uhura (Nichelle Nichols), the starship's "glorified telephone operator," to use Nichols's own words. The pants for women were gone too, replaced by micro-miniskirts with matching panties. It would take 30 years for *Star Trek*'s TV franchise to produce a female starship captain via *Voyager*'s Kathryn Janeway (Kate Mulgrew), and, yes, she wore pants.

Science fiction gives its creators the chance to imagine the roles women might play in future societies when they are not bound by tradition and stereotype. Fantasy offers even more freedom, allowing writers to envision any sort of woman without being shackled by the rules of science. And, yet, televised SF/fantasy, especially prior to the 90s, often revealed a tension between imagination and conformity, where networks and sometimes the creators themselves were bound by their perceptions of what would offend audiences, thereby limiting their vision in the quest for high ratings.

In 1950, when television was still young, only a third of women participated in the labor force. While woman's place may have been in the home at that time, the space operas of the era took women as far away from home as they could get, often across the galaxy, and portrayed them as having scientific achievements, piloting skills, and courage—not merely as damsels in distress. Men were still the leaders, of course, but women were an invaluable part of the team, even if they made their contributions while wearing the ever practical, futuristic short skirt.

*Space Patrol* (1950–1955) featured two such trailblazing women, Tonga (Nina Bara), a reformed criminal once known as "The Lady of Diamonds," and Carol Carlisle (Virginia Hewitt), the all–American girl, both of whom patrolled the dangerous space lanes with Commander Buzz Corry (Ed Kemmer) of the United Planets. Dr. Joan Dale (Margaret Garland) of *Tom Corbett, Space Cadet* (1950–55) taught teenaged cadets at the Space Academy, while contributing brilliant technological innovations and piloting *Orion*, her own rocketship. *Rocky Jones, Space Ranger* (1954) had it's own all–American girl with Vena Ray (Sally Mansfield), the spirited translator and navigator of the rocketship *Orbit Jet*, but also featured an arch villainess in Cleolanthe (Patsy Parsons), the beautiful and bejeweled queen of the planet Ophiuchus. In *Flash Gordon* (1954–1955), Dale Arden (Irene Champlin), a scientist for the Galactic Bureau of Investigation, served as a true partner to the hunky title character (Steve Holland), while battling German-accented villains in the far reaches of space.

Lois Lane also worked outside the home, albeit closer to home, in *Adventures of Superman* (1952–1958). Lois was a reporter for *The Daily Planet* in Metropolis, working beside newsman Clark Kent (George Reeves), who just happened to be Superman, the Man of Steel. As portrayed by Phyllis Coates in the first season, Lois was one tough cookie, who didn't wait for Superman to rescue her and took a swing at bad guys about once per episode. After Coates departed the series due to other commitments, her successor in the role, Noel Neill, portrayed a softer Lois Lane, still out to best Clark in the newsroom, but more demure and with a developing romantic attraction to Superman. Neill's Lois was the typical single woman of the 50s (except that she knew a superhero), while Coates's Lane was ahead of her time and would have been at home in the ladies-with-attitude era of our new millennium.

Although *The Feminine Mystique* (1963) by Betty Friedan had offered some cautions on the "housewife as career" option for American women, domesticity was in bloom on 60s television, especially when it came to fantasy sitcoms, which were all the rage. Samantha Stephens (Elizabeth Montgomery), a bona fide witch, had promised to give up her powers in favor of suburban bliss with husband Darrin (Dick York) in *Bewitched* (1964–1972). Morticia Addams (Carolyn Jones) was a traditional stay-at-home mom like June Cleaver—traditional, except for the fact that she wore tentacled dresses and cultivated a carnivorous plant in *The Addams Family* (1964–1966). Lily Munster (Yvonne De Carlo), the daughter of Dracula and wife of the Frankenstein monster, "dusted" by spreading dirt around the house in *The Munsters* (1964–1966).

The female protagonists of 60s fantasy sitcoms always had naysayers around them who tried to curtail their special powers, which were seen as a nuisance in the normal world. In *Bewitched*, Samantha, her mother Endora (Agnes Moorehead), and daughter Tabitha (Erin Murphy) all ran afoul of Darrin's shortsighted "no witchcraft" policy. Jeannie (Barbara Eden), the personal "genie" for astronaut Tony Nelson (Larry Hagman) in *I Dream of Jeannie* (1965–1970), often caused problems for her "master," especially at NASA, by attempting to fulfill his every wish. In *The Flying Nun* (1967–1970), Sister Bertrille (Sally Field), a novice nun in Puerto Rico, learned that her habit gave her the ability to fly, much to the consternation of her mother superior (Madeleine Sherwood).

Domesticity may have been fine for the suburbs, but it didn't mix well with espionage in the jet-setting world of 60s spy-fi. Television's female spies of the era were single, beautiful, stylish, and able to take care of themselves—when allowed. Cathy Gale (Honor Blackman) and Emma Peel (Diana Rigg) used their judo skills and high IQs in equal measure, when confronted with outré crimes in *The Avengers* (1961–1969), a British import. But April Dancer (Stefanie Powers) was more confused about how a "girl" spy should comport herself in *The Girl from U.N.C.L.E.* (1966–1967), often content to await rescue by partner Mark Slate (Noel Harrison). Cinnamon Carter (Barbara Bain), a former top model, was a seasoned operative with the Impossible Missions Force, able to resist psychological torture if need be in *Mission: Impossible* (1966–1973). Agent 99 (Barbara Feldon) was brainier than her bumbling partner Maxwell Smart (Don Adams) in *Get Smart* (1965–1970), usually making the brilliant deductions, while Max handled the fisticuffs. She did break the mold for 60s female spies, however, going on to get married and later giving birth to twins as TV's first "spy mom."

In addition to a spy mom, 60s television also produced a "space mom"—Maureen Robinson (June Lockhart) on *Lost in Space* (1965–1968). Although the earliest episodes mentioned Maureen's PhD, her main jobs were preparing meals, tending the garden, and fretting over the safety/whereabouts of her children on an uncharted planet. Like Maureen's daughter, Judy (Marta Kristen), most other female space travelers on 60s TV were unmarried, including Lieutenant Uhura of *Star Trek* (1966–1969). Although Uhura wasn't much of a trailblazer when it came to her job as a "glorified telephone operator" (albeit on a starship), she certainly broke new ground as an African American woman, moving beyond the traditional TV role of domestic servant with her portrayal of a bridge officer, equal in dignity, if not always in rank, with other members of the crew.

With the second wave of feminism, a.k.a. the Women's Liberation Movement, in full swing during the 70s, a spate of female superheroes hit the small screen, and as lead characters, to boot. They were gorgeous, sweet as apple pie, and slender (never brawny), but they got to engage in modest action, which was something new, especially on American television. For the younger set, there was *Isis* (1975–1976), wherein Andrea Thomas (JoAnna Cameron), just your average high school science teacher, transformed herself into the goddess of the title, gaining limitless abilities to fight evil (or at least the bad choices of her students). Also aimed at the Saturday-morning crowd was *Electra Woman and Dyna Girl* (1976), originally broadcast as part of *The Krofft Supershow*, which brought us a pair of female caped crusaders, Electra Woman (Deidre Hall) and Dyna Girl (Judy Strangis), who fought crime with an array of gadgets. *The Bionic Woman* (1976–1978) entertained adults (and kids) in the evening, with Lindsay Wagner as Jaime Sommers, a former tennis player fitted with cybernetic replacement parts after an accident, parts which gave her special abilities and a new career as a secret agent.

Wonder Woman (Lynda Carter) wore her feminist heart on her sleeve (or would have if she'd worn a sleeve) on *Wonder Woman* (1975–1979). "Women are the wave of the future and sisterhood is stronger than anything," she said in the pilot movie for the series. Although Wonder Woman had grown up in a female-only society of Amazons, she'd left her home on Paradise Island to help Major Steve Trevor (Lyle Waggoner) in America's fight against the Nazis during World War II. Wonder Woman frequently rescued Steve from dangerous situations, thereby reversing the "damsel in distress" trope so popular at the time. In the second season, the series flashed forward 30 years to the 70s, where Wonder Woman found a new Trevor to assist, Steve Jr. (Waggoner again), in his job for the U.S. Inter-Agency Defense Command. The camp quotient rose even higher here than in the first season, with Hitler clones, diabolical rock stars, and robot hijinks, while the feminist aphorisms diminished. Season three was more youth-oriented, with lots of teenage boys in trouble and even a special skateboarding costume (cool!) for Wonder Woman. While Carter was iconic in her role, a more consistent identity would have enhanced the character's already trailblazing stature.

There was (and still is) a difference of opinion on whether *Wonder Woman* was truly a feminist statement. Some feminists criticized Wonder Woman's skimpy costume (which got skimpier in season two) and its obvious purpose of attracting the male gaze. A similar difference of opinion exists on *Star Maidens*

(1976), a lesser-known UK/West German import that ran in U.S. syndication. Like *Wonder Woman*, *Star Maidens* featured female leads in revealing costumes and portrayed a female-centric society. *Star Maidens* went a step further, however, by making men subservient to women, not on Earth, but on the planet Medusa, and by depicting the males as sex objects. (That'll teach 'em!) Pretty much everyone agreed that *Star Maidens* and *Wonder Woman* were campy, but the agreement ended there. The messages the shows conveyed were sometimes muddled due to the collaborative nature of the television business. Then, too, what is and isn't feminist is often in the eye of the beholder.

Except for *Star Maidens*, space operas of the 70s featured male leads, although a few women succeeded in attaining co-starring status. *Space: 1999* (1975–1977) starred Martin Landau as Commander John Koenig and Barbara Bain as Dr. Helena Russell, medical chief of Moonbase Alpha, which was hurtling through space because of a nuclear accident. *Buck Rogers in the 25th Century* (1979–1981) featured Gil Gerard as Captain Buck Rogers and Erin Gray as Colonel Wilma Deering, commander of Earth's space defenses after a—nuclear—war. (A science-fiction trope is emerging.) Not only did the actresses have better billing, but their characters had higher ranks than Lieutenant Uhura and Nurse Chapel had enjoyed ten years earlier on *Star Trek*. And the space opera short skirts had finally been replaced by pants, although the pants were usually of the slinky catsuit variety, especially for Colonel Deering, because, above all else, women must look sexy while roaming the galaxy.

The 80s served as an interregnum between the superhero 70s and the action-hero 90s for women of SF/fantasy television. Wonder Woman and the Bionic Woman were gone, and their 80s sisters returned to the more traditional role of "superhero's girlfriend." In *The Greatest American Hero* (1981–1983), William Katt portrayed a schoolteacher who became a reluctant superhero after receiving a special suit from aliens, while Connie Sellecca was his lawyer-girlfriend and sometimes helper. *Superboy* (1988–1992) rewound the adventures of the Man of Steel back to his Boy of Steel days, focusing on the college adventures of Clark Kent (John Haymes Newton) and his high school girlfriend Lana Lang (Stacy Haiduk) as they battled various baddies between classes.

Although women were the second bananas in the superhero shows of the decade, they managed to be the center of attention in SF/fantasy sitcoms. "Little women," peculiar little women, were the focus of kid-oriented comedies, as science fiction got a "terminal" case of the cutes. In *Small Wonder* (1985–1989), Tiffany Brissette portrayed a 10-year-old girl who was actually a sophisticated robot adopted by her creator's family. *Out of This World* (1987–1991) starred Maureen Flannigan as a 13-year-old girl with special powers inherited from her extraterrestrial father.

Fantasy caught the sitcom bug as well, but here the peculiar women were all grown up. *Jennifer Slept Here* (1983–1984) starred Ann Jillian as Jennifer Farrell, a former movie star, now poltergeist, who haunted her Beverly Hills manse and dispensed advice to teenage occupant Joey Elliott (John P. Navin, Jr.). In *Down to Earth* (1984–1987), Carol Mansell portrayed angel-in-waiting Ethel MacDoogan, who hoped to earn her wings by helping a family on Earth and especially its youngest, Jay Jay Preston (Randy Josselyn). *The Charmings* (1987–1988) featured two peculiar women, Snow White (Caitlin O'Heaney) and Queen Lillian (Judy Parfitt), who had been transported to modern-day California along with the rest of the Charming clan because of the Queen's too-powerful curse. (Shades of *Once Upon a Time*.)

The science fiction dramas of the decade included women who were so peculiar that they were out of this world. *V* (1984–1985) featured Diana (Jane Badler), supreme commander of the "visitors," aliens who looked like humans, but were actually carnivorous reptiles underneath their thin skins. *Star Trek: The Next Generation* (1987–1994) beamed us Deanna Troi (Marina Sirtis), a half-human/half-alien (Betazoid), who had the ability to sense people's emotions and served as the *Enterprise*'s counselor/psychologist. Troi wore various slinky, low-cut bodysuits, in keeping with space opera's sexy costuming tradition for women, if not with the usual sartorial standards of the psychology profession. (What would Freud say?)

The 90s were a watershed period for women on science fiction and fantasy television. Strong female characters became the order of the day, and women flourished as series leads.

Female action heroes returned after a decade of absence, and displayed more convincing physical power than had their 70s predecessors.

Xena (Lucy Lawless) slashed her way across the ancient world in *Xena: Warrior Princess* (1995–2001), battling mortals and gods alike, to help the helpless while atoning for a prior life of evil. Gabrielle (Renée O'Connor) accompanied Xena on her amazingly far-flung travels, starting out as a naïve peasant girl, but going on to become an Amazon warrior in her own right. Xena was as tough as any man, and her height in addition to her toned, but not willowy body, made her look convincing as a warrior. Still, like Wonder Woman before her, Xena did spur disagreement over whether she was truly a feminist icon. Once again there was concern over a costume, this time a revealing leather bustier-minidress, and Gabrielle's clothing became more eye-popping as the seasons wore on too. The series also prompted debate over whether Xena and Gabrielle were lovers—a relationship which was hinted at, but never spelled out in the series.

Fantasy television's second female warrior of the decade didn't exactly look the part. In *Buffy the Vampire Slayer* (1997–2003), Buffy Summers (Sarah Michelle Gellar) learned that she was "The Slayer," a girl endowed with special powers to fight vampires, demons, and a panoply of evil creatures. Buffy's skills had been handed to her by fate, but it was more delicious that she was a petite, blonde cheerleader, the stereotypical horror victim turned modern horror savior. Since Buffy's high school was located directly over a Hellmouth, she had plenty of slaying to keep her busy, and she called upon a close-knit circle of friends, nicknamed the Scooby Gang, to help her with occult research and even serve as an army when needed. One of the Scoobies, Willow Rosenberg (Alyson Hannigan), began to discover that she had magical powers, and later embarked upon a lesbian relationship with another witch, a pairing portrayed in a realistic way (witchcraft aside) rather than as sensationalistic ratings fodder.

Witches, in fact, cast a spell on television in the 90s, as they became the subjects of two series that were particularly popular with young females. In *Sabrina the Teenage Witch* (1996–2003), Sabrina Spellman (Melissa Joan Hart) discovered on her 16th birthday that she was a witch, and spent the rest of the series learning how to wield her powers while navigating two worlds, the mortal one and the magical "Other Realm." *Charmed* (1998–2006) featured the beautiful Halliwell sisters (Shannen Doherty, Alyssa Milano and Holly Marie Combs), who learned they were witches with the "Power of Three," once they had reunited as twentysomethings in their ancestral home.

This sudden onset of power, "girl power," was a prevalent metaphor on 90s television. In addition to Buffy, Sabrina, and the Halliwell sisters, Alex Mack (Larisa Oleynik) experienced a surge of power(s) in *The Secret World of Alex Mack* (1994–1998), but not as the result of a supernatural occurrence. Alex, a junior high school student, received her strange gifts, such as telekinesis and levitation, because she was accidentally doused with a top-secret chemical from a nearby factory.

Of course, female TV heroes of the 90s weren't just celebrated for physical strength or supernatural abilities—some had BRAIN power. In *The X-Files* (1993–2002, 2016–), FBI Agent Dana Scully (Gillian Anderson), a medical doctor, investigated weird, unsolved cases with her trademark intelligence and rationalism. Scully became the thinking person's sex symbol, although (or maybe because) she wore only conservative suits. *So Weird* (1999–2001) featured Cara DeLizia as teenager Fi Phillips, a mini–Scully, who investigated paranormal activity with her trusty laptop and even engaged in that favorite 90s pastime—witchcraft—with abilities inherited from her grandmother.

In 1995, *Star Trek*'s television franchise introduced its first female captain and series lead, Kathryn Janeway, in *Star Trek: Voyager* (1995–2001). A former science officer, Janeway was tough and by the book, believing that rules and ethics still applied, even while her starship was stranded far from home. She had a regal bearing, but was cranky without her coffee, famously saying "there's coffee in that nebula," when depleted energy reserves were affecting food preparation. In the course of their adventures, Janeway and company rescued a human/Borg (cybernetic organism), known as Seven of Nine (Jeri Ryan), who joined *Voyager*'s crew. Seven of Nine adopted a skin-tight, silver bodysuit that left little to the imagination (and made Ryan an omnipresent sex symbol). Janeway, on the other hand, wore the conservative Starfleet uniform of military-style jacket and pants, which took her light years away from Uhura's miniskirt of the original series. *Voyager* took two steps forward and one step back in regard to practical space opera costuming for women, but it made one giant leap on the girl power—make that woman power—front with its commanding, indomitable Captain Janeway.

Women of color made some small progress as series leads on SF/fantasy television in the 90s, although not on the major networks. *Beyond Reality* (1991–1993), a USA Network offering, starred African American actress Shari Belafonte as Laura Wingate, a university professor who investigated reports of ghosts, telekinesis, and other weird phenomena with her skeptical associate J.J. Stillman (Carl Marotte). Tia Carrere, an actress of Filipino, Chinese, and Spanish descent, portrayed professor, archaeologist, and adventurer Sydney Fox in *Relic Hunter* (1999–2002), a first-run syndication series. Sydney was the Indiana Jones of the piece, using both brains and brawn, the latter in the form of martial arts skills, to battle evil competitors, while her diffident assistant Nigel Bailey (Christien Anholt) had the "damsel in distress" role usually reserved for women.

In the new millennium, actresses of color emerged as lead characters on the major networks, albeit sporadically. Jessica Alba, an actress of Mexican-American descent, starred in the Fox network series *Dark Angel* (2000–2002) as Max Guevara, a genetically enhanced supersoldier, who tries to stay one step ahead of her former captors. Oscar-winner Halle Berry brought her movie-star wattage to the small screen in the CBS series *Extant* (2014–2015), portraying Molly Woods, an astronaut who returns to Earth inexplicably pregnant. Nicole Beharie was Abbie Mills, a police lieutenant called upon to fight the coming apocalypse alongside Ichabod Crane (Tom Mison) in Fox's *Sleepy Hollow* (2013– ). While a forceful presence and role model as an African American detective, Beharie's character was written out of the series after the third season, shocking and disappointing fans, who noticed that *Sleepy Hollow* had diminished its roles for actors of color since the first season.

On cable's Disney Channel, African American actress Raven-Symoné (credited simply as "Raven"), once of *The Cosby Show*, made a big splash as

Raven Baxter, a psychic teen with cloudy clairvoyance in *That's So Raven* (2003–2007). Baxter's flamboyant personality, flair for fashion, and catchphrase-littered speech (oh, snap!) made her a favorite with the younger set. Grown-ups noticed too, and the NAACP bestowed five of its Image Awards between 2004 and 2008 to Raven-Symoné in the Outstanding Performance by a Youth category. She holds the record for most wins to this day.

Disney found success with another teen queen, Selena Gomez, in *Wizards of Waverly Place* (2007–2012), a two-time Emmy winner for Outstanding Children's Program. Gomez portrayed Alex Russo, a pretty underachiever living in Greenwich Village, who went to school like other kids, but also competed with her two brothers to become the Family Wizard. Alex followed in the footsteps of other sitcom spellcasters, such as Samantha Stephens and Sabrina Spellman, who used magic to solve problems, only to create more problems. She was of mixed lineage, with a Mexican mortal mom, and an Italian wizarding dad. Selena Gomez, also of Mexican and Italian heritage (but not descended from wizards, as far as we know), won the ALMA (American Latino Media Arts Award) in 2009 for her positive portrayal of a Latina in a television comedy.

Lesbian and bisexual characters gained prominence at the turn of the 21st century after some implied appearances during the 1990s. Xena and Gabrielle had been constant companions in *Xena: Warrior Princess*, but a sexual relationship was never depicted on screen, although many fans had assumed (and even insisted) it was there. Similar assumptions were made about Susan Ivanova (Claudia Christian) of *Babylon 5* (1994–1998), who hosted a sleepover for Talia Winters (Andrea Thompson), but had disappeared during the night, leaving matters to viewers' imaginations. Jadzia Dax (Terry Farrell) shared a "lesbian" kiss with Lenara Kahn (Susanna Thompson) on *Star Trek: Deep Space Nine* (1993–1999), but Dax had been a male in a prior incarnation (long story), leaving observers wondering if this truly constituted a same-sex kiss.

In the next decade, lesbian and bisexual relationships weren't just implied—they were clearly depicted. *Buffy the Vampire Slayer* had introduced the apparently straight character of Willow Rosenberg in 1997, but starting in 2000, Willow had embarked upon a love affair with fellow witch Tara Maclay (Amber Benson), culminating in a watershed on-screen kiss in "The Body" (2001). *Hex* (2004–2005) featured another important kiss, this one between Thelma Bates (Jemima Rooper), a boarding school ghost, and Cassie Hughes (Christina Cole), her former roommate, who herself had been granted a brief stay in the spirit realm. *Lost Girl* (2010–2016) chronicled the adventures of pansexual succubus Bo Dennis (Anna Silk), who learned self-control from her lover Lauren Lewis (Zoie Palmer), so she wouldn't accidentally kill her partners during sexual encounters. *The 100* (2014– ) featured the first bisexual lead on network

TV in Clarke Griffin (Eliza Taylor), but created controversy when Griffin's female lover was killed, a victim of "dead lesbian syndrome," many thought, a TV affliction wherein lesbian characters meet too frequent demises (as had *Buffy*'s Tara).

Despite the trend toward more diverse casts, SF/fantasy shows in the new millennium didn't offer many opportunities for older women, continuing a long-standing tradition. While mystery series through the decades had managed to produce a few leading roles for women over 50 (and even 60), such as Jessica Fletcher in *Murder, She Wrote* (1984–1996), Vera Stanhope in *Vera* (2011– ), and various incarnations of Miss Marple, SF/fantasy was pretty much a young woman's game. Agnes Moorehead, while not the lead character in *Bewitched*, was one exception, a memorable and formidable presence as Endora, witch, mother, grandmother, and mother-in-law, all to son-in law Darrin's dismay. Another screen actress, Joan Bennett, received top billing (amongst a large ensemble cast) as Elizabeth Collins Stoddard, matriarch of a wealthy, but cursed family, in *Dark Shadows* (1966–1971). Almost three decades later Della Reese portrayed Tess, a tough, but caring supervisor to apprentice angel Monica (top-billed Roma Downey) in *Touched by an Angel* (1994–2003). Otherwise, older women were usually consigned to smaller roles, such as Grandmama Addams (Blossom Rock) on *The Addams Family*, and there were few such parts at that.

Flash forward to the 21st century, and there's not much improvement. Older women, if you can call them that, sometimes appear among the large ensemble casts of science fiction series, but usually they are barely 50 (and look younger). Mary McDonnell, age 52 at the time, portrayed Laura Roslin, President of the Twelve Colonies, in *Battlestar Galactica* (2004–2009), with top billing going to Edward James Olmos as William Adama. Ming-Na Wen, also in her early 50s, stars as Melinda May, pilot, weapons expert, and right-hand woman to Phil Coulson (Clark Gregg) in *Agents of S.H.I.E.L.D.* (2013– ). Paige Turco, born in 1965, portrays Abby Griffin, medical officer and mother of lead character Clarke Griffin, both survivors of a nuclear apocalypse in *The 100*. Rarely do we see women over 60, and when we do, they're usually in supporting roles, such as CCH Pounder, who was a recurring, but unforgettable presence in *Warehouse 13* (2009–2014) as Irene Frederic, a woman who (appropriately enough) never seemed to age, although Pounder turned 60 midway through the show's five seasons.

In 2015, ABC brought *Agent Carter*, a spin-off from the film *Captain America: The First Avenger*, to the small screen. Peggy Carter (Hayley Atwell), a secret agent with the Strategic Scientific Reserve (SSR) in 1946, was mourning the (apparent) death of her true love, Steve Rogers/Captain America (Chris Evans). She returned after World War II to an office full of men who underestimated her investigative abilities and asked her to make coffee. It was the men who were out of their depth, however, since under their noses Peggy was on a clandestine crusade to clear the name of Howard Stark (Dominic Cooper), a Howard Hughes–esque inventor accused of treason.

Carter, a character set in the 40s, but depicted in the new millennium, was perfectly placed to comment on the history of women on and off television in the postwar years. She often highlighted the sexism of her colleagues, even if the word "sexism" wasn't used in that era, but one speech in particular transcended the rest. "You think you know me, but I've never been more than what each of you has created. To you, I'm the stray kitten, left on your doorstep to be protected. The secretary turned damsel in distress. The girl on the pedestal, transformed into some daft whore."

Peggy Carter reminded us. Let's not forget where we've been.

# Television's Women of Science Fiction and Fantasy by Character Last Name and by Series Title

**Adair, Devon** (*Earth 2*)
Billionaire who leads an expedition to an Earth-like planet in hopes of curing her son of an illness.
See: *Earth 2* (**1994–1995, 22 episodes, USA**)

**Adams, Bo** (*Believe*)
Young girl sought by a secret organization because of her prodigious psychic abilities.
See: *Believe* (**2014, 13 episodes, USA**)

**The Addams Family (1964–1966, 64 episodes, USA)**
*Based on:* The *New Yorker* cartoons of Charles Addams
*Created by:* David Levy
*Production Co.:* Filmways Television
*Originally Aired:* ABC
*Main Cast:* John Astin, Carolyn Jones, Jackie Coogan, Ted Cassidy, Blossom Rock, Ken Weatherwax, Lisa Loring

A weird little comedy gem from the 60s, *The Addams Family* stars Carolyn Jones as **Morticia Addams** and John Astin as her husband Gomez, eccentric (to say the least) soulmates. Morticia and Gomez live with their children, extended family, and servants at 0001 Cemetery Lane, a street as dark as the Cleavers' is bright. Black-clad Morticia is a refined woman who specializes in cultivating roses, which she beheads, preferring to keep their beautiful thorns. Cigar-chomping Gomez, a wealthy man who never seems to work, pursues fascinating hobbies as well, such as blowing up model trains, when he's not distracted by his scintillating "Tish." Other members of the bizarre household include Morticia's Uncle Fester (Jackie Coogan), who can illuminate a lightbulb by placing it in his mouth and Grandmama Addams (Blossom Rock), who likes to brew potions. Lurch (Ted Cassidy), their harpsichord-playing butler, presents his towering, ghastly frame at the sound of the servant's gong. (His "You rang?" became a popular catchphrase.) Equally indispensable is "Thing" (usually played by Ted Cassidy, but credited as "Itself"), a disembodied hand which pops up from strategically placed boxes to lift a phone receiver or pour some tea.

The Addamses prefer to stay insulated from the outside world, but sometimes interlopers, in the form of truant officers, salespeople, burglars, and even spies, pay a call on this creepy and "kooky, mysterious and spooky" clan. The result is a fiendishly funny clash of cultures.

See also: **Addams, Morticia (*The Addams Family*)**

Morticia Addams (Carolyn Jones) trades her signature tentacled dress for a Santa suit when *The Addams Family* celebrates Christmas (ABC Television).

### Addams, Morticia (*The Addams Family*)

Morticia Addams (Carolyn Jones) is just your typical 60s suburban mother, typical, that is, if your address is 0001 Cemetery Lane. As mothers do, Mrs. Addams keeps a watchful eye on her children, Pugsley (Ken Weatherwax), who enjoys spending time with his exotic pets, including Aristotle, the octopus, and adorable Wednesday (Lisa Loring), who likes to behead her dolls, appropriately named Marie Antoinette and Mary Queen of Scots. Sultry Morticia, who wears a long black dress with fabric tentacles at the bottom of its "hobble skirt," still sparks ardor in husband Gomez (John Astin), moving him to uncontrollable (G-rated) passion when she speaks French. Like her Uncle Fester (Jackie Coogan), who has his own illumination abilities, Morticia can light candles with her fingertips and also loves a good smoke— no cigarettes required, since the smoke emanates directly from her body. She has a green thumb, which she manages to keep attached to her hand while feeding her carnivorous plant, an African Strangler she calls Cleopatra. At the same time, Morticia is a sensitive soul, who will not allow her children to be subjected to life's cruelties, such as accounts of dragon-slaying: "What a lovely name, Grimm. How could he write such terrible stories?"

In a less "ooky" world, Morticia Addams might have been June Cleaver.

See also: *The Addams Family* (1964–1966, 64 episodes, USA)

## Addams, Morticia (*The New Addams Family*)

Darkly seductive wife and doting mother in a household full of oddball characters and creatures.

See: *The New Addams Family* (1998–1999, 65 episodes, Canada/USA)

## *The Adventures of Superboy*

See: *Superboy* (1988–1992, 100 episodes, USA)

## *Adventures of Superman* (1952–1958, 104 episodes, USA)

*Based on:* The DC Comics character Superman created by Jerry Siegel, Joe Shuster
*Originally Aired:* In Syndication
*Main Cast:* George Reeves, Phyllis Coates, Noel Neill, Jack Larson, John Hamilton, Robert Shayne

**Lois Lane (Phyllis Coates) and The Man of Steel (George Reeves) investigate strange mysteries in the "dark series" of *Adventures of Superman* (Motion Pictures for Television/Photofest).**

The Man of Steel leaped to the small screen for the first time in this classic 50s series, starring George Reeves as Superman and his alter ego, newspaper reporter Clark Kent. Clark works for *The Daily Planet* in Metropolis, where he gets the inside scoop on mysteries, crimes, and disasters which may require Superman's prodigious powers for resolution. Working with Kent at The Planet are **Lois Lane** (Phyllis Coates and later Noel Neill), an experienced newshound, Jimmy Olsen (Jack Larson), a cub reporter, and Perry White (John Hamilton), the newspaper's irascible editor. The first season of Superman has a noir sensibility, dark in both look and tone, focusing on mystery and crime, and directed at an adult audience. Lois Lane (Phyllis Coates) has her inquisitive nose buried deep in most of the mysteries and crimes during this "dark series" of *Adventures of Superman*. Later seasons, however, are lighter in nature, and with the shift to color episodes in 1954, the series takes on a more cartoonish feel, aimed at the young fans who were flocking to the show at the time.

Light or dark, the episodes lived on in reruns and now, in the digital age, are immortal, just like the Man of Steel himself. George Reeves died in 1959 of an apparent suicide, so he never got to see that *Adventures of Superman* would live so far beyond him.

See also: **Lane, Lois (*Adventures of Superman*)**

## *Agent Carter* (2015–2016, 18 episodes, USA)
*Based on:* The Marvel Comics character created by Stan Lee, Jack Kirby
*Created by:* Christopher Markus, Stephen McFeely
*Production Co.:* ABC Studios, Marvel Television
*Originally Aired:* ABC
*Main Cast:* Hayley Atwell, James D'Arcy, Chad Michael Murray, Enver Gjokaj, Shea Whigham, Wynn Everett, Reggie Austin, Bridget Regan, Dominic Cooper

Hayley Atwell portrays Peggy Carter, an agent with the Strategic Scientific Reserve (SSR) in 1946. Peggy is mourning the (apparent) death of her true love, Steve Rogers/Captain America (Chris Evans), which occurred in the Marvel Cinematic Universe film *Captain America: The First Avenger*. She returns after World War II to an office full of men who underestimate her investigative abilities and treat her like an unqualified assistant. It's the men, however, who are out of their depth, since under their noses Peggy is on a clandestine crusade to clear the name of Howard Stark (Dominic Cooper), a Howard Hughes–esque inventor and weapons-maker accused of treason. In this personal mission, Peggy has the assistance of Edwin Jarvis (James D'Arcy), Stark's prim British butler, who exchanges witty banter with Carter even while their lives are in danger.

The scene shifts from New York to Los Angeles in season two, where Carter works with Daniel Sousa (Enver Gjokaj), chief of the SSR's local office. While these two try to figure out exactly what their relationship is, their investigations lead to a new and deadly physical force called Zero Matter and a screen actress named Whitney Frost (Wynn Everett). Frost, who is also a brilliant scientist (shades of Hedy Lamarr), eventually absorbs the Zero Matter into her body, causing all kinds of problems for the SSR, and ultimately goes insane for her trouble.

Agent 19

**Peggy Carter (Hayley Atwell) runs a clandestine operation under the noses of her male colleagues (left to right, Enver Gjokaj, Chad Michael Murray, and Shea Whigham) in *Agent Carter* (ABC/Photofest).**

*Agent Carter*'s emphasis on story over frenetic action makes it a breath of fresh air within the Marvel Cinematic Universe, but may also have doomed it with the franchise's mayhem-loving fans. The series was canceled after two seasons, totaling a mere 18 episodes. While *Agent Carter*'s television stay was short, the series is unforgettable both for its beautiful 40s aesthetic and its skill at portraying strong, smart women without forgetting the limitations they faced during the pre-feminist era.

"I conducted my own investigation because no one listens to me. I got away with it because no one looks at me. Because unless I have your reports, your coffee, or your lunch, I'm invisible."

We'll miss you, Peg.

## Agent 99 (*Get Smart*)

Agent 99 works for super-secret government agency CONTROL alongside "top" operative Maxwell Smart (Agent 86) to battle the evil forces of KAOS. As portrayed by Barbara Feldon, Agent 99 is long, cool, and competent, while Don Adams's Max is none of those things. For some unfathomable reason, though, the sleek 99, whose real name is never revealed in the series, is enamored of her bumbling partner. In "Too Many Chiefs" (1965), Agent 99, sporting a stylish holster/belt accented by a lace hanky, reveals her jealous side when Max must guard a beautiful refugee in his apartment. It's Max's turn to be jealous in "Kisses for KAOS" (1966), when 99 must feign interest in a wealthy art gallery owner to investigate exploding paintings. Otherwise, it's business as usual, as in "Shipment to Beirut" (1966), when 99 goes undercover as a fashion model to thwart a smuggling operation and is almost turned into a mannequin for her trouble. "With Love and Twitches" (1968) finds the couple finally ready to wed, but 99's big day may be in jeopardy when an important map surfaces as a rash on Maxwell's body. Agent 99 and her unlikely hubby go on to produce even more unlikely spy-twins in the two-part "And Baby Makes Four" (1969), proving that 99 is a trooper 100 percent of the time.

See also: *Get Smart* (1965–1970, 138 episodes, USA)

### Agents of S.H.I.E.L.D. (2013– , 66 episodes, USA)

*Based on:* The comic book feature "Nick Fury, Agent of S.H.I.E.L.D." by Stan Lee, Jack Kirby
*Created by:* Joss Whedon, Jed Whedon, Maurissa Tancharoen
*Production Co.:* ABC Studios, Marvel Television, Mutant Enemy Productions
*Originally Aired:* ABC
*Main Cast:* Clark Gregg, Ming-Na Wen, Brett Dalton, Chloe Bennet, Iain De Caestecker, Elizabeth Henstridge, Henry Simmons

The agents of Strategic Homeland Intervention, Enforcement and Logistics Division (S.H.I.E.L.D.) battle threats to the U.S. and planet Earth, such as a CEO who wants to control the planet's gravity, a street performer with pyrokinetic abilities, and an international organization of evildoers with its tentacles in everything (the aptly named, Hydra). It's just your everyday spy outfit—if you're a character in the Marvel Cinematic Universe, that is.

Leading the way for S.H.I.E.L.D. is Agent Phil Coulson (Clark Gregg), who has been mysteriously resurrected after his death in *The Avengers*, the blockbuster movie hit from 2012. Coulson assembles a team of crack field operatives to investigate weird phenomena around the globe, and to dispatch any related threats, whether of this world or someplace more exotic. Melinda May (Ming-Na Wen), nicknamed "The Cavalry," is Coulson's right-hand woman, a veteran pilot and weapons expert, who is loyal to Coulson, despite her secret assignment to monitor him after his resurrection. In "Melinda" (2015), the story behind May's nickname is explained,

Ming-Na Wen of *Agents of S.H.I.E.L.D.* in a 2016 public appearance at WonderCon (from a color photograph by Gage Skidmore, CC BY-SA 3.0).

revealing both her bravery, and the lasting trauma she suffered after having to shoot a dangerous child.

Skye (Chloe Bennet), a computer hacker and orphan, is captured by the team, but later joins the unit at Coulson's behest, while continuing to investigate her mysterious origins. Jemma Simmons (Elizabeth Henstridge), the crew's life sciences expert, works closely with Leo Fitz (Iain De Caestecker), the engineering and weapons guy, in this uber-high-tech environment. Coulson's talented, but trouble-prone team chases bad guys while their loyalties are continually questioned and tested. In "Turn, Turn, Turn" (2014), they even learn that one of their own, Grant Ward (Brett Dalton), a specialist in black ops, is actually an agent of the dreaded Hydra.

Although this series is chock full of fancy gadgets, at its core, it's still about that most powerful of weapons—secrets.

## Albright, Mary (*3rd Rock from the Sun*)

Anthropology professor sharing an office with a physics professor, who's actually an extraterrestrial.

See: *3rd Rock from the Sun* (1996–2001, 139 episodes, USA)

## *Alcatraz* (2012, 13 episodes, USA)

*Created by:* Elizabeth Sarnoff, Steven Lilien, Bryan Wynbrandt
*Production Co.:* Bonanza Productions, Bad Robot Productions, Warner Bros. Television
*Originally Aired:* FOX
*Main Cast:* Sarah Jones, Jorge Garcia, Jonny Coyne, Parminder Nagra, Sam Neill, Jason Butler Harner, Robert Forster

Science fiction thriller à la *The 4400*, wherein the prisoners and guards of Alcatraz Federal Penitentiary, all of whom mysteriously disappeared in 1963, suddenly reappear in modern-day San Francisco, without having aged and with no memories of the missing time. Emerson Hauser (Sam Neill) heads a secret government unit tasked with finding and capturing the returning prisoners, known as "63s," who are continuing their criminal ways but with a hidden agenda. SFPD homicide detective Rebecca Madsen (Sarah Jones) is drawn into the Alcatraz mystery while searching for a killer, and has a family member among the returning inmates. Rebecca works with Hauser and Alcatraz historian Dr. Diego "Doc" Soto (Jorge Garcia) to stop the inmates' crime spree and learn the secrets behind their return.

Due to the short run of this series, most of the secrets of the 63s are still safe today.

## *ALF* (1986–1990, 102 episodes, USA)

*Created by:* Paul Fusco, Tom Patchett
*Production Co.:* Alien Productions, Lorimar-Telepictures
*Originally Aired:* NBC
*Main Cast:* Paul Fusco, Max Wright, Anne Schedeen, Andrea Elson, Benji Gregory

What if a furry, sarcastic extraterrestrial came to live with your family, disrupting its suburban bliss? That's the premise of this popular series, which wasn't as popular behind the scenes, due to the technical demands and long hours of working with puppets.

Gordon Shumway, who hails from the recently exploded planet of Melmac, crash-lands on the garage of the Tanner family in the San Fernando Valley. Willie Tanner (Max Wright), the family patriarch, nicknames the visitor ALF (Alien Life Form), and agrees to take him in, although wife Kate (Anne Schedeen) has doubts, and with good reason. ALF (voiced by Paul Fusco) is sloppy, unpleasant, and opinionated, commenting on Earth's customs with his trademark wisecracks. Surliness notwithstanding, ALF does help the family solve its problems, but often because he has an ulterior motive. In "Mother and Child Reunion" (1987), Kate must deal with the arrival of her overbearing mother (Anne Meara), and ALF counsels a confrontational approach, but only so he can get back into the house after exile to the garage. Sometimes his motives are more selfless, as in "Oh, Pretty Woman" (1987), when he enters Tanner daughter Lynn (Andrea Elson) into a beauty contest after she is dumped by her boyfriend for a prettier girl. ALF gets the opportunity to observe customs surrounding human childbirth in "Having My Baby" (1989), when little Eric joins the Tanner family, a plot device added to explain Schedeen's real-life pregnancy.

*ALF* became a minor pop-culture phenomenon, spawning dolls and video games, but cast members couldn't share the joy because they were miserable on set. No one wanted to play second fiddle to a puppet, especially one which required lots of prep time on a set filled with trap doors. Elson developed bulimia and Schedeen called the group a "big, dysfunctional family."

*ALF* learned a lot from these human encounters, perhaps more than was originally intended.

### *Alien Nation* (1989–1990, 22 episodes, USA)
*Based on:* Characters created by Rockne S. O'Bannon
*Created by:* Kenneth Johnson
*Production Co.:* Kenneth Johnson Productions, 20th Century–Fox Television
*Originally Aired:* Fox
*Main Cast:* Gary Graham, Eric Pierpoint, Michele Scarabelli, Lauren Woodland, Sean Six, Terri Treas, Jeff Marcus, Ron Fassler

"Theirs was a slave ship, carrying a quarter million beings, bred to adapt and labor in any environment. But they'd washed ashore on Earth, with no way to get back to where they came from."

*Starsky & Hutch* meets the *Coneheads* in this buddy-cop show with a twist— one of the partners is from another planet! Matthew Sikes (Gary Graham) is a detective for the LAPD whose partner, George Francisco (Eric Pierpoint), is a "Newcomer" from the planet Tencton. The Tenctonese are humanoid, but have large heads with spots on their scalps instead of hair. The Newcomers face prejudice and discrimination in our world, but are trying to adapt to Earth's customs five years after their arrival. Susan Francisco (Michele Scarabelli), George's wife, works in an advertising agency, while raising their two children, Emily (Lauren Woodland), age 9, and

Buck (Sean Six), a troubled teen. Eventually the couple decides to have a third offspring, and their mating ritual involves three parties, Susan, George, and fellow Newcomer Albert Einstein (Jeff Marcus)—no relation to the relativity guy (as far as we know). Pregnant Susan later transfers the incubation pod to George, who gives birth to the child. (Simple!) Romantic rituals are center stage again in "Green Eyes" (1990), when Detective Matt's attraction to Newcomer Cathy Frankel (Terri Treas), a biochemist, leads to a first kiss and emotional complications.

"Green Eyes" ended with a cliffhanger, as a group of human radicals infected Newcomers, including Susan and Emily, with deadly bacteria. At this point, fledgling network Fox canceled the series, which was up against stiff competition from CBS ratings powerhouse *Murphy Brown*. But many thought the series had been canceled too soon, and apparently Fox agreed, bringing *Alien Nation* back for not one, but five TV movies. The first one, *Alien Nation: Dark Horizon* (1994), resolved the "Green Eyes" cliffhanger, sparing the lives of Susan and Emily.

Lucky Newcomers! Humans rarely return from television's cancellation limbo.

**Alonso, Emma (*Every Witch Way*)**
High school student who learns that she is the Chosen One, the world's most powerful witch.
See: ***Every Witch Way* (2014–2015, 85 episodes, USA)**

*Alphas* **(2011–2012, 24 episodes, USA)**
*Created by:* Zak Penn, Michael Karnow
*Production Co.:* BermanBraun, Universal Cable Productions
*Originally Aired:* Syfy
*Main Cast:* David Strathairn, Ryan Cartwright, Warren Christie, Azita Ghanizada, Laura Mennell, Malik Yoba

Science fiction series about people with enhanced natural abilities, known as "Alphas," who work with the Defense Department to fight crimes committed by others of their kind. Dr. Lee Rosen (David Strathairn), a psychiatrist and non–Alpha, leads this exceptional group, serving as neurological expert, counselor, and father figure. Five Alphas fill out the team, including Ryan Cartwright as Gary Bell, an autistic savant with the ability to track communication sources with his mind, and Malik Yoba as Bill Harken, a former FBI agent able to enhance his strength and endurance by amping up his fight-or-flight response. Azita Ghanizada portrays Rachel Pirzad, the "sensitive" Alpha, who can heighten any one of her five senses to track someone by scent or view evidence at a microscopic level. Nina Theroux (Laura Mennell) has the power to "push" people into doing her bidding, which allows her to get past security guards or erase inconvenient memories from witnesses. Together, the team battles Alphas who are unable or unwilling to control their abilities, such as the radical group Red Flag, which espouses the primacy of Alphas. Along the way, Rosen's group wrestles with the problems generated by their own Alpha abilities, such as social isolation, health issues, and lack of self-control.

### Alston, Penny (*Turnabout*)
Cosmetics executive who accidentally switches bodies with her husband thanks to a gypsy's statue.
See: *Turnabout* (1979, 7 episodes, USA)

### Amanda (*Highlander: The Raven*)
A 1200-year-old thief who uses her immortality to battle evil.
See: *Highlander: The Raven* (1998–1999, 22 episodes, Canada/France)

### *Andromeda* (2000–2005, 110 episodes, Canada/USA)
*Created by:* Gene Roddenberry; Robert Hewitt Wolfe
*Production Co.:* Tribune Entertainment, Fireworks Entertainment, et al.
*Originally Aired:* In Syndication (2000–2004), Syfy (2004–2005)
*Main Cast:* Kevin Sorbo, Lisa Ryder, Keith Hamilton Cobb, Lexa Doig, Laura Bertram, Gordon Michael Woolvett, Brandy Ledford

"The long night has come. The Systems Commonwealth, the greatest civilization in history, has fallen. But now one ship, one crew, have vowed to drive back the night and rekindle the light of civilization."

Modern television space opera loves motley crews and abundant concepts, and Gene Roddenberry's *Andromeda* shot for the moon (or sentient sun) with its profusion of worlds, alien races, and themes. Dylan Hunt (Kevin Sorbo), Captain of the Commonwealth starship *Andromeda Ascendant*, had been frozen in time for 300 years before his rescue by the salvage ship *Eureka Maru*. Hunt asks the crew of the *Maru* to join his quest to restore the Systems Commonwealth, a utopian federation comprising three major galaxies, which had fallen to the enemy Nietzscheans during his stasis. Members of the *Maru* decide to comply, but not always with the best of intentions.

Rebecca "Beka" Valentine (Lisa Ryder), Captain of the *Maru*, becomes *Andromeda*'s first officer and pilot, going along, at least initially, to enjoy *Andromeda*'s more comfortable accommodations, while hoping to find a big score along the way. Self-interest is Beka's usual modus operandi, but she develops feelings of loyalty for Dylan, which are tested (naturally). Beka becomes the founding matriarch of the enemy Nietzschean race when her DNA samples travel back in time (long story).

The *Maru*'s Trance Gemini (Laura Bertram), a mysterious alien with pre-cognitive abilities (and a tail), becomes *Andromeda*'s resident medic and botanist. Naïve and purple-skinned at the beginning, Trance later transforms mentally and physically, becoming worldly-wise and golden-skinned, when she changes places with her future self, thanks to a time-folding machine. It turns out that Trance is actually an energy being, the avatar of a sentient sun (another long story).

Rommie (Lexa Doig) is not from the *Maru*, but was part of the original *Andromeda Ascendant* crew—sort of. She started out as a holograph of *Andromeda*'s artificial intelligence system, but became "Rommie" when engineer Seamus Harper (Gordon Michael Woolvett) made her "flesh" in the form of an android, a beautiful android. (Is there any other kind?) Rommie develops emotions, as the best androids do, so she sometimes disagrees with her more logical AI manifestation. Eventually Rommie receives a new android body called Doyle (Brandy Ledford) to cover for Lexa Doig's real-life pregnancy (pregnant androids are hard to explain), but Rommie later returns, and the two droids overcome their differences to work together as dual avatars of the ship.

More long stories later, the Earth is annihilated, but the Commonwealth is saved when Trance uses her Sun to destroy an enemy known as the Abyss.

And you thought your life was complicated.

## *Angel* (1999–2004, 110 episodes, USA)
*Created by:* Joss Whedon, David Greenwalt
*Production Co.:* Mutant Enemy Productions, Sandollar Television, et al.
*Originally Aired:* WB
*Main Cast:* David Boreanaz, Charisma Carpenter, Alexis Denisof, J. August Richards, Amy Acker, Glenn Quinn, Vincent Kartheiser, Andy Hallett

Angel (David Boreanaz), the vampire with a soul, moves from Sunnydale to Los Angeles in this spin-off from *Buffy the Vampire Slayer*. Brooding Angel wants to find redemption in the City of Angel(s), hoping to atone for his bloodthirsty past by helping those afflicted by supernatural forces. Offering help on whom to help is Doyle (Glenn Quinn), a half-demon who receives migraine-inducing visions sent by "The Powers That Be." Doyle's first lead brings Angel face to face with Sunnydale shallow girl **Cordelia Chase** (Charisma Carpenter), who has fallen on hard times while waiting for her big break in Hollywood. After Angel saves Cordelia from a vampire playboy, she hits upon the idea of Angel Investigations (AI), where she will work with Angel and Doyle to save Angeleno souls, at least until she achieves her "inevitable stardom."

As the agency battles vampires, demons, and the evil law firm of Wolfram & Hart, new members join the AI team, including Wesley Wyndam-Pryce (Alexis Denisof), a former Watcher for Buffy, and Charles Gunn (J. August Richards), a gang leader who protects his turf from vamps. The extended team rescues another recruit, Winifred "Fred" Burkle (Amy Acker), from a demon dimension known as Pylea, where she had been held as a slave for five years. Fred, a former UCLA grad student in physics, overcomes the trauma of captivity and re-acclimates to human life in Los Angeles. She becomes a successful strategist, inventor, and warrior for Angel Investigations until her body is taken over by an ancient demon named Illyria.

The show was canceled at that point, but a subsequent comic book series *Angel: After the Fall*, also known as *Angel: Season 6*, picks up the story of Angel, Illyria, et al. after the demonic partners of Wolfram & Hart have sent Los Angeles to Hell. Literally. (No wisecracks.)

Even the WB's pointy stick of cancellation couldn't kill the hunky vampire with a soul.

See also: **Chase, Cordelia (***Buffy the Vampire Slayer*; *Angel***)**

### Angelique (*Dark Shadows*)
Witch in a love/hate relationship with a vampire whose "undeath" she caused via a curse.
See: ***Dark Shadows* (1966–1971, 1225 episodes, USA)**

### ANI (*Mercy Point*)
Android Nursing Interface setting impossible standards for her colleagues on the frontiers of space.
See: ***Mercy Point* (1998–1999, 7 episodes, USA)**

### Anna (*V*)
Beautiful extraterrestrial who seemingly comes in peace, but has plans to conquer Earth.
See: ***V* (2009–2011, 22 episodes, USA)**

### Apple, Gillian (*You Wish*)
Single mother who accidentally releases a genie from 2000 years of captivity.
See: ***You Wish* (1997–1998, 13 episodes, USA)**

### Arden, Dale (*Flash Gordon*)
Scientist and agent for the Galactic Bureau of Investigation who battles exotic villains with a hunky partner.
See: ***Flash Gordon* (1954–1955, 39 episodes, France/USA/West Germany)**

### Ark II (1976, 15 episodes, USA)
*Created by:* Martin Roth
*Production Co.:* Filmation Associates
*Originally Aired:* CBS
*Main Cast:* Terry Lester, Jean Marie Hon, Jose Flores

"For millions of years, Earth was fertile and rich. Then pollution and waste began to take their toll. Civilization fell into ruin. This is the world of the 25th Century."

Apocalypse as the premise for a Saturday morning kiddie show?

It's the year 2476, and the Earth has become an uncivilized wasteland, thanks not to nuclear war, but to pollution and neglect. If that doesn't sound exactly perky, there IS a cool, sleek, high-tech RV called the Ark II and a jetpack called the Jet Jumper to distract the kids from all that bleakness.

For Ark II (the first ark was Noah's, of course), the handful of remaining scientists on Earth have trained three intrepid, young, crew members: Jonah (Terry Lester), the dashing captain, Ruth (Jean Marie Hon), the team's pretty medic and scientist, and Samuel (Jose Flores), the requisite teen genius. Make that four crew members, if you include Adam, the talking, chess-playing chimp. (And apparently we are supposed to include him.) The team looks great in their spandex uniforms (even Adam) and their well-coiffed 'dos (well, not so much Adam), while everyone else is in rags à la *Mad Max*. But our heroes bring the promise of a new civilization, encountering tiny villages suffering from superstition, plague, and technophobia (imagine!), and setting them on the path to tomorrow.

What that tomorrow will be is anyone's guess. After all, as Ruth points out in "The Cryogenic Man" (1976), "There are no Democrats or Republicans anymore...."

Maybe there is hope after all.

### Austen, Kate (*Lost*)

Kate Austen (Evangeline Lilly) is one of 72 survivors of a plane crash on a mysterious (to put it mildly) island in the South Pacific. Kate hadn't been traveling on a pleasure trip—she was flying from Sydney to Los Angeles in the custody of a U.S. Marshal who had been pursuing her for killing her abusive father. The vicissitudes of Kate's prior life have prepared her well for the island's rigors, at least as well as anyone could be prepared for a "smoke monster" that kills, an apocalypse-averting computer system, and MORE. As a quintessential survivor, she becomes a prominent voice among the castaways, along with Jack Shepard (Matthew Fox), a medical doctor, and Jack's rival for her affection, James "Sawyer" Ford (Josh Holloway), a con man. Sawyer calls Kate "Freckles," but her innocent beauty belies both the secrets she keeps and the reserves of strength she calls upon during their many trials, as when she and Sawyer are caged by the nefarious (or are they?) "Others" in "A Tale of Two Cities" (2006). Kate eventually escapes the island with five other castaways, and begins a relationship with Jack, but all six return to save the ones left behind in "316" (2009). She escapes once again in series finale "The End" (parts one and two, 2010), but her "happily ever after" with Jack is more "after" than usual, when she meets Jack in the afterlife, where all the castaways "move on" together.

Kate's smudged good looks, especially her frequent appearances in a dirty tank top, placed her on several lists of "sexiest" TV characters, but her spiritual grit is more attractive still.

See also: ***Lost*** **(2004–2010, 118 episodes, USA)**

### The Avengers (1961–1969, 161 episodes, UK)

*Created by:* Sydney Newman
*Production Co.:* ABC Weekend Television, Associated British Corporation
*Originally Aired:* ABC
*Main Cast:* Patrick Macnee, Ian Hendry, Honor Blackman, Diana Rigg, Linda Thorson

Groundbreaking British spy-fi series known for its wit, style, and strong female characters. Through many incarnations and cast changes, Patrick Macnee is the one *Avengers* constant, portraying John Steed, dapper secret agent and crime fighter. Steed works with a succession of partners, the most notable of whom is Mrs. **Emma Peel** (Diana Rigg), a brilliant, sexy, sardonic, leather-suited, judo-chopping amateur agent. Her immediate predecessor, Dr. **Cathy Gale** (Honor Blackman), an anthropologist, is cut from the same cloth (or leather) in her intelligence, bravery, and martial arts expertise. Tara King (Linda Thorson), Mrs. Peel's successor, is less worldly than Steed's other partners, but is a bona fide, though inexperienced, agent. The various *Avengers* pairings investigate outré crimes and circumstances, such as killer robots, haunted castles, mind-transference devices, machine-gun-wielding nuns, and lethal pussycats. But evildoers are no match for Steed's steel-plated bowler hat, Mrs. Peel's IQ, or Cathy's indomitable spirit.

See also: **Gale, Cathy** (*The Avengers*); **Peel, Emma** (*The Avengers*)

### Babylon 5 (1994–1998, 110 episodes, USA)
*Created by:* J. Michael Straczynski
*Production Co.:* Babylonian Productions, Inc., Warner Bros. Television
*Originally Aired:* PTEN (1994–1997), TNT (1998)
*Main Cast:* Bruce Boxleitner, Claudia Christian, Jerry Doyle, Mira Furlan, Richard Biggs, Andrea Thompson, Bill Mumy, Peter Jurasik, Andreas Katsulas, Stephen Furst, Michael O'Hare, Jason Carter, Tracy Scoggins, Patricia Tallman, Jeff Conaway

"The Babylon Project was our last, best hope for peace. A self-contained world five miles long, located in neutral territory. A place of commerce and diplomacy for a quarter of a million humans and aliens."

Space station Babylon 5 is a nexus for diplomacy, commerce, intrigue, and conflict in the early 23rd century. A human military officer serves as commander of the station, first Jeffrey Sinclair (Michael O'Hare) and later John Sheridan (Bruce Boxleitner). This "shining beacon in space" is also home to alien species, some with long

Captain John Sheridan (Bruce Boxleitner) and Minbari Ambassador Delenn (Mira Furlan) develop an emotional bond while working side by side on space station *Babylon 5* (Warner Bros. Television/Photofest).

histories of hostility, and ambassadors from the great powers serve on Babylon 5's Council, which tries to arbitrate disputes.

Ambassador Delenn (Mira Furlan) represents the Minbari Federation on the Council. Delenn begins her diplomatic work on the station as a full-blooded Minbari, but undergoes a mysterious transformation at the end of the first year, morphing into a Human/Minbari hybrid. Delenn's metamorphosis is emblematic of a secret genetic link between Humans and Minbari, but is also symbolic of the crucial role the two species will play in fighting the Shadows, an ancient, militaristic race which has resurfaced after 1000 years. The Vorlons, who hold a seat on the Babylon 5 Council, test Delenn with torture to assess her readiness for leadership in "Comes the Inquisitor" (1995). Delenn proves she is willing to sacrifice her life to save the life of another, unmotivated by fame and glory. Captain Sheridan passes the same test, showing that he and Delenn are "the right people, in the right place, at the right time," according to their inquisitor, Jack, the Ripper (long story). Delenn and Sheridan marry in "Rising Star" (1997), after forming a new Interstellar Alliance when the Shadows have left the galaxy.

Babylon 5's second in command is Susan Ivanova (Claudia Christian), an exceptional soldier, loyal and honest. Ivanova has latent telepathic abilities, but no love for Psi Corps, the earth agency which controls the lives of telepaths and ruined her mother's life, leading her to suicide. Susan warms up a bit to Psi Corps, however, or at least to one of its members, Talia Winters (Andrea Thompson), with whom she begins a friendship and possibly more. But her hatred for the agency is renewed when Talia reveals a deadly sleeper personality, which obliterates all aspects of her true identity in "Divided Loyalties" (1995). Ivanova's "all love is unrequited" pattern reaches its unfortunate nadir with Marcus Cole (Jason Carter), who literally transfers his life energy into her, saving her from death, but leaving her alone once again. Christian departed the series at this point, although the principals disagree over whether she quit or was fired.

While we take such things for granted now, *Babylon 5* was innovative both in its use of CGI effects and in featuring a multi-year story arc. Creator J. Michael Straczynski even had enough B5 story remaining to produce a sequel, *Crusade*, with another planned five-year arc. Alas, the series premiered as an already canceled series after TNT experienced a quick case of buyer's remorse.

The TV world has Shadows of its own.

### Baird, Eve (*The Librarians*)

Former soldier, now Guardian for a group of librarians who save the world from magic.

See: *The Librarians* (2014– , 20 episodes, USA)

### Baptiste, Maggie (*Stitchers*)

Former CIA assassin, now an operative for a covert program which accesses the minds of dead people.

See: *Stitchers* (2015– , 21 episodes, USA)

### Bates, Dianne (*Ocean Girl*)

Divorced marine biologist who studies whale song and meets a girl from an ocean planet.
See: *Ocean Girl* (1994–1997, 78 episodes, Australia)

### Bates, Thelma (*Hex*)

Boarding school ghost in love with her former roommate, a witch with supernatural powers of her own.
See: *Hex* (2004–2005, 19 episodes, UK)

### Batgirl (*Batman*)

A librarian who dons the cowl to help Batman and Robin fight crime.
See: *Batman* (1966–1968, 120 episodes, USA)

### *Batman* (1966–1968, 120 episodes, USA)

*Based on:* The comic book series by Bob Kane, Bill Finger
*Created by:* William Dozier
*Production Co.:* Greenway Productions, 20th Century–Fox Television
*Originally Aired:* ABC
*Main Cast:* Adam West, Burt Ward, Alan Napier, Neil Hamilton, Stafford Repp, Madge Blake, Yvonne Craig

Campy, superhero action series starring Adam West as Batman/Bruce Wayne and Burt Ward as Robin/Dick Grayson. When summoned by Gotham City's Police Commissioner Gordon (Neil Hamilton), the dynamic duo springs into action, sliding down Batpoles to the Batcave, suiting up, and screeching off in the Batmobile to meet the villain of the week. Well-known actors lined up to play the colorful evildoers, including Cesar Romero as the Joker, Vincent Price as Egghead, Frank Gorshin as the Riddler, and Burgess Meredith as the Penguin. Julie Newmar and later Eartha Kitt portrayed Batman's *purr*-fect female foil, Catwoman, who pursues feline-related treasures, such as cat-shaped jewels, while vacillating

Eartha Kitt as Catwoman, the *purr*-fect foil for the caped crusaders in *Batman* (ABC Television).

between her attraction to Batman and desire to kill him. (You know how cats can be.)

Yvonne Craig later joins the series as Barbara Gordon, daughter of the Commissioner, in "Enter Batgirl, Exit Penguin" (1967). Gordon is a librarian with a few secrets of her own, including a cape, a cowl, and a Batgirlcycle. Batgirl unites with the caped crusaders, who are unaware of her true identity, and the terrific trio pursues more Batadventures, which culminate in climactic fight scenes, punctuated by superimposed, comics-style action words…

BAM! POW!

## *Battlestar Galactica* (2004–2009, 75 episodes, USA)

*Based on:* The TV series *Battlestar Galactica* created by Glen A. Larson
*Created by:* Ronald D. Moore
*Production Co.:* David Eick Productions, R&D TV, et al.
*Originally Aired:* Syfy
*Main Cast:* Edward James Olmos, Mary McDonnell, Katee Sackhoff, Jamie Bamber, James Callis, Tricia Helfer, Grace Park, Michael Hogan, Aaron Douglas, Tahmoh Penikett, Alessandro Juliani, Kandyse McClure

Dark reimagining of the *Star Wars*–esque *Battlestar Galactica* from 1978. In this version, human survivors of a war with the Cylons, androids created by the humans themselves, escape their decimated planets known as the Twelve Colonies to search for a fabled planet called Earth. Battlestar *Galactica* leads the way under the command of William Adama (Edward James Olmos), a grim, experienced veteran of a prior war with the Cylons.

The 70s edition of *Battlestar Galactica* was a macho affair, with only men, including Richard Hatch and Lorne Green, listed in the opening titles. The 2004 version had a much larger female presence, starting with Mary McDonnell, listed second in the credits, as Laura Roslin, who had no analog in the 70s *BSG*. Roslin had been Secretary of Education for the Colonies, but assumed the presidency when the 42 people in the line of succession before her were killed during the Cylon attack. Roslin rises to the occasion, while dealing with a potentially terminal breast cancer diagnosis, becoming a strong and sometimes even ruthless leader.

In the 1978 *BSG*, "Starbuck" (Dirk Benedict) had been a hotshot pilot and ladies' man. Flash forward to 2004, and Starbuck is an actual lady (er, woman), Lieutenant Kara "Starbuck" Thrace (Katee Sackhoff), also a hotshot pilot who enjoys a good cigar. Distaff Starbuck is fierce, competitive, and trouble-prone, haunted by guilt at the death of her fiancé Zak Adama (Tobias Mehler), who was her student at flight school.

Another "sex change" from the original series occurred with the character of "Boomer" (Herb Jefferson, Jr.), who became Sharon "Boomer" Valerii (Grace Park) in the revival. The new Boomer is actually a humanoid Cylon, model "Number Eight." Boomer/Number Eight believes she is human, but eventually follows her programming to shoot Adama, while a different version of Number Eight goes on to give birth to a human/Cylon child.

Number Six (Tricia Helfer) is another Cylon infiltrator. She seduces Dr. Gaius Baltar (James Callis) and gains access to the Colonial Defense System, opening the door to the Cylon attack. While shielding Baltar from a nuclear blast, she dies, but later appears to him repeatedly as a virtual being and even messenger from God. In this incarnation, Number Six is a blond bombshell à la Marilyn Monroe and often wears a revealing, iconic red dress. (God sure has changed.)

Critically acclaimed for most of its run, *Battlestar Galactica* was more than just a whiz-bang space opera. It contained elements of political drama, especially an analogy to the war on terror, questions about religion, and examinations of the moral implications of war. Awards were plentiful, including a Peabody Award for the series in 2005, a Saturn Award for Katee Sackhoff in 2006, and a Saturn for Mary McDonnell in 2009.

*Battlestar Galactica* generated a prequel spinoff called *Caprica* in 2010, but Syfy pulled it before all 19 of its episodes had aired. Apparently no one was interested in how the Cylons were created. It's also possible that viewers found war more interesting than peace. Who knew?

## Baxter, Raven (*That's So Raven*)

Psychic teen with a big personality, a love of fashion design, and a nose for trouble.

See: ***That's So Raven* (2003–2007, 100 episodes, USA)**

## Baywatch Nights (1995–1997, 44 episodes, USA)

*Based on:* Characters from the TV series *Baywatch*
*Created by:* Michael Berk, Gregory J. Bonann, David Hasselhoff, Douglas Schwartz
*Production Co.:* The Baywatch Company, Tower 18 Production Company, All American Television, et al.
*Originally Aired:* In Syndication
*Main Cast:* David Hasselhoff, Gregory Alan Williams, Angie Harmon, Lisa Stahl, Lou Rawls, Eddie Cibrian, Donna D'Errico, Dorian Gregory

Spin-off from the long-running lifeguard series *Baywatch*, wherein two of the beach folk decide to give the P.I. biz a try, although they stay close to the ocean in their new line of work. Garner Ellerbee (Gregory Alan Williams) and Mitch Buchannon (David Hasselhoff) are the industrious dudes in question, joined in their investigations by the beautiful Ryan McBride (Angie Harmon). The first season focuses on standard detective fare, as the team pursues murderers, drug dealers, smugglers, and burglars, often by means of outré undercover operations. In "976 Ways to Say I Love You" (1995), Ryan overcomes her personal misgivings to go undercover as a phone-sex operator in hopes of catching a killer.

The second season shifts to a paranormal universe, with vampires, mummies, sea monsters, time travel, and UFOs. (Think *X-Files* at the beach.) Alas, this wasn't *The X-Files*. It wasn't even *Baywatch*.

## Beauchamp, Joanna, Wendy, Ingrid, and Freya (*Witches of East End*)

Beautiful, but benighted family of witches battling ancient curses and bad romantic decisions.

See: ***Witches of East End* (2013–2014, 23 episodes, USA)**

## *Beauty and the Beast* (1987–1990, 56 episodes, USA)
*Based on:* The fairy tale by Jeanne-Marie Leprince de Beaumont
*Created by:* Ron Koslow
*Production Co.:* Witt/Thomas Productions, Republic Pictures
*Originally Aired:* CBS
*Main Cast:* Linda Hamilton, Ron Perlman, Roy Dotrice, Jay Acovone, Ren Woods, Jo Anderson, Stephen McHattie

*Beauty and the Beast* is a modern take on the well-known fairy tale, updated with gritty New York locations and a new-age sensibility, whereby the beast never becomes a handsome prince, because he's beautiful INSIDE. (And because he's kind of hunky already.) **Catherine Chandler** (Linda Hamilton) is the beauty of the piece, a glamorous corporate attorney with her father's law firm. Catherine's privileged life takes a seemingly tragic turn, when she is jumped by thugs, who beat her, slash her face, and dump her out of their van. But salvation is at hand in the form of Vincent (Ron Perlman), a cowled man-beast with leonine features, who takes her to a secret world below the city. There he and "Father" (Roy Dotrice), his foster parent and the de facto leader of the "World Below," tend to Catherine's needs, and she recovers under their care. Catherine eventually returns to the world above, but she and Vincent have forged a spiritual link, and even a psychic one, whereby Vincent can sense when she is in danger. While they cannot be together because of their different worlds (and possibly different species), they "will never, ever be apart."

The series hummed along nicely, achieving cult status with a mostly female audience, until Hamilton became pregnant and departed after the first two episodes of season three. Her character was killed off, but not before Catherine had given birth to Vincent's son, although their relationship had always been depicted as chaste. Jo Anderson joined the cast as Diana Bennett, a criminal profiler, who investigated Catherine's death, leading her to the World Below, where she became an ally to the community, as Catherine had been before her.

It's hard to replace a lead actress, especially one who convincingly portrays a character in a will-they-or-won't-they relationship with a lion-man who has the soul of a poet. Even with George R.R. Martin (pre–*Game of Thrones*) as a writer and supervising producer, and beastly makeup work by Rick Baker, the series never recovered.

*Grrr…*

See also: **Chandler, Catherine (*Beauty and the Beast*)**

## *Beauty & the Beast* (2012– , 68 episodes, Canada/USA)
*Based on:* The TV series *Beauty and the Beast* created by Ron Koslow
*Production Co.:* CBS Television Studios, Take 5 Productions, Whizbang Films
*Originally Aired:* The CW

*Main Cast:* Kristin Kreuk, Jay Ryan, Sendhil Ramamurthy, Max Brown, Austin Basis, Nina Lisandrello, Brian White, Nicole Gale Anderson

Loosely based on the 1987 series of the same title (give or take an ampersand), the 2012 edition reimagines Catherine Chandler (Kristin Kreuk) as a homicide detective who witnessed her mother's murder, but was saved from harm herself by a mysterious creature. Nine years later, a murder investigation leads Cat to Vincent Keller (Jay Ryan), a doctor and Army veteran, supposedly deceased, but clearly very much alive and living a shadow life in New York. Vincent had been the victim of a "super-soldier" experiment gone awry, which transformed him into "a beast" with heightened senses and extraordinary strength, but only when agitated. Catherine realizes that Vincent was her savior many years before, and the two form an alliance, which quickly becomes complicated by romantic feelings, old loves, and secrets from the past. Some of those secrets involve an organization called Muirfield, the group responsible for unleashing enhanced "beasts" upon the world and the former employer of Cat's deceased mother. Helping to protect Vincent's secret(s) are J.T. Forbes (Austin Basis), a university professor who once had ties to Muirfield, and Tess Vargas (Nina Lisandrello), Cat's partner on the force and best friend, the only person in New York who doesn't seem to have a connection to Muirfield.

After many, and not the usual, relationship ups and downs (kidnapping, brainwashing), Catherine and Vincent finally marry in the season three finale, "Destined" (2015), but the honeymoon is cut short (naturally) in the season four opener, "Monsieur et Madame Bête" (2016). Alas, happily ever after is still several episodes in the future, as a black-market buyer of beasts causes problems for the Bête household.

Black market? Definitely not your mother's (or Mr. Disney's) *Beauty*.

## Becker, Liz (*Star Maidens*)

Earth scientist held hostage on a planet where women rule and men are treated as second-class citizens.

See: ***Star Maidens*** **(1976, 13 episodes, UK/West Germany)**

## Being Human (2011–2014, 52 episodes, Canada/USA)

*Based on:* The UK series *Being Human* created by Toby Whithouse
*Created by:* Jeremy Carver, Anna Fricke
*Production Co.:* Muse Entertainment Enterprises, Zodiak USA, et al.
*Originally Aired:* Syfy
*Main Cast:* Sam Witwer, Meaghan Rath, Sam Huntington, Kristen Hager, Eddy Kariti

A vampire, a werewolf, and a ghost walk into a bar… That sounds like the setup for a joke, but it's not far off from the premise of this series, which is based on a UK show of the same title.

Aidan Waite (Sam Witwer), a vampire since the Revolutionary War, moves into a Boston brownstone with Josh Levison (Sam Huntington), a werewolf in search of a cure for his hirsute condition. These two unusual men are hoping to help each other lead normal lives with the goal of "being human."

While they're not off to the best start in the normalcy department, things get even more peculiar when they find they have a surprise "roommate," Sally Malik (Meaghan Rath), a ghost who haunts their house. Sally had been murdered in the house by her fiancé seven months earlier, but doesn't remember the incident, and is initially unable to leave the brownstone. She later learns from another ghost how to teleport to other locations, and she decides to haunt her ex for a while, finally remembering the truth about her demise. Later Sally goes through a number of transformations, returning to human form, but subsequently becoming a zombie, a witch, etc.

When it comes to fantasy tropes, the more, the merrier.

## *Believe* (2014, 13 episodes, USA)
*Created by:* Alfonso Cuarón, Mark Friedman
*Production Co.:* Bad Robot Productions, Esperanto Filmoj, Warner Bros. Television, Bonanza Productions
*Originally Aired:* NBC
*Main Cast:* Jake McLaughlin, Johnny Sequoyah, Jamie Chung, Kyle MacLachlan, Delroy Lindo, Kerry Condon, Katie McClellan

Psychic powers never seem to go out of TV fashion, although some series lose their telepathic hold on audiences sooner than others. This one, created by Academy Award–winner Alfonso Cuarón, established a weak link, lasting just a half-season.

Bo Adams (Johnny Sequoyah) is a 10-year-old girl with amazing psychic abilities, including telekinesis, precognition, and levitation. Bo was raised mostly by scientists in a government-sanctioned project called Orchestra, but was removed by Dr. Milton Winter (Delroy Lindo) when he began to doubt the intentions of his partner, Dr. Roman Skouras (Kyle MacLachlan). Since Bo is not yet in control of her prodigious powers, she needs protection from Skouras and Orchestra, so Winter enlists the help of William Tate, Jr. (Jake McLaughlin), a death-row inmate who also happens to be Bo's biological father. Winter's team breaks Tate out of prison minutes before his execution (simple plans are the best). After some Orchestra-induced mayhem, Bo, Winter, Tate and Janice Channing (Jamie Chung), Orchestra's former head of security, go on the run, trying to stay one step ahead of Skouras's nefarious plans which involve establishing an army of psychics.

Bo sometimes sees a blue butterfly, which helps lead her in the right direction. Too bad the creative team here didn't have a blue butterfly of its own.

## Bennet, Claire (*Heroes*)

"Save the cheerleader, save the world."

Claire Bennet (Hayden Panettiere) has the weight of the world on her shoulders. As a high school student and cheerleader, she deals with the usual teenage woes, but when she discovers she has the ability to heal from any injury, her life changes forever. Claire begins to test her ability by injuring herself repeatedly, eventually rescuing a man from a fiery train wreck in "Genesis" (2006). An attempted rape by the high school quarterback leaves Claire dead in "One Giant Leap" (2006), but she revives during the autopsy and flees. Ever-beleaguered, she runs into a serial killer who steals special powers in "Homecoming" (2006), but is saved by Peter Petrelli (Milo Ventimiglia), who has been told he must "Save the cheerleader, save the world" because some sort of cataclysm is coming. While Claire has been hiding her "gift" from her family, she learns in "Fallout" (2006) that her adoptive father, Noah Bennet (Jack Coleman), already knows her secret and has LOTS of secrets of his own when it comes to the special powers brigade. Claire's relationship with Noah, as well as with her birth father, Nathan Petrelli (Adrian Pasdar), becomes a roller-coaster ride thereafter, as their ambiguous motives and connections to vast conspiracies play themselves out.

Hayden Panettiere won a Saturn Award in 2007 for her performance as Claire Bennet. Claire's good heart, tenacity, and strength are constants throughout *Heroes*, or as constant as they can be in a series which adopts and abandons alternate timelines with—well, abandon.

See also: ***Heroes* (2006–2010, 77 episodes, USA)**

### Bennett, Bonnie (*The Vampire Diaries*)

High-school student and powerful witch with the bad habit of dying and returning from the dead.

See: ***The Vampire Diaries* (2009– , 155 episodes, USA)**

### Bennett, Diana (*Beauty and the Beast*)

Criminal profiler who meets a mysterious man-beast from a world below the streets of New York.

See: ***Beauty and the Beast* (1987–1990, 56 episodes, USA)**

### Bennigan, Claire (*The Whispers*)

FBI Agent investigating children with an "imaginary" friend who may not be of this world.

See: ***The Whispers* (2015, 13 episodes, USA)**

### Benson, Kate (*Special Unit 2*)

Chicago detective who deals with "Links," missing links between apes and humans.

See: ***Special Unit 2* (2001–2002, 19 episodes, USA)**

### Bering, Myka (*Warehouse 13*)

Myka Bering is a Secret Service Agent with an exceptionally secret secret. Myka (Joanne Kelly) works at Warehouse 13, a repository for the world's supernatural artifacts, located in a remote corner of South Dakota. Partnered with fellow Secret Service Agent Pete Lattimer (Eddie McClintock), Myka searches the world for strange occurrences, always finding an "artifact" as the root cause, such as Man Ray's Camera, which steals the youth of supermodels, causing rapid aging in "Age before Beauty" (2010). At first, Myka, the detail-oriented, straight arrow clashes with Pete, the fun-loving manchild, but soon they learn that their styles are complementary, making them an effective team. Myka has a prodigious knowledge of books, gained at her father's bookstore, and her familiarity with the Bard comes in handy when Shakespeare's

Lost Folio starts killing people in "The New Guy" (2011). Agent Bering survives ovarian cancer, the loss of a colleague, her boss's psychotic break, and all manner of Warehouse *mishigas*, finally realizing that she is in love with partner Pete in series finale "Endless" (2014).

See also: ***Warehouse 13* (2009–2014, 64 episodes, USA)**

### Betty I and Betty II (*Quark*)

Identical women who pilot an interstellar garbage scow and argue over which is the clone.

See: ***Quark* (1977–1978, 8 episodes, USA)**

### Bewitched (1964–1972, 254 episodes, USA)

*Created by:* Sol Saks
*Production Co.:* Screen Gems, Ashmont Productions
*Originally Aired:* ABC
*Main Cast:* Elizabeth Montgomery, Dick York, Dick Sargent, Agnes Moorehead, David White, Erin Murphy

Long-running fantasy sitcom about a beautiful witch who tries to live a normal suburban existence to please her mortal husband, but fails thanks to her interloping relatives. The witch in question is **Samantha Stephens** (Elizabeth Montgomery),

Witchcraft leads to unexpected time travel for Samantha Stephens (Elizabeth Montgomery) and husband Darrin (Dick Sargent) on *Bewitched* (ABC Television).

who reveals her magical side to husband Darrin (Dick York and later Dick Sargent) on their wedding night, but promises to forgo witchcraft in hopes of becoming the All-American wife. The marriage comes as bad news to interloper-in-chief Endora (Agnes Morehead), Samantha's sartorially resplendent mother, who purposely botches Darrin's name at every turn, calling him "Durwood" or "Dumbo." Many episodes focus on Endora's supernatural schemes to separate the couple or to coax Samantha into using her witchly ways. Magical matters are further complicated by the arrival of Tabitha (Erin Murphy), an adorable daughter for Samantha and Darrin, who takes after her mother's side of the family, and is unable to control her nascent "wishcraft." Other in-laws making Darrin's life a misery include forgetful Aunt Clara (Emmy winner Marion Lorne), grandiose father of the bride Maurice (Maurice Evans), and Samantha's mischievous look-alike cousin Serena (Elizabeth Montgomery credited as "Pandora Spocks"). Larry Tate (David White), Darrin's ad agency boss, is a frequent mortal lightning rod for all the magical sparks, continually barging into the Stephens home with clients in need of wooing.

The special effects on *Bewitched* were both special and effective, particularly for a 60s sitcom, and the performances were first-rate, especially that of Elizabeth Montgomery, who brought charm and unending enthusiasm to her role of a witch torn between two worlds.

See also: **Stephens, Samantha (*Bewitched*)**

## *Beyond Reality* (1991–1993, 44 episodes, Canada/USA)
*Created by:* Richard Manning, Hans Beimler
*Production Co.:* Glen Warren Productions
*Originally Aired:* USA Network
*Main Cast:* Shari Belafonte, Carl Marotte, Nicole de Boer

Shari Belafonte stars as Laura Wingate, a university parapsychologist who investigates strange phenomena around the world. Her partner in paranormality is J.J. Stillman (Carl Marotte), a clinical psychologist, who has more traditional scientific training, so is Scully to her Mulder two years before *The X-Files*. The duo looks into reports of telekinesis, astral projection, ghosts, precognition, and more, later with the help of graduate assistant Celia Powell (Nicole de Boer). In "Let's Play House" (1993), a man transports Celia into a 50s sitcom universe (pre–*Pleasantville*), where she is unwillingly cast as the doting housewife in the perfect suburban home. Laura and J.J. follow, adopting various roles, such as civil defense worker and FBI agent, to point out that, with red scares and fallout shelters, staying in the 50s is no bargain.

In addition to being ahead of its time on the creative front, *Beyond Reality* also featured a lead actress of color, a rarity for the 90s. While not literally a lost treasure, this one deserves to be better known.

## Bingum, Jane (*Drop Dead Diva*)

Plus-sized attorney who receives the soul of an aspiring model after a heavenly mishap.

See: ***Drop Dead Diva* (2009–2014, 78 episodes, USA)**

## The Bionic Woman (1976–1978, 58 episodes, USA)

*Based on:* The novel *Cyborg* by Martin Caidin
*Created by:* Kenneth Johnson
*Production Co.:* Universal TV, Harve Bennett Productions
*Originally Aired:* ABC (1976–1977), NBC (1977–1978)
*Main Cast:* Lindsay Wagner, Richard Anderson, Martin E. Brooks

The story of the bionic woman begins on *The Six Million Dollar Man*, when **Jaime Sommers** (Lindsay Wagner), a tennis star, is injured while parachuting with her bionic fiancé, Col. Steve Austin (Lee Majors). With Steve's intercession, Oscar Goldman (Richard Anderson) of the Office of Scientific Investigations agrees to allow an operation that will save Jaime by fitting her with bionic replacement parts. As *The Bionic Woman* opens, a now-recovered Jaime is working as a schoolteacher in Ojai, California, while undertaking missions as an agent for the OSI. Jaime's super-hearing, lightning speed, massive strength and other abilities make her a special, special agent, although the special effects used to demonstrate her powers are sometimes not so special, such as using slow motion whenever she's running or a close-up of her ear to demonstrate her profound hearing. Lindsay Wagner's sweet sincerity as Jaime, however, adds conviction to this SF/adventure series.

Jaime Sommers (Lindsay Wagner) goes undercover as a showgirl to investigate an army of "Fembots" in *The Bionic Woman* (NBC Television).

See also: **Sommers, Jaime** (*The Bionic Woman*)

## Bionic Woman (2007, 8 episodes, USA)

*Created by:* David Eick
*Production Co.:* GEP Productions, David Eick Productions, Universal Media Studios
*Originally Aired:* NBC
*Main Cast:* Michelle Ryan, Miguel Ferrer, Molly Price, Lucy Hale, Will Yun Lee, Chris Bowers

A reimagining of the classic Lindsay Wagner series from the 70s, this short-lived SF drama stars Michelle Ryan as the retooled bionic woman. In the modern telling, Jaime Sommers is a bartender who must juggle work, home life with rebellious younger sister Becca (Lucy Hale), and romance with boyfriend Will Anthros (Chris Bowers). Jaime's life changes forever when she is almost killed in a car accident, but is saved by a miraculous operation, performed by boyfriend Will, which replaces her damaged body parts with bionic prosthetics and implants. Now with enhanced strength, speed, hearing, and eyesight, Jaime begins working for the Berkut Group, a private intelligence outfit responsible for her bionics surgery. Jaime undertakes missions for the organization, investigating terrorist threats, rescuing Americans in distress, and thwarting assassination plots.

Viewers may not have been ready for the darker tone of the rebooted series, and a strike by the Writers Guild of America which halted production may not have helped, but, whatever the case, there was no resuscitation for this one after its eight-episode run.

### *Birds of Prey* (2002–2003, 13 episodes, USA)
*Based on:* The comic book series created by Chuck Dixon, Jordan B. Gorfinkel, Gary Frank
*Created by:* Laeta Kalogridis
*Production Co.:* Warner Bros. Television, DC Entertainment, Tollin/Robbins Productions
*Originally Aired:* WB
*Main Cast:* Ashley Scott, Dina Meyer, Rachel Skarsten, Shemar Moore, Ian Abercrombie, Mia Sara

What is Gotham City to do once Batman leaves town? Enter Helena Kyle (Ashley Scott), also known as Huntress, the daughter of Batman and Catwoman, who possesses "metahuman" abilities, such as super-strength, enhanced agility, and a sixth sense for danger. Helena accepts the caped crusader's crime-fighting mantle with the help of Barbara Gordon (Dina Meyer), who used to be Batgirl, but had to leave the bat-life behind due to a paralyzing gunshot wound from the Joker. Barbara has rechristened herself as Oracle, and uses computers to battle baddies, while Huntress takes the non-virtual approach to confronting super-villains. Assisting Huntress and Oracle is teenager Dinah Lance (Rachel Skarsten), another metahuman, who has telepathic and telekinetic abilities (but who apparently was absent the day they handed out the cool superhero names). The Birds seek their prey in (now) New Gotham, assisted by Detective Jesse Reese (Shemar Moore), and thwarted at every turn by Harley Quinn (Mia Sara), the Joker's former lover, who masquerades as psychiatrist Dr. Harleen Quinzel, an expert on violent criminals. You needed a scorecard to keep track of all these characters and their alter-egos, but you didn't need it for long, because these birds were shot down after only 13 episodes.

### *Black Scorpion* (2001, 22 episodes, USA)
*Created by:* Roger Corman, Craig J. Nevius
*Originally Aired:* Syfy
*Main Cast:* Michelle Lintel, Scott Valentine, B.T., Enya Flack, Steven Kravitz, Guy Boyd

The Black Scorpion is a vigilante superhero/crime-fighter in the Batman mold, but on the distaff side. By day, the Scorpion is Darcy Walker (Michelle Lintel), a police detective in Angel City, who never received justice for the murder of her father. By night, the Black Scorpion takes the law into her own hands, battling supervillains with clever names, such as Aerobicide, Clockwise, Flashpoint, Polutia, and Vox Populi. She has no superpowers per se, but relies on high-tech gadgets, such as her "Scorpionmobile," a super-car with the capability to disguise itself, and a ring which transforms her street clothing at an atomic level into the skimpy Black Scorpion costume. (Convenient!) Darcy/Scorpion is a martial arts expert and computer whiz, who somehow finds time for a relationship with Detective Steve Rafferty (Scott Valentine), but manages to keep the identity of her alter-ego a secret from him. In an otherworldly twist, Darcy's father is resurrected from the dead in series finale "Zodiac—Part 2" (2001), and the two battle the combined power of four supervillains together.

### Blacke, Helen (*Highcliffe Manor*)
Happily oblivious widow who inherits a Gothic mansion full of mad scientists. See: *Highcliffe Manor* (1979, 6 episodes, USA)

### Blade: The Series (2006, 13 episodes, USA)
*Based on:* The comic book character created by Marv Wolfman, Gene Colan
*Created by:* David S. Goyer
*Production Co.:* Marvel Entertainment, Phantom Four Films, New Line Television
*Originally Aired:* Spike
*Main Cast:* Kirk "Sticky" Jones, Jill Wagner, Nelson Lee, Jessica Gower, Neil Jackson

Kirk Jones (a.k.a. rapper Sticky Fingaz) tries to fill the big shoes left behind by Wesley Snipes in this sequel to the *Blade* movie series. Jones/Fingaz stars as Eric Brooks, a half-human/half-vampire known as Blade, a leather-clad warrior who hunts down vampires in Detroit. Krista Starr (Jill Wagner) joins forces with Blade when she returns from military service to find that her brother has been killed by a vampire. And not just any vampire, but the big kahuna, Marcus Van Sciver (Neil Jackson), the rich and powerful ruler of the House of Chthon, a vampire crime family. Bloody complications ensue, when Marcus sets his undead cap for Krista and turns her into a vampire. Not to worry, though, as Blade injects Krista with the same serum he uses to control his own vampiric urges, although Krista struggles at times to balance her vampire and human sides. Now seemingly an evil bloodsucker, Krista infiltrates the House of Chthon to gain intel on the plans of Marcus and his minions, including platinum blonde vamp(ire) Chase (Jessica Gower).

The series had a successful premiere episode, catering to fledgling network Spike's predominantly male audience with plenty of sex, blood, gore, and sex. Ratings dropped precipitously after the premiere, however, and it didn't help that *Blade* was an expensive series to produce. It died after one short season with the vampiric equivalent of a quick bloodletting.

### Blake, Allison (*Eureka*)
Dr. Allison Blake (Salli Richardson-Whitfield) works in picture-perfect Eureka, where the "small-town ambience" hides big, sometimes COSMIC secrets. Eureka is home to Global Dynamics, a cutting-edge research facility, where Blake serves as

liaison for the Department of Defense. Sounds simple enough, but GD employs the world's most brilliant scientists, whose experiments, sometimes accidentally, and sometimes intentionally place lives and even the planet's existence in jeopardy. It's then up to Blake, alongside Eureka's sheriff, Jack Carter (Colin Ferguson), to set things right before the next disaster occurs. In "Founders' Day" (2010), the disaster is so big it actually disrupts the timeline, when Blake, Carter, and associates accidentally travel to 1947, returning to different futures than the ones they left behind.

Blake is a busy and able woman, with two PhDs, a demanding job, an autistic son, and a complicated love life, both with her estranged husband Nathan Stark (Ed Quinn), which produces another child, and with Carter, whom she later marries.

How does she do it? Anything is possible in Eureka.

See also: *Eureka* (2006–2012, 77 episodes, USA)

## Blake, Cassie (*The Secret Circle*)

Teen who learns she is descended from a long line of witches and connected to a coven.

See: *The Secret Circle* (2011–2012, 22 episodes, Canada/USA)

## Blake, Octavia (*The 100*)

Teen delinquent sent with her peers to determine the Earth's habitability after a nuclear war.

See: *The 100* ("The Hundred," 2014– , 45 episodes, USA)

## *Blood Ties* (2007–2008, 22 episodes, Canada)

*Based on:* The novels of Tanya Huff
*Created by:* Peter Mohan
*Production Co.:* Insight Film Studios, Chum Television
*Originally Aired:* Lifetime
*Main Cast:* Christina Cox, Kyle Schmid, Dylan Neal, Gina Holden

Christina Cox stars as Victoria "Vicki" Nelson, a former Toronto homicide detective who leaves the force because of failing eyesight and opens her own private investigation firm. In the course of a gruesome murder investigation, Vicki meets Henry Fitzroy (Kyle Schmid), a centuries-old vampire, the kind who likes to help out attractive mortal women in need, and the illegitimate son of Henry VIII to boot. Their partnership leads Vicki to pursue unusual cases with supernatural overtones, much to the consternation of Detective Mike Celluci (Dylan Neal), Vicki's former partner on the police force, and sometimes lover. While the trio tries to navigate the dimensions of this otherworldly love triangle, Vicki, with Henry's assistance, battles demons, ghosts, zombies, mummies, and even Medusa herself.

Not your typical villains, not your typical P.I.

## Bloom, Sydney (*VR.5*)

Computer enthusiast who discovers a new level of virtual reality which can change events in the real world.

See: *VR.5* (1995, 13 episodes, USA)

### Breslauer, Haylen and Dru (*Mercy Point*)

Sisters/doctors dealing with trust issues while ministering to patients on the fringes of the galaxy.
See: ***Mercy Point* (1998–1999, 7 episodes, USA)**

### Buchanan, Leila (*The Event*)

Kidnap victim who escapes her captor only to learn that her father is an extraterrestrial.
See: ***The Event* (2010–2011, 22 episodes, USA)**

### *Buck Rogers* (1950–1951, 36 episodes, USA)

*Based on:* The novella *Armageddon 2419 A.D.* by Philip Francis Nowlan
*Originally Aired:* ABC
*Main Cast:* Kem Dibbs, Robert Pastene, Harry Sothern, Lou Prentis, Eva Marie Saint, Harry Kingston, Sanford Bickart

No kinescopes are known to exist of this early television series which was made on a shoestring budget and broadcast live. During the show's short run several actors portrayed Buck Rogers, including Kem Dibbs and Robert Pastene. In this version, 20th century Buck went into suspended animation because of a mining accident, and woke up in 2430 near Niagara, the capital of the new world. Buck soon met beautiful Wilma Deering (Eva Marie Saint and Lou Prentis) and the two fought intergalactic villainy from a secret lab inside a small cave. Lending scientific support to their cramped, albeit brave efforts was brilliant Dr. Huer (Harry Sothern and Sanford Bickart). Even claustrophobia couldn't stand in the way of such intrepid heroes!

### *Buck Rogers in the 25th Century* (1979–1981, 37 episodes, USA)

*Based on:* The novella *Armageddon 2419 A.D.* by Philip Francis Nowlan
*Created by:* Glen A. Larson, Leslie Stevens
*Production Co.:* Glen A. Larson Productions, Universal Television
*Originally Aired:* NBC
*Main Cast:* Gil Gerard, Erin Gray, Pamela Hensley, Tim O'Connor, Felix Silla, Mel Blanc, Eric Server, Thom Christopher, Jay Garner, Wilfrid Hyde-White

"The year is 1987, and NASA launches the last of America's deep space probes. In a freak mishap, Ranger 3 and its pilot, Captain William "Buck" Rogers, are blown out of their trajectory into an orbit which freezes his life support systems, and returns Buck Rogers to Earth ... 500 years later."

Captain Buck Rogers (Gil Gerard) returns to Earth after 500 years of suspended animation and learns that the place has changed a bit after a nuclear war. Buck finds work with the Earth Defense Directorate, under the leadership of Dr. Elias Huer (Tim O'Connor), and battles alien invaders who drop by our planet with distressing frequency in the 25th century. Colonel Wilma Deering (Erin Gray), a strong and intelligent officer with the Directorate, helps Buck with his sometimes secret missions, as in "Cruise Ship to the Stars" (1979), where the attractive duo must protect a galactic beauty queen, Miss Cosmos (Dorothy Stratten), from mysterious attacks. Buck must also fend off the advances, both territorial and romantic, of Princess

Ardala (Pamela Hensley), who attacks Earth in hopes of marrying Buck (unique approach) and never meets a revealing costume she doesn't like.

In season two, the tone shifts from campy adventure to preachy space opera, and several characters disappear including Dr. Huer and Princess Ardala. Wilma Deering remains, but becomes less assertive and more feminine, as her character is relegated to the background in the show's new setting, a spaceship. Her costumes change too, from form-fitting, spandex pantsuits (but, at least, PANTS) to an incongruous short-skirted uniform that makes her look like a 50s carhop. Hawk (Thom Christopher), a birdlike creature, completes the show's dramatic makeover in a season that was shortened by an actors' strike. It all proved too much for confused audiences, who fled the series after its season premiere.

In the words of Twiki, Buck's robot sidekick: "Bidi-bidi-bidi." Roughly translated, that means, "If it ain't broke..."

## *Buffy the Vampire Slayer* (1997–2003, 144 episodes, USA)
*Created by:* Joss Whedon
*Production Co.:* Mutant Enemy Productions, Sandollar Television, 20th Century–Fox Television, Kuzui Enterprises
*Originally Aired:* WB (1997–2001), UPN (2001–2003)
*Main Cast:* Sarah Michelle Gellar, Nicholas Brendon, Alyson Hannigan, Charisma Carpenter, Anthony Stewart Head, David Boreanaz, Seth Green, James Marsters, Marc Blucas, Emma Caulfield, Michelle Trachtenberg, Amber Benson, Kristine Sutherland

"In every generation there is a chosen one. She alone will stand against the vampires, the demons, and the forces of darkness. She is the Slayer."

What sounds like the most shallow of teen horror premises, with a title that seals the superficial deal, becomes something rich and deep in the hands of creator/executive producer Joss Whedon, lead actor Sarah Michelle Gellar, and the rest of the company in *Buffy the Vampire Slayer*. Whedon's "high school as hell" concept mingled supernatural horrors with the (sometimes) terrifying rites of adolescence. What's more, the capable and irreverent protagonist of the title became the avatar of "girl power" in the 90s, a strong female character embraced by girls and women alike.

**Buffy Summers** (Sarah Michelle Gellar) arrives for sophomore year at Sunnydale High School in California, carrying both literal and figurative baggage. Buffy had been expelled from her prior school for burning down the gymnasium, but rather than being a troubled teen, she had been pursuing her mystical calling of "Slayer," rooting out a nest of local vampires. At her new school, Buffy soon meets the stuffy librarian, Rupert Giles (Anthony Stewart Head), who has been assigned as her "Watcher," the person tasked with training her for the harrowing battles ahead and contributing the knowledge he gleans from his vast collection of occult books.

It's lucky that no one uses the library at Sunnydale High, because it becomes the headquarters for the "Scooby Gang," a group of students who learn Buffy's secret and assist her in defeating the weekly villain(s) as well as each season's "Big Bad." Foremost among the Scoobies is **Willow Rosenberg** (Alyson Hannigan), soon

Buffy's BFF, a shy student who excels at doing computer research for the group, but later discovers magical powers as a witch. Xander Harris (Nicholas Brendon), the regular guy of the piece, is eager to help in any way he can, especially since it puts him closer to pretty Buffy. The Slayer, however, only has eyes for Angel (David Boreanaz), who is about as far from a regular guy as you can get, a centuries-old vampire, but one with a soul. Angel and Buffy consummate their forbidden love in season two, but their happiness is short-lived, when complications from a gypsy's curse ensue. Eventually Angel moves to Los Angeles and finds his own spin-off, the aptly titled *Angel*, taking resident shallow girl and reluctant Scooby **Cordelia Chase** (Charisma Carpenter) with him after season three.

As the series progresses, Buffy, Willow, and the gang deal with issues of love and loss, life and death, but never more so than in "The Body" (2001), when Buffy's mother Joyce (Kristine Sutherland) passes away. Buffy always wanted to live a normal life, and she gets her chance in series finale "Chosen" (2003), when a spell cast by Willow activates all the potential Slayers in the world, lightening Buffy's peculiar burden.

*Buffy the Vampire Slayer* was known for its innovative storytelling techniques, including the use of almost no dialogue in the Emmy-nominated (and terrifying) "Hush" (1999). The series was embraced by academe, with courses, papers, books, and conferences, all devoted to "Buffy Studies."

Not bad for a girl who got expelled from school.

See also: **Summers, Buffy** (*Buffy the Vampire Slayer*); **Rosenberg, Willow** (*Buffy the Vampire Slayer*); **Chase, Cordelia** (*Buffy the Vampire Slayer*; *Angel*)

### Burkle, Winifred "Fred" (*Angel*)

Grad student held as a slave in a demon dimension, now an operative for a supernatural detective agency.

See: *Angel* (1999–2004, 110 episodes, USA)

### Burton, Sally (*The Girl with Something Extra*)

Newlywed who reveals to her husband on their wedding night that she has ESP.

See: *The Girl with Something Extra* (1973–1974, 22 episodes, USA)

### Caffrey, Molly Anne (*Threshold*)

Contingency analyst whose emergency plan is activated when an alien object attacks a U.S. ship.

See: *Threshold* (2005–2006, 13 episodes, UK/USA)

### Calvert, Rosalee (*Grimm*)

Apothecary with cures both natural and supernatural, who can turn into a fox-like creature.

See: *Grimm* (2011– , 110 episodes, USA)

### Cameron (*Terminator: The Sarah Connor Chronicles*)

Android assassin from the future reprogrammed to defend a teenage boy destined to save the world from machines.

See: *Terminator: The Sarah Connor Chronicles* (2008–2009, 31 episodes, USA)

### Cameron, Kiera (*Continuum*)

Police officer in the year 2077 who is pulled to 2012 and must work to preserve the future she knows.

See: *Continuum* (2012–2015, 42 episodes, Canada)

### Carlisle, Carol (*Space Patrol*)

Glamorous, but daring spaceship crewmember and espionage expert in the 30th century.

See: *Space Patrol* (1950–1955, 210 episodes, USA)

### Carter, Cinnamon (*Mission: Impossible*)

Cinnamon Carter (Barbara Bain) is an elite operative with the Impossible Missions Force (IMF), a team of secret agents specializing in assignments which involve intricate planning, large-scale deceptions, and futuristic technology. Under the leadership of Jim Phelps (Peter Graves), Cinnamon works with master of disguise Rollin Hand (Martin Landau) et al. to effect coups, rescue prisoners, and foil assassination plots. As a former top model, Cinnamon uses her physical attractiveness to advantage, luring powerful men to work against their own evil interests. Carter, though, is not just window-dressing for the squad—she is intelligent and forceful, never breaking under psychological torture in "The Exchange" (1969), never giving up her colleagues to their adversaries. She is also adept at role-playing, posing as a psychic, a photographer, or a lost princess.

Barbara Bain won three consecutive Emmy Awards for her portrayal of superspy Cinnamon Carter. She departed the series after her third season, making a fourth consecutive Emmy her own "mission: impossible."

See also: *Mission: Impossible* (1966–1973, 171 episodes, USA)

### Carter, Peggy (*Agent Carter*)

Agent with the Strategic Scientific Reserve in 1946 who battles threats to the world with a rich man's butler.

See: *Agent Carter* (2015–2016, 18 episodes, USA)

### Carter, Samantha (*Stargate SG-1*)

Samantha Carter (Amanda Tapping) is a theoretical astrophysicist and an Air Force captain. Carter's brainy and brawny skill set is just what the General ordered, when she joins the most special of special ops teams, one which will use an alien portal called a "Stargate" to travel the Milky Way galaxy and beyond. Carter is a compassionate soldier, who sometimes bucks her superiors when orders conflict with her moral code. In "Ascension" (2001), Sam works with a sensitive being named Orlin (Sean Patrick Flanery), who has literally followed her home from another planet, to stop activation of a dangerous alien weapon coveted by Stargate Command. Carter is no cream puff, however, and she fights her assailants tooth and nail when she is kidnapped for medical experimentation in "Desperate Measures" (2001).

Needless to say, it's hard for a woman with a top-secret job to have a love life. It's even more complicated when that woman harbors romantic feelings for her commanding officer that neither can act upon due to their professional relationship. When Sam finally accepts a marriage proposal from another man, Pete Shanahan (David DeLuise), she soon breaks it off in "Threads" (2005), leaving hope that she and Colonel Jack O'Neill (Richard Dean Anderson) may find themselves together in a future where their careers are no longer an issue.

Carter is a main character in all 10 seasons of *Stargate SG-1* and in one season of the spin-off series *Stargate Atlantis*. Amanda Tapping received the 2004 Saturn Award and Leo Awards in 2003, 2004, and 2005 for her performance as Samantha Carter.

Colonel O'Neill once called Carter "one of this country's natural resources, if not national treasures." It's hard to disagree with that.

See also: ***Stargate SG-1* (1997–2007, 214 episodes, Canada/USA)**

### Casey, Lisa (*Mission: Impossible*)

Disguise expert working with a team of secret agents on elaborate cons/assignments.

See: ***Mission: Impossible* (1966–1973, 171 episodes, USA)**

### Castle, Jane (*Space Precinct*)

Police officer in Demeter City, "the crime capital of the galaxy," on the planet Altor.

See: ***Space Precinct* (1994–1995, 24 episodes, UK)**

### Catlyn (*Roar*)

Former slave, now a bow-toting warrior allied with an orphaned prince to unite the Celtic tribes against Rome.

See: ***Roar* (1997, 13 episodes, Australia/USA)**

### Catwoman (*Batman*)

Supervillain attracted to feline-related treasures and (sometimes) to Batman in Gotham City.

See: ***Batman* (1966–1968, 120 episodes, USA)**

### *The Champions* (1968–1969, 30 episodes, UK)

*Created by:* Dennis Spooner, Monty Berman
*Production Co.:* ITC Entertainment
*Originally Aired:* NBC
*Main Cast:* Stuart Damon, Alexandra Bastedo, William Gaunt, Anthony Nicholls

"...their mental and physical capacities fused to computer efficiency; their sight, sense and hearing raised to their highest, futuristic stage of mental and physical growth."

SF/espionage hybrid chronicling the adventures of three secret agents who work for Nemesis, an international law-enforcement agency based in Geneva. During the course of a mission, the operatives crash-land in the remote mountains of Tibet, and are rescued by an advanced civilization which bestows enhanced powers, such as telepathy, precognition, and superior strength. The team, consisting of Craig Stirling (Stuart Damon), Sharron Macready (Alexandra Bastedo), and Richard Barrett (William Gaunt), attempts to keep their new abilities secret, while continuing their work for Nemesis, where said hidden talents often come in handy. The Champions battle Nazis, prevent foreign assassinations, investigate mysterious phenomena, such as ghost planes and cryogenic storage, and generally bring light to the world. Sixties-supermodel good looks accompany the amazing superpowers of Macready and Stirling, in particular.

## Chandler, Catherine (*Beauty and the Beast*)

"He comes from a secret place, far below the city streets, hiding his face from strangers, safe from hate and harm. He brought me there to save my life ... and now, wherever I go, he is with me, in spirit."

Linda Hamilton portrays Catherine Chandler, the "beauty" in this updated version of the well-known fairy tale. Her "beast" is Vincent (Ron Perlman), a lion-man of unknown origin, who rescues Catherine after a brutal beating and face-slashing, taking her to an intricate civilization below the streets of Manhattan, called the "World Below." There he tends to her wounds, while reading her sonnets in his gentle, sonorous voice. A spiritual link is forged between the two, which withstands the big reveal of Vincent's appearance when the bandages finally come off Catherine's face.

Catherine returns to the world above, and after some cosmetic surgery, decides to switch from corporate law to more meaningful work as an investigator in the Manhattan District Attorney's office. Catherine's new job places her in frequent jeopardy, but she can take care of herself thanks to the martial arts skills she cultivated after her attack. Sometimes baddies come in bunches, however, and in those cases Vincent can sense her fear using his uncanny psychic link to her. He rushes to the rescue, running across the city or sometimes splaying himself (he is part cat, after all) across the top of a hurtling subway car, if great distances are involved. (Great distances meaning travel to downtown Manhattan or Brooklyn.)

The "romance" between Catherine and Vincent was of the forbidden variety, with longing looks, stilted speech, and no kissing. It came as a surprise then, when Catherine turned up pregnant with Vincent's baby at the beginning of season three. (It was less surprising if you'd heard that actress Hamilton was also pregnant.) Hamilton departed the series, and the character of Catherine was killed off, but not before leaving Vincent a bouncing baby boy.

Catherine lived on, albeit briefly, in novelizations of series episodes published by Avon Books. But she lives forever in the hearts of *Beauty and the Beast* fans, who continue to write fan fiction set in a universe where the events of season three never happened.

*Beauty and the Beast* is a fairy tale, after all. There has to be a happy ending.

See also: ***Beauty and the Beast* (1987–1990, 56 episodes, USA)**

### Chandler, Catherine "Cat" (*Beauty & the Beast*)

New York homicide detective in love with a mutated man/beast.

See: ***Beauty & the Beast* (2012– , 68 episodes, Canada/USA)**

### Channing, Janice (*Believe*)

Former head of security for a secret organization, now on the run to protect a psychic girl.

See: ***Believe* (2014, 13 episodes, USA)**

### Chapel, Christine (*Star Trek*)

Starship nurse who harbors romantic feelings for an unemotional half-human.

See: ***Star Trek* (1966–1969, 79 episodes, USA)**

### Charles, Charlotte "Chuck" (*Pushing Daisies*)

Former "dead girl" who now serves pie and solves murders with her glum boyfriend.

See: ***Pushing Daisies* (2007–2009, 22 episodes, USA)**

### *Charmed* (1998–2006, 178 episodes, USA)

*Created by:* Constance M. Burge
*Production Co.:* Spelling Television, Paramount Television, et al.
*Originally Aired:* WB
*Main Cast:* Holly Marie Combs, Alyssa Milano, Shannen Doherty, Rose McGowan, Brian Krause, Dorian Gregory, Julian McMahon, T.W. King

Witches took 90s television by storm: Sabrina Spellman and her wacky aunts on *Sabrina the Teenage Witch* (1996–2003), Willow Rosenberg and (later) Tara Maclay on *Buffy the Vampire Slayer* (1997–2003), and the three Halliwell sisters, Prue, Piper and Phoebe, on *Charmed*.

After inheriting a Victorian house from their grandmother, the twentysomething Halliwell sisters learn that they are descended from a long line of witches. Even more startling, each sister suddenly manifests a power different from that of the other two. Prue (Shannen Doherty), an appraiser at an auction house and the oldest of the three, is able to move objects with her mind. Piper (Holly Marie Combs), a restaurant manager and the middle sister, can freeze people and objects in time. Phoebe (Alyssa Milano), an unemployed free spirit and the youngest, is able to see the future. While the sisters' lives had been demon-free prior to attaining their gifts, now every warlock in town has their address, paying a call in hopes of grabbing their nascent powers, usually leading to nasty business. The "Charmed Ones" learn to fight back with incantations from *The Book of Shadows*, an heirloom hidden from prying eyes in their attic, and they are strongest when they use the "Power of Three," reciting the book's spells in unison.

The powers of the sisters increase over time, but they aren't enough to save Prue from a demonic assassin in "All Hell Breaks Loose" (2001), directed by Doherty. The magic of the sisters might have worked better had it focused on the real problem, the ill will between actresses Doherty and Milano, which had developed during the third season. Doherty's disenchantment with the show's storylines didn't help, and she was ultimately dismissed from the series in a replay of her exit from another Aaron Spelling show, *Beverly Hills, 90210*. Doherty was replaced by Rose McGowan who took the part of Paige Matthews, a recently (and conveniently) discovered half-sister of The Charmed Ones. It was a risky move replacing the popular Doherty on a popular show, but the gamble paid off, and *Charmed* lasted three more seasons with a newly configured "Power of Three."

The 90s were all about girl power, and witches were the ultimate powerful girls. The Halliwell sisters, with their beauty, trendy clothing, cool careers, man-troubles, and sunny, San Francisco lifestyles, made witchcraft less exotic, but also more relatable. It was a potent brew.

### *The Charmings* (1987–1988, 21 episodes, USA)
*Created by:* Prudence Fraser, Robert Sternin
*Production Co.:* Sternin & Fraser Ink, Embassy Television
*Originally Aired:* ABC
*Main Cast:* Christopher Rich, Caitlin O'Heaney, Carol Huston, Judy Parfitt, Cork Hubbert, Brandon Call, Garette Ratliff Henson, Paul Eiding, Dori Brenner, Paul Winfield

"... with a spell so powerful even she couldn't control it, she put the Charmings to sleep for 1,000 years."

What if Snow White and Prince Charming were followed to the modern world by the evil queen? No, this isn't *Once Upon a Time*, but a short-lived 80s sitcom called *The Charmings*. Snow White (Caitlin O'Heaney and later Carol Huston) and Prince Eric (Christopher Rich) wake up in modern-day Van Oaks, California, the victims of a revenge curse gone awry. The spellcaster, Queen Lillian White (Judy Parfitt), has accidentally included herself in the curse, and a couple of others to boot, Luther (Cork Hubbert), one of the seven dwarfs, and her snarky Magic Mirror (Paul Winfield). The Charmings and their two sons try to adapt to modern life, while Lillian, who is Snow's stepmother, lives upstairs from the couple whose happiness makes her unhappy. Sometimes Lillian uses magic to cause dissension, usually by throwing a pretty woman in handsome Eric's path. At other times, her spells accidentally call forth more fairytale characters (shades of *Once Upon a Time* again), such as Cinderella and the giant from Jack and the Beanstalk.

Poor Snow. Having a wicked stepmother who's bad at magic isn't exactly charming.

### Chase (*Blade: The Series*)
Platinum blond vamp(ire) working for the leader of an undead crime family.
See: *Blade: The Series* (2006, 13 episodes, USA)

### Chase, Cordelia (*Buffy the Vampire Slayer; Angel*)

The character of Cordelia Chase (Charisma Carpenter) begins life on *Buffy the Vampire Slayer* as a mean girl at the top of the social pyramid at Sunnydale High School. Beautiful, vain Cordelia serves as a foil for series protagonist Buffy Summers (Sarah Michelle Gellar), who is also beautiful, but must always remain an outsider due to her fate-ordained role as a vampire slayer and savior of the world. Cordelia taunts social outcast Buffy and her friends, but begins to learn that Sunnydale, despite its name, is full of darkness, when she is kidnapped and tortured by an invisible student in "Out of Mind, Out of Sight" (1997). Thereafter she becomes a reluctant member of Buffy's "Scooby Gang," and dates one of its members, Xander Harris (Nicholas Brendon), bringing about her own social ostracism in "Bewitched, Bothered, and Bewildered" (1998). While battling vampires, demons, and other supernatural baddies, Cordelia must also fight her own superficial nature, usually with mixed results.

When Cordy arrives in Los Angeles via *Angel*, a spin-off from *Buffy the Vampire Slayer*, she's seeking her "inevitable stardom" as an actress after her parents have fallen on hard times. She runs into Angel (David Boreanaz), the vampire with a soul, and insults him, whereupon Angel notes, "It's nice to see that she's grown as a person." But Cordelia's journey to hero is about to begin, as she joins Angel in forming Angel Investigations, a detective agency specializing in supernatural cases. She soon begins to receive clues about whom to help in the form of migraine-inducing visions from "The Powers That Be." In "To Shanshu in L.A." (2000), a demon inundates her with visions of those in need, bringing her to catatonia and the point of death. After experiencing the pain of the world, however, Cordelia vows to help others, whatever the cost.

Cordelia departs this earth and the series in *Angel*'s 100th episode, "You're Welcome" (2004), but not before getting some ghostly closure with Angel, including a long-awaited kiss. She briefly returns as a higher power in *Angel: After the Fall*, a subsequent comic book series.

Somehow an elevated status in the afterlife seems appropriate for former queen bee Cordelia. Totally.

See also: ***Buffy the Vampire Slayer* (1997–2003, 144 episodes, USA);** ***Angel* (1999–2004, 110 episodes, USA)**

### Chennault, Commander (*Space Rangers*)

Leader of an Earth colony called Fort Hope on the far-off planet Avalon.

See: ***Space Rangers* (1993, 6 episodes, USA)**

### Chiana (*Farscape*)

Thief, con artist, and prostitute on the run from her conformity-loving government.

See: ***Farscape* (1999–2003, 88 episodes, Australia/USA)**

### *Chuck* (2007–2012, 91 episodes, USA)

*Created by:* Josh Schwartz, Chris Fedak

*Production Co.:* College Hill Pictures, Fake Empire Productions, Wonderland Sound and Vision, Warner Bros. Television
*Originally Aired:* NBC
*Main Cast:* Zachary Levi, Yvonne Strahovski, Adam Baldwin, Joshua Gomez, Sarah Lancaster, Ryan McPartlin, Mark Christopher Lawrence, Vik Sahay, Scott Krinsky, Bonita Friedericy

Chuck Bartkowski is all nerd. He works at the local Buy More (read: Best Buy) as part of its "Nerd Herd" of computer repair experts, and is happily underachieving after his expulsion from Stanford University. One day Chuck (Zachary Levi) opens an e-mail and downloads "The Intersect," the entire CIA/NSA database, into his BRAIN, and his life changes forever.

The Intersect needs government babysitting, of course, so operatives are dispatched, CIA Agent **Sarah Walker** (Yvonne Strahovski) and Major John Casey (Adam Baldwin) of the NSA. Sarah takes the cover identity of Chuck's girlfriend, working at a yogurt shop near the Buy More, while Casey must suffer the indignity of becoming a sales associate at the electronics superstore. The trio must fight off repeated attempts by enemy spy organizations, large and small, to steal/kidnap the Intersect for the valuable information it/he contains. In the meantime, faux couple Sarah and Chuck start to develop genuine feelings for each other, complicating missions, especially at the times when Chuck is considered expendable. But as *Scarecrow and Mrs. King* showed us, spies and civilians make strange, but lasting bedfellows, so a little thing like having every coveted piece of spy information in your brain isn't going to get in their way.

See also: **Walker, Sarah (*Chuck*)**

### Cillian, Cassandra (*The Librarians*)

Mathematician with tumor-induced hallucinations who works to save the world from magic.

See: *The Librarians* (2014– , 20 episodes, USA)

### Clark, Kirsten (*Stitchers*)

Caltech grad student whose consciousness is inserted into the minds of dead people to solve crimes.

See: *Stitchers* (2015– , 21 episodes, USA)

### Clark, Marissa (*Early Edition*)

Confidante of a man who receives newspapers with the next day's news, allowing him to avert disasters.

See: *Early Edition* (1996–2000, 90 episodes, USA)

### Cleo (*Cleopatra 2525*)

Exotic dancer "defrosted" in the year 2525 to help battle robots who have taken over the Earth.

See: *Cleopatra 2525* (2000–2001, 28 episodes, USA)

## Cleolanthe (*Rocky Jones, Space Ranger*)

Suzerain of the planet Ophiuchus and beautiful space nemesis of Rocky Jones.

See: *Rocky Jones, Space Ranger* (1954, 39 episodes, USA)

## Cleopatra 2525 (2000–2001, 28 episodes, USA)

*Created by:* R.J. Stewart, Rob Tapert
*Production Co.:* Renaissance Pictures, Universal Network Television
*Originally Aired:* In Syndication
*Main Cast:* Gina Torres, Victoria Pratt, Jennifer Sky, Elizabeth Hawthorne, Patrick Kake, Joel Tobeck

There are concepts, and there are CONCEPTS. An exotic dancer is cryogenically frozen after her breast augmentation surgery goes awry, and is accidentally awakened 500 years later by two female warriors who are battling robots for control of the Earth. That's the premise for this syndicated series from 2000 that no one would mistake for cinéma vérité.

Cleo (Jennifer Sky) is defrosted, as it were, by Hel (Gina Torres) and Sarge (Victoria Pratt), two women who fight against the Baileys, flying robots who have driven humans into underground tunnels in the year 2525. Hel is the team's leader, receiving orders from the "Voice" (Elizabeth Hawthorne), who heads the resistance against the Baileys. Cleo joins the cause, spouting lines from 20th-century pop culture at the drop of a hat, such as "Live long and prosper" and "Make my day." In addition to the Baileys, the women must battle Betrayers, robots who have the ability to become perfect clones of people, but have a few deadly weapons up their sleeves. Another nemesis is Creegan (Joel Tobeck), a human scientist who is mad (his demonic clown makeup is a dead giveaway) and turns out to be none other than Dr. George Bailey, creator of the menacing Baileys. Assisting the scantily clad warriors is Mauser (Patrick Kake), a Betrayer who has been repurposed to help the team.

In other words, take *The Terminator*, throw in some bellybuttons and cleavage, and you have the cheesy fun known as *Cleopatra 2525*.

## Connor, Sarah (*Terminator: The Sarah Connor Chronicles*)

Sarah Connor, one of science fiction's great and most beloved female characters, began life on the silver screen in *The Terminator* (1984), a small movie that went on to do big things. Sarah (Linda Hamilton), a fun-loving college student and waitress, learns she will give birth to a son who will go on to save the world from deadly machines, led by the menacing Skynet, if she can stay alive long enough to fulfill her destiny.

By 1999, when *Terminator: The Sarah Connor Chronicles* begins, Sarah (Lena Headey) is a hardened fugitive, living with her teenage son, the future savior of humanity, John Connor (Thomas Dekker). Sarah, John, and Cameron (Summer Glau), a Terminator sent from the future to protect John, now work to prevent Skynet from being built. Sarah tries hard to be a loving mother to John, but their bloody encounters with "metal" put her in the position of military commander over her son, leaving little time for tenderness. When her stress level after a brutal battle with a Terminator leads to nightmares and sleepwalking in "Complications" (2008), she seeks the help of a psychiatrist, but must hide the true story of machines from the future. Romance is a luxury she can't afford, and she flees her engagement to Charley Dixon (Dean Winters) without warning, only to involve him in her dangerous life later, leading to tragic consequences in "To the Lighthouse" (2009).

Lena Headey was initially a controversial choice for Sarah, her body seen as too thin and not as "buff" as the Sarah portrayed by Hamilton in *Terminator 2: Judgment Day* (*T2*). But tough isn't just about buff, and Headey showed she could infuse the role with her own brand of wounded strength and intensity.

As for Hamilton, she is slated to return as her iconic character in a movie sequel to *T2*, scheduled for release in 2019. Life sometimes imitates art, and Hamilton can now use the line made famous by co-star Arnold Schwarzenegger in the first Terminator movie.

"I'll be back."

See also: **Terminator: The Sarah Connor Chronicles (2008–2009, 31 episodes, USA)**

## Continuum (2012–2015, 42 episodes, Canada)

*Created by:* Simon Barry
*Production Co.:* Reunion Pictures, Boy Meets Girl Film Company, Shaw Media, et al.
*Originally Aired:* Syfy
*Main Cast:* Rachel Nichols, Victor Webster, Erik Knudsen, Stephen Lobo, Roger Cross, Lexa Doig, Omari Newton, Luvia Petersen, Jennifer Spence, Brian Markinson

Kiera Cameron (Rachel Nichols) is a police officer with the Vancouver City Protective Services in the year 2077. When a group of rebels known as "Liber8" travels to the past, Kiera is unexpectedly pulled with them to the year 2012, where she works to thwart their plans, which involve changing the past to affect the future. Kiera must keep her origins secret, although her "new" partner in the 2012 Vancouver Police Department, Detective Carlos Fonnegra (Victor Webster), eventually learns the truth, and is further shocked when two Kieras appear after more time-travel mishaps. The Kiera from the original timeline survives, while the one they call "Green Kiera" dies, and Fonnegra agrees to conceal the body. While the death of Green Kiera keeps things (relatively) simple for "Red Kiera," two Alec Sadlers (Erik Knudsen), also referred to as Green and Red, create further complications, especially since Alec is a computer genius who will go on to found one of the mega-corporations ruling the world in 2077. (Scorecard, anyone?)

Will Kiera unify the timeline so she can get back to the future where her husband and son are waiting? The answer is revealed in the series finale "Final Hour" (2015), but, as you might expect from a series with multiple timelines, the answer is not a simple one, and raises one more question.

Are two Kieras better than one?

**Cooke, Rema** (*Mercy Point*)
Doctor fighting for the rights of patients, human and extraterrestrial, on the fringes of the galaxy.
See: **Mercy Point** (**1998–1999, 7 episodes, USA**)

**Corrigan, Rachel** (*Poltergeist: The Legacy*)
Psychiatrist who joins an ancient society which investigates occult happenings to fight supernatural evil.
See: **Poltergeist: The Legacy** (**1996–1999, 88 episodes, Canada/USA**)

**Cowgirl** (*TekWar*)
Freelance hacker in 2045 who penetrates computer networks with a wave of her hand.
See: **TekWar** (**1994–1996, 18 episodes, Canada/USA**)

**Crabtree, Gladys "Mother"** (*My Mother the Car*)
Lawyer's deceased mother who is reincarnated as a 1928 Porter automobile.
See: **My Mother the Car** (**1965–1966, 30 episodes, USA**)

## The Crow: Stairway to Heaven (1998–1999, 22 episodes, Canada)
*Based on:* The comic book series by James O'Barr
*Created by:* Bryce Zabel
*Production Co.:* Alliance Atlantis Communications, Crescent Entertainment
*Originally Aired:* In Syndication
*Main Cast:* Mark Dacascos, Marc Gomes, Sabine Karsenti, Katie Stuart

"People once believed that when someone dies the crow carries their soul to the land of the dead. But sometimes something so bad happens that a terrible sadness is carried with it and the soul can't rest."

Based on the comic book series by James O'Barr and the hit movie starring the late Brandon Lee, *The Crow: Stairway to Heaven* stars Mark Dacascos as Eric Draven, a rock musician who is brutally murdered. Draven returns to Earth one year later as The Crow, a being neither alive nor dead, who appears to be human, but has a supernatural alter-ego who looks like he got carried away at the goth makeup store. Draven wants revenge for the murder and rape of his fiancée, Shelly Webster (Sabine Karsenti), who can't move on to the afterlife with Eric until he resolves his issues. Alas, Eric's mandate grows larger when he's back on earth, and he becomes a crime-fighting avenger, bringing justice to victims of wrongdoing, so Shelly will have to wait a lot longer. Draven gets moral support from Sarah Mohr (Katie Stuart), a 13-year-old girl with street smarts, who lives in his seedy apartment building. (You didn't know crows live in apartment buildings?) In "Like It's 1999" (1998), Sarah goes missing when she infiltrates a cult to save her best friend, and Draven comes to the rescue. Rounding out The Crow's human posse is Daryl Albrecht (Marc Gomes), the detective assigned to his case, who becomes an ally after initially suspecting Eric of Shelly's murder.

The first-season cliffhanger was never resolved due to cancellation of the series, leaving Eric Draven stranded in limbo once again.

### Crusher, Beverly (*Star Trek: The Next Generation*)
Chief medical officer aboard a starship and mother of a teenage prodigy.
See: *Star Trek: The Next Generation* (1987–1994, 178 episodes, USA)

### Cruz, Andi (*Every Witch Way*)
High school student who is the best friend and guardian of the world's most powerful witch.
See: *Every Witch Way* (2014–2015, 85 episodes, USA)

### Cutter, Helen (*Primeval*)
Scientist with a mysterious connection to temporal anomalies and a lack of connection to her husband.
See: *Primeval* (2007–2011, 36 episodes, UK)

### Dale, Joan (*Tom Corbett, Space Cadet*)
Professor, scientist, and adventurer at a space academy for teens "in the world beyond tomorrow."
See: *Tom Corbett, Space Cadet* (1950–1955, 58 episodes, USA)

### Dancer, April (*The Girl from U.N.C.L.E.*)
Secret agent who battles the enemies of good while wearing the latest mod fashions.
See: *The Girl from U.N.C.L.E.* (1966–1967, 29 episodes, USA)

### Danvers, Alex (*Supergirl*)
Alien-hunter at the Department of Extra-Normal Operations, who just happens to be Supergirl's adoptive sister.
See: *Supergirl* (2015– , 20 episodes, USA)

### Danvers, Kara (*Supergirl*)
Mild-mannered assistant at a media conglomerate, who protects the citizens of National City as Supergirl.
See: *Supergirl* (2015– , 20 episodes, USA)

### Dark Angel (2000–2002, 43 episodes, USA)
*Created by:* James Cameron, Charles H. Eglee
*Production Co.:* Cameron/Eglee Productions, 20th Century–Fox Television
*Originally Aired:* Fox
*Main Cast:* Jessica Alba, Michael Weatherly, Richard Gunn, J.C. MacKenzie, Valarie Rae Miller, John Savage

Jessica Alba stars as Max Guevara, a genetically enhanced super-soldier on the run from a secret government project. Guevara, designated X5-452, had escaped from a military facility when she was nine, along with 11 of her uncanny "siblings."

Ten years later Max continues to elude capture by government agents, led by ruthless Colonel Donald Lydecker (John Savage), while searching for her lost super-siblings when she can. She receives help in her quest from Logan Cale, a.k.a. Eyes Only (Michael Weatherly), a wealthy underground cyberjournalist, hacker, and vigilante. In return, she uses her enhanced strength, super-speed, lightning reflexes, heightened senses, et al. to serve as Logan's agent and soldier after he is shot, losing the use of his legs.

Max holds down a day job in Seattle, where amenities are few in 2019, thanks to a terrorist-generated electromagnetic pulse, which knocked out computers and communications for a time. She works with a motley (to say the least) crew of misfits at Jam Pony, a bicycle messenger service, including "Normal" (J.C. MacKenzie), her uptight boss, and "Sketchy" (Richard Gunn), her—er, sketchy friend. Max's coworkers at Jam Pony are mostly caricatures, although her best friend, Cynthia "Original Cindy" McEachin (Valarie Rae Miller), manages some "original" moments, breaking TV ground as an African American lesbian character.

Jessica Alba (*Dark Angel*) at San Diego Comic-Con International in 2014 (from a color photograph by Gage Skidmore, CC BY-SA 2.0).

Max continued the trend of kick-ass female characters on television which had started in the 90s, but *Dark Angel* never achieved the resonance or longevity of *Buffy the Vampire Slayer*. Alba was chosen from more than 1000 women for the part of Max, and she has the swagger down cold (some might say hot), but her expertise here is mostly on the action front, with a year of special training in gymnastics, martial arts, and motorcycle-riding. Still, she won a Saturn Award in 2001 as Best Television Actress in a deep field including Gillian Anderson, Kate Mulgrew, and Sarah Michelle Gellar.

Nothing wrong with being an action hero. As Max herself once said, "Girls kick ass—says so on a t-shirt."

## *Dark Shadows* (1966–1971, 1225 episodes, USA)

*Created by:* Dan Curtis
*Production Co.:* Dan Curtis Productions
*Originally Aired:* ABC
*Main Cast:* Joan Bennett, Grayson Hall, Jonathan Frid, Nancy Barrett, Alexandra Moltke, Louis Edmonds, Kathryn Leigh Scott, David Selby, David Henesy, Lara Parker, Thayer David

*Dark Shadows* was a supernatural soap opera which ran five days a week for six seasons, racking up an astonishing 1225 episodes. Sixties teens rushed home from school each day to revel in the Gothic melodrama, especially when it introduced evil vampire Barnabas Collins (Jonathan Frid) and tortured, but gorgeous ghost Quentin Collins (David Selby). Quentin's addition was even responsible for a hit on the Billboard charts in 1969, when "Quentin's Theme (Shadows of the Night)," the ghost's own haunting melody, was released as a single.

*Dark Shadows* is the story of the wealthy, but benighted Collins family of Collinsport, Maine. The family's matriarch, Elizabeth Collins Stoddard (Joan Bennett), harbors the traditional deep, dark, secret, and hasn't left the family mansion for 17 years. Matriarchs need help, of course, so Victoria Winters (Alexandra Moltke) comes to the family estate, Collinwood, to serve as a governess for Elizabeth's nephew David Collins (David Henesy). At the time of her hire, Victoria is unaware that her job description will include time travel back to 1795, where her knowledge of the future will bring about accusations of witchcraft.

The extended Collins family includes Roger Collins (Louis Edmonds), father of David and brother of Elizabeth, who brings his lovely bride Cassandra home to meet the family. It turns out that Cassandra is actually Angelique (Lara Parker), a witch who 200 years earlier had placed a curse on Barnabas Collins which brought about his "undeath." Dr. Julia Hoffman (Grayson Hall), a local psychologist who had tried to cure Barnabas of his vampirism, also does some time-traveling, via I-Ching (don't ask), to save Barnabas from death in 1897.

The hard-working actors often portray several parts, characters from the show's present day and their look-alike ancestors. Things get even more confusing when a portal to a parallel time is discovered in another wing of the mansion (as often happens). Storylines for present, past, present parallel, and past parallel times challenged the show's fans (not to mention its creative team). Viewers began to lose interest, ratings dropped, and ABC replaced the series with *Password*, a show which teenagers did not rush home to catch, but was cheaper to produce.

A primetime revival of the series, also created by Dan Curtis, lasted for a few months in 1991. That show, however, was merely a specter, a ghostly apparition in the Gothic mansion that is American series television. Cue "Quentin's Theme."

### Davidson, Pam (*The Greatest American Hero*)

Civilian member of a crime-fighting trio with her superhero boyfriend and his G-man partner.

See: *The Greatest American Hero* (**1981–1983, 44 episodes, USA**)

### Davies, Tru (*Tru Calling*)

Morgue worker with the ability to rewind a day so she can save the lives of people who have died.

See: *Tru Calling* (**2003–2005, 27 episodes, Canada/USA**)

### Davis, Laura and Lydia (*Three Moons Over Milford*)

Mother and daughter who cope with crises cosmic and domestic when the moon breaks into three pieces.

See: *Three Moons Over Milford* (**2006, 8 episodes, USA**)

**Dax, Jadzia (*Star Trek: Deep Space Nine*)**
    Space station science officer comprising two species, a humanoid female and a slug-like symbiont.
    See: ***Star Trek: Deep Space Nine* (1993–1999, 176 episodes, USA)**

**Dead Like Me (2003–2004, 29 episodes, USA)**
*Created by:* Bryan Fuller
*Production Co.:* John Masius Productions, MGM Television, DLM Productions
*Originally Aired:* Showtime
*Main Cast:* Ellen Muth, Laura Harris, Callum Blue, Jasmine Guy, Cynthia Stevenson, Mandy Patinkin, Britt McKillip, Christine Willes

What's next when you're 18 years old and you've just been killed by a falling toilet seat from the Mir space station? For Georgia Lass (Ellen Muth), "next" is the job of Grim Reaper, a collector of souls, who escorts the dearly departed to the afterlife. "George," as she is known, works in the Reapers' "External Influence" division, which deals with accidents and homicides, where she receives assignments on post-it notes from father-figure Rube Sofer (Mandy Patinkin), who calls her "Peanut." Since reaping isn't a paying gig, George must also find earthly employment, taking a job at Happy Time Temporary Services under the name "Mildred Hagen," who has a different physical appearance from George, the Reaper.

George learns it's not easy to deal with death all the time—her own, the deaths she reaps, and even those of her fellow Reapers. In "Curious George" (2003), George causes problems by visiting her family, whom she misses, while co-reaper Roxy Harvey (Jasmine Guy) mourns the 21st anniversary of her own death in "Business Unfinished" (2003). But life goes on (sort of), as George experiences a human right of passage, losing her virginity in "Death Defying" (2004). She also engages in the mundane rituals of life, such as meeting her colleagues at an after-work hangout, but since it's her REAPER colleagues she meets at "Der Waffle Haus," any sense of normalcy is illusory.

Death/undeath is always lively for the Reaper affectionately known as "Toilet Seat Girl."

**Dee, Ella (*Hex*)**
    Centuries-old witch, now a boarding school student tasked with killing the spawn of a fallen angel.
    See: ***Hex* (2004–2005, 19 episodes, UK)**

**Deering, Wilma (*Buck Rogers*)**
    Beautiful woman in the 25th century who fights intergalactic evil with a man revived from suspended animation.
    See: ***Buck Rogers* (1950–1951, 36 episodes, USA)**

**Deering, Wilma (*Buck Rogers in the 25th Century*)**
    Colonel with the Earth Defense Directorate, who battles alien invaders with a 20th century astronaut.
    See: ***Buck Rogers in the 25th Century* (1979–1981, 37 episodes, USA)**

### DeLauro, Emma (*Mutant X*)
Woman with highly developed mental powers, working with a team of "New Mutants."
See: *Mutant X* (2001–2004, 66 episodes, Canada/USA)

### Delenn (*Babylon 5*)
Alien ambassador who undergoes a mysterious transformation to human hybrid aboard a 23rd-century space station.
See: *Babylon 5* (1994–1998, 110 episodes, USA)

### DeLuca, Maria (*Roswell*)
Waitress and student in a love/hate relationship with an extraterrestrial boy.
See: *Roswell* (1999–2002, 61 episodes, USA)

### Dennis, Bo (*Lost Girl*)
Succubus who opens a detective agency with a fast-talking thief, while investigating her strange origins.
See: *Lost Girl* (2010–2015, 77 episodes, Canada)

### DeWitt, Adelle (*Dollhouse*)
Head of a high-tech facility in Los Angeles which programs the minds of its operatives to suit wealthy clients.
See: *Dollhouse* (2009–2010, 26 episodes, USA)

### Diana (*V*)
Commander of the Visitors, aliens who look human, but hide secrets, some that are only skin deep.
See: *V* (1984–1985, 19 episodes, USA)

### Diana, Queen (*Roar*)
Roman ruler working with an evil wizard to conquer Celtic tribes in ancient Ireland.
See: *Roar* (1997, 13 episodes, Australia/USA)

### Dinallo, Gloria (*Misfits of Science*)
Troubled telekinetic teen who finds her calling with scientists out to save the world.
See: *Misfits of Science* (1985–1986, 16 episodes, USA)

### Doctor Who (1963–1989, 2005– , 821 episodes, UK)
*Created by:* Sydney Newman
*Production Co.:* British Broadcasting Corporation (BBC), BBC Wales
*Originally Aired:* In Syndication (1963–1989), Syfy (2006–2008), BBC America (2010– )
*Main Cast:* Tom Baker, William Hartnell, Jon Pertwee, Patrick Troughton, Elizabeth Sladen, Jacqueline Hill, Matt Smith, David Tennant, Peter Capaldi, Jenna Coleman, Karen Gillan, Billie Piper, Freema Agyeman

There's never been anything on television like *Doctor Who*. Not only is it the longest-running science fiction show on TV, but it has retained its viewership over the decades while juggling series leads—an astounding 12 different Doctors since 1963. If 12 Doctors aren't enough to confuse you, his companions will make your head spin—more than 50 by most counts. Yet the Doctor continues to dazzle.

Doctor Who is a Time Lord, a human-looking extraterrestrial who journeys through time and space, battling foes to save the universe or parts thereof. He travels in a time machine called the "TARDIS" (Time and Relative Dimension in Space), which looks like a blue British police box, but is a cavernous vessel inside. The Doctor can regenerate when he is near death, taking on a new body and even personality, providing the producers with a handy mechanism for replacing actors due to poor health, dismissal, etc. The most well-known Doctor from the show's classic run is The Fourth Doctor (Tom Baker), who appeared in 172 episodes, while The Tenth Doctor (David Tennant) is most recognized from the show's revival in the new millennium.

The Doctor travels with companions—LOTS of companions. They are usually human and mostly female, initially serving as audience surrogates, but later receiving more character development. **Sarah Jane Smith** (Elizabeth Sladen), an investigative reporter, traveled with the Third and Fourth Doctors, returned for the revived series to assist the Tenth Doctor, and went on to become the protagonist of her own series in *The Sarah Jane Adventures*. Other notable companions include Rose Tyler (Billie Piper), a working-class London teen and the first companion in the revived show, Martha Jones (Freema Agyeman), a medical student and the Doctor's first black female companion, and Clara Oswald (Jenna Coleman), who has managed to interact with every doctor since the first due to the magic of modern editing.

How to keep this all straight? You'll have to become a Time Lord to figure that out.

See also: **Smith, Sarah Jane** (*Doctor Who*)

## *Dollhouse* (2009–2010, 26 episodes, USA)

*Created by:* Joss Whedon
*Production Co.:* Mutant Enemy Productions, 20th Century–Fox Television, Boston Diva Productions
*Originally Aired:* Fox
*Main Cast:* Eliza Dushku, Harry Lennix, Fran Kranz, Tahmoh Penikett, Enver Gjokaj, Dichen Lachman, Olivia Williams Muscat

Eliza Dushku stars as Echo, an operative for a shadowy organization called the Rossum Corporation. Echo has a codename, but not much else. All of her memories have been wiped by Rossum so that she can be imprinted with a myriad of personalities to suit the company's well-heeled clients. Echo and her fellow Actives or "Dolls" take on the identities of hackers, bank robbers, sex slaves, bodyguards, politicians—whatever the paying customer desires. When not on assignment, the Actives exist in a blank state at the Los Angeles "Dollhouse," a high-tech underground facility.

In her former life, Echo was Caroline Farrell, a college student and political activist who discovered some of Rossum's dirty secrets. She was captured by Adelle DeWitt (Olivia Williams), the head of the Los Angeles Dollhouse, who forced her to sign a five-year contract. FBI Special Agent Paul Ballard (Tahmoh Penikett), who is investigating the Dollhouse, receives mysterious packages containing pictures and videos of Caroline/Echo during her college days, and he becomes obsessed with rescuing her.

Things are humming along nicely, or as nicely as they can under Rossum's virtual enslavement, when Echo begins to retain some memories after her personality wipes. As she continues to gain self-awareness, she works with Ballard to take down Rossum. Many mind-swaps later, Echo and her team save the world from Rossum's imprinting technology, which has turned into an apocalyptic nightmare, in "Epitaph Two: Return" (2010), the series finale.

*Dollhouse* ran for two brief, ratings-challenged seasons. Its main character was essentially a different person every episode, especially at the beginning, making it difficult for audiences to form an attachment. How ironic that a series so concerned with issues of identity suffered from its own identity crisis.

### Donner, Lindsay (*Psi Factor: Chronicles of the Paranormal*)

Data analyst and agent for a covert organization investigating paranormal activity.

See: ***Psi Factor: Chronicles of the Paranormal*** (1996–2000, 88 episodes, Canada)

### Donovan, Claudia (*Warehouse 13*)

Claudia Donovan (Allison Scagliotti) is a techie wunderkind at Warehouse 13, a repository for supernatural artifacts located in the Badlands of South Dakota. Claudia's mechanical expertise and hacking skills come in handy at the warehouse, both in locating artifacts around the world and in designing devices to defeat them. After a period of apprenticeship and warehouse-bound duties, Claudia moves into fieldwork, partnering with Steve Jinks (Aaron Ashmore), who becomes her BFF. In "An Evil Within" (2012), Claudia uses an artifact, Johann Maelzel's Metronome, to bring Steve back to life after a warehouse catastrophe, but experiences unintended consequences when she feels the pain of any injuries Steve receives. Teenaged Claudia is an

*Warehouse 13*'s Allison Scagliotti at the 2012 Comic-Con International in San Diego (from a color photograph by Gage Skidmore, CC BY-SA 3.0).

orphan, but finds a substitute, albeit cranky, father in Warehouse 13's Agent in Charge, Artie Nielsen (Saul Rubinek). While Claudia grows into her role as field agent, she learns she is destined to become the future caretaker of the warehouse, replacing inimitably spooky Mrs. Frederic (CCH Pounder), a destiny that is fulfilled with Claudia's typical cool in series finale "Endless" (2014).

See also: ***Warehouse 13*** **(2009–2014, 64 episodes, USA)**

## Down to Earth (1984–1987, 106 episodes, USA)
*Created by:* Sam Harris, Bruce H. Newberg
*Production Co.:* Procter & Gamble Productions
*Originally Aired:* TBS
*Main Cast:* Carol Mansell, Stephen Johnson, Dick Sargent, David Kaufman, Kyle Richards, Randy Josselyn, Marla Rubinoff, Lester Fletcher, Ronnie Schell, Michael Delano, Rip Taylor

Ethel MacDoogan (Carol Mansell) had been a flapper during the Roaring Twenties, perishing prematurely after an unfortunate encounter with a trolley. ("Golly!") Ethereal Ethel, a.k.a. Angel 972, waits patiently in heaven for 60 years, hoping to earn her wings, and gets her chance when young Jay Jay Preston (Randy Josselyn) prays for an angel to help his family. Ethel is soon back on Earth, working for the Prestons as a maid, and much of the early humor revolves around Ethel's lack of familiarity with modern-day customs and devices. In "Food for Thought" (1984), Ethel does the grocery shopping by home computer, but ends up ordering 10 of everything at the store. She must also deal with a succession of heavenly supervisors, including Mr. Divine (Lester Fletcher) and Lester Luster (Ronnie Schell). In "Lester Gets Stuck" (1984), Ethel sends Luster's jacket to the cleaners, which promptly burns down, destroying Lester's wings and grounding him on Earth. And that's just an average day in the life of this endearing, but daffy guardian angel.

## The Dresden Files (2007, 12 episodes, Canada/USA)
*Based on:* The novels of Jim Butcher
*Production Co.:* Dresden Files Productions, Saturn Films, Lionsgate Television
*Originally Aired:* Syfy
*Main Cast:* Paul Blackthorne, Valerie Cruz, Terrence Mann, Conrad Coates, Raoul Bhaneja

Harry Dresden (Paul Blackthorne) is the only wizard listed in the Chicago Yellow Pages. Dresden won't perform at your party, but if you've lost something or think you're being haunted by a ghost, Harry's your man. Given his profession, Harry has a lot of unusual events swirling around him, which tend to draw the attention of the police, most of whom don't believe in magic. Lt. Connie Murphy (Valerie Cruz), however, is on the fence, disavowing magic, but turning to Harry for help on cases which might best be described as "hinky."

In "Hair of the Dog" (2007), Murphy seeks Dresden's assistance in solving murders where the victims' hair and teeth are taken, and Harry realizes werewolves are involved—as victims. Not surprisingly, there is some romantic frisson between handsome Harry and comely Connie, but, like "Bob" (Terrence Mann), Harry's spirit-friend trapped for eternity in a skull, their unfulfilled romance is a specter, ensnared forever in the black box of premature series cancellation.

## Drop Dead Diva (2009–2014, 78 episodes, USA)
*Created by:* Josh Berman
*Production Co.:* Storyline Entertainment, Sony Pictures Television, et al.
*Originally Aired:* Lifetime
*Main Cast:* Brooke Elliott, Margaret Cho, April Bowlby, Kate Levering, Jackson Hurst, Josh Stamberg, Ben Feldman, Lex Medlin, Brooke D'Orsay

You don't often find plus-sized women as series leads on television, and when you do, their weight is always a prominent theme, as in *Drop Dead Diva*. This dramedy/fantasy/legal procedural inspires when making the point that a woman's weight shouldn't matter in work or in life, but it still employs some female stereotypes along the way.

Aspiring model Deb Dobkins (Brooke D'Orsay), a sweet, but shallow blonde, is killed in a car crash while driving to her audition for a game show. Due to the inattention of a clerical worker at the Pearly Gates, Deb returns to Earth in the body of a recently deceased shooting victim, Jane Bingum (Brooke Elliott). Deb wakes up to the shock of Jane's size-16 body, and must learn to accept a new exterior as well as a rearranged interior life. "Jane" now has Deb's memories, but still retains her own brilliant legal mind and career. If that's not complicated enough, Deb's boyfriend, Grayson Kent (Jackson Hurst), begins to work at the same law firm as Jane, so Deb must see her former love every day, without revealing her true identity, although she is often tempted. Jane/Deb somehow manages to keep her sanity, with the help of Stacy Barrett (April Bowlby), a sweet, but ditzy blonde (yes, stereotypes), who knows her secret. At work, she stays on the rails thanks to Teri Lee (Margaret Cho), her wisecracking assistant, who fills in Jane's memory blanks, which Teri thinks were caused by the shooting.

As Jane/Deb tries to catch Grayson's eye, she continues to accept cases, many, just by coincidence, involving women and their weight. In "The F Word" (2009), "F" stands for fat, as Jane's client, a waitress at a trendy bar, sues the establishment for terminating her employment because she gained 50 pounds. Jane later reverses roles, becoming a client of her law firm in "The Dress" (2009), when she sues a Beverly Hills boutique for not carrying plus-sizes. She is represented in the action, albeit grudgingly, by office rival and sometime mean girl Kim Kaswell (Kate Levering), who is also a rival for Grayson's affections.

More body-swapping ensues in later seasons, when Grayson dies and comes back as a convicted murderer, and the original Jane comes back as a model. (Turnabout is fair play.)

In the universe of *Drop Dead Diva*, heaven's efficiency is less than divine.

## DuBois, Allison (*Medium*)
Allison DuBois sees dead people—usually when she's asleep, but sometimes even when she's awake. She uses her psychic abilities to help murder victims find

peace, and her job as a consultant in the Phoenix District Attorney's Office puts her in an ideal position to see that justice is done. But her visions, like the dreams that bring them, are often incoherent and sometimes surreal, making it difficult to make immediate sense of them. In "Being Mrs. O'Leary's Cow" (2005), Allison (Patricia Arquette) has confusing dreams about a pilot who may or may not save a plane from crashing, and who may or may not have murdered his wife. Allison and husband Joe (Jake Weber) must also raise three daughters, all of whom are beginning to display psychic abilities. In "Mother's Little Helper" (2007), Allison and eldest daughter Ariel (Sofia Vassilieva) have a series of interconnected dreams, and must work together to interpret their visions if they are to solve the double homicide of a mother and daughter.

Patricia Arquette won an Emmy Award for her portrayal of Allison, a woman who is tenacious and strong, yet vulnerable and sympathetic. She convinced us on a weekly basis that seeing dead people is a tough way to make a living.

See also: *Medium* (2005–2011, 130 episodes, USA)

**Dunham, Olivia (*Fringe*)**

FBI agent with a federal task force investigating weird science and unexplained phenomena.

See: *Fringe* (2008–2013, 100 episodes, USA)

**Dyna Girl (*Electra Woman and Dyna Girl*)**

Magazine reporter who transforms into a caped alter-ego to fight crime.

See: *Electra Woman and Dyna Girl* (1976, 16 episodes, USA)

**Dyna Girl (*Electra Woman and Dyna Girl*)**

Los Angeles superhero relegated to sidekick status because of a glamorous partner.

See: *Electra Woman and Dyna Girl* (2016, 8 episodes, USA)

**Early Edition (1996–2000, 90 episodes, USA)**
*Created by:* Ian Abrams, Patrick Q. Page, Vik Rubenfeld, Bob Brush
*Production Co.:* Three Characters, Angelica Films, CBS Productions, et al.
*Originally Aired:* CBS
*Main Cast:* Kyle Chandler, Shanésia Davis-Williams, Fisher Stevens, Kristy Swanson, Billie Worley, Myles Jeffrey, Ron Dean

Gary Hobson (Kyle Chandler) receives a copy of the *Chicago Sun-Times* every day. That doesn't sound like much of a TV show premise, does it? But add the fact that Gary is mysteriously receiving the NEXT day's newspaper one day early, giving him the chance to avert disasters, and the possibilities become clear.

A former stockbroker whose wife has shown him the door, Gary reverses his personal tailspin with his new, albeit reluctant, mission to help people he identifies in the newspaper, which is delivered daily and protected by an orange cat. The devil on Gary's shoulder is his friend Chuck Fishman (Fisher Stevens), who knows about the strange newspaper and would like to use it for selfish ends, usually involving quick cash. Marissa Clark (Shanésia Davis-Williams), is the angel to Chuck's devil,

Gary's blind former co-worker who helps him make moral decisions when the paper presents difficult choices. In "March in Time" (1997), for example, Gary questions whether he should save the life of a white supremacist, but Marissa, who is black, convinces him that he should.

*Early Edition* went from middling to poor ratings, and was canceled after its fourth season. Gary should have seen that coming.

### Earp, Waverly (*Wynonna Earp*)

Research expert in Earp family history, who helps her sister kill demons due a generational curse.

See: ***Wynonna Earp*** (2016– , 13 episodes, Canada/USA)

### Earp, Wynonna (*Wynonna Earp*)

Great-great-granddaughter of Wyatt Earp tasked with killing demons originally dispatched by her ancestor.

See: ***Wynonna Earp*** (2016– , 13 episodes, Canada/USA)

### *Earth 2* (1994–1995, 22 episodes, USA)

*Created by:* Michael Duggan, Carol Flint, Mark Levin, Billy Ray
*Production Co.:* Amblin Entertainment, Universal Television
*Originally Aired:* NBC
*Main Cast:* Debrah Farentino, Joey Zimmerman, Clancy Brown, J. Madison Wright, Sullivan Walker, Jessica Steen, Rebecca Gayheart, John Gegenhuber, Antonio Sabàto, Jr.

Debrah Farentino stars as Devon Adair, a billionaire living on a space station in the year 2192. Even space-faring billionaires have problems, however, and Devon's is "the syndrome," a usually fatal illness afflicting her eight-year-old son Ulysses (Joey Zimmerman). Devon assembles an expedition to an Earth-like planet, G889, believing that exposure to sunlight and fresh air might cure Uly of his malady, thought to be a type of space-station environmental illness.

After crash-landing on the planet, the remaining members of The Eden Project, as the expedition is called, begin a trek to the proposed site of their colony, New Pacifica. The survivors include John Danziger (Clancy Brown) and his troubleprone daughter True (J. Madison Wright), hunky pilot Alonzo Solace (Antonio Sabàto, Jr.), and cyborg tutor Yale (Sullivan Walker). Before long they encounter some spooky humanoid locals, the aptly named "Terrians," who tunnel through the sandy Earth and communicate telepathically. The Terrians manage to heal Uly, but Devon's problems are far from over, as she and the pioneers must deal with a traitor in their midst, Dr. Julia Heller (Jessica Steen), an agent for a government group with its own plans for G889. But no one has asked the planet what it wants, and the Terrians, who have a symbiotic link with their world, may see the colonists as a threat.

Communications with the group were lost at that point, when NBC canceled the series after one season.

### *Eastwick* (2009, 13 episodes, USA)

*Based on:* The novel *The Witches of Eastwick* by John Updike

*Created by:* Maggie Friedman
*Production Co.:* Curly Girly, Warner Bros. Television, Bonanza Productions
*Originally Aired:* ABC
*Main Cast:* Jaime Ray Newman, Rebecca Romijn, Lindsay Price, Paul Gross, Matt Dallas, Sara Rue, Ashley Benson, Jon Bernthal, Veronica Cartwright, Johann Urb, Darren Criss, Cybill Shepherd, Mia Hayes

Three beautiful, but unhappy women in the idyllic town of Eastwick make a wish for something to change in their lives. Their wish seemingly summons a mysterious and charismatic stranger, Darryl Van Horne (Paul Gross), who reveals that the women have untapped supernatural powers. Kat Gardener (Jaime Ray Newman), a nurse and mother of five caught in a loveless marriage, begins to display control over the elements and later exhibits healing abilities. Joanna Frankel (Lindsay Price), a shy journalist with an unrequited crush on her coworker, finds that she can hypnotize men and soon discovers telekinetic abilities. Roxie Torcoletti (Rebecca Romijn), a sculptor and widow scandalizing the town by dating a younger man, learns that she can see the future and read others' thoughts, including those of the dead. The witches, one blonde, one brunette, and one redhead, use their gifts to improve their lives, while growing increasingly concerned that Van Horne may have a hidden, if not dark agenda. (Is that Van Horne or Van Horned?)

Witches had led a charmed (ahem) existence on TV up until this point in long-running hits such as *Bewitched* and *Sabrina the Teenage Witch*. *Eastwick* more resembled *Charmed*, with its three witches' learning to control their powers, but *Charmed* had lasted an enchanting eight seasons, while *Eastwick* was cursed/canceled after nine episodes. If only these women had discovered their powers earlier—some clairvoyance from Roxie, a little mind-control from Joanna, and a hint of lightning (just for show) from Kat would have done the trick.

### Echo (*Dollhouse*)

Operative whose mind is programmed with various personalities to suit the tastes of an organization's rich clients.
See: ***Dollhouse*** **(2009–2010, 26 episodes, USA)**

### Edison, Eve (*Mann & Machine*)

Police officer who is actually a sophisticated robot under the skin.
See: ***Mann & Machine*** **(1992, 9 episodes, USA)**

### Edison, Tina (*Maniac Mansion*)

Eccentric scientist's brilliant daughter who helps out around the lab while dealing with adolescence.
See: ***Maniac Mansion*** **(1990–1993, 66 episodes, Canada/USA)**

### Electra Woman (*Electra Woman and Dyna Girl*)

Superhero who fights cleverly named criminals with gobs of gadgets.
See: ***Electra Woman and Dyna Girl*** **(1976, 16 episodes, USA)**

### Electra Woman (*Electra Woman and Dyna Girl*)
Caped crusader who gains the spotlight at the expense of her less glamorous partner.

See: *Electra Woman and Dyna Girl* (2016, 8 episodes, USA)

### *Electra Woman and Dyna Girl* (1976, 16 episodes, USA)
*Created by:* Joe Ruby, Ken Spears
*Production Co.:* Sid & Marty Krofft Television Productions
*Originally Aired:* ABC
*Main Cast:* Diedre Hall, Judy Strangis, Norman Alden

A pastiche of the popular *Batman* TV series and comic books, *Electra Woman and Dyna Girl*, originally broadcast as part of *The Krofft Supershow*, brings us a pair of female caped crusaders who fight crime in spandex. Deidre Hall is Lori/Electra Woman and Judy Strangis portrays Judy/Dyna Girl, two magazine reporters who use their alter-egos and an array of gadgets (most with the prefix "Electra") to battle baddies, such as "Glitter Rock," "The Spider Lady," and "Empress of Evil." Professor Frank Heflin (Norman Alden) assists the Dyna duo at ElectraBase, manning the CrimeScope computer and feeding the superheroes information via their Electra-Coms, amazing wrist-worn devices with a variety of functions, including a force field and tractor beam. Holy Electra-Change!

### *Electra Woman and Dyna Girl* (2016, 8 episodes, USA)
*Based on:* The TV series created by Joe Ruby, Ken Spears
*Production Co.:* Legendary Digital Media, Sid & Marty Krofft Pictures
*Originally Aired:* Streaming on Fullscreen, Google Play, iTunes
*Main Cast:* Grace Helbig, Hannah Hart, Christopher Coutts, Matreya Fedor

Reboot of the 1976 series, introducing the female superheroes to the digital generation with a big Electra-smirk. YouTube comedy stars Grace Helbig and Hannah Hart portray the distaff caped crusaders, who are tired of anonymity and decide to get some attention by filming their exploits. Their video goes viral, natch, and the duo is picked up by CMM (Creative Masked Management), which handles PR for the tights-wearing crowd. Our heroes promptly move from Akron, Ohio, to Los Angeles, where the action is, but a rift develops once they're in the spotlight. Electra Woman (Helbig), a statuesque beauty, becomes famous, while Dyna Girl (Hart), who sports a short haircut to match her short body, is relegated to sidekick status.

Gadget guy Frank Heflin (Christopher Coutts) and The Empress of Evil (Matreya Fedor) are back for this reimagining, which spoofs superhero films, Hollywood culture, and the Internet. That's a tall order for a short series of 11-minute episodes, but if anyone can pull it off, it's the dynamic duo of Helbig and Hart.

### Elizabeth (*V*)
A human/extraterrestrial hybrid who chooses one side of her heritage over the other in a battle for Earth.

See: *V* (1984–1985, 19 episodes, USA)

## Endora (*Bewitched*)

Sartorially resplendent witch, none too happy about her daughter's marriage to a mortal.

See: ***Bewitched*** (1964–1972, 254 episodes, USA)

## Engelson, Camille (*Stitchers*)

Caltech grad student and operative for a covert program which accesses the minds of dead people.

See: ***Stitchers*** (2015– , 21 episodes, USA)

## Enterprise

See: ***Star Trek: Enterprise*** (2001–2005, 98 episodes, USA)

## Eureka (2006–2012, 77 episodes, USA)

*Created by:* Andrew Cosby, Jaime Paglia
*Production Co.:* Universal Cable Productions, NBC Universal Television
*Originally Aired:* Syfy
*Main Cast:* Colin Ferguson, Salli Richardson-Whitfield, Joe Morton, Jordan Hinson, Ed Quinn, Erica Cerra, Neil Grayston, Niall Matter

Eureka is a fictional town in the Pacific Northwest, home to a cadre of brilliant scientists, most of whom work for Global Dynamics, a cutting-edge research facility under the aegis of the Department of Defense. While Eureka contributes technological advances to modern society, misuses of science, whether accidental or intentional, do occur (on almost a weekly basis), and someone must step in to ferret out the mysterious circumstances and clean up the mess. Town Sheriff Jack Carter (Colin Ferguson), though not a genius himself, has a knack for getting to the truth of the matter through intuition and common sense. Dr. **Allison Blake** (Salli Richardson-Whitfield), the liaison between DOD and GD, uses her intelligence and two PhDs to puzzle out the science of the matter. Among others assisting the sheriff and the doctor is Deputy Sheriff **Josefina "Jo" Lupo** (Erica Cerra), who goes by the book in keeping order among the eccentrics, not an easy job, especially when alternate timelines make things confusing. But this is Eureka, where thought is exalted, and problems made by the mind can be solved by the mind.

See also: **Blake, Allison** (*Eureka*); **Lupo, Josefina "Jo"** (*Eureka*)

## Evans, Erica (*V*)

FBI agent Erica Evans has a lot of secrets. While seemingly working to protect extraterrestrial "Visitors" from terrorist attacks in her day job, she conspires with resistance fighters and the Visitors' own Fifth Column by night to thwart the plans of evil alien leader Anna (Morena Baccarin). Erica, as portrayed by Elizabeth Mitchell, also hides the truth about the visitors' real intentions and reptilian undercarriage from everyone, including her impressionable teenage son Tyler (Logan Huffman), who is enamored with the aliens, especially Anna's pretty daughter Lisa (Laura Vandervoort). Somehow, though, Agent Evans manages to keep it all straight, juggling all her lies and lives, even going on to become the leader of the global Fifth Column in "Uneasy Lies the Head" (2011).

See also: *V* **(2009–2011, 22 episodes, USA)**

### Evans, Isabel (*Roswell*)

Extraterrestrial teen adopted by an Earth family and trying to discover her origins.

See: *Roswell* **(1999–2002, 61 episodes, USA)**

### *The Event* (2010–2011, 22 episodes, USA)

*Created by:* Nick Wauters
*Production Co.:* Universal Media Studios, Steve Stark Productions
*Originally Aired:* NBC
*Main Cast:* Jason Ritter, Sarah Roemer, Laura Innes, Ian Anthony Dale, Scott Patterson, Taylor Cole, Lisa Vidal, Bill Smitrovich, Clifton Collins, Jr., Željko Ivanek, Blair Underwood

Complex SF thriller about the arrival of a small group of extraterrestrials on our planet at the end of World War II, and the political and worldwide ramifications of their secret existence here, extending to the present day. Enter Sean Walker (Jason Ritter), an amiable everyman, who is thrust into the middle of the international conspiracy, when his girlfriend, Leila Buchanan (Sarah Roemer), is kidnapped during a Caribbean cruise. Leila's kidnapper is Vicky Roberts (Taylor Cole), a former CIA operative turned private security contractor/assassin, whose conscience leads her in unexpected directions. It turns out that Leila is half-extraterrestrial on her father's side, and must search for her kidnapped sister after her own escape.

The small skirmishes fought by Sean, Leila, and company are mirrored by big battles at the top between the extraterrestrials, led by Sophia Maguire (Laura Innes), and the U.S. government, fronted by President Elias Martinez (Blair Underwood). Sophia, who looks human, but ages very slowly, has been held with other extraterrestrials at a detention facility in Alaska for almost 70 years. Some of Sophia's people, however, had escaped capture, and are now sleepers among the human population.

Double-crosses, assassination attempts, and alien technology were just the tip of the iceberg for *The Event*, which retained more secrets than originally planned due to its cancellation after just one season.

### *Every Witch Way* (2014–2015, 85 episodes, USA)

*Based on:* The TV series *Grachi*
*Production Co.:* Cinemat, Nickelodeon Productions
*Originally Aired:* Nickelodeon
*Main Cast:* Paola Andino, Nick Merico, Paris Smith, Daniela Nieves, Tyler Alvarez, Autumn Wendel, Denisea Wilson, Zoey Burger, Michele Verdi, Rahart Adams

*Every Witch Way* is an apt title for this tween-oriented sitcom which has witches every which way you turn. Paola Andino portrays Emma Alonso, the new kid at Iridium High, who soon learns that she's a witch. That's a lot to take in for a teen, but, to make matters worse, Emma soon runs afoul of Maddie Van Pelt (Paris Smith), the most popular girl in school, who is also a witch. Next she makes an enemy of Principal Torres (Michele Verdi), not for any academic reason, but because the principal is (you guessed it) a witch. Torres wants to steal Emma's powers because Emma is not just any witch, but the Chosen One, the world's most powerful witch. (For some reason, at least since *Buffy the Vampire Slayer*, Chosen Ones must be pretty girls in high school.) Romance leads Emma astray as well, especially when her love interest, Jax Novoa (Rahart Adams), turns out to be a wizard hoping to steal her magical energy. (A pattern is emerging.) Ultimately Emma gets by with a little help from her (MANY) friends, overcoming romantic rivals, magical challengers, evil clones, and even a "continuum break," which alters reality.

*Every Witch Way* ran for four seasons and generated an immediate sequel, *WITS Academy*, spinning off several characters, including Andi Cruz (Daniela Nieves). Andi, Emma's best friend, is a non-witch allowed to attend the supernatural school so she can become a Guardian to witches and wizards.

Alas, the spin-off lasted only one season, failing to master ratings magic.

### Evil Queen (*Once Upon a Time*)

Mayor of a Maine town whose curse has stripped its residents of their enchanted pasts.

See: *Once Upon a Time* (2011– , 111 episodes, USA)

### Extant (2014–2015, 26 episodes, USA)

*Created by:* Mickey Fisher
*Production Co.:* Amblin Television, CBS Television Studios, 22 Plates
*Originally Aired:* CBS
*Main Cast:* Halle Berry, Goran Visnjic, Pierce Gagnon, Jeffrey Dean Morgan, Grace Gummer, Hiroyuki Sanada, Camryn Manheim, Tyler Hilton, Michael O'Neill, Henderson Wade

Halle Berry stars as Molly Woods, an astronaut on a solo mission in outer space, who returns home after 13 months to find herself inexplicably pregnant. Molly tries to settle back into a normal home life, or as normal as it can be, since her "son" Ethan (Pierce Gagnon) is a human-appearing robot engineered by her husband, John Woods (Goran Visnjic). She continues to investigate the strange circumstances behind her pregnancy, learning that extraterrestrial forces are involved, not to mention the requisite governmental conspiracy. Soon enough, Molly's boys, robot Ethan

Halle Berry (*Extant*) speaks at San Diego Comic-Con International in 2013 (from a color photograph by Gage Skidmore, CC BY-SA 3.0).

and extraterrestrial Ahdu (Henderson Wade), come to hold the very future of our planet in their hands, and it's up to Mother Molly to make sure the Earth endures.

While the narrative arc sounds silly enough, this SF thriller is gripping in its first season, when secret after secret is revealed within the context of realistic science, but it loses steam in its second year, thanks to a large reboot that attempted to add more action and violence into the mix. Alas, *Extant* went extinct after season two, leaving Molly, Ethan, et al. trapped in the alternate universe known as premature series cancellation.

### *The Fantastic Journey* (1977, 10 episodes, USA)
*Production Co.:* Bruce Lansbury Productions, Columbia Pictures Television
*Originally Aired:* NBC
*Main Cast:* Jared Martin, Ike Eisenmann, Carl Franklin, Katie Saylor, Roddy McDowall

"Lost in the Devil's Triangle, trapped in a dimension with beings from the future and other worlds, a party of adventurers journey through zones of time back to their own time."

Even the opening narration can't clarify what's going on in this short-lived series that suffered from too many concepts. A research expedition is surrounded by a mysterious green cloud in the Bermuda Triangle and ends up shipwrecked on an uncharted island. Soon the group meets Varian (Jared Martin), a man from the 23rd century, who explains exactly what kind of mess they've gotten themselves into. It seems that the island is the center of a space/time warp, and people from various eras and even worlds are trapped there. Varian becomes the guide for the remaining members of the expedition, teenager Scott Jordan (Ike Eisenmann) and medical doctor Fred Walters (Carl Franklin), hoping to lead them to a promised land which is the gateway back home. As they travel through different time periods/zones on the island, each with its own community, they encounter Liana (Katie Saylor), the "daughter of an Atlantian father and an extra-

Liana (Katie Saylor) has a unique lineage and peculiar powers in *The Fantastic Journey* (NBC Television).

terrestrial mother." (Yes, lots of concepts here.) Liana possesses superior physical strength and has a companion cat with whom she can communicate telepathically. Liana befriends the group, but is kidnapped by Dr. Jonathan Willoway (Roddy McDowall), a 60s scientist, who is leading a community of robots. Eventually Willoway joins the band too, and they are off for further adventures until another unnatural force, the National Broadcasting Company, wields its invisible, but mighty axe, cutting off their last hope of returning home.

### Farrell, Jennifer (*Jennifer Slept Here*)
Deceased 60s movie star who offers ghostly guidance to a teenaged boy.
See: *Jennifer Slept Here* (1983–1984, 13 episodes, USA)

### *Farscape* (1999–2003, 88 episodes, Australia/USA)
*Created by:* Rockne S. O'Bannon
*Production Co.:* Jim Henson Productions, Hallmark Entertainment, et al.
*Originally Aired:* Syfy
*Main Cast:* Ben Browder, Claudia Black, Virginia Hey, Anthony Simcoe, Gigi Edgley, Paul Goddard, Lani Tupu, Wayne Pygram, Jonathan Hardy, Tammy MacIntosh

John Crichton (Ben Browder), an astronaut for the International Aeronautics and Space Administration, takes a test flight aboard an experimental prototype, but faces a bigger test than he bargained for when a wormhole flings his spacecraft to an unknown part of the galaxy. The commander suddenly finds himself in the midst of a fierce battle between two groups, the incongruously named Peacekeepers and a small band of prisoners, who are attempting to escape via a biomechanical ship called *Moya*.

During *Moya*'s escape, she literally pulls Crichton and one of the Peacekeepers, Aeryn Sun (Claudia Black), along with her. Sun is a Peacekeeper pilot and officer of the human-appearing Sebacean species, who initially becomes a prisoner of the rebels, but eventually becomes a fellow fugitive. At the start of her encounter with Crichton and the various alien species aboard *Moya*, Aeryn is emotionally cold due to her Peacekeeper indoctrination, but begins to learn how to play nicely with her crewmates. Her training in weapons and hand-to-hand combat makes her physically superior to John, placing her in the traditional "male" role, while John gets the "damsel in distress" treatment during their adventures.

Crichton meets his first plant person in Pa'u Zotoh Zhaan (Virginia Hey), a priestess and member of the Delvian species, who is blue from (bald) head to toe. Zhaan had murdered her lover, who was a Peacekeeper collaborator, and now uses her empathic and telepathic abilities to assist *Moya*'s crew. She later sacrifices herself to save the other fugitives in "Self-Inflicted Wounds (Part 2): Wait for the Wheel" (2001), when *Moya* becomes fused with another vessel. Zhaan's death coincided with Virginia Hey's request for a lighter workload, when her health began to suffer from the long hours in her character's stunning, but toxic makeup.

Chiana (Gigi Edgley), a thief, con artist, and prostitute of the gray-skinned Nebari species, later joins the fugitives on *Moya*, when she effects an escape from a

Nebari agent. Her conformity-loving government, appropriately known as The Establishment, had sentenced Chiana to be "cleansed" (mind-wiped) for her rebellious and freedom-loving ways. She helps the crew with her fighting skills, developed during a life on the run, and she gains precognitive abilities in "Losing Time" (2001), which allow her to alter the course of problematic events.

As the crew works to evade the Peacekeepers, and John searches for a wormhole back to Earth, John and Aeryn grow closer. Aeryn becomes pregnant, although there is some confusion over paternity for a time due to the sudden presence of a "twin" John (this being science fiction, and all). In the series finale, "Bad Timing" (2003), Aeryn accepts John's proposal of marriage, and the two are promptly obliterated by an alien intruder. That certainly wasn't the ending fans were hoping for, but it seems that Syfy (then the Sci-Fi Channel) had abruptly canceled the series before the producers could finish their arc, which would have revived the couple. Pressure from fans helped to bring about a two-part miniseries, *Farscape: The Peacekeeper Wars* (2004), wherein John and Aeryn were reanimated by aliens. This more fitting sendoff allowed John, Aeryn, and baby-makes-three to find their happily ever after.

Aww.

### Feigelsteen, Miranda (*Mysterious Ways*)

Introverted research assistant working with a professor who searches for proof of miraculous phenomena.

See: *Mysterious Ways* **(2000–2002, 44 episodes, Canada/USA)**

### Fi (*The Lost Saucer*)

Time-traveling android from the year 2369 who accidentally kidnaps a 70s youth and his babysitter.

See: *The Lost Saucer* **(1975–1976, 16 episodes, USA)**

### Figalilly, Phoebe "Nanny" (*Nanny and the Professor*)

Young British nanny whose strange charms captivate a widowed professor and his three children.

See: *Nanny and the Professor* **(1970–1971, 54 episodes, USA)**

## *Firefly* (2002, 14 episodes, USA)

*Created by:* Joss Whedon
*Production Co.:* Mutant Enemy Productions, 20th Century–Fox Television
*Originally Aired:* Fox
*Main Cast:* Nathan Fillion, Gina Torres, Alan Tudyk, Morena Baccarin, Adam Baldwin, Jewel Staite, Sean Maher, Summer Glau, Ron Glass

Most shows canceled in the middle of their first season "go gentle into that good night," becoming footnotes in television reference books. On rare occasion, however, a short-lived series refuses to leave quietly, making an indelible impression on its fans, and, in the case of *Firefly*, finding new life in different media.

Created by Joss Whedon of *Buffy the Vampire Slayer* fame, *Firefly* is a space western about renegades and resisters on the frontiers of space in 2517. Nathan Fillion portrays Mal Reynolds, captain of his own transport ship, *Serenity*, a "Firefly" class spaceship, that resembles, well—a firefly. Mal had fought on the losing side of a civil war against The Alliance, and he copes with the new world order, while trying to preserve his independence.

If it's a space opera, there must be a motley crew, and Mal's is the most ragtag of the ragtag. Zoe Washburne (Gina Torres), who had served with Reynolds during the Unification War, is his second-in-command on *Serenity*. Given their wartime history, Zoe is fiercely loyal to Mal, often to the consternation of her husband, "Wash" Washburne (Alan Tudyk), *Serenity*'s pilot, who calls his wife a "warrior woman." But Zoe shows where her loyalty ultimately lies, when she is given the "Zoe's choice" of saving her husband or her captain in "War Stories" (2002).

Other members of the nine-person crew include Kaylee Frye (Jewel Staite), the ship's talented and sunny engineer, Inara Serra (Morena Baccarin), a high-class courtesan called a "Companion," who actually confers prestige on *Serenity* by her presence, and Simon Tam (Sean Maher), the resident physician. Simon smuggles his teenaged sister, River Tam (Summer Glau), onto *Serenity* after freeing her from an Alliance school that served as cover for a program to create an army of assassins. Because of the program's medical experiments, River is sometimes delusional and even violent, but she also possesses psychic abilities and almost superhuman combat skills, which she uses to assist the crew in life-threatening situations.

*Firefly* was canceled by Fox after only 11 episodes had aired, but the series had already gained an avid cult following, whose continued interest sparked the release of a feature film, *Serenity*, by Universal Pictures in 2005. Several comic book series ensued, while *Firefly* continued to show up on magazine lists of the top cult shows ever. As *Entertainment Weekly* said on its own list of best cult shows in 2012: "…martyrdom has only enhanced its legend."

### The Flash (2014– , 46 episodes, USA)
*Based on:* The DC Comics character created by Robert Kanigher, Carmine Infantino
*Created by:* Greg Berlanti, Andrew Kreisberg, Geoff Johns
*Production Co.:* Warner Bros. Television, DC Entertainment, et al.
*Originally Aired:* The CW
*Main Cast:* Grant Gustin, Candice Patton, Danielle Panabaker, Rick Cosnett, Carlos Valdes, Tom Cavanagh, Jesse L. Martin, Keiynan Lonsdale

Even Ancestry.com would have a hard time keeping track of all the characters who have gone by the name "Flash" throughout DC Comics history, but television's focus has been on the Barry Allen incarnation, first in *The Flash* (1990–1991), and now in this series, which has shown more staying power than its predecessor.

Grant Gustin stars as Barry Allen, a forensic scientist who is struck by lightning after a particle accelerator accident in Central City. Waking up from a coma nine months later, Barry learns that he has superhuman speed, later becoming the Flash, a superhero who will battle the supervillains created by the same superaccident. (Convenient!) Barry's childhood friend and future love interest Iris West (Candice Patton) writes about the Flash on her blog, graduating to the job of reporter for

Central City Picture News. In a break from the comic books, which depicted her as Caucasian, Iris is African American in this reimagining.

Since SF shows and comics like to mix things up with parallel universes and alternate timelines, Iris is a police detective on Earth Two, an alternate dimension revealed in season two. (There is even an Earth-38, but let's not go there.) Back on Earth One, Iris assists Barry on "Team Flash," along with Dr. Caitlin Snow (Danielle Panabaker), a bio-engineer at S.T.A.R. Labs. Caitlin has a double on Earth Two, of course, who even has her own alter ego, a meta-human named Killer Frost. Since her Earth Two doppelgänger is evil, Caitlin is concerned that darkness may hide inside her.

Not surprisingly, given the main character's speed, *The Flash* is light on its feet. Enjoy the fun, but have a scorecard handy to keep track of all those universes and doppelgängers.

## *Flash Gordon* (1954–1955, 39 episodes, France/USA/ West Germany)

*Based on:* The comic strip created by Alex Raymond
*Production Co.:* Intercontinental Television Films, La Telediffusion, Interwest Film
*Originally Aired:* In Syndication, DuMont
*Main Cast:* Steve Holland, Irene Champlin, Joseph Nash

When people of a certain age picture Flash Gordon, they usually think of Buster Crabbe, who portrayed the square-jawed hero in three multi-chapter movie serials, later shown on television during the 50s and beyond. Lesser known is Steve Holland, the Flash of this one-season wonder, who shows off his cover-model good looks by taking off his shirt at least once per episode. The Dale Arden of the piece is Irene Champlin, who along with Flash and Dr. Hans Zarkov (Joseph Nash), works for the Galactic Bureau of Investigation, battling exotic villains to keep the cosmos safe. Champlin's Dale isn't merely a damsel in distress, although, like all space opera heroes, she needs rescuing occasionally, as in "Escape into Time" (1954), when she is kidnapped by a notorious criminal with time-traveling on his mind. Dale is a true partner to Flash, as well as a trained scientist, repeatedly making her case for accompanying him on a mission which might expose them to radiation in "The Claim Jumpers" (1954). Dale performs many of her missions in pants, but can also be seen in the shortest of short skirts, not much more than a tunic really, continuing the sf miniskirt trend seen in shows such as *Space Patrol*.

In a departure from the other space shows, however, *Flash Gordon* featured villains and aliens with German accents, a byproduct of filming episodes in West Germany. Whether that adds an element of charm, kitsch, or both to this obscure series is in the eye of the beholder.

In 2007, Alex Raymond's comic book hero flashed across the small screen again, with Eric Johnson as the title character and Gina Holden as Dale Arden. *Flash Gordon* ran for 21 episodes on Syfy (then the Sci-Fi Channel), and was canceled after one season due to low ratings and abysmal reviews.

Ming the Merciless is laughing somewhere.

## *FlashForward* (2009–2010, 22 episodes, USA)
*Based on:* The novel *Flashforward* by Robert J. Sawyer
*Created by:* Brannon Braga, David S. Goyer
*Production Co.:* HBO Entertainment, ABC Studios, Phantom Four Films
*Originally Aired:* ABC
*Main Cast:* Joseph Fiennes, John Cho, Jack Davenport, Zachary Knighton, Peyton List, Dominic Monaghan, Brían F. O'Byrne, Courtney B. Vance, Sonya Walger, Christine Woods

Complex, character-laden SF mystery about a brief worldwide loss of consciousness wherein (almost) everyone receives a glimpse of their lives six months into the future. The FBI is immediately on the case, trying to determine the who/what/why of the matter, with Assistant Director Stanford Wedeck (Courtney B. Vance) in charge, Mark Benford (Joseph Fiennes) as the lead agent in the field, and a bevy of associates, including Special Agent Janis Hawk (Christine Woods). Clues in the tangled scientific puzzle take the agents from their home base of Los Angeles to Somalia, where a smaller, but similar event had occurred years earlier. Janis, who becomes pregnant, has her hands full as a double (triple?) agent, infiltrating the blackout conspiracy at the behest of the CIA, while hiding that fact from the FBI in "Goodbye Yellow Brick Road" (2010). In the meantime, the team grapples with some of the personal revelations of their flashforwards, such as infidelity, alcoholism, and even death.

## *The Flying Nun* (1967–1970, 82 episodes, USA)
*Based on:* The novel *The Fifteenth Pelican* by Tere Ríos
*Created by:* Bernard Slade, Harry Ackerman, Max Wylie
*Production Co.:* Screen Gems Television
*Originally Aired:* ABC
*Main Cast:* Sally Field, Madeleine Sherwood, Marge Redmond, Shelley Morrison, Alejandro Rey, Linda Dangcil, Vito Scotti

Sally Field stars as Sister Bertrille, a novice nun at a convent in San Juan, Puerto Rico. While that doesn't sound like much of a sitcom premise, when you add the fact that Sister Bertrille can FLY, the comic possibilities become apparent.

Sister Bertrille (Sally Field) makes the psychedelic scene with a rock-star friend (Paul Petersen) in *The Flying Nun* (ABC Television).

The former Elsie Ethrington finds upon donning a habit that her 90-pound weight, plus her order's huge, bird-shaped cornette (headpiece), and the high ocean winds of the area allow her to lift off, soaring through the skies in search of problems to solve (or, more likely, to create). Word of Sister Bertrille's flying ability does not come as welcome news to the Reverend Mother Placido (Madeleine Sherwood), the conservative woman who runs the convent. More accepting of the new novice and her ways are fun-loving Sister Jacqueline (Marge Redmond), who also narrates Sister Bertrille's adventures, and Sister Sixto (Shelley Morrison), a Puerto Rican nun who has humorous problems with English idioms, such as "sharp as a tick." Since nuns frequently have contact with playboy casino owners, Alejandro Rey fills that role as handsome Carlos Ramirez, who was raised by the Sisters.

Many madcap adventures ensue, as when a pelican falls in love with Sister Bertrille in "With Love from Irving" (1967), and when the flying novice is mistaken for a UFO in "Two Bad Eggs" (1968). Since Sister Bertrille is young and hip (by convent standards), she gets involved in the contemporary rock scene as a songwriter in "Song of Bertrille" (1968) and via a car accident with "hippies" in "When Generations Gap" (1970). But her "bad trips" are confined to rough landings after her flights—Sister Bertrille never made it to Woodstock (as far as we know).

### Fogg, Rebecca (*The Secret Adventures of Jules Verne*)

British Secret Service operative during an alternate Victorian Era.

See: *The Secret Adventures of Jules Verne* (2000, 22 episodes, Canada/UK)

### Forbes, Caroline (*The Vampire Diaries*)

Overachieving honors student who recovers from a serious car accident by becoming a vampire.

See: *The Vampire Diaries* (2009– , 155 episodes, USA)

### Forever Knight (1992–1996, 70 episodes, Canada/West Germany)

*Created by:* Barney Cohen, James D. Parriott
*Production Co.:* Glen Warren Productions, Paragon Entertainment Corporation, Tele München Fernseh Produktionsgesellschaft, TriStar Television, USA Network
*Originally Aired:* CBS
*Main Cast:* Geraint Wyn Davies, Catherine Disher, Nigel Bennett, Ben Bass, Deborah Duchene, Blu Mankuma, Natsuko Ohama, John Kapelos, Lisa Ryder, Gary Farmer

"He was brought across in 1228, preyed on humans for their blood. Now he wants to be mortal again...."

*Forever Knight* is the story of vampire Nicholas Knight (Geraint Wyn Davies), an immortal full of remorse for centuries of bloodthirsty sins, who wants to make amends, and become human again. In his current incarnation, Nick is a detective for the Toronto police department, and uses his supernatural powers to solve crimes and bring evildoers to justice. He partners first with boorish Detective Don Schanke (John Kapelos), and later with police commissioner's daughter **Tracy Vetter** (Lisa Ryder), neither of whom know that Nick is a vampire. The revolving roster of precinct captains includes Amanda Cohen (Natsuko Ohama), who dies in a plane bombing along with Detective Schanke at the beginning of season three. Nick's love interest is medical examiner Dr. Natalie Lambert (Catherine Disher), constantly searching for a cure for Nick's vampirism, so their love can finally be consummated. The villain of the piece is Nick's sire Lucien LaCroix (Nigel Bennett), who tries to ensure that Nick remains in the vampire family, and urges him to embrace his animal nature. In an unusual twist, Nick's conflict appears to end tragically in series finale, "Last Knight" (1996).

See also: **Vetter, Tracy (*Forever Knight*)**

### *The 4400* (2004–2007, 44 episodes, USA)
*Created by:* René Echevarria, Scott Peters
*Production Co.:* American Zoetrope, Renegade 83, 4400 Productions, CBS Paramount Network Television
*Originally Aired:* USA Network
*Main Cast:* Joel Gretsch, Jacqueline McKenzie, Mahershalalhashbaz Ali, Laura Allen, Patrick Flueger, Megalyn Echikunwoke, Chad Faust, Kaj-Erik Eriksen, Samantha Ferris, Jenni Baird, Brooke Nevin, Conchita Campbell, Karina Lombard, Bill Campbell, Peter Coyote

SF thriller about the return to Earth of 4400 people who had disappeared inexplicably in the years since World War II. The returnees suddenly appear near Mount Rainier in Washington state, and The National Threat Assessment Command (NTAC) investigates the circumstances surrounding the abduction and reappearance of the 4400. Lead agents Tom Baldwin (Joel Gretsch) and **Diana Skouris** (Jacqueline McKenzie) interview and track returnees, but their task is made more difficult when members of the 4400 begin to manifest special abilities such as telekinesis, healing powers, enhanced strength and precognition. Work intersects with family for both agents, since Tom's son Kyle (Chad Faust) is a 4400, and Diana adopts Maia (Conchita Campbell), a returnee child with the ability to predict the future. Factions within the U.S. government and among the 4400 press their agendas, sometimes with violence, ensuring that Tom and Diana will have their loyalties tested within the new world order.

See also: **Skouris, Diana (*The 4400*)**

### Foster, Micki (*Friday the 13th: The Series*)
Woman who inherits a store full of cursed antiques after her uncle breaks his deal with the devil.

See: ***Friday the 13th: The Series*** (1987–1990, 72 episodes, Canada)

### Fowler, Peggy (*Mysterious Ways*)
Hospital psychiatrist working with a professor who searches for proof of miraculous phenomena.

See: ***Mysterious Ways*** (2000–2002, 44 episodes, Canada/USA)

### Fox, Shalimar (*Mutant X*)
Woman with enhanced physical abilities via animal DNA, who works with other "New Mutants."
See: ***Mutant X* (2001–2004, 66 episodes, Canada/USA)**

### Fox, Sydney (*Relic Hunter*)
Professor and archaeologist who searches for relics around the world in between classes.
See: ***Relic Hunter* (1999–2002, 66 episodes, Canada/France)**

### Fraiser, Janet (*Stargate SG-1*)
Chief medical officer for an Air Force team which travels the galaxy via an alien portal.
See: ***Stargate SG-1* (1997–2007, 214 episodes, Canada/USA)**

### Francisco, Susan (*Alien Nation*)
Extraterrestrial female trying to adapt to Earth's customs with her husband and two children.
See: ***Alien Nation* (1989–1990, 22 episodes, USA)**

### Frankel, Cathy (*Alien Nation*)
Alien biochemist and former slave attracted to a human detective for the LAPD.
See: ***Alien Nation* (1989–1990, 22 episodes, USA)**

### Frankel, Joanna (*Eastwick*)
Journalist who discovers she has mind-control abilities as two other women in town exhibit special powers.
See: ***Eastwick* (2009, 13 episodes, USA)**

### Frederic, Irene (*Warehouse 13*)
Imposing caretaker of a centuries-old warehouse full of supernatural artifacts.
See: ***Warehouse 13* (2009–2014, 64 episodes, USA)**

## *Friday the 13th: The Series* (1987–1990, 72 episodes, Canada)
*Created by:* Frank Mancuso, Jr., Larry B. Williams
*Production Co.:* Lexicon Productions, Variety Artists International, Hometown Films, et al.
*Originally Aired:* In Syndication
*Main Cast:* Louise Robey, John D. LeMay, Steve Monarque, Chris Wiggins

"Lewis Vendredi made a deal with the devil to sell cursed antiques. But he broke the pact, and it cost him his soul. Now, his niece Micki, and her cousin Ryan have inherited the store ... and with it, the curse. Now they must get everything back— and the real terror begins."

Despite the title, you won't see Jason Voorhees or his hockey mask in this series which has a different premise and characters than the long-running *Friday the 13th* movie franchise. Micki Foster (Louise Robey) and her cousin Ryan Dallion (John

D. LeMay) inherit a store from her uncle, who had agreed to sell cursed antiques in an unusual consignment deal with the devil. Joined by Jack Marshak (Chris Wiggins), an occultist, they seek out the cursed antiques and place them in a magically secured vault below the store. (How *Warehouse 13* of them.)

It's dangerous work, and Micki even dies once, but some devil worshipers are tricked into bringing her back to life in "Tails I Live, Heads You Die" (1988). There's not much time for romance, and Micki breaks off her engagement in "Root of All Evil" (1987), so the boys won't go it alone while searching for demon mulchers, murderous scalpels, and killer scarecrows. Micki is almost involved in a marriage of a different sort when the devil hopes to impregnate her with his demon spawn in "Wedding in Black" (1989), but she is able to escape from this, er, hellish scenario.

The series was abruptly canceled late in its third season, no doubt due to a cursed television set that had escaped the team's notice.

### *Fringe* (2008–2013, 100 episodes, USA)
*Created by:* J.J. Abrams, Alex Kurtzman, Roberto Orci
*Production Co.:* Bad Robot Productions, Warner Bros. Television, Fringe Element Films
*Originally Aired:* Fox
*Main Cast:* Anna Torv, Joshua Jackson, John Noble, Jasika Nicole, Lance Reddick, Blair Brown, Kirk Acevedo, Seth Gabel, Mark Valley

Science fiction drama about a Joint Federal Task Force known as the Fringe Division, which investigates weird science and unexplained phenomena a là *The X-Files*. Leading the way for the government is Olivia Dunham (Anna Torv), an FBI agent who is well suited to her assignment, given that she has special abilities gained from an experimental chemical administered to her as a child. Among other powers, Olivia is able to discern when an object originates in a parallel universe, a handy talent when an alternate dimension causes problems (as often happens). Olivia works with Dr. Walter Bishop (John Noble), a researcher on the hinterlands of science, who was institutionalized for many years, making him the "mad scientist" of the piece. Olivia recruits Walter's estranged son, Peter Bishop (Joshua Jackson), to work with his father, although, like any family, they have their problems, such as the fact that Walter kidnapped Peter from the alternate universe, when his own Peter had died (as often happens). The principals do what they can to diminish the interdimensional confusion of alternate characters and storylines by giving clever names to their doppelgängers, such as "Fauxlivia" for Olivia and "Walternate" for Walter. It turns out that Olivia and the boys are fighting for nothing less than the world as we know it.

Anna Torv received a record four Saturn Awards for her portrayal of Olivia Dunham in this intricate, mythology-rich series, where past is future is past.

### Frost, Whitney (*Agent Carter*)
Screen actress and brilliant scientist who runs afoul of a new physical force called Zero Matter.

See: *Agent Carter* (2015–2016, 18 episodes, USA)

### Frye, Kaylee (*Firefly*)

Sunny engineer on a spaceship full of renegades after a civil war between confederations of planets.

See: *Firefly* (2002, 14 episodes, USA)

### Fulvia (*Star Maidens*)

Supreme Councillor on the planet Medusa, where women rule and men are treated as sex objects.

See: *Star Maidens* (1976, 13 episodes, UK/West Germany)

### Gabrielle (*Xena: Warrior Princess*)

Gabrielle (Renée O'Connor) is a peasant girl living in a small village when she meets the woman who will change her life forever, Xena (Lucy Lawless), a warrior who has turned from the dark side to fight for the innocent. Since Gabrielle isn't interested in an arranged marriage, she follows Xena on her path through the ancient world, hoping for adventure and the chance to sharpen her bardic skills along the way. While Gabrielle starts out as Xena's fangirl, she is destined to become a hero in her own right, a journey which begins in "Hooves & Harlots"(1995), when she becomes an Amazon princess, replacing another who has died. Gabrielle receives a fighting staff and discards her conservative peasant attire for increasingly skimpy outfits, which are conveniently de rigueur for female warriors in the ancient world. By the time of "Beware Greeks Bearing Gifts" (1996), Gabrielle is fighting with the staff, but she still harbors bardic aspirations, as in "Athens City Academy of the Performing Bards" (1996). It's a good thing Gabrielle persisted in her craft, since Xena's amazing adventures wouldn't have survived until this day if Gabrielle hadn't written them down in "The Xena Scrolls" (1997).

Gabrielle walks at Xena's side for six seasons, while both find scattered moments to pursue love interests. As the country girl, Gabrielle has innocent flirtations with men like Iolaus (Michael Hurst), but she eventually marries Perdicas (Scott Garrison), the man she had left behind in her village of Potidaea. Poor Perdicas didn't last long, however, thanks to Xena's nemesis Callisto (Hudson Leick), but that left Gabrielle free to continue her travels with Xena, who may have been her greatest love of all. Although an explicit relationship between the two women is never depicted, there are hints along the way that one exists, especially in the series finale, "A Friend in Need, Part 2" (2001). when Gabrielle tries to revive Xena with what she hopes are life-giving kisses.

At the beginning of their adventures, Gabrielle says to Xena, "You've got to take me with you, teach me everything you know." By the end, Xena had done just that, although she had lost her life in the process. But Gabrielle was ready, with Xena's trusty weapon, the Chakram, on her belt, and Xena's spirit in her heart, to follow in her footsteps.

See also: *Xena: Warrior Princess* (1995–2001, 134 episodes, USA)

### Gale, Cathy (*The Avengers*)

Dr. Cathy Gale, anthropologist, finds herself in the unlikely role of amateur operative when she assists secret agent John Steed (Patrick Macnee) on a case in "Mr. Teddy Bear" (1962). As portrayed by Honor Blackman, Cathy is smart, independent, assertive, and adept at hand-to-hand combat, whether attired in street clothes or her signature black leather suit and boots. She and Steed handle some strange cases, such as the "Death of the Great Dane" (1962), wherein a dead millionaire turns up in a burial plot at a pet cemetery. Cathy distinguishes herself from a trio of talented amateurs, going on to become Steed's regular partner in "Brief for Murder" (1963). All good things must come to an end, however, and Cathy departs after "Lobster Quadrille" (1964), having blazed a trail that other female spies, including her successor, **Emma Peel**, will follow.

See also: *The Avengers* (1961–1969, 161 episodes, UK)

### Gardener, Kat (*Eastwick*)

Nurse who begins to display control over the elements after the arrival of a mysterious stranger in town.

See: *Eastwick* (2009, 13 episodes, USA)

### Garland, Evie (*Out of This World*)

California girl who learns on her 13th birthday that her father is an extraterrestrial.

See: *Out of This World* (1987–1991, 96 episodes, USA)

### Gemini, Trance (*Andromeda*)

Mysterious alien with pre-cognitive abilities who becomes the resident medic on a starship.

See: *Andromeda* (2000–2005, 110 episodes, Canada/USA)

### Gentry, Laura (*Space Academy*)

Psychic sibling, who with her older brother, attends a school for gifted students in outer space.

See: *Space Academy* (1977, 15 episodes, USA)

### *Get Smart* (1965–1970, 138 episodes, USA)

*Created by:* Mel Brooks, Buck Henry
*Production Co.:* Talent Associates, CBS Productions (1969–1970)
*Originally Aired:* NBC (1965–1969), CBS (1969–1970)
*Main Cast:* Don Adams, Barbara Feldon, Edward Platt, Robert Karvelas

Maxwell Smart, Agent 86, works for CONTROL, a secret U.S. counterintelligence agency based in our nation's capital. While 86 (Don Adams) is a top agent, his success is based mostly upon accident, coincidence, dumb luck, and the skill of his partner, **Agent 99** (Barbara Feldon). Supervising the bumbling Smart is the long-suffering "Chief" of CONTROL (Edward Platt), whose office "Cone of Silence" serves only to hinder his communications with Max, while broadcasting them to the outside world.

As the enemy of control is chaos, so the enemy of CONTROL is KAOS, an international organization of evil, frequently fronted by the German-accented Siegfried (Bernie Kopell). Smart and 99 thwart the aspirations of KAOS and other evildoers with the help of a motley crew of fellow agents, including Hymie, the robot (Richard Gautier), and Fang, the dog. Just a few of the pleasures of this innovative comedy series include the classic opening-title sequence with the automated underground doors, Max's "shoe-phone," and the many catchphrases, especially, "Sorry about that, Chief."

A short-lived sequel of the same title appeared in 1995, with Adams and Feldon reprising their roles as Smart and 99, but it lasted only seven episodes. As Smart would say, "Missed it by *that* much."

See also: **Agent 99 (*Get Smart*)**

Stylish Agent 99 (Barbara Feldon) uses a gun as a mod accessory on *Get Smart* (NBC Television).

## *The Ghost & Mrs. Muir* (1968–1970, 50 episodes, USA)

*Based on:* The novel by R.A. Dick
*Created by:* Jean Holloway
*Production Co.:* 20th Century–Fox Television
*Originally Aired:* NBC (1968–1969), ABC (1969–1970)
*Main Cast:* Hope Lange, Edward Mulhare, Reta Shaw, Harlen Carraher, Kellie Flanagan, Charles Nelson Reilly

Widowed writer Carolyn Muir (Hope Lange) rents a charming cottage in Schooner Bay, Maine, unaware it is inhabited by a ghost. The poltergeist in question, Daniel Gregg (Edward Mulhare), a sea captain who had died 100 years earlier, is none too happy about the intruder, who has brought along her two children, a housekeeper (Reta Shaw), and a scruffy dog named Scruffy. The captain's insipid great-nephew Claymore Gregg (Charles Nelson Reilly), who fears his great-uncle's spectral anger, has nonetheless been forced to rent out the cottage or see it torn down. The ghost reveals himself to Mrs. Muir, and they are immediately at odds, given his 19th-century worldview, not to mention his ability to appear and disappear at will. But Carolyn is comely and Daniel is dashing, so sparks begin to fly, at least as much as they can fly between this world and the astral plane.

Hope Lange won two consecutive Emmy Awards for her portrayal of Carolyn Muir, but awards weren't enough to save the series, which jumped from NBC to ABC and then off the air. It is said, however, that the ghost still appears to those who summon him via DVD.

## Ghost Whisperer (2005–2010, 107 episodes, USA)
*Created by:* John Gray
*Production Co.:* Sander/Moses Productions, Touchstone Television, ABC Studios, Paramount Network Television, et al.
*Originally Aired:* CBS
*Main Cast:* Jennifer Love Hewitt, David Conrad, Aisha Tyler, Camryn Manheim, Jay Mohr, Christoph Sanders, Jamie Kennedy, Connor Gibbs

"I might be just like you. Except that from the time I was a little girl I knew I could talk to the dead."

In *The Sixth Sense* (1999), Haley Joel Osment spoke the memorable line, "I see dead people." It wasn't long before movie and TV characters were seeing dead people everywhere, and in 2005, two such characters hit the small screen, Allison DuBois (Patricia Arquette) in *Medium* and Melinda Gordon (Jennifer Love Hewitt) in *Ghost Whisperer*. While DuBois's stories were gritty, focusing on justice for murder victims, Gordon's were more sentimental, emphasizing love and forgiveness.

Carolyn Muir (Hope Lange) rents a charming cottage, but learns it is inhabited by the spirit of a sea captain in *The Ghost and Mrs. Muir* (NBC Television).

Melinda Gordon tries to lead a normal life despite her unusual gift, but even on her wedding day a ghost stalks her, interrupting her minutes-old wedded bliss with husband Jim Clancy (David Conrad). Jim himself will go on to become one of Melinda's ghostly clients in "Threshold" (2008), after he is killed, but refuses to cross over into the light. Things get even more complicated when Jim enters the recently deceased body of Sam Lucas, essentially re-animating him, so Jim won't have to leave Melinda alone on earth. Eventually Melinda marries/remarries Sam/Jim, and they have a son Aiden Lucas (Connor Gibbs), who is Jim's son from before he was killed. (Following along at home?) When the series jumps five years ahead, it is revealed that Aiden can see spirits too, and is even more powerful than Melinda.

Inspired in part by the work of "spirit communicators" James Van Praagh and

Mary Ann Winkowski, *Ghost Whisperer* depicts a woman in love with her gift. When Melinda temporarily loses it, as in "The Vanishing" (2006), she is bereft, knowing that her ability helps people, corporeal or not, to find peace.

Melinda also loves to wear low-cut dresses, and given their frequency of appearance, one can only conclude that such attire strengthens the link between this world and the next. And here we thought it was all about crystal balls and tarot cards.

### Gilbert, Elena (*The Vampire Diaries*)
High-school student in a love triangle with a pair of vampire brothers.
See: *The Vampire Diaries* (2009– , 155 episodes, USA)

### Girardi, Joan (*Joan of Arcadia*)
Maryland teen who receives instructions directly from God, causing complications in her personal life.
See: *Joan of Arcadia* (2003–2005, 45 episodes, USA)

### The Girl from U.N.C.L.E. (1966–1967, 29 episodes, USA)
*Created by:* Norman Felton
*Production Co.:* Arena Productions, MGM Television
*Originally Aired:* NBC
*Main Cast:* Stefanie Powers, Noel Harrison, Leo G. Carroll

Spoofy spy spin-off from *The Man from U.N.C.L.E.*, starring Stefanie Powers as "The Girl," a.k.a. April Dancer, an agent for The United Network Command for Law and Enforcement. April, along with partner Mark Slate (Noel Harrison), travels the globe battling the evil organization THRUSH and other enemies of good. Under the command of chief Alexander Waverly (Leo G. Carroll), April carries a purse full of gadgets and wears the latest mod fashions, while never engaging in much gunplay or fisticuffs, although she can call upon martial arts skills when needed. The tone of the episodes is broad, occasionally hitting farcical high notes, as in "The Mother Muffin Affair" (1966), with an in-drag Boris Karloff as the villainous Mother Muffin, who moons over her enemy Napoleon Solo (guest star Robert Vaughn), while despising April for her youth and proximity to the man from U.N.C.L.E. "The Atlantis Affair" (1966) finds April and Mark searching for a gateway to the famed lost continent in an episode penned by legendary SF/horror writer Richard Matheson. But many of the episodes slide into sheer silliness, dissipating the obvious potential of this spy-fi series.

### The Girl with Something Extra (1973–1974, 22 episodes, USA)
*Created by:* Bernard Slade
*Production Co.:* Screen Gems Television
*Originally Aired:* NBC
*Main Cast:* Sally Field, John Davidson, Teri Garr, Henry Jones, Zohra Lampert

On the heels of hit supernatural comedy *Bewitched* came this similar but shorter-lived sitcom about a woman with special powers and the husband who would contain them. The newlywed wife this time is Sally Burton (Sally Field) who reveals to husband John (John Davidson) on their wedding night that she has ESP. John's none too thrilled to learn that Sally has been able to read his mind all along (scary thought!), and now that he knows, he wants her to ignore her gift. But it's not easy for Sally to turn off her ability, so marital friction ensues, as when John has difficulty hiding a birthday present from his psychic wife in "A Gift for the Gifted" (1973). Sometimes Sally uses her power to help others, and in "How Green Was Las Vegas" (1973), she tries to assist John's brother Jerry (Jack Sheldon) by using ESP to win money at the casino, but John wants her to return the cash (how Darrin Stephens of him).

Alas, *The Girl with Something Extra* was unable to divine the secret to high ratings and permanently closed her psychic channel after one season.

## *Good Witch* (2015– , 19 episodes, Canada/USA)
*Based on:* The TV movie *The Good Witch* written by Rod Spence
*Created by:* Craig Pryce, Sue Tenney
*Production Co.:* Whizbang Films
*Originally Aired:* Hallmark Channel
*Main Cast:* Catherine Bell, Bailee Madison, James Denton, Rhys Matthew Bond, Catherine Disher, Anthony Lemke, Peter MacNeill, Kylee Evans

Is Cassandra Nightingale a witch? This G-rated, family-friendly series is ambiguous on that point, depicting Cassie (Catherine Bell) as a dark-haired beauty who possesses a keen intuition about people and a special ability to manipulate events, bringing good things to all who know her. But, a witch? That's in the eye of the beholder.

Cassie, who was introduced in a series of TV movies, owns a shop called Bell, Book & Candle in Middleton, a picturesque, "Main Street" type of town. Her shop's inventory is new age, but eclectic, and she always seems to have that rare item that someone needs, something that will reveal an important truth to them. Busy Cassie also runs a bed and breakfast at historic Grey House, where she lives with her teenaged daughter Grace Russell (Bailee Madison). Grace shares Cassie's special intuitive gifts, as when she knows her half-brother Brandon Russell (Dan Jeannotte) is in trouble during a blizzard in "Together We Stand…" (2015).

While Cassie is recovering from the death of her husband, a handsome, albeit grumpy doctor, Sam Radford (James Denton), moves in next door with his sullen teenage son Nick (Rhys Matthew Bond). Needless to say, Cassie and Sam soon embark upon the common fictional path marked, "we're destined for each other, but let's pretend not to notice." Cassie and Sam have different views on Western medicine, since Cassie provides herbal remedies for her customers.

Middleton's Mayor Martha Tinsdale (Catherine Disher) provides broad comic relief as a self-important busybody, who seems like she accidentally found her way from a 30s screwball comedy. In fact, a lack of subtlety is the main problem with *Good Witch* in general. There is much promise here, with an appealing lead and an intriguing concept, but the strict adherence to Hallmark's romantic formula can leave you feeling like you've been hit over the head with a bag of sugar.

## The Good Witch of Laurel Canyon
See: *Tucker's Witch* (1982–1983, 12 episodes, USA)

## Gordon, Barbara (*Batman*)
A librarian who dons the cowl to help Batman and Robin fight crime.
See: *Batman* (1966–1968, 120 episodes, USA)

## Gordon, Barbara (*Birds of Prey*)
Former caped crusader, now paralyzed, who still fights crime via computer.
See: *Birds of Prey* (2002–2003, 13 episodes, USA)

## Gordon, Melinda (*Ghost Whisperer*)
Woman who can talk to dead people, helping to resolve their earthly problems so they can cross over into the light.
See: *Ghost Whisperer* (2005–2010, 107 episodes, USA)

## The Greatest American Hero (1981–1983, 44 episodes, USA)
*Created by:* Stephen J. Cannell
*Production Co.:* Stephen J. Cannell Productions
*Originally Aired:* ABC
*Main Cast:* William Katt, Robert Culp, Connie Sellecca, Michael Paré, Faye Grant

The Greatest American Hero is a caped superhero without a supername. (Superman? Already taken.) Ralph Hinkley (William Katt), a special education teacher in Los Angeles, receives a red suit from extraterrestrials while on a field trip in the desert. The suit gives Ralph extraordinary powers such as the ability to fly, invulnerability to injury, holographic vision, and more, but only while he is wearing the suit. A complication quickly develops when Ralph loses the instruction manual for the suit, and must learn its powers on the fly (so to speak), with smooth landings proving particularly difficult.

The aliens have instructed Ralph to work with FBI Special Agent Bill Maxwell (Robert Culp), a gung-ho G-man with a 50s mindset. The crime-fighting duo becomes a trio, when Ralph's pretty girlfriend, Pam Davidson (Connie Sellecca), joins the team. Davidson is Ralph's divorce attorney, now girlfriend, whose main assignments seem to be waiting in the car and verbally sparring with Neanderthal Bill when he says sexist things (which is often). Pam goes from the role of superhero's girlfriend to superhero's wife in "The Newlywed Game" (1983), but not without some wedding crashers who may be Russian spies!

In 1986, the cast reunited for a pilot movie, *The Greatest American Heroine*, wherein Ralph passes the red suit to a woman—or "skirt," as Bill calls her. The pilot didn't air, but it provided closure for the original series and was eventually re-edited for inclusion with syndication broadcasts of the show.

Although *The Greatest American Hero* was never a ratings giant, it has seeped into the popular consciousness, helped by its memorable theme song, which was a Billboard hit in the summer of 1981, "Believe It or Not."

### Griffin, Abby (*The 100*)

Doctor aboard an Earth-orbiting space station which houses the survivors of a nuclear holocaust.

See: *The 100* ("The Hundred," 2014– , 45 episodes, USA)

### Griffin, Clarke (*The 100*)

Leader of a group of teens who must learn to survive on Earth after a nuclear apocalypse.

See: *The 100* ("The Hundred," 2014– , 45 episodes, USA)

### *Grimm* (2011– , 110 episodes, USA)

*Created by:* Stephen Carpenter, David Greenwalt, Jim Kouf
*Production Co.:* Universal Television, GK Productions, Hazy Mill Productions
*Originally Aired:* NBC
*Main Cast:* David Giuntoli, Russell Hornsby, Bitsie Tulloch, Silas Weir Mitchell, Sasha Roiz, Reggie Lee, Bree Turner, Claire Coffee, Robert Blanche, Damien Puckler, Jacqueline Toboni

"There once was a man who lived a life so strange, it had to be true. Only he could see what no one else can—the darkness inside, the real monster within, and he's the one who must stop them. This is his calling. This is his duty. This is the life of a Grimm."

Nick Burkhardt is a "Grimm." If that sounds "grim," it is, as Nick (David Giuntoli) has inherited the ability to recognize and fight supernatural creatures called Wesen, who look like humans, but have alter-egos right out of Grimms' Fairy Tales. As his battles begin, Nick gains the help of a good Wesen named Monroe (Silas Weir Mitchell), a wolf-like creature called a Blutbad, who has an encyclopedic knowledge of the Wesen. Also assisting Nick is Munro's love interest and future wife Rosalee Calvert (Bree Turner), a fox-like Wesen called a Fuchsbau, who runs a local spice shop and has experience with cures both natural and supernatural. Rosalee's apothecarial acumen comes in handy when Nick's girlfriend, Dr. Juliette Silverton (Bitsie Tulloch), a veterinarian, is scratched by a cat and later falls into a coma. The cat is no ordinary feline (surprise!), and has been given a potion by Adalind Schade (Claire Coffee), a Hexenbiest or witch, who resembles a decaying corpse when in Wesen form. More magic ensues, as Nick's relationship with Juliette is tested, ancient conspiracies swirl, and creatures of myth and fairytale come to life.

Nick later gains a protégé in Theresa Rubel (Jacqueline Toboni), nicknamed "Trubel" (pronounced "Trouble"), a young Grimm on the run from foster homes and potential madness, as no one has explained to her why she keeps seeing monsters. Trubel is tough and street-smart, eventually taking to the life of a Grimm, which helps a lot when Nick loses his powers (long story). Shocking events ensue as Trubel kills Juliette, who was trying to kill Nick, who soon has a newborn son by Adalind (the once and future and once and future Hexenbiest), and learns that Juliette has been re-animated as Eve.

Lots to keep track of on this one. Even the Brothers Grimm would be out of their depth.

**Groves, Larkin (*Invasion*)**
TV reporter in Homestead, Florida, investigating weird lights and mysterious disappearances after a hurricane.
See: *Invasion* (2005–2006, 22 episodes, USA)

**Guevara, Max (*Dark Angel*)**
Genetically enhanced super-soldier on the run from government agents in post-apocalyptic Seattle.
See: *Dark Angel* (2000–2002, 43 episodes, USA)

**Guinan (*Star Trek: The Next Generation*)**
Survivor of a race of "listeners," now tending bar and dispensing wisdom aboard a starship.
See: *Star Trek: The Next Generation* (1987–1994, 178 episodes, USA)

**Guinevere "Gwen" (*Merlin*)**
Kind and loyal woman who rises from maidservant to Queen of Camelot.
See: *Merlin* (2008–2012, 65 episodes, UK)

**Halliwell, Phoebe, Piper, and Prue (*Charmed*)**
Sisters living in San Francisco who discover they are descended from a long line of witches.
See: *Charmed* (1998–2006, 178 episodes, USA)

**Hamilton, Betty (*Land of the Giants*)**
"Stewardess" on a flight which crashes on a planet where the people are 12 times the size of humans.
See: *Land of the Giants* (1968–1970, 51 episodes, USA)

**Hanadarko, Grace (*Saving Grace*)**
Oklahoma City police detective whose bad behavior brings her in contact with an angel.
See: *Saving Grace* (2007–2010, 46 episodes, USA)

**Harris, Rebecca (*Limitless*)**
FBI agent working with a man whose mental powers have been enhanced by a dangerous drug.
See: *Limitless* (2015–2016, 22 episodes, USA)

**Hathaway, Michelle, Taylor, and Frankie (*The Haunted Hathaways*)**
Mother and two daughters who move to a house inhabited by a family of male ghosts.
See: *The Haunted Hathaways* (2013–2015, 48 episodes, USA)

**The Haunted Hathaways (2013–2015, 48 episodes, USA)**
*Created by:* Robert Peacock

*Production Co.:* Bugliari/McLaughlin Productions
*Originally Aired:* Nickelodeon
*Main Cast:* Amber Montana, Curtis Harris, Benjamin "Lil' P-Nut" Flores, Jr., Breanna Yde, Ginifer King, Chico Benymon

Here's the story of a lovely lady, who was bringing up two very lovely girls... While that sounds like the start of *The Brady Bunch* (minus one lovely girl), this Nickelodeon series makes a swift twist and a fast turn, when the male members of the blended family turn out to be GHOSTS, and African American ones at that.

Michelle Hathaway (Ginifer King), a divorced mother, reboots her life by moving to New Orleans and opening a bakery called Hathaway's Pie Squared. She takes up residence above the bakery with her daughters, 14-year-old Taylor (Amber Montana) and nine-year-old Frankie (Breanna Yde), but the Hathaways soon discover they are not alone. The house is already occupied by the Preston family, Ray (Chico Benymon), a jazz musician, his 13-year-old son Miles (Curtis Harris), and his younger boy Louie (Benjamin "Lil' P-Nut" Flores, Jr.). The Prestons, it seems, have a lease of a different sort—they are ghosts.

Michelle gives the ghostbusting routine a try, but Taylor and Miles have already bonded, so the families decide to coexist. They begin to cooperate to solve problems, often causing bigger problems, in true supernatural sitcom style. In "Haunted Viking" (2014), Taylor needs help with her Viking report for school, and Louie summons a Viking ghost, who is too in touch with his marauding past.

Eventually the Hathaways and the Prestons surmount their racial, gender, and ethereal differences to become a different type of blended family. *The Haunted Hathaways* manages to transmit that positive message, while retaining the requisite tweener viewpoint, fart humor and all, for the Nickelodeon crowd.

## *Haven* (2010–2015, 78 episodes, Canada/USA)

*Based on:* The novel *The Colorado Kid* by Stephen King
*Created by:* Jim Dunn, Sam Ernst
*Production Co.:* Entertainment One, Big Motion Pictures Productions, Piller/Segan/Shepherd, Universal Networks International
*Originally Aired:* Syfy
*Main Cast:* Emily Rose, Lucas Bryant, Eric Balfour, Richard Donat, John Dunsworth, Nicholas Campbell, Adam Copeland

When FBI Agent Audrey Parker (Emily Rose) chases an escaped prisoner to the picturesque, seaside town of Haven, Maine, little does she know that her life is about to change forever. It turns out that Haven is home not only to the fishing industry, but also to "The Troubles," psychic and supernatural powers that manifest in a large group of the townspeople every few decades, usually causing, well, troubles. It also turns out that Parker possesses the ability to help those who are "troubled," so she stays in Haven, joining the local police department. There she can also investigate her own murky past, when a photo surfaces of her look-alike mother, whom she had never known. It further turns out that the photo may actually be of Audrey herself, who has not aged over the decades, hinting that her memory has somehow been erased. All of this is just the tip of the iceberg, as information about cyclical meteor storms, time travel, and an alternate world is revealed. Helping Audrey sort through these exotic mysteries are two handsome hunks, who are also rivals for her affection. Nathan Wuornos (Lucas Bryant), Audrey's detective partner, has no sense of touch due to The Troubles, but is able to feel Audrey, giving them a unique connection. Duke Crocker (Eric Balfour), a suspected smuggler and charming bad boy, learns via an old diary that his late father wanted him to kill Audrey, but even Duke isn't that bad.

Obviously Haven, despite its name and its breathtaking beauty (the series is actually filmed in Nova Scotia), should not be your destination for a quiet vacation.

### Hawk, Janis (*FlashForward*)

FBI agent investigating a brief, worldwide loss of consciousness.
See: ***FlashForward* (2009–2010, 22 episodes, USA)**

### Hel (*Cleopatra 2525*)

Leader of a band of beautiful female warriors who battle robots in the year 2525.
See: ***Cleopatra 2525* (2000–2001, 28 episodes, USA)**

### Heller, Julia (*Earth 2*)

Doctor on an expedition to an Earth-like planet, who turns out to be a government spy.
See: ***Earth 2* (1994–1995, 22 episodes, USA)**

### *Heroes* (2006–2010, 77 episodes, USA)

*Created by:* Tim Kring
*Production Co.:* Tailwind Productions, Universal Media Studios
*Originally Aired:* NBC
*Main Cast:* Hayden Panettiere, Jack Coleman, Milo Ventimiglia, Masi Oka, Greg Grunberg, Ali Larter, Adrian Pasdar, Sendhil Ramamurthy, James Kyson Lee, Zachary Quinto, Cristine Rose, Ashley Crow

The premise is simple enough, even familiar—everyday people discover they have superpowers. But with its abundance (some might say, "excess") of characters and a preference for elliptical storytelling, *Heroes* turns out to be anything but simple.

*Heroes* employs the style and structure of comic books to follow 12 major characters throughout its first season. While that's a lot of narrative arcs, the characters are linked by family ties, a shadowy organization known as The Company, and a possible apocalyptic event. The linchpin for season one and much of the series is **Claire Bennet** (Hayden Panettiere), a teenage cheerleader who has the ability to heal from any injury, no matter how life-threatening. Claire appears to be the key to preventing a cataclysmic explosion in New York, or so believes Hiro Nakamura (Masi Oka), a Japanese computer programmer with the ability to teleport. When Hiro takes a short, accidental trip to the future, he learns that he must "save the cheerleader, save the world," as Claire is in danger from a serial killer named Sylar (Zachary Quinto), who has the power to steal super-abilities from others. Not to worry, though, as Claire's uncle, Peter Petrelli (Milo Ventimiglia), who can absorb abilities from others (but not in Sylar's yucky way), saves Claire, only to become the actual threat to New York City as a human bomb. Not to worry (again), however, as Peter's brother and Claire's biological father, Nathan Petrelli (Adrian Pasdar), who has the power to fly, scoops up Peter in the nick of time and shoots into the stratosphere, where the bomb detonates, saving New York.

Peter and Nathan are back for season two (surprise!), as new characters with different "gifts" enter the crowded picture. Old friends (and enemies) return too, including Claire, Syler, and Noah Bennet (Jack Coleman), Claire's adoptive father, who continues to pursue those with powers for his ever ambiguous reasons, while his love for "Claire Bear" remains constant. Niki Sanders (Ali Larter), who has superhuman strength via her violent alter ego Jessica, meets her demise, but is reborn (sort of) in the season three character of Tracy Strauss (Ali Larter again), who is her fellow genetically modified triplet. (Following along at home?) Tracy has the ability to freeze whatever she touches, including people, a definite no-no in her chosen career of political adviser. Another political guru of sorts is Angela Petrelli (Cristine Rose), who had hoped to push her son Nathan toward the U.S. Presidency by allowing New York City to blow up. Angela is able to see the future via her dreams, a power of dubious benefit, since these heroes nip in and out of the timeline, which tends to rearrange the prophesied futures.

*Heroes* is a dizzying experience—shifting alliances, powers acquired and lost, futures revealed and abandoned. Season one was a critical and ratings success, but viewers fled in droves every season thereafter. Still, the series managed to survive four seasons and even spun off a 13-episode miniseries in 2015, *Heroes Reborn*.

Season one of *Heroes* will probably be enough for most viewers, as it comes to a satisfying, natural conclusion. Only true TV heroes will see the show through to the bitter end.

See also: **Bennet, Claire (*Heroes*)**

## *Hex* (2004–2005, 19 episodes, UK)

*Created by:* Julian Jones, Lucy Watkins
*Production Co.:* Shine Limited, Sony Pictures Television International
*Originally Aired:* BBC America
*Main Cast:* Christina Cole, Jemima Rooper, Michael Fassbender, Laura Pyper, Jamie Davis, Amber Sainsbury, Colin Salmon, Joseph Beattie

Cassie Hughes (Christina Cole) is England's answer to Buffy, a blonde student at Medenham Hall, who discovers strange, supernatural powers after touching an antique vase. Like Buffy, Cassie is drawn to a mysterious stranger from a dark realm. While Buffy's monster/man was named Angel, Cassie's is an actual ANGEL, but one of the fallen variety, named Azazeal (Michael Fassbender). Eventually Cassie falls under Azazeal's (literal) spell and they conceive a fast-developing child named Malachi (Joseph Beattie), who later attends the same school (giving advanced placement new meaning).

Even more Buffy-like is Ella Dee (Laura Pyper), a 400-year-old witch and last of the "anointed ones," who has been charged with preventing Azazeal from breeding with witches of Cassie's lineage. Too late! Ella enrolls at Medenham with a new mission—to kill Malachi, the demon, er, angel spawn. Ella teams up with Cassie and her friend Thelma Bates (Jemima Rooper) to dispatch Malachi, but things don't go as planned, when Cassie sacrifices herself for her son at the last minute. Thelma, a ghost who had been in love with Cassie, remains to help Ella in her battle with Azazeal and later Malachi. More mythology is revealed, and complications both supernatural and romantic ensue, just like in *Buffy the Vampire Slayer*.

What *Hex* was missing, however, was Buffy's staying power, critical accolades, and cultural impact. Apparently the producers had no hex for that.

## *Highcliffe Manor* (1979, 6 episodes, USA)
*Created by:* Brad Buckner
*Production Co.:* Alan Landsburg Productions
*Originally Aired:* NBC
*Main Cast:* Shelley Fabares, Stephen McHattie, Eugenie Ross-Leming, Gerald Gordon, Jenny O'Hara, Chris Marlowe, Audrey Landers, Ernie Hudson

Gone-in-a-flash Gothic horror parody starring Shelley Fabares as Helen Blacke, a widow who inherits a spooky mansion populated by mad scientists, when her husband perishes in a laboratory explosion. Helen's not exactly welcome at the manor, but she seems happily oblivious to the warnings of danger offered by eerie maid Rebecca (Jenny O'Hara). The scientists, it seems, are out to clone the world's leaders, because nothing goes better with mad science than world domination. One of the megalomaniacs, Dr. Frances Kisgadden (Eugenie Ross-Leming), has even created a man, Bram Shelley (Chris Marlowe), from erector set pieces and stolen body parts. (His name is appropriated as well, but appropriately so, from horror greats Bram Stoker and Mary Shelley). Other members of the crowded mansion include womanizing missionary the Rev. Ian Glenville (Stephen McHattie) and sexy secretary Wendy Sparkles (also appropriately named), portrayed by Audrey Landers.

While the premise sounded promising, even Dr. Frankenstein couldn't have reanimated this one after the network pulled the plug with only a few episodes aired.

## *Highlander: The Raven* (1998–1999, 22 episodes, Canada/France)
*Based on:* A character from *Highlander: The Series*
*Production Co.:* Gaumont Television, Fireworks Entertainment, Davis-Panzer Productions, Chum Television, et al.
*Originally Aired:* In Syndication
*Main Cast:* Elizabeth Gracen, Paul Johansson

Short-lived spin-off from *Highlander: The Series*, starring Elizabeth Gracen as immortal Amanda, a 1200-year-old thief who, like others of her kind, can die only if she is beheaded. Amanda's daring capers bring her to the attention of Detective Nick Wolfe (Paul Johansson), who later leaves the police force for private security work and learns of Amanda's immortality. Together, they battle evil immortals, help the helpless, solve crimes, and deal with ghosts from Amanda's past, while keeping the secrets of immortality safe.

Amanda's talent for grand larceny proves useful along the way, as in "Immunity" (1998), when she and Nick attempt to steal documents from an embassy. But her amazing propensity to run into vengeful immortals does tend to slow them down, and she has a surprise in store for Nick, who has been poisoned by one of her immortal enemies, in series finale, "Dead on Arrival" (1999).

## Hoffman, Julia (*Dark Shadows*)

Maine psychologist who tries to cure a vampire of his "undeath."
See: *Dark Shadows* (1966–1971, 1225 episodes, USA)

## *Honey, I Shrunk the Kids* (1997–2000, 66 episodes, USA)

*Based on:* The film directed by Joe Johnston
*Created by:* Ed Ferrara, Kevin Murphy
*Production Co.:* Plymouth Productions, St. Clare Entertainment, Walt Disney Television
*Originally Aired:* In Syndication
*Main Cast:* Peter Scolari, Barbara Alyn Woods, Hillary Tuck, Thomas Dekker, George Buza

The "science gone awry" SF trope is on steroids in this Disney series about an eccentric inventor whose gadgets create chaos for his family. Peter Scolari stars as Wayne Szalinski, the absent-minded professor of the piece, who does indeed shrink the family in series premiere "Honey, We've Been Swallowed by Grandpa" (1997). Barbara Alyn Woods portrays Wayne's long-suffering wife, Diane Szalinski, a lawyer who isn't above using one of Wayne's unpredictable inventions for her own purposes. In "Honey, You Drained My Brain" (1998), Diane employs the "Thinky Ring" to soup up her brain for a court case, but ends up draining the brains of others. (Don't try this at home.) Wayne and Diane have a daughter named Amy (Hillary Tuck), who experiences the usual teenage growing pains, such as sibling rivalry, bad skin, and unrequited love for her teacher. But Amy doesn't live in the usual suburban household, so she uses Dad's time machine to meet her teacher during the 70s, when he's just the right age, in "Honey, We're Stuck in the 70s" (1997). The final member of this nutty nuclear family is Amy's younger brother Nicholas (Thomas Dekker), a precocious nerd and Wayne's "Mini-Me" when it comes to inventing gadgets and getting in trouble.

The series ended after three seasons in keeping with Disney's 65-episode rule of the time, no doubt prompting the question, "Honey, Why Can't We Have More Episodes?"

## Horne, Audrey (*Twin Peaks*)

Sultry teen whose crush on an FBI agent endangers her life in a charming, but off-kilter town.
See: *Twin Peaks* (1990–1991, 30 episodes, USA)

### Houston, Sam (*TekWar*)

Former police lieutenant, now a risk-taking operative at a private security firm in 2045.

See: *TekWar* (1994–1996, 18 episodes, Canada/USA)

### Hughes, Cassie (*Hex*)

British boarding school student with supernatural powers, who bears the child of a fallen angel.

See: *Hex* (2004–2005, 19 episodes, UK)

### *The 100* ("The Hundred," 2014– , 45 episodes, USA)

*Based on:* The novel by Kass Morgan
*Created by:* Jason Rothenberg
*Production Co.:* Alloy Entertainment, Warner Bros. Television, et al.
*Originally Aired:* The CW
*Main Cast:* Eliza Taylor, Paige Turco, Marie Avgeropoulos, Bob Morley, Christopher Larkin, Devon Bostick, Isaiah Washington, Henry Ian Cusick, Lindsey Morgan, Richard Harmon, Ricky Whittle, Alycia Debnam-Carey

Ninety-seven years after a nuclear apocalypse has devastated the earth, the known survivors are living on an orbiting space station. Their leaders confront another existential crisis, when the station, appropriately called "The Ark," shows signs that its life-support system is failing. What to do? The powers that be send 100 of their juvenile delinquents to Earth to see if the planet is once again habitable by humans. While this premise may sound hokey, *The 100* is deadly serious, dealing with the question of how far people are willing to go to survive. The answer, by the way, is much farther than you'd think.

Once on the ground, the teen survivors gravitate toward two natural leaders, Clarke Griffin (Eliza Taylor) and Bellamy Blake (Bob Morley), who each have their own adherents and agendas. Clarke serves as medic for the 100, as they confront the dangers of new Earth, both environmental and human, including a hostile group of survivors known as the Grounders. While Clarke works to preserve life, she later takes it on a large scale at Mount Weather, where the Mountain Men, another group of survivors, imperil the settlers. She and Bellamy use radiation to wipe out over 300 people in order to save 47 of their own in "Blood Must Have Blood, Part 2" (2015). After this, the Grounders call Clarke "*Wanheda*," the Commander of Death.

During the Battle of Mount Weather, Clarke also saves the life of her mother, Dr. Abby Griffin (Paige Turco), the Chief Medical Officer of the Ark, who had escaped to Earth with other inhabitants of the space station. Clarke and her mother have a strained relationship, since Abby had betrayed Clarke's father on the Ark, setting in motion a chain of events that had led to his execution. The two women face off as leaders of their respective groups in "Coup de Grâce" (2015), and Clarke, already hardened by her time on earth, gets Abby, now Chancellor of the new arrivals, to back down.

Postapocalyptic life, both on the Ark and on the ground, hinges on alliances, which frequently turn on a dime. Bellamy's first allegiance is to his sister, Octavia Blake (Marie Avgeropoulos), who had lived most of her life hidden on the Ark due to a strict one-child-per-family law. While loyal to the 100, Octavia's experience on the Ark has given her an outsider's viewpoint, and she becomes sympathetic to the Grounders, especially Lincoln (Ricky Whittle), from whom she learns the skills of a warrior.

The 100 featured the first bisexual lead on network TV in Clarke, who took a Grounder lover, Lexa (Alycia Debnam-Carey), but controversy ensued when Lexa was killed not long after having a sexual encounter with Clarke. Many saw Lexa's fate as a continuation of the trope known variously as "bury your gays" or "dead lesbian syndrome," wherein gay or lesbian characters meet frequent demises, especially after a fleeting moment of happiness.

The series won a Saturn Award as Best Youth-Oriented Series on Television in 2015, but given its violence and mature themes, viewer discretion is advised, as the saying goes. Its visuals often employ the "shaky cam" technique, so that's another warning, for those susceptible to motion sickness. For everyone else, enjoy the strong female characters and complicated moral landscape of *The 100*.

Eliza Taylor talks about her series, *The 100*, at WonderCon in 2016 (from a color photograph by Gage Skidmore, CC BY-SA 3.0).

## *I Dream of Jeannie* (1965–1970, 139 episodes, USA)
*Created by:* Sidney Sheldon
*Production Co.:* Sidney Sheldon Productions, Screen Gems Television
*Originally Aired:* NBC
*Main Cast:* Barbara Eden, Larry Hagman, Bill Daily, Hayden Rorke, Barton MacLane, Emmaline Henry

When the space capsule of astronaut Tony Nelson (Larry Hagman) veers off course, landing on a South Pacific island, he finds a genie in a bottle, literally. This genie isn't a portly man in a turban, but a beautiful, blonde woman in a harem costume who has materialized from a puff of smoke. **Jeannie** (Barbara Eden), as he soon calls her, "blinks" a rescue helicopter into existence, and Tony frees her from service in gratitude for being saved. But Jeannie won't be discarded that easily, as she is already in love with Tony (2000 years in a bottle after all), and surreptitiously hitches a ride back to Florida with him, where she will cause him weekly headaches by trying to fulfill his every wish.

Upon Tony's return, he is examined by NASA psychiatrist Dr. Alfred Bellows

A quick trip to ancient Persia brings Jeannie (Barbara Eden) and Tony (Larry Hagman, right) face to face with the formidable Ali (Richard Kiel) in *I Dream of Jeannie* (NBC Television).

(Hayden Rorke). Tony mistakenly blabs about his encounter with Jeannie, and Bellows embarks upon an eternal quest to prove that Tony is crazy. Jeannie's magical meddling unwittingly fuels the doctor's obsession, but Bellows inevitably looks like a fool, especially in the eyes of General Martin Peterson (Barton MacLane).

Tony's best friend, fellow astronaut Roger Healey (Bill Dailey), soon learns Jeannie's secret, and he becomes her "master," hoping to advance his usual schemes of getting rich and finding women. Eventually Jeannie returns to Tony and redoubles her efforts to become his bride, using her powers to thwart potential rivals. After several years, Jeannie finally succeeds in becoming Mrs. Nelson, but the couple's happily ever after is brief, as the show was soon canceled.

Sidney Sheldon created the series after the spectacular first-season success of another magical lady in *Bewitched*. Although *I Dream of Jeannie* was never as highly rated as its witchy predecessor, nor as long-running, it was a ratings blockbuster in rerun syndication and became an international hit. It also spawned two TV movie sequels, although Hagman did not return as Tony Nelson. Eden, however, remained ageless in her signature role, fitting for a 2000-year-old-genie.

See also: **Jeannie (*I Dream of Jeannie*)**

## Invasion (2005–2006, 22 episodes, USA)
*Created by:* Shaun Cassidy
*Production Co.:* Shaun Cassidy Productions, Warner Bros. Television
*Originally Aired:* ABC
*Main Cast:* William Fichtner, Eddie Cibrian, Kari Matchett, Lisa Sheridan, Tyler Labine, Alexis Dziena, Evan Peters, Ariel Gade, Aisha Hinds

The mysteries of *Invasion* were never fully revealed due to its cancellation after one season, but essentially it's *Invasion of the Body Snatchers* with a dash of watery luminescence. When a hurricane hits Homestead, Florida, weird lights fall from the sky. Park Ranger Russell Varon (Eddie Cibrian) and his conspiracy-obsessed brother-in-law Dave Groves (Tyler Labine) begin to investigate, but Dave is attacked by SOMETHING in the water. As people disappear and reappear, Russell's TV reporter wife, Larkin Groves (Lisa Sheridan), gets in on the action, continually placing herself in jeopardy to get some answers to their questions. In the meantime, the town's sheriff, Tom Underlay (William Fichtner), quarantines the town and seems to be standing in the way of the Varon/Groves family's inquiries. (The name "Underlay" provides a hint that he might have some secrets buried deep.) Tom's wife and Russell's ex-wife, Dr. Mariel Underlay (Kari Matchett), begins to behave peculiarly, exhibiting signs that she might be an alien "hybrid." All of this affects the "yours, mine, and ours" children of Russell, Mariel and Tom, whose familial relationships you need the help of ancestry.com to keep straight.

Although critically acclaimed, *Invasion* was unable to retain the ratings of its popular lead-in, *Lost*, and was canceled after one season. If only the alien hybridization campaign had reached the network honchos in time.

## The Invisible Man (2000–2002, 45 episodes, USA)
*Created by:* Matt Greenberg
*Production Co.:* Stu Segall Productions
*Originally Aired:* Syfy
*Main Cast:* Vincent Ventresca, Paul Ben-Victor, Shannon Kenny, Eddie Jones, Mike McCafferty, Brandy Ledford

"There once was a story about a man that could turn invisible. I thought it was only a story until it happened to me."

There's something about an invisible man, at least as far as television producers are concerned. No fewer than three weekly TV series have been inspired by the classic 1897 novel of the same title by H.G. Wells. In the 1958 series, which ran for 26 episodes, an uncredited actor voiced the title character, while the 1975 entry, starring David McCallum, lasted just 13 episodes. The winner, in terms of longevity, is this millennial edition, which racked up 45 episodes for Syfy (then the Sci-Fi Channel).

Through a sequence of complicated (surprise!) circumstances, Darien Fawkes (Vincent Ventresca), a career criminal, is implanted with a special "Quicksilver" gland which makes him invisible, but also, on occasion, criminally insane. Darien works for the Agency, a shadowy, er—agency—of the U.S. government, alongside Bobby Hobbes (Paul Ben-Victor), a paranoid intelligence operative. Claire "The

Keeper" Keeply (Shannon Kenny), a medical doctor, keeps Fawkes alive and more or less sane with an antidote for "Quicksilver madness," which must be administered periodically. Alex Monroe (Brandy Ledford) later joins the Agency to pursue her vendetta against Chrysalis, an organization of evil (there's always one of those), which took her surrogate child. (Long story.) As Fawkes and friends pursue assassins and other bad guys, Claire bucks her Agency superiors and fixes Darien's Quicksilver gland, freeing him from the madness, while allowing him to retain his invisibility.

The series was canceled at this point, fading to invisibility on Syfy's schedule.

## *Isis* (1975–1976, 22 episodes, USA)
*Created by:* Marc Richards
*Production Co.:* Filmation Associates
*Originally Aired:* CBS
*Main Cast:* JoAnna Cameron, Brian Cutler

Andrea Thomas is just your average high school science teacher until she finds an ancient Egyptian amulet on an archaeological dig. With this amazing talisman, Andrea (JoAnna Cameron) can transform herself into the goddess Isis, gaining limitless abilities, such as superhuman strength or command of earth, air, fire and water. Andrea uses these gifts to fight evil, but since she's a long way from ancient Egypt, the evil she confronts tends to be less exotic and more sophomoric, often involving poor judgment by her students. In "Scuba Duba" (1975), Andrea/Isis must save a student, when the boy flouts SCUBA diving safety rules and is trapped underwater. "Fool's Dare" (1975) brings the goddess to the rescue of a girl who, after accepting a dare, stumbles upon a ring of car thieves. "Oh, Mighty Isis!"

## *It's About Time* (1966–1967, 26 episodes, USA)
*Created by:* Sherwood Schwartz
*Production Co.:* Redwood Productions, Gladasya Productions, United Artists Television
*Originally Aired:* CBS
*Main Cast:* Frank Aletter, Jack Mullaney, Imogene Coca, Joe E. Ross, Mary Grace, Pat Cardi, Cliff Norton, Mike Mazurki

Marooning people on an island had proved to be a winning concept for creator/producer Sherwood Schwartz with *Gilligan's Island*, so why not strand folks in TIME? That's the premise of this one-season-wonder about two astronauts, Mac MacKenzie (Frank Aletter) and Hector Canfield (Jack Mullaney), who find themselves in the prehistoric era after a spacefaring misadventure. There they meet the typical Stone Age family, led by Shad (Imogene Coca, listed as "Shag" in early episodes) and Gronk (Joe E. Ross), a fur-clad couple who have two typical Stone Age teens, Mlor (Mary Grace) and Breer (Pat Cardi). A major clash of cultures ensues, where the astronauts try to bring some civilization to the cave-dwellers, apparently unconcerned about changing the course of human history and development. In "Me Caveman—You Woman" (1966), Hec describes a courtship custom where men give women flowers rather than dragging them around by their hair, and Shad likes what she hears, trying to domesticate Gronk.

Low ratings led to a mid-season retooling, where the astronauts repair their spaceship and return to the 20th century in the company of Gronk, Shad and the kids, who were about to be killed by their tribe. Now the prehistoric family must adapt to modern ways, which, among other things, involves being discovered as a rock group (that 60s sitcom staple) in "The Cave Family Swingers" (1967).

Alas, jumping forward in time didn't help this series about time which ran out of time before its time. One way or another, "it's about time."

### Ivanova, Susan (*Babylon 5*)

Exceptional soldier and space station first officer for whom love always ends in tragedy.

See: *Babylon 5* (1994–1998, 110 episodes, USA)

### *Jack of All Trades* (2000, 22 episodes, New Zealand/USA)
*Created by:* Eric Morris
*Production Co.:* Renaissance Pictures
*Originally Aired:* In Syndication
*Main Cast:* Bruce Campbell, Angela Dotchin, Stuart Devenie

Campy comedy-adventure starring Bruce Campbell as American spy Jack Stiles and Angela Dotchin as Emilia Rothschild, his British counterpart, who work together on a South Pacific island in the early 1800s to thwart Napoleon's imperialistic designs. Emilia supplies the brains and Jack the brawn, as their madcap escapades take them from rescuing Ben Franklin in "The Floundering Father" (2000) to searching for King George's crown on the Marquis de Sade's island in "X Marquis the Spot" (2000). Emilia is also an inventor, furnishing miraculous creations when the need arises, while Jack calls upon his alter ego, The Daring Dragoon, a masked hero who swashes his buckle when secrecy is required. In "Shark Bait" (2000), Emilia and Jack search for an alleged sea monster in her hand-cranked, pre-steampunk submarine and find more adolescent humor than the ocean is able to hold.

Add a dash of romantic tension, a sprinkling of anachronisms, and a soupçon of satire, and you have the bouillabaisse known as *Jack of All Trades*.

### Janeway, Kathryn (*Star Trek: Voyager*)

"You've come a long way, baby." So said the famous ad campaign for Virginia Slims cigarettes, which launched in 1968, emphasizing women's rising independence. In the same year, the last season of *Star Trek* aired, featuring that most macho of starship captains, that king of the flying drop kick, James Tiberius Kirk (William Shatner). Although women had indeed "come a long way" by 1968, there was a long way to go, both in the real world and on the small screen. It wasn't until 1995, almost 30 years later, that *Star Trek*'s TV franchise produced a female starship captain and series lead in Kathryn Janeway, portrayed by Kate Mulgrew.

Janeway commands the crew of USS *Voyager*, a small Federation vessel, which is stranded about 75 years' travel from home. A former science officer, Janeway is able to see beyond science to the big picture, especially when a lot is at stake. In "The

Omega Directive" (1998), she insists upon destroying particles with the potential to eradicate warp travel, even though her science advisers, particularly Seven of Nine (Jeri Ryan), would prefer to retain some for study.

When her leadership skills aren't enough to solve problems in deep space, Janeway relies upon her creativity. In "Bride of Chaotica!" (1999), she assumes the role of Arachnia, Queen of the Spider People, in a *Flash Gordon*–esque holographic program. Armed conflict has broken out, because aliens have mistaken the simulation for reality. Janeway/Arachnia must charm Chaotica, a villain à la Ming, the Merciless, posing as his prospective bride, and adapting to changing circumstances as the simulation plays out.

**Kathryn Janeway (Kate Mulgrew) shatters the glass ceiling for female starship captains on** *Star Trek: Voyager* **(Paramount/Photofest).**

Mulgrew won a 1998 Saturn Award in the "Best Actress on Television" category for her performance as groundbreaking, stereotype-busting Kathryn Janeway. *Star Trek* captains had indeed come a long way, as Janeway noted in her own inimitable style...

"Ma'am is acceptable in a crunch, but I prefer Captain."

See also: ***Star Trek: Voyager* (1995–2001, 172 episodes, USA)**

## Jeannie (*I Dream of Jeannie*)

Is that Jeannie or genie? When astronaut Tony Nelson (Larry Hagman) frees Jeannie (Barbara Eden) from 2000 years of captivity in a pretty but decidedly cramped bottle, she immediately falls in love with him. Following her new "master" back to Cocoa Beach, the beautiful genie tries to grant his every wish, while hoping he will learn to reciprocate her love. Jeannie takes up residence with Nelson in his well-appointed bachelor home (the scandal!), but decorum is maintained as she continues to sleep in her old bottle, the genie's version of a granny flat.

Jeannie is a jealous genie, and she sabotages Tony's dates at every turn, as in "Who Needs a Green Eyed Jeannie?" (1966), when she locks him up in a cage to keep him from a rendezvous. As if one Jeannie isn't enough, Jeannie has a sister, a genie also named Jeannie (Barbara Eden in a dual role), who looks just like Jeannie, except for her brown hair. Jeannie II also has eyes for genie-magnet Tony, and tries to drive a wedge between her sister and the astronaut, even after they are married, as in "My Sister, the Homewrecker" (1969).

Although she wears a pink harem costume, Jeannie is a modest genie. The censors at NBC would not allow the character to show her navel, and her gauzy harem pants were lined so she wouldn't show any leg. If she entered Nelson's bedroom, she had to be shown exiting it in those oh-so-quaint days before cohabitation.

While no one would ever accuse *I Dream of Jeannie* of being a feminist statement, Jeannie was at least independent-minded, especially for a genie, often imposing her own will on Tony. If she called her husband "master" even after their marriage, well, let's just call that an anachronistic endearment.

See also: *I Dream of Jeannie* (1965–1970, 139 episodes, USA)

### *Jennifer Slept Here* (1983–1984, 13 episodes, USA)

*Created by:* Larry Rosen, Larry Tucker
*Production Co.:* Columbia Pictures Television, The Larry Larry Company
*Originally Aired:* NBC
*Main Cast:* Ann Jillian, John P. Navin, Jr., Georgia Engel, Brandon Maggart, Mya Stark, Glenn Scarpelli

Ann Jillian portrays Jennifer Farrell, a movie star who had an unfortunate encounter with an ice cream truck, leading to her untimely demise in 1963. Twenty years later, Jennifer is still kicking around her old manse, but she's just a shadow of her former self now, or, more precisely, a spirit. When the Elliott family takes up residence in Jennifer's Beverly Hills home, Joey Elliott (John P. Navin, Jr.), the teenage son of George (Brandon Maggart) and Susan (Georgia Engel), is the only family member able to see Jennifer, but no one believes his ghostly tales. Jennifer is very real to Joey, however, and the glamour queen helps him navigate the troubled waters of adolescence, which seem to involve girls, bullies, girls, school, and girls. In the meantime, Jennifer deals with problems of her own, including a surprising number of ghostly visitors, not the least of whom is her mother, Alice Farrell (Debbie Reynolds).

Alas, this unusual experiment in ghostly guidance-counseling came to an end when NBC sent Jennifer to the other side after 13 episodes.

### Jennings, Norma (*Twin Peaks*)

Diner owner supervising troubled teens in a town beset by sinister spirits.
See: *Twin Peaks* (1990–1991, 30 episodes, USA)

### Jessi (*Kyle XY*)

Teen with more than the usual share of problems, such as being the product of a scientific experiment.
See: *Kyle XY* (2006–2009, 43 episodes, Canada/USA)

### *Jessica Jones* (2015– , 13 episodes, USA)

*Based on:* The Marvel Comics character created by Brian Michael Bendis, Michael Gaydos
*Created by:* Melissa Rosenberg
*Production Co.:* Marvel Television, ABC Studios
*Originally Aired:* Netflix

*Main Cast:* Krysten Ritter, Mike Colter, Rachael Taylor, Wil Traval, Erin Moriarty, Eka Darville, Carrie-Anne Moss, David Tennant

Jessica Jones (Krysten Ritter) is a retired superhero. She hung up her tights at a young age due to the trauma she suffered at the hands of a sadistic villain known as Kilgrave (David Tennant), who possessed formidable mind-control abilities. Jessica had been Kilgrave's slave, committing heinous crimes, while smiling (and worse) on command. Now free from Kilgrave's control, Jessica binge-drinks to deal with her PTSD, a practice which eminently qualifies her for her new occupation of hard-boiled private eye in New York's Hell's Kitchen. Jessica's powers of super-strength, near-invulnerability, and (tentative) flight also come in handy, but she uses them sparingly. She accepts a simple missing persons case in "AKA Ladies Night" (2015), but the trail leads to her nemesis, Kilgrave, whom she thought was dead. A cat-and-mouse game ensues for the rest of the first season, with LOTS of collateral damage, ending when Jones, now immune to Kilgrave's power, snaps his neck.

Despite its superhero trappings and connection to the Marvel Cinematic Universe, *Jessica Jones* is not for children. It includes graphic torture, and examines adult issues such as recovery from abuse, and the nature of rape and consent. While not for everyone, if your tastes lean toward noir-tinged psychological horror and strong female antiheroes, *Jessica Jones* might be up your darkest of dark alleys.

## *Joan of Arcadia* (2003–2005, 45 episodes, USA)
*Created by:* Barbara Hall
*Production Co.:* Barbara Hall Productions, CBS Productions, Sony Pictures Television
*Originally Aired:* CBS
*Main Cast:* Amber Tamblyn, Joe Mantegna, Mary Steenburgen, Jason Ritter, Michael Welch, Chris Marquette, Becky Wahlstrom, Wentworth Miller

Joan of Arc was a 15th-century teenager who received visions from saints, became a French military hero, and was executed for heresy. Joan of Arcadia is a 21st-century teen who talks directly to God, deals with the usual adolescent woes, and sometimes looks crazy when she follows God's instructions. On the bright side, there's no Inquisition.

Joan Girardi (Amber Tamblyn), a high-school student in Arcadia, Maryland, starts to have weird encounters with strangers who claim to be God. Although initially skeptical, Joan begins to believe that God is talking to her, and she follows God's mysterious instructions, although they often cause embarrassment and sometimes make her appear unbalanced. Joan must proceed on faith, as God never explains the reasons behind the instructions, although Joan usually sees the good that comes from each of her assignments. In "Just Say No" (2003), God's seemingly mundane instruction that Joan hold a garage sale leads her to disturbing paintings created by her mother, Helen (Mary Steenburgen), and the ultimate revelation that Helen had been raped in college. Joan has her first crisis of faith in "The Devil Made Me Do It" (2003), when her assignment to remove a friend's sculpture from an art show leads to her suspension from school and the alienation of her friend, Adam Rove (Chris Marquette), who later becomes her love interest.

Joan's trials continue until "Something Wicked This Way Comes" (2005), when God tells Joan that the recent past has been prelude to her biggest challenge yet. Alas, *Joan of Arcadia* was canceled at this point, so the series never delivered upon its tantalizing promise that Joan would have a sinister adversary who also talks to God, a millionaire newspapermen named Ryan Hunter (Wentworth Miller).

God appeared to Joan in more than 50 incarnations, including a rich woman (Susan Sullivan), a little girl (Juliette Goglia), an old lady (Kathryn Joosten), a homeless man (Larry Hankin), and a dog walker (Russ Tamblyn, Amber's father). The concept was an echo of the show's opening theme, "One of Us," sung by Joan Osborne, especially the line, "What if God was one of us?"

**Johnson, Shelly (*Twin Peaks*)**
Diner waitress married to a sadistic trucker in a town plagued by supernatural forces.
See: *Twin Peaks* (1990–1991, 30 episodes, USA)

**Jones, Jessica (*Jessica Jones*)**
New York private eye who retired from the superhero business due to a past trauma.
See: *Jessica Jones* (2015– , 13 episodes, USA)

**Jones, Martha (*Doctor Who*)**
Medical student who travels through space and time with a human-looking extraterrestrial.
See: *Doctor Who* (1963–1989, 2005– , 821 episodes, UK)

**Joyner-Kersee, Jackie (*The Neighbors*)**
One of a group of extraterrestrials who have taken the names of famous athletes and reside in New Jersey.
See: *The Neighbors* (2012–2014, 44 episodes, USA)

**Kali (*Sheena*)**
African shaman who adopts an orphan girl and teaches her the secrets of shapeshifting.
See: *Sheena* (2000–2002, 35 episodes, USA)

**Keeply, Claire "The Keeper" (*The Invisible Man*)**
Medical doctor at a shadowy government agency who must keep an invisible man from going insane.
See: *The Invisible Man* (2000–2002, 45 episodes, USA)

**Kerby, Marion (*Topper*)**
Fun-loving ghost who haunts the home of a staid banker with the help of her husband and a tipsy St. Bernard.
See: *Topper* (1953–1955, 78 episodes, USA)

## Killjoys (2015– , 19 episodes, Canada)
*Created by:* Michelle Lovretta
*Production Co.:* Bell Media, Temple Street Productions
*Originally Aired:* Syfy
*Main Cast:* Hannah John-Kamen, Aaron Ashmore, Luke Macfarlane, Tamsen McDonough, Rob Stewart

Bounty hunters in space! That sounds like a high concept, but it becomes an ultra-complicated fictional universe in this series, which follows the mythology-heavy style of contemporary speculative television.

Yalena "Dutch" Yardeen (Hannah John-Kamen) is a Reclamation Agent or "Killjoy," a bounty hunter who pursues warrants across the Quad, a planetary system in a distant star cluster. Killjoys swear an oath that renounces citizenship and declares loyalty only to the warrant, summed up in the rule, "The warrant is all." Smoldering Dutch heads a reclamation team which includes Johnny Jaqobis (Aaron Ashmore), her dyslexic technical expert, and D'avin Jaqobis (Luke Macfarlane), Johnny's older brother, a former soldier who now has PTSD. Dutch, the boys, and their spaceship named Lucy (voiced by Tamsen McDonough) undertake dangerous assignments, involving fertility cults, memory blockers, genetic bombs, green plasma, mummies, and secrets. (There must be SECRETS.) Dutch's hidden truths involve a mysterious childhood mentor named Khylen (Rob Stewart), who trained her as an assassin while she was in a harem. (Yes, harem.)

Although Dutch is tortured by her past, she copes in the present with a deadly sense of humor: "I have a headache, a badge, and a gun. Behave."

### King, Chloe (*The Nine Lives of Chloe King*)
San Francisco teen who learns on her 16th birthday that she is descended from cat-people.
See: *The Nine Lives of Chloe King* (2011, 10 episodes, USA)

### King, Tara (*The Avengers*)
Novice British agent who investigates outré crimes with a dapper veteran.
See: *The Avengers* (1961–1969, 161 episodes, UK)

### Kira, Nerys (*Star Trek: Deep Space Nine*)
Former resistance fighter on an occupied planet, now First Officer to the commander of a strategic space station.
See: *Star Trek: Deep Space Nine* (1993–1999, 176 episodes, USA)

### Kisgadden, Frances (*Highcliffe Manor*)
Mad scientist who creates a man from erector set pieces and stolen body parts.
See: *Highcliffe Manor* (1979, 6 episodes, USA)

### Krux, Marguerite (*The Lost World*)
Heiress who funds an expedition to the Amazon in search of prehistoric creatures.
See: *The Lost World* (1999–2002, 66 episodes, Australia/Canada/USA)

**Kwon, Sun (*Lost*)**
Survivor of a plane crash on a mysterious Pacific island, who hides secrets from her possessive husband.
See: ***Lost* (2004–2010, 118 episodes, USA)**

**Kyle, Helena (*Birds of Prey*)**
The daughter of Batman and Catwoman, who protects New Gotham as superhero Huntress.
See: ***Birds of Prey* (2002–2003, 13 episodes, USA)**

**Kyle XY (2006–2009, 43 episodes, Canada/USA)**
*Created by:* Eric Bress, J. Mackye Gruber
*Production Co.:* ABC Studios, ABC Family Original Productions, Kyle XY Productions, BenderSpink Productions
*Originally Aired:* ABC Family
*Main Cast:* Matt Dallas, Jaimie Alexander, Marguerite MacIntyre, April Matson, Kirsten Prout, Chris Olivero, Jean-Luc Bilodeau, Bruce Thomas

Kyle Trager (Matt Dallas) is not your typical teen. Suffering from total amnesia and strangely missing a bellybutton, he is taken home as a foster child by psychologist Nicole Trager (Marguerite MacIntyre) and learns about life while blending with her family. It turns out that Kyle is the product of a scientific experiment and that there is another like him, Jessi (Jaime Alexander), who is sent to get intel on Kyle, but ends up falling in love with him. This places Kyle at the center of a love triangle between Jessi and the true object of his affections, next door neighbor Amanda Bloom (Kirsten Prout). As if love, high school, and finding out their true identities aren't enough challenges for Kyle and Jessi, organizations with names like Zzyzx and Latnok ruthlessly pursue the pair for their own agendas in this fascinating hybrid of teen drama and SF thriller.

And you thought getting through high school was tough.

**Lambert, Natalie (*Forever Knight*)**
Medical Examiner who tries to cure her love, a vampire, of his bloodthirsty ways.
See: ***Forever Knight* (1992–1996, 70 episodes, Canada/West Germany)**

**Lance, Dinah (*Birds of Prey*)**
Teenager with telekinetic abilities who works with female superheroes in New Gotham.
See: ***Birds of Prey* (2002–2003, 13 episodes, USA)**

**Land of the Giants (1968–1970, 51 episodes, USA)**
*Created by:* Irwin Allen
*Production Co.:* Irwin Allen Productions, Kent Productions, 20th Century–Fox Television
*Originally Aired:* ABC

The "little people" (left to right, Don Matheson, Heather Young, Kurt Kasznar, Deanna Lund, Gary Conway, and Don Marshall) find themselves stranded in the Land of the Giants (ABC Television).

*Main Cast:* Gary Conway, Don Matheson, Kurt Kasznar, Don Marshall, Stefan Arngrim, Deanna Lund, Heather Young

In 1983, a suborbital passenger ship on its way to London from the U.S. encounters a space anomaly and crash-lands on an unknown planet. The survivors soon discover that they are marooned in a land of giants, where the inhabitants, although human-appearing, are actually 12 times the size of the castaways. The ship's captain, Steve Burton (Gary Conway), becomes the leader of the crash victims, assisted by his crew, co-pilot Dan Erickson (Don Marshall) and flight attendant (then called stewardess) Betty Hamilton (Heather Young). The passengers they serve are Mark Wilson (Don Matheson), an engineer, Valerie Scott (Deanna Lund), a glamorous jet-setter, Alexander Fitzhugh (Kurt Kasznar), a bank robber disguised as a Navy man, and Barry Lockridge (Stefan Arngrim), a young boy with his dog.

The giants aren't fans of the "little people," as they call them, preferring to capture them for study or to display them as curiosities. Although the crew and passengers work hard to survive, hoping to find materials to repair the spacecraft for a return to Earth, their main occupation is rescuing other members of their party who have been kidnapped by the giants. Animals also pose a threat, as in "The Marionettes"

(1970), when a giant ape carries off Valerie, who is freed, but not before Betty becomes caught in an animal trap. Further rescues ensue.

The special effects were grand for the time, with lots of giant props, such as phones, guns, and chessboards, and the actors did many of the stunts themselves. But special effects are expensive, too expensive to keep this series afloat for a third season, leaving the little people "lost in space," not unlike other characters from the imagination of creator Irwin Allen.

## *Land of the Lost* (1974–1976, 43 episodes, USA)
*Created by:* David Gerrold (uncredited), Sid Krofft, Marty Krofft, Allan Foshko
*Production Co.:* Sid & Marty Krofft Television Productions
*Originally Aired:* NBC
*Main Cast:* Spencer Milligan, Wesley Eure, Kathy Coleman, Phillip Paley, Ron Harper

In addition to the usual rigors of river rafting, one must be concerned about falling over an earthquake-induced waterfall and sliding into an alternate universe, or so the creators of *Land of the Lost* would have us believe. Although the series looks cheesy by today's standards, it had lots of SF wattage behind it, with episodes penned by Larry Niven, Ben Bova, Theodore Sturgeon, and more.

The hapless Marshall family encounters dinosaurs in this land of the lost, as well as creatures unknown to humans, such as "Sleestak" (lizard people). Rick Marshall (Spencer Milligan) and his kids, Will (Wesley Eure), an adventurous teen, and Holly (Kathy Coleman), a tweener with blonde braids à la Cindy Brady, try to make the best of a bad situation, while hoping to find their way back home. Holly likes to name the dinosaurs they meet, such as "Dopey," a baby *Brontosaurus* she adopts as a pet. All is not sweetness, however, as the family must stay clear of a T. rex named "Grumpy" and other creatures who want to capture or kill them. In "The Paku Who Came to Dinner" (1974), Holly is kidnapped by humanoid primates called the Pakuni, who are attracted to her perfume.

The series ended without rescue for the marooned family, although the first-season episode "Elsewhen"(1974) offered a tantalizing hint from a future Holly that the castaways would eventually return home. The Kroffts' 1991 remake of their own series didn't provide any clues to the Marshalls' fate, as new folks, the Porters, were stranded (albeit with better special effects), leaving two families now forsaken in the *Land of the Lost*.

## Lane, Lois (*Adventures of Superman*)
Lois Lane is a reporter for *The Daily Planet* in Metropolis, working alongside newsman Clark Kent (George Reeves), who just happens to lead a double-life as Superman, the Man of Steel. Lois likes to beat Clark to scoops, and, as portrayed by Phyllis Coates in the first season, is one tough cookie, who doesn't back down even when confronted by killers or kidnappers. Her nose for news involves her in dark investigations, such as "Mystery of the Broken Statues" (1952), where her inquisitiveness gets her abducted, but leads to the recovery of a priceless gem. Coates's Lois doesn't wait for Superman to rescue her, using a nearby statue as a bludgeon, when

threatened by her kidnapper. For all her trailblazing, Phyllis Coates turned down a second season of *Adventures of Superman* due to other commitments.

Her successor, Noel Neill, portrays a softer Lois Lane, still inquisitive and out to best Clark in the newsroom, but more demure and with a developing romantic attraction to Superman. In "The Wedding of Superman" (1956), Lois marries the Man of Steel, but wakes up to find it was only a heartbreaking dream.

But tough or soft, in black-and-white or color, Lois Lane breaks new TV ground, because it takes a real superman to beat this newswoman to a byline.

See also: ***Adventures of Superman* (1952–1958, 104 episodes, USA)**

### Lane, Lois (*Lois & Clark: The New Adventures of Superman*)

Premier investigative reporter who's in love with a superhero, his alter ego, or both.

See: ***Lois & Clark: The New Adventures of Superman* (1993–1997, 87 episodes, USA)**

### Lane, Lois (*Smallville*)

Tenacious reporter for a metropolitan newspaper who learns that her boyfriend is a superhero.

See: ***Smallville* (2001–2011, 217 episodes, USA)**

### Lang, Lana (*Smallville*)

High school sweetheart of a superhero who later gains special powers in her own right.

See: ***Smallville* (2001–2011, 217 episodes, USA)**

### Lang, Lana (*Superboy*)

College student and frequent kidnap victim, always rescued by the Boy of Steel.

See: ***Superboy* (1988–1992, 100 episodes, USA)**

### Lass, Georgia "George" (*Dead Like Me*)

Teenager who becomes a Grim Reaper after she's killed by a falling toilet seat from the Mir space station.

See: ***Dead Like Me* (2003–2004, 29 episodes, USA)**

### Lawrence, Minx (*The Whispers*)

D.C.–area child with an "imaginary" friend who may not be of this world.

See: ***The Whispers* (2015, 13 episodes, USA)**

### Layton, Veronica (*The Lost World*)

"Untamed beauty" who lives in the Amazon jungle with prehistoric creatures.

See: ***The Lost World* (1999–2002, 66 episodes, Australia/Canada/USA)**

### Lewis, Lauren (*Lost Girl*)

Scientist who teaches a succubus self-control and falls in love with her.

See: ***Lost Girl* (2010–2015, 77 episodes, Canada)**

**Liana (*The Fantastic Journey*)**
Bermuda Triangle castaway, the daughter of an Atlantian father and an extraterrestrial mother.
See: *The Fantastic Journey* (1977, 10 episodes, USA)

**The Librarians (2014– , 20 episodes, USA)**
*Based on:* The TV-movie series *The Librarian* created by David Titcher
*Created by:* John Rogers
*Production Co.:* Kung Fu Monkey Productions, Electric Entertainment
*Originally Aired:* TNT
*Main Cast:* Christian Kane, Rebecca Romijn, Lindy Booth, John Harlan Kim, John Larroquette, Noah Wyle

A show about the Dewey Decimal Classification System this isn't. The librarians of the title work at a special, special library, one which stores the knowledge and artifacts they collect to keep the world's citizens safe from the chaos of magic (not unlike *Warehouse 13*). Rebecca Romijn is Colonel Eve Baird, not one of the librarians per se, but their Guardian, a former counter-intelligence officer for NATO, well-chosen to defend the librarians on their dangerous assignments. Eve is beautiful, but tough (surprise!), and protects not just the lives of the librarians, but even their immortal souls, as in "And the Infernal Contract" (2015), when the team encounters none other than Mephistopheles (John DeLancie) amidst small-town politics in New Hampshire.

The librarians themselves are a colorful crew. Cassandra Cillian (Lindy Booth) is a mathematician, who has been coping with a brain tumor since childhood. Her "brain grape," while dangerous, also gives her hallucinations which help the team, as well as synesthesia, something like two senses for the price of one, where numbers appear to her as colors and science as musical notes.

Cassandra works with two other librarians, Jacob Stone (Christian Kane), an art history expert, formerly (and incongruously) a pipeline laborer, and Ezekiel Jones (John Harlan Kim), a master thief and hacker. Along with tactician Eve, the librarians deal with some pretty eldritch stuff, such as a tentacled Lovecraftian monster summoned from another dimension in "And the Cost of Education" (2015).

Perhaps this show will FINALLY lay to rest the stereotype of the prim librarian—the one who wears her hair in a bun and glasses on a chain. That would be magical.

**Limitless (2015–2016, 22 episodes, USA)**
*Based on:* The film *Limitless* directed by Neil Burger
*Created by:* Craig Sweeny
*Production Co.:* K/O Paper Products, Relativity Television, Action This Day!, CBS Television Studios
*Originally Aired:* CBS
*Main Cast:* Jake McDorman, Jennifer Carpenter, Hill Harper, Mary Elizabeth Mastrantonio, Bradley Cooper

Brian Finch (Jake McDorman) is a struggling musician and confirmed underachiever living in the Big Apple. His life changes forever when a friend gives him NZT, a pill which unlocks all his brain's potential—intelligence, creativity, and memory—transforming Brian from a muddle-headed slacker into a mental giant, but only as long as he continues to take the pill. The problem is (it couldn't be that simple, right?) NZT has ravaging and often deadly side effects. Enter a mysterious United States Senator, Eddie Morra (Bradley Cooper), who appears out of nowhere with an immunity inoculation for Brian, a hidden agenda, and a demand that Brian keep the NZT cure a secret.

When Brian becomes a suspect in a murder investigation, he shows up on the radar of FBI Special Agent Rebecca Harris (Jennifer Carpenter). Rebecca herself has a special connection to NZT, believing that the drug played a part in the death of her father, an artist, and hoping to solve the mystery of his early demise. Rebecca and her boss, Nasreen "Naz" Pouran (Mary Elizabeth Mastrantonio), believe that Brian is somehow immune to the effects of NZT, and know nothing of Morra's involvement. Naz agrees to take Brian on as a consultant, feeding him one NZT pill each day to make the most of his prodigious drug-enhanced brain.

Brian and Rebecca descend into the hidden world of NZT, while occasionally investigating crimes involving murder and terrorism. In the process, Brian must tell lie after lie to Rebecca, although he sincerely tries to gain her trust. Emotional contradictions are as much a challenge for his brain as the crime puzzles he must solve.

## Lisa (*V*)

Extraterrestrial visitor who grows conflicted about her mother's plans for Earth.
See: ***V*** **(2009–2011, 22 episodes, USA)**

## Lisa (*Weird Science*)

Computer-generated genie who comes to life and teaches two teenage boys about the opposite sex.
See: ***Weird Science*** **(1994–1998, 88 episodes, USA)**

## Littleton, Claire (*Lost*)

Survivor of a plane crash on a mysterious island, who must deal with threats to her baby before and after he is born.
See: ***Lost*** **(2004–2010, 118 episodes, USA)**

## *Lois & Clark: The New Adventures of Superman* (1993–1997, 87 episodes, USA)

*Based on:* The DC Comics character Superman created by Jerry Siegel, Joe Shuster
*Created by:* Deborah Joy LeVine
*Production Co.:* December 3rd Productions, Gangbuster Films Inc., Roundelay Productions, Warner Bros. Television
*Originally Aired:* ABC
*Main Cast:* Dean Cain, Teri Hatcher, Lane Smith, Eddie Jones, K Callan, Justin Whalin, Michael Landes, Tracy Scoggins, John Shea

Superman was aptly named. The character's strength and staying power throughout all media have been legendary, and his conquest of our TV screens was no exception. Starting with George Reeves in *Adventures of Superman* (1952–1958), continuing (albeit backwards) to the character's boy of steel days in *Superboy* (1988–1992) and later *Smallville* (2001–2011), and coming back to the future with his adult adventures in *Lois & Clark*, there seems to be no TV kryptonite that will take out new incarnations of the Man of Steel.

*Lois & Clark* brings us Dean Cain as Superman/Clark Kent and Teri Hatcher as his newsroom competitor Lois Lane. As the title suggests, this iteration focuses on the relationship between Lois and Clark, which is more of a triangle, especially at the beginning, when Lois pines for Superman, but doesn't know his true identity. When Lois thinks there's no hope for a relationship with her super guy, she falls for Lex Luthor (John Shea), a smarmy billionaire badguy who controls almost everything in Metropolis except Superman. Clark, who loves Lois, notes the irony that the *Daily Planet*'s premier investigative reporter is unable to see her fiancé for what he is. (And viewers may wonder about this choice for the character as well.) A conflicted Lois agrees to marry Luthor, but comes to her senses at the altar (where else?) in the season one finale "The House of Luthor" (1994).

Finally realizing that Superman is Clark, Lois accepts his marriage proposal in "Ultra Woman" (1995), after flying a mile in his cape, so to speak, when red kryptonite transfers his prodigious powers to her. "The course of true love never did run smooth," however, especially when networks want to string along their romance-loving audiences for high ratings. The Clark/Lois wedding was hyped for Valentine's Day sweeps in season three, but Clark ended up marrying only a clone of Lois in "I Now Pronounce You..." (1996), thanks to the cunning of the resurrected Lex Luthor. The real wedding occurred at last in the appropriately titled season-four episode "Swear to God, This Time We're Not Kidding" (1996), which coincided with the DC Comics release of *Superman: The Wedding Album*.

The series was abruptly canceled at the end of season four after a big drop in the ratings. Many believe "the wedding" was to blame, but which wedding is a matter of debate. The phony Valentine's Day wedding broke faith with fans and disappointed their expectations. The real wedding gave fans what they wanted, but also dissipated the sexual tension between the leads, a common problem in "will they or won't they" series such as *Moonlighting*.

TV love is often problematic when driven by ratings rather than story. As Lois herself once said, "You know, it's true what they say. Love stinks."

## *Lost* (2004–2010, 118 episodes, USA)
*Created by:* Jeffrey Lieber, J.J. Abrams, Damon Lindelof
*Production Co.:* Bad Robot Productions, Touchstone Television, ABC Studios
*Originally Aired:* ABC
*Main Cast:* Naveen Andrews, Emilie de Ravin, Matthew Fox, Jorge Garcia, Josh Holloway, Daniel Dae Kim, Yunjin Kim, Evangeline Lilly, Dominic Monaghan, Terry O'Quinn, Harold Perrineau, Elizabeth Mitchell, Michael Emerson, Henry Ian Cusick

A passenger jet bound for Los Angeles from Sydney, Australia crashes on a South Pacific island, stranding 72 survivors. The premise sounds simple enough—a dramatic (albeit crowded) *Gilligan's Island*. But with its elliptical storytelling, serialized plots, and SF/fantasy elements, *Lost* is anything but simple.

The complexity extends to the characters themselves, not just their tangled histories and emotions, but also their sheer number, with 14 regular speaking parts in the first season alone. Jack Shepard (Matthew Fox), a medical doctor, emerges as a reluctant leader of the castaways, tending to their injuries, and using his analytical skills to solve problems, while coping with demons from his past. (The island virtually teems with demons from the past.) **Kate Austen** (Evangeline Lilly), a fugitive in federal custody at the time of the plane crash, assists Jack, and becomes a second prominent voice among the survivors. James "Sawyer" Ford (Josh Holloway), the handsome bad boy of the piece, sneers and growls a lot, but may have a heart underneath, which he is saving for Kate, if hers isn't already committed to virtuous Jack. Claire Littleton (Emilie de Ravin), a young, pregnant woman, had planned to give her baby up for adoption in Los Angeles, and now fights emotional and physical threats to her pregnancy and later to her son Aaron. Jin Kwon (Daniel Dae Kim), an enforcer for his father-in-law, is overly protective of his wife, and keeps her isolated from the other survivors. Sun Kwon (Yunjin Kim), Jin's seemingly subservient wife, had planned to escape Jin at the Sydney airport, but relented at the last minute. She hides her knowledge of English from her husband, who speaks only Korean, but they eventually reconcile, bound by the daily crises of island life.

By the time the series ends, the castaways have discovered a second group of survivors from their flight, a mysterious and unfriendly colony of "Others" living on the island, a network of scientific bunkers designed to avert an unspecified apocalypse, a polar bear, a smoke monster that kills, the smoke monster's human alter-ego and, yes, much MORE. Some will escape the island (or will they?) and some will travel back in time, while flashes back and forward reveal their past and future connections, even those in the afterlife.

If you were lost after the big series finale in season six, you weren't alone. Welcome to the island.

See also: **Austen, Kate (*Lost*)**

## *Lost Girl* (2010–2015, 77 episodes, Canada)
*Created by:* Michelle Lovretta
*Production Co.:* Prodigy Pictures
*Originally Aired:* Syfy
*Main Cast:* Anna Silk, Kris Holden-Ried, Ksenia Solo, K.C. Collins, Zoie Palmer, Rick Howland, Cle Bennett

"Life is hard when you don't know who you are. It's harder when you don't know what you are."

A succubus detective—talk about a high concept. The succubus in question is Bo Dennis (Anna Silk), a young woman raised by humans, who begins to suspect she is "different," when she accidentally kills her boyfriend during her first sexual encounter. On the run for years, and leaving behind a trail of dead bodies after she has drained their life force, Bo learns who she really is from The Fae, an ancient, supernatural society. Bo is supposed to decide which side to serve in the Fae world, "Light" or "Dark," but instead she remains neutral, preferring the company of humans, especially her new friend Kenzi Malikov (Ksenia Solo), a fast-talking thief. Bo and Kenzi decide to open a private investigation business, catering to both humans and Fae, while Bo continues to learn more about her origins and the ways of the multi-specied Fae. In "(Dis)Members Only" (2010), Bo and Kenzi investigate a missing person at a country club, where Bo and her wolf-shapeshifter boyfriend, Dyson (Kris Holden-Ried), a homicide detective in the human world, go undercover as just your average married couple. Bo also has a romantic relationship with Lauren Lewis (Zoie Palmer), a doctor and scientist in service to the Light Fae, who teaches Bo the handy talent of self-control, the practice of which allows Bo's human and Fae partners to remain alive after sexual encounters with her. Bo continues to face challenges, both in her ultra-complicated sex life and in her chosen middle ground between Light and Dark Fae, whose truce is always tenuous and whose adherents are hatching plots at every turn. But in series finale "Rise" (2015), Bo achieves some clarity in her love life with Lauren, and the warring Fae take a big leap forward.

The life of a succubus may sound like fun, but it's never easy.

## *Lost in Space* (1965–1968, 83 episodes, USA)

*Created by:* Irwin Allen
*Production Co.:* Irwin Allen Productions, Van Bernard Productions, 20th Century–Fox Television, CBS, et al.
*Originally Aired:* CBS
*Main Cast:* Guy Williams, June Lockhart, Mark Goddard, Marta Kristen, Angela Cartwright, Billy Mumy, Jonathan Harris

This series about a space-faring *Swiss Family Robinson* took a quick detour after its original, unaired pilot, when the creative team decided to add a foil for the show's wholesome family. Thenceforth *Lost in Space*, while ostensibly about the Robinsons, was really about Dr. Zachary Smith (Jonathan Harris), a scheming saboteur and scientist, while the family members, with the exception of young Will Robinson (Billy Mumy), were assigned seats at the back of the spaceship.

In 1997, the United States develops a

Judy Robinson (Marta Kristen) is marooned with her family on an uncharted planet in *Lost in Space* (CBS Television).

program to colonize a planet in the Alpha Centauri system, and selects a talented (and photogenic) family to be their guinea pigs—er, astronauts. Professor John Robinson (Guy Williams), pilot, astrophysicist, and father, heads the expedition, which crash-lands on an unknown planet due to Dr. Smith's bumbling attempt at sabotage. Robinson's wife, Maureen (June Lockhart), has a PhD in biochemistry, but she is more "space mom" in their temporary home, preparing meals, tending the garden, and fretting over the safety of her children, especially Will, who spends too much time with Smith. But her other children are not immune to the problems of a hostile planet. Middle child Penny (Angela Cartwright), an intelligent and compassionate young teen, falls into a dimension containing a monster (as often happens) in "The Magic Mirror" (1966). Maureen's eldest daughter, Judy (Marta Kristen), is pulled into a fiery realm (or dimension—a pattern is emerging) with Dr. Smith's help in "A Visit to Hades" (1966).

*Lost in Space* was more highly rated than its contemporary *Star Trek* during their original runs, but it was never the franchise-spawning, inspiration-factory that *Star Trek* became. Despite its respectable ratings, *Lost in Space* was abruptly canceled after its third season, leaving the Robinsons, Dr. Smith, Major Don West (Mark Goddard), and The Robot stranded for decades. A feature-film reboot in 1998 wasn't lucrative enough to generate a sequel, so these intrepid travelers remain lost in space to this day.

### The Lost Saucer (1975–1976, 16 episodes, USA)
*Created by:* Dick Morgan, Si Rose
*Production Co.:* Sid & Marty Krofft Television Productions
*Originally Aired:* ABC
*Main Cast:* Jim Nabors, Ruth Buzzi, Jarrod Johnson, Alice Playten, Larry Larsen

The Lost Saucer stars Jim Nabors and Ruth Buzzi as Fum and Fi, two time-traveling androids from the year 2369, who land their flying saucer on Earth. Fi and Fum are a friendly pair and invite two terrans aboard their ship, young Jerry (Jarrod Johnson) and his babysitter Alice (Alice Playten). As a crowd gathers and the police arrive, Fi and Fum get spooked and take off with Jerry and Alice still on board. Returning them home should be easy, but the ship's controls get damaged, and Fi and Fum are not the most competent pilots. Sometimes they end up in the distant past or the far-off future, where their passengers (and the kids in the Saturday-morning audience) can learn valuable lessons about society and the environment. In "Fat Is Beautiful" (1975), the travelers find themselves in a land where being thin is against the law (as if), and people rely too much on mechanized help (sounds more familiar). Throw in a "dorse," a dog with the head of a horse (but actually Larry Larsen in a shaggy suit), and you have the short-lived kidvid known as *The Lost Saucer*, a show which makes Nabors's *Gomer Pyle, U.S.M.C.* and Buzzi's Gladys Ormphby (*Laugh-In*) look like high art by comparison.

### The Lost World (1999–2002, 66 episodes, Australia/Canada/USA)
*Based on:* The novel by Sir Arthur Conan Doyle

*Production Co.:* Coote Hayes Productions, St. Clare Entertainment, et al.
*Originally Aired:* In Syndication
*Main Cast:* Peter McCauley, Rachel Blakely, William Snow, Jennifer O'Dell, David Orth, Michael Sinelnikoff

Professor George Challenger (Peter McCauley) leads an expedition to the Amazon circa 1920 in hopes of proving the existence of a lost world filled with prehistoric creatures. Since the London Zoological Society is understandably skeptical, Challenger receives funding from a gorgeous heiress, Marguerite Krux (Rachel Blakely), whose only requirement is that she be allowed to tag along on the expedition. Challenger, Marguerite, and company reach their destination, but the dangers are many (cannibals!), and they are fortunate to receive the assistance of Veronica Layton (Jennifer O'Dell), "an untamed beauty" who has been living in the jungle for years since the disappearance of her parents. Trapped on a plateau with man-eating dinosaurs, giant bees, evil lizard men, and even alien invaders, they face danger at every turn. (Imagine!) Cleavage seems to come in—er, handy in these harrowing situations, as both Veronica, in her leather bikini, and Marguerite, in her low-cut blouses, display it at every turn.

Will these intrepid adventurers ever escape the plateau? We'll never know, since financial problems prevented production of *The Lost World*'s fourth season. As the show's producers learned, in the real world, there's never an heiress with money to burn when you need one.

### Lupo, Josefina "Jo" (*Eureka*)

Deputy Sheriff Jo Lupo works in a small town with a quaint main street, which sounds like an easy gig, but the small town is Eureka, home to a bevy of geniuses, who have a tendency to get into catastrophic, sometimes cosmic trouble. Jo (Erica Cerra) assists Sheriff Jack Carter (Colin Ferguson) in keeping the peace, using her skills as a former U.S. Army Ranger and a no-nonsense attitude to combat the craziness around her. Her relationship with Zane Donovan (Niall Matter) is short-circuited by a shift in the timeline, wherein they have never dated and she is head of security at Global Dynamics, Eureka's giant scientific research facility. Love finds a way, however, in series finale, "Just Another Day" (2012), when Zane accepts Josefina's marriage proposal.

See also: ***Eureka* (2006–2012, 77 episodes, USA)**

### MacDoogan, Ethel (*Down to Earth*)

Heaven-sent angel and former 20s flapper, who helps an 80s family with their problems.

See: ***Down to Earth* (1984–1987, 106 episodes, USA)**

### MacGregor, Ann (*The Time Tunnel*)

Scientist working on a time travel experiment beneath the Arizona desert.

See: ***The Time Tunnel* (1966–1967, 30 episodes, USA)**

## Mack, Alex (*The Secret World of Alex Mack*)
Junior-high student who acquires strange powers after being doused with a top-secret chemical.
See: *The Secret World of Alex Mack* (1994–1998, 78 episodes, USA)

## Macready, Sharron (*The Champions*)
Secret agent with enhanced powers bestowed by an ancient civilization.
See: *The Champions* (1968–1969, 30 episodes, UK)

## Madigan, Lisa (*RoboCop*)
Police officer who knows the secrets of her cyber-cop partner in Delta City/Old Detroit.
See: *RoboCop* (1994, 23 episodes, Canada)

## Madsen, Rebecca (*Alcatraz*)
SFPD detective investigating the mass disappearance and reappearance of Alcatraz inmates.
See: *Alcatraz* (2012, 13 episodes, USA)

## *The Magicians* (2015– , 13 episodes, USA)
*Based on:* The novel by Lev Grossman
*Created by:* Sera Gamble, John McNamara
*Production Co.:* Groundswell Productions, Universal Cable Productions
*Originally Aired:* Syfy
*Main Cast:* Jason Ralph, Stella Maeve, Olivia Taylor Dudley, Hale Appleman, Arjun Gupta, Summer Bishil, Jade Tailor, Rick Worthy

Quentin Coldwater (Jason Ralph) and his childhood friend Julia Wicker (Stella Maeve) find themselves suddenly whisked to Brakebills University for Magical Pedagogy, a graduate school that teaches students to find their inner magical selves. Quentin passes the entrance exam, but Julia fails, and an administrator purges her memory of the event, or so it appears. While Julia refuses to forget about magic, Quentin begins his classes at Brakebills, where the twenty-something grad students indulge in too much drinking, sex, and unauthorized spellcasting. During one such spell, Quentin and classmates Alice Quinn (Olivia Taylor Dudley), "Penny" Adiyodi (Arjun Gupta), and Kady Orloff-Diaz (Jade Tailor) accidentally summon a beast from another world, who conducts a grisly attack on the schools's Dean, Henry Fogg (Rick Worthy). Quentin discovers that The Beast is from Fillory, the setting of his beloved childhood fantasy books, which apparently were more historical than fantastical.

As the students train to battle The Beast, Quentin begins a romantic relationship with Alice, who is a brilliant student, but awkward and intense. The relationship provides them both with more trouble than comfort, however, especially when Quentin engages in a post-spell, drunken threesome with fellow students Eliot Waugh (Hale Appleman) and Margo Hanson (Summer Bishil). In the meantime, Julia practices illicit spellcasting in New York City with Hedge Witches, people on the fringes of magical society, and gets in lots of trouble of her own. There's never any doubt, though, that Julia and Quentin will eventually reunite to face The Beast with the help of Quentin's new friends.

Although the initial concept sounds like it's straight out of *Harry Potter*, this Syfy series has plenty of its own imagination, atmosphere, and wonder. At the same time, there are several instances of sexual assault, handled in a mostly restrained manner, and scattered scenes of blood and gore, so sensitive viewers are hereby forewarned. Hogwarts this isn't.

## Magnus, Ashley (*Sanctuary*)

Jack, the Ripper's daughter, who has the ability to teleport, and gets caught in a war over other "Abnormals."

See: ***Sanctuary*** **(2008–2011, 59 episodes, Canada)**

## Magnus, Helen (*Sanctuary*)

Doctor who ages slowly, due to a serum based on vampire blood, and protects other "Abnormals."

See: ***Sanctuary*** **(2008–2011, 59 episodes, Canada)**

## Maguire, Sophia (*The Event*)

Leader of an extraterrestrial group held at a detention facility in Alaska since World War II.

See: ***The Event*** **(2010–2011, 22 episodes, USA)**

## Maitland, Abby (*Primeval*)

Zookeeper who deals with creatures sent to the present via temporal anomalies.

See: ***Primeval*** **(2007–2011, 36 episodes, UK)**

## Mal Doran, Vala (*Stargate SG-1*)

Con artist who joins a special ops team which uses an alien portal to travel the galaxy.

See: ***Stargate SG-1*** **(1997–2007, 214 episodes, Canada/USA)**

## Malik, Sally (*Being Human*)

A ghost in a peculiar "roommate" situation with a vampire and a werewolf.

See: ***Being Human*** **(2011–2014, 52 episodes, Canada/USA)**

## Malikov, Kenzi (*Lost Girl*)

Petty criminal who opens a detective agency with a succubus.

See: ***Lost Girl*** **(2010–2015, 77 episodes, Canada)**

## Maniac Mansion (1990–1993, 66 episodes, Canada/USA)

*Based on:* The computer game by Lucasfilm Games
*Created by:* Eugene Levy, Michael Short, John Hemphill, Paul Flaherty
*Production Co.:* Lucasfilm, Atlantis Films

*Originally Aired:* The Family Channel
*Main Cast:* Joe Flaherty, Deborah Theaker, Kathleen Robertson, Avi Phillips, George Buza, Mary Charlotte Wilcox, John Hemphill

A bizarre comedy with a *Second City Television* (*SCTV*) lineage, *Maniac Mansion* stars Joe Flaherty as Fred Edison, an eccentric scientist and inventor, who has a powerful meteorite in his basement laboratory. Fred's mansion houses other maniacs, a.k.a. his extended family, including long-suffering wife Casey Edison (Deborah Theaker), brother-in-law Harry Orca (John Hemphill), who has been accidentally turned into a housefly with a human head, and four-year-old son Turner (George Buza), who looks like a 250-pound man via more weird science. Fred also has a 10-year-old son named Ike (Avi Phillips) and a brilliant teenaged daughter, Tina (Kathleen Robertson), who assists Fred in his lab. Tina goes through the usual adolescent problems, but not in the usual adolescent ways, as in "Trapped Like Rats" (1990), when she and Ike must work through their sibling rivalry after "little" bro Turner locks them in "The Andromeda Chamber," but doesn't remember the combination to get them out. Tina also learns lessons about beauty and friendship, when she eats some experimental food which doesn't do much for her looks in "Ugly Like Me" (1991).

Given its Family Channel residency, *Maniac Mansion* was more offbeat sitcom and less B-movie horror than its videogame predecessor. No homicidal maniacs at this mansion.

### *Manimal* (1983, 8 episodes, USA)

*Created by:* Glen A. Larson, Donald R. Boyle
*Production Co.:* 20th Century–Fox Television, Glen A. Larson Productions
*Originally Aired:* NBC
*Main Cast:* Simon MacCorkindale, Melody Anderson, Michael D. Roberts, Reni Santoni

Dr. Jonathan Chase (Simon MacCorkindale) has a secret ... a BIG secret. Jonathan has learned a technique whereby he can transform himself into any animal—a hawk, a panther, a dolphin, or a bear. The handsome doctor uses this ability to fight crime, assisting beautiful police detective Brooke McKenzie (Melody Anderson) with her cases. Rounding out the exotic detective team is Ty Earl (Michael D. Roberts), Jonathan's buddy from the Vietnam War.

"Night of the Scorpion" (1983) pits Jonathan, Brooke, and Ty against Russian agents, who are searching for a mysterious list and an heiress who may hold the key to its whereabouts. While at the beach in "Scrimshaw," the trio discovers a skeleton with a scrimshaw clutched in its bony fingers and sets out to investigate the mystery.

Alas, Manimal's crime-fighting days were short-lived, with only eight adventures on record. To add insult to injury, *TV Guide* ranked *Manimal* as number 15 on its list of the "50 Worst TV Shows of All Time" in 2002. Grr...

### *Mann & Machine* (1992, 9 episodes, USA)

*Created by:* Robert De Laurentiis, Dick Wolf
*Production Co.:* Wolf Films, Universal TV

*Originally Aired:* NBC
*Main Cast:* Yancy Butler, David Andrews, S. Epatha Merkerson

Cop shows love the mismatched-partners premise, and this one took it to the hilt, pairing an off-the-shelf wisecracking maverick with a female ROBOT. Yancy Butler is Sgt. Eve Edison, to all appearances a sexy (of course) female officer, who under the skin is a sophisticated robot capable of learning and emotion. Her none-too-willing partner is Detective Bobby Mann (David Andrews), who must teach Eve not only about police work, but also about what it means to be human. In "Billion Dollar Baby" (1992), Eve starts to develop maternal instincts, when she cares for a genetically engineered child sought by baby brokers. She learns about death and dying in "Cold, Cold Heart," when her case involves a terminally ill cryonics scientist.

Alas, her life lessons were cut short when this series went offline after only a handful of episodes.

## Manning, Sarah (*Orphan Black*)

A con artist who runs into a deadly conspiracy when she learns that she is one of several clones.

See: *Orphan Black* (2013– , 40 episodes, Canada)

## Marshall, Holly (*Land of the Lost*)

Preteen stranded with her father and brother in an alternate dimension of dinosaurs and strange creatures.

See: *Land of the Lost* (1974–1976, 43 episodes, USA)

## Marvel's Agent Carter

See: *Agent Carter* (2015–2016, 18 episodes, USA)

## Marvel's Agents of S.H.I.E.L.D.

See: *Agents of S.H.I.E.L.D.* (2013– , 66 episodes, USA)

## Marvel's Jessica Jones

See: *Jessica Jones* (2015– , 13 episodes, USA)

## Mastriani, Jess (*Missing*)

Young psychic whose visions help the FBI locate missing people.

See: *Missing* (2003–2006, 56 episodes, Canada/USA)

## Matthews, Paige (*Charmed*)

Newly discovered half-sister of two witches who fills out their triumvirate after the loss of another sister.

See: *Charmed* (1998–2006, 178 episodes, USA)

## May, Melinda (*Agents of S.H.I.E.L.D.*)

Pilot and weapons expert for a unit that investigates weird phenomena around the world.

See: *Agents of S.H.I.E.L.D.* (2013– , 66 episodes, USA)

### Maya (*Space: 1999*)
Extraterrestrial science officer with the ability to transform herself into any lifeform.
See: *Space: 1999* (1975–1977, 48 episodes, Italy/UK)

### McBride, Ryan (*Baywatch Nights*)
Part of a team of private investigators who like to stick close to the beach.
See: *Baywatch Nights* (1995–1997, 44 episodes, USA)

### McConnell, Mindy (*Mork & Mindy*)
Colorado woman who meets a man from the planet Ork and tutors him in human behavior.
See: *Mork & Mindy* (1978–1982, 95 episodes, USA)

### McCullough, Suzanne and Debi (*War of the Worlds*)
Microbiologist mother and her daughter who battle successive extraterrestrial invasions of Earth.
See: *War of the Worlds* (1988–1990, 43 episodes, Canada/USA)

### McKenzie, Brooke (*Manimal*)
Police detective who receives assistance from a doctor with a big secret.
See: *Manimal* (1983, 8 episodes, USA)

### Meade, Diana (*The Secret Circle*)
Teen witch in a love triangle with her boyfriend and her half-sister, all part of the same coven.
See: *The Secret Circle* (2011–2012, 22 episodes, Canada/USA)

### *Medium* (2005–2011, 130 episodes, USA)
*Based on:* The real-life experiences of Allison DuBois
*Created by:* Glenn Gordon Caron
*Production Co.:* Picturemaker Productions, Grammnet Productions, CBS Paramount Network Television (2006–2009), et al.
*Originally Aired:* NBC (2005–2009), CBS (2009–2011)
*Main Cast:* Patricia Arquette, Jake Weber, Miguel Sandoval, Sofia Vassilieva, Maria Lark, David Cubitt

Patricia Arquette stars as **Allison DuBois**, a clairvoyant who uses her psychic gifts to help the Phoenix District Attorney's Office prosecute cases and solve murders. Allison's visions arrive by way of her dreams, which jolt her awake, causing sleepless nights for her and dutiful husband Joe (Jake Weber). Although Allison develops a great track record, D.A. Manuel Devalos (Miguel Sandoval) and Detective Lee Scanlon (David Cubitt) are frequently skeptical, seemingly forgetting each week that it takes five or six nights of dreams for Allison to sort through the misleading and jumbled visions to get at the truth. In the meantime, Allison and Joe struggle to provide their three daughters, all of whom seem to have inherited Allison's gifts, with some semblance of a normal life.

See also: **DuBois, Allison** (*Medium*)

## Mercy Point (1998–1999, 7 episodes, USA)
*Created by:* Trey Callaway, David Simkins, Milo Frank
*Production Co.:* Mandalay Television, Columbia TriStar Television
*Originally Aired:* UPN
*Main Cast:* Joe Morton, Maria del Mar, Alexandra Wilson, Brian McNamara, Julia Pennington, Gay Thomas, Salli Richardson, Jordan Lund, Joe Spano

Every now and again a series is noteworthy because it bombs so completely. *Mercy Point* is one of those series.

The premise sounds promising enough. *ER* in space! (Or *ER* meets *Star Trek*! Or *Star Trek* meets *M\*A\*S\*H*!). It's the 23rd century, and someone must tend to the medical needs of humans and extraterrestrials on the fringes of the galaxy. Enter the talented doctors and nurses of Mercy Point, a hospital space station. Grote Maxwell (Joe Morton), a legendary alien physiologist and surgeon, spends his spare time searching for estranged family members. His boss, Dr. Haylen Breslauer (Maria del Mar), doesn't have to look far for her own estranged family members, when her half-sister Dru Breslauer (Alexandra Wilson) shows up at the facility as a new resident intern. Haylen has trust issues with her little sister, who has a history of addiction, poor choices, and irresponsibility. ANI (Julia Pennington) is an Android Nursing Interface, so she is a perfect nurse and perfectly gorgeous, making her colleagues jealous because of the impossible standards she sets in every department. As an android, she is unable to recognize their feelings at first, but she later begins to develop emotions of her own. Dr. Rema Cooke (Gay Thomas) fights for the rights of patients in this frontier setting, but she isn't all-work when there's an attractive paramedic nearby.

Of course, it takes more than a promising premise to make a successful series, and it doesn't help when your network is still experiencing growing pains. (What kind of doctor do you call for that?) Due to low ratings, *Mercy Point* was placed on hiatus after just three episodes, and its final four episodes aired during the summer. Mercy!

## Merlin (2008–2012, 65 episodes, UK)
*Created by:* Julian Jones, Jake Michie, Johnny Capps, Julian Murphy
*Production Co.:* Shine Limited
*Originally Aired:* NBC (2009), Syfy (2010–2013)
*Main Cast:* Colin Morgan, Bradley James, Angel Coulby, Katie McGrath, Richard Wilson, Anthony Head, John Hurt

"In a land of myth, and a time of magic, the destiny of a great kingdom rests on the shoulders of a young boy. His name.... Merlin."

*Merlin* simultaneously updates and rewinds Arthurian legend, depicting Merlin (Colin Morgan) as a callow warlock and Arthur (Bradley James) as a spoiled prince, both of whom will forge a bond that will make Arthur the King of Camelot. When Merlin first arrives at court to serve as an apprentice to physician Gaius (Richard Wilson), he learns that King Uther Pendragon (Anthony Head) has outlawed magic, also called the Old Religion. But Merlin will need his wizardry, because he is destined to protect Arthur and help him unite Albion (England), or so he is told by the Great Dragon (voiced by John Hurt). In fact, there's lots of magic right under Uther's prejudiced nose. His ward and illegitimate daughter, Morgana Pendragon (Katie McGrath), learns that she is a seer, but must hide this fact, finally turning to the dark side and (many) plots to take over Camelot. Morgana's maidservant Guinevere, called "Gwen" (Angel Coulby), while not of royal blood, cannot be corrupted like her lady, and is a loyal friend to Merlin. Eventually Gwen and Arthur fall in love, overcoming many obstacles, including Uther's disapproval and Morgana's machinations, to be married in "The Sword in the Stone: Part 2" (2011). Alas, they don't live happily ever after, as Arthur succumbs in a battle with Morgana's army, leaving Gwen the Queen of Camelot in series finale "The Diamond of the Day: Part 2" (2012).

The casting of Angel Coulby, a mixed-race actress, as Guinevere sparked some controversy about historical accuracy, but *Merlin* is fantasy fiction, not history. You can tell because there's a dragon.

### Miller, Rhoda (*My Living Doll*)

Statuesque beauty whose smooth skin hides the inner workings of a robot. See: *My Living Doll* (1964–1965, 26 episodes, USA)

### Mills, Abbie (*Sleepy Hollow*)

Abbie Mills (Nicole Beharie) is a police lieutenant in the not-so-sleepy hamlet of Sleepy Hollow. Upon meeting Ichabod Crane (Tom Mison), a resurrected Revolutionary war soldier, Abbie learns that Sleepy Hollow is ground zero for the coming apocalypse, and that she and Crane are the two biblically prophesied witnesses with the ability to stop Armageddon. As a child, Abbie and her sister Jenny (Lyndie Greenwood) had seen something nasty in the woods, specifically the demon Moloch, ringleader for the forces of evil in the coming showdown. The incident and its aftermath had led to an estrangement between the sisters and repeated institutionalizations for Jenny, but in "The Lesser Key of Solomon" (2013), Abbie and Jenny become allies in the fight against Moloch and his minions. Abbie's work takes her out of the real world and into purgatory, where she is trapped in "Bad Blood" (2014), but later escapes with Ichabod's help.

Crane and Abbie eventually defeat Moloch, but not without releasing demons trapped in purgatory, including Pandora (Shannyn Sossamon). In defeating Pandora's master, the Hidden One, Abbie sacrifices herself to save the world once again.

While her character's gesture was noble, the departure of lead actress Nicole Beharie in the season three finale, "Ragnarok" (2016), shocked and disappointed fans. The Twitter hashtag #AbbieMillsDeservesBetter demonstrated fans' disenchantment with the show's treatment of Beharie's character, a grievance which extended all the way back to season two of the series. There was concern that the parts of Abbie and other characters of color had been inexplicably diminished after a successful first season, while more emphasis was put on Crane and other white characters.

A tragic end, in more ways than one, for a strong and vibrant female character.
See also: **Sleepy Hollow (2013– , 49 episodes, USA)**

## Misfits of Science (1985–1986, 16 episodes, USA)
*Created by:* James D. Parriott
*Production Co.:* Universal Television, James D. Parriott Productions
*Originally Aired:* NBC
*Main Cast:* Dean Paul Martin, Kevin Peter Hall, Mark Thomas Miller, Courteney Cox, Jennifer Holmes, Max Wright, Mickey Jones

One person's misfit is another person's superhero, as in *Heroes*, and its more fun-loving predecessor *Misfits of Science*. Dr. Billy Hayes (Dean Paul Martin), a handsome, but "normal," scientist, studies "human anomalies" at the Humanidyne Institute. Billy conducts research alongside Dr. El Lincoln (Kevin Peter Hall), a seven-footer who has the ability to shrink to Ken-doll size at a moment's notice. (He carries a petite set of clothes in his pocket for reasons of decency.) Younger misfits join the incredibly good-looking team, including Johnny B. (Mark Thomas Miller), a rock musician who is able to zap blue lightning from his fingertips. (Cool!) Courtney Cox, fresh off her appearance in Bruce Springsteen's "Dancing in the Dark" video, portrays Gloria Dinallo, a troubled telekinetic teen with a history of shoplifting. Gloria just wants to be normal, but begins to embrace her power, as the team shifts into save-the-world mode. In "The Avenging Angel" (1986), Gloria uses her telekinetic gifts to rescue an elderly couple from an attack, giving a man the mistaken impression that he's a powerful wrestler.

Bad reviews aside, this one never stood a chance, as it was scheduled against CBS's ratings-powerhouse *Dallas*. Courtney Cox went on to achieve fame and fortune with *Friends*, but bad luck was otherwise associated with this short-lived series. Dean Paul Martin and Kevin Peter Hall both died prematurely at the age of 35, a sad footnote to a light-hearted 80s series.

## Missing (2003–2006, 56 episodes, Canada/USA)
*Based on:* The *1–800-WHERE-R-YOU* series of novels by Meg Cabot
*Created by:* Glenn Davis, William Laurin
*Production Co.:* NDG Productions, Lions Gate Television, Missing Productions II
*Originally Aired:* Lifetime
*Main Cast:* Caterina Scorsone, Gloria Reuben, Vivica A. Fox, Mark Consuelos, Justina Machado, Dean McDermott, Justin Louis

Originally titled *1-800-Missing*, this crime/paranormal drama stars Caterina Scorsone as Jess Mastriani, a young woman whose psychic visions help to locate missing people. In the first season, Jess works as a consultant for the FBI, partnering with Brooke Haslett (Gloria Reuben), who is highly skeptical of Jess's abilities, especially since her visions are more like puzzles, which are almost as difficult to solve as the crimes themselves. A major reboot occurred in season two, with not only the change in title, but also a new lead for the series in Vivica A. Fox as FBI Agent Nicole Scott. Caterina/Jess becomes the second banana, now a full-fledged, if junior, agent, but there's less emphasis on her visions and more attention to her partnership with rule-breaking, sassy, supercop Nicole. As an iconoclast, Nicole does immediately accept the validity of Jess's visions, and finds the information gained from them useful, when she can slow down long enough to hear it. With a new boss, John Pollock (Justin Louis), who loves to grab all the credit, and a partner who has problems with authority, rookie Jess certainly has her hands full.

### *Mission: Impossible* (1966–1973, 171 episodes, USA)
*Created by:* Bruce Geller
*Production Co.:* Desilu Productions, Paramount Television
*Originally Aired:* CBS
*Main Cast:* Steven Hill, Barbara Bain, Greg Morris, Peter Lupus, Peter Graves, Martin Landau, Leonard Nimoy, Lynda Day George

"As always, should you or any of your I.M. Force be caught or killed, the Secretary will disavow any knowledge of your actions."

Fast-paced espionage series chronicling the exploits of the Impossible Missions Force (IMF), a team of secret agents led by Jim Phelps (Peter Graves), who receives instructions via a tape-recording which self-destructs seconds after reaching its conclusion. Phelps selects operatives for each sensitive and dangerous assignment based on their unique skills, and his favorites include master of disguise Rollin Hand (Martin Landau), top model turned undercover specialist **Cinnamon Carter** (Barbara Bain), and (later) disguise expert Lisa Casey (Lynda Day George). The team topples dictators, rescues hostages, and prevents assassinations, using impossibly intricate plans, split-second timing, and technology we still don't possess today, aided by the skills of electronics genius Barney Collier (Greg Morris) and strongman Willy Armitage (Peter Lupus). Most missions involve an elaborate ruse, such as an impersonation, culminating in a big reveal, where one of the agents rips off a mask to display their true identity to the startled mark.

*Mission: Impossible*, as its title suggests, is all about the mission, and we learn little about the personal lives of the IMF or who their bosses might be. That just adds to the intrigue and élan of this imaginative series.

See also: **Carter, Cinnamon (*Mission: Impossible*)**

### *Mission: Impossible* (1988–1990, 35 episodes, USA)
*Created by:* Bruce Geller
*Production Co.:* Paramount Network Television
*Originally Aired:* ABC
*Main Cast:* Peter Graves, Thaao Penghlis, Tony Hamilton, Phil Morris, Jane Badler, Bob Johnson

Peter Graves reprises his role as Jim Phelps in this sequel to the 1966 TV series of the same title. Phelps comes out of retirement to lead the Impossible Missions Force, with a new dossier of agents and more advanced high-tech gadgets at his disposal. Joining Phelps for dangerous duty around the world are Thaao Penghlis as Nicholas Black, master of disguise; Phil Morris as Grant Collier, electronics expert and son of Barney Collier (Phil's real-life father Greg Morris) from the original series;

Former model Cinnamon Carter (Barbara Bain) works with Rollin Hand (Martin Landau, left) and Daniel Briggs (Steven Hill) on an elite team of secret agents in *Mission: Impossible* (CBS Television).

and Jane Badler as Shannon Reed, a former Secret Service Agent and role-playing specialist. The IMF fights neo–Nazis, thwarts invasions, destroys druglords, and even saves the planet, as in "Target Earth," when Shannon finds herself trapped on an orbiting spacecraft hijacked by terrorists. In short, the new team is much like the old team, just with better toys for a digital age.

**Mohr, Sarah** (*The Crow: Stairway to Heaven*)
Street kid who helps a man, neither alive nor dead, right wrongs on Earth and find redemption.
See: *The Crow: Stairway to Heaven* (1998–1999, 22 episodes, Canada)

**Monica** (*Touched by an Angel*)
Angel who travels the countryside in human form, helping people at pivotal points in their lives.
See: *Touched by an Angel* (1994–2003, 212 episodes, USA)

**Monroe, Alex** (*The Invisible Man*)
Secret agent with a personal vendetta against an evil organization which took her surrogate child.
See: *The Invisible Man* (2000–2002, 45 episodes, USA)

## *Moonlight* (2007–2008, 16 episodes, USA)
*Created by:* Ron Koslow, Trevor Munson
*Production Co.:* Warner Bros. Television, Silver Pictures Television
*Originally Aired:* CBS
*Main Cast:* Alex O'Loughlin, Sophia Myles, Jason Dohring, Shannyn Sossamon

Alex O'Loughlin stars as Mick St. John, a Los Angeles private detective with a bloody little secret—he's a vampire. At a murder scene, Mick runs into Internet reporter **Beth Turner** (Sophia Myles), and vampire and mortal find themselves drawn together in crime, while flashbacks reveal a prior (un)deadly connection between the two that Beth only partially remembers. Soon Beth learns Mick's secret and is introduced to the shadowy underworld of L.A. vampiredom, which includes Mick's is-she-or-isn't-she-undead late wife Coraline (Shannyn Sossamon) and his boyish but wealthy friend Josef (Jason Dohring), a 400-year-old vampire. In the meantime, tortured Mick and spirited Beth continue to hear the call of forbidden love, while finding time to solve crime and fight evil in both their worlds.

See also: **Turner, Beth** (*Moonlight*)

**Moreau, Alexandra "Alex"** (*Poltergeist: The Legacy*)
Researcher and psychic for a secret society dedicated to protecting humans from supernatural evil.
See: *Poltergeist: The Legacy* (1996–1999, 88 episodes, Canada/USA)

## *Mork & Mindy* (1978–1982, 95 episodes, USA)
*Created by:* Garry Marshall, Dale McRaven, Joe Glauberg
*Production Co.:* Henderson Productions, Paramount Television, Miller-Milkis Productions
*Originally Aired:* ABC
*Main Cast:* Robin Williams, Pam Dawber, Conrad Janis, Ralph James, Elizabeth Kerr, Tom Poston, Jay Thomas, Gina Hecht, Jonathan Winters

Robin Williams portrays Mork, a visitor from the planet Ork who travels to Earth in an egg-shaped spaceship to observe human behavior. After landing in

Colorado, Mork meets Mindy McConnell (Pam Dawber), who's just had to fight off an amorous date in a woodsy lovers' lane. Mindy takes Mork back to her apartment, thinking he's a kind, albeit peculiar, priest, because Mork has his business suit, supplied to help him blend in with the locals, on backwards. When Mindy discovers the haberdashery error, Mork reveals his true identity and mission, and Mindy, an open-minded and caring soul, agrees to help. Thus begins this zany, four-year romp, wherein Mork moves into Mindy's attic as the strangest roommate on Earth, learns about our customs under Mindy's tutelage, and later marries her and even has HER baby, Orkan physiology differing a wee bit from our own.

A lot of supporting characters moved in and out of the series, as its phenomenal success in the first season, due mostly to the manic improvisations of Williams, led the powers that were to conclude that a little tinkering could only improve their number THREE showing in the ratings. Fred McConnell (Conrad Janis), Mindy's overprotective father, appears in season one as the owner of a music store, disappears as a regular in season two, and reappears in season three, now the conductor of the Boulder Symphony Orchestra, to help tinker with the tinkering that had dropped the series to number 27 in the ratings. Mearth (Jonathan Winters) arrives in season four after a further ratings drop, as Mork and Mindy's BIG baby, who looks like a middle-aged man because Orkans age backwards.

Mork frequently says "Shazbot," an Orkan profanity, but it might just translate to "don't tinker with a hit."

### Muir, Carolyn (*The Ghost & Mrs. Muir*)
Widowed writer who rents a cottage inhabited by a sea captain's ghost.
See: ***The Ghost & Mrs. Muir* (1968–1970, 50 episodes, USA)**

### Munster, Lily (*The Munsters*)
Vampire housewife with a (Frankenstein's) monster for a husband and a werewolf son.
See: ***The Munsters* (1964–1966, 70 episodes, USA)**

### Munster, Lily (*The Munsters Today*)
Vampire who awakens in the 80s and resumes her role as homemaker in a family of monsters.
See: ***The Munsters Today* (1988–1991, 72 episodes, USA)**

### Munster, Marilyn (*The Munsters*)
Blonde beauty, considered the ugly duckling in a family of vampires and werewolves.
See: ***The Munsters* (1964–1966, 70 episodes, USA)**

### Munster, Marilyn (*The Munsters Today*)
Niece of a vampire and a monster who starts to recognize her human beauty in the 1980s.
See: ***The Munsters Today* (1988–1991, 72 episodes, USA)**

## *The Munsters* (1964–1966, 70 episodes, USA)
*Created by:* Allan Burns, Chris Hayward, Ed Haas, Norm Liebmann
*Production Co.:* Kayro-Vue Productions, CBS Television Network
*Originally Aired:* CBS
*Main Cast:* Fred Gwynne, Yvonne De Carlo, Al Lewis, Beverly Owen, Pat Priest, Butch Patrick

They're creepy and they're kooky, but the Addams Family they ain't. The Munsters, a different mysterious and spooky clan, were the CBS entry in television's 1964 weird family sweepstakes. Herman Munster (Fred Gwynne) is the blue-collar head of household, a regular Ralph Kramden, except for the fact that he looks like Frankenstein's monster. His wife Lily (Yvonne De Carlo) pursues the typical 60s role of housewife, although her "cleaning" routine involves spreading trash and cobwebs around the house. Occasionally Lily's aspirations extend beyond the home, as when she opens a beauty salon in "The Most Beautiful Ghoul in the World" (1966), but the business quickly folds because of Lily's confused belief that women wish to emulate her vampiric beauty. Lily pursues this venture with her niece Marilyn (Pat Priest), a "plain" girl in the eyes of her family, who is actually a blonde knockout (à la Marilyn Monroe) in the "normal" world. The Munsters, Marilyn included, believe that her inability to keep a boyfriend is due to HER physical unattractiveness rather than their own monstrous looks.

Other members of the extended family living at 1313 Mockingbird Lane include Herman and Lily's son Eddie (Butch Patrick), a werewolf (don't try to figure out those genetics), and Lily's father, "Grandpa" (Al Lewis), a centuries-old vampire. Most of the humor is of the culture-clash variety, as in "Far out Munsters" (1965), when a rock group rents out the Munster manse for a weekend (pre–Airbnb), but the family returns home because their hotel room is horrifyingly clean. The Munsters crash the "long hair" fun at the party, and everyone performs, including Lily, who plays the harp and sings "He's Gone Away" in a standout performance by De Carlo.

*The Munsters* lasted only two seasons, but rose from the dead for several movies (some with original cast members) and a television sequel, *The Munsters Today* (1988–1991), with a completely different cast. Given Hollywood's penchant for remakes, *The Munsters* will no doubt have the longevity of Sam Dracula, a.k.a. "Grandpa" Munster.

## *The Munsters Today* (1988–1991, 72 episodes, USA)
*Based on:* The TV series *The Munsters* created by Allan Burns, Chris Hayward, Ed Haas, Norm Liebmann
*Production Co.:* The Arthur Company
*Originally Aired:* In Syndication
*Main Cast:* John Schuck, Lee Meriwether, Howard Morton, Jason Marsden, Hilary Van Dyke

The Munsters awake from a 22-year nap in 1988, occasioned by one of Grandpa's experiments gone awry, and find that their faces have altered because they are in "a brand new show" (per the theme song). This sequel to *The Munsters* has the same

Lily Munster (Yvonne De Carlo), the daughter of Dracula, pursues a peculiar vision of 60s domesticity with hubby Herman (Fred Gwynne) in *The Munsters* (CBS Television).

characters and premise as the original, but uses different actors, cheaper sets, and (too much) color to depict the loving, but monstrous clan at 1313 Mockingbird Lane.

John Schuck portrays Herman Munster, who looks like Frankenstein's monster, but is amiable in his uniquely goofy way. Herman's vampire wife, Lily (Lee Meriwether), resumes her homemaker role, but is sometimes lured outside the home, as in "Designing Munsters" (1988), wherein Lily becomes a fashion designer, while Herman does the household chores. Pretty niece Marilyn (Hilary VanDyke) is still considered an ugly duckling by her warped relatives, but begins to realize her own beauty. She even finds a boyfriend, Dustin Nelson (Scott Reeves), who isn't scared off by the family, but his parents are another matter in "Two Left Feet" (1989).

The new version lasted just two more episodes than the original, indicating that the average shelf life for this "high" concept is 71 episodes.

## Murphy, Connie (*The Dresden Files*)

Chicago police lieutenant who consults with a professional wizard on bizarre cases.

See: *The Dresden Files* (2007, 12 episodes, Canada/USA)

## *Mutant X* (2001–2004, 66 episodes, Canada/USA)

*Created by:* Avi Arad
*Production Co.:* Fireworks Entertainment, Marvel Studios, et al.
*Originally Aired:* In Syndication
*Main Cast:* Forbes March, Victoria Pratt, Lauren Lee Smith, Victor Webster, John Shea, Tom McCamus, Karen Cliche

This *X-Men* clone (with the lawsuits to prove it) chronicles the exploits of genetically enhanced humans with extraordinary powers here called "New Mutants." Adam Kane (John Shea) had worked to create the mutants as part of a covert government program, but came to regret his part in the experiments. He assembles a team of New Mutants under the name Mutant X to locate and protect others of their kind, who face capture at the hands of Kane's former colleague Mason Eckhart (Tom McCamus).

Shalimar Fox (Victoria Pratt) joins Mutant X after Kane finds her in a fleabag motel, where she had been close to starvation. Fox is a Feline Feral who has a combination of human and animal DNA, giving her enhanced strength and speed, acute senses, including a spidey sense for danger, and accelerated healing. Sometimes her eyes glow in feline gold, although she never purrs. (*Meow?*) In "Where Evil Dwells" (2003), Shalimar assists her New Mutant friend, a criminal profiler, to find a serial killer, but Fox learns that evil can reside close to home in the New Mutant world.

Shalimar's colleague Emma DeLauro (Lauren Lee Smith) is a Psionic mutant with highly developed mental abilities, including telepathy, mind control, and precognition. Emma dies in an explosion at the end of season two (precognition has its limits), and is replaced by Lexa Pierce (Karen Cliche), a "Chromatic Molecular," who can make herself invisible and shoot lasers from her fingertips. (Cool!)

The women work alongside New Mutants Jesse Kilmartin (Forbes March) and Brennan Mulwray (Victor Webster) to solve mutant-related crimes, while playing cat and mouse with a shadowy organization known as The Dominion. Alas, the fate of our heroes was left unresolved in the season-ending cliffhanger "The Assault" (2004), after which the series was canceled due to the sale of production company Fireworks Entertainment.

It turned out that *Mutant X* wasn't a bad title for a series that was kind of a TV mutant, starting off with lawsuits and ending with the dissolution of a company.

## *My Living Doll* (1964–1965, 26 episodes, USA)
*Created by:* Bill Kelsay, Al Martin
*Production Co.:* Jack Chertok Television Productions, Columbia Broadcasting System
*Originally Aired:* CBS
*Main Cast:* Bob Cummings, Julie Newmar, Jack Mullaney, Doris Dowling

The "living doll" in question is one Rhoda Miller (Julie Newmar), a statuesque beauty whose smooth skin hides the inner workings of a robot. Rhoda, also known as "AF 709," is an Air Force prototype whose care is entrusted to base psychiatrist Dr. Bob McDonald (Bob Cummings). Bob sets out to teach Rhoda what it means to be a human female, but since Bob is proceeding from the mid–60s male viewpoint, he thinks Rhoda should be obedient and subservient. Needless to say, he's met the wrong robot. In "Rhoda's First Date" (1964), the android accepts a dinner date with Bob's colleague and neighbor Peter Robinson (Jack Mullaney), who promptly concludes that Rhoda is the girl for him. While trying to keep her secret from Peter, trouble-prone Rhoda forges a Picasso in "Color Me Trouble" and steals some jewelry in "The Kleptomaniac," but actually manages to help both men with some precision pool shooting in "Pool Shark" (1965).

The show displayed some SF ingenuity, as when Rhoda suffered a bad case of vertigo, and the cause turned out to be *Alice in Wonderland*, or more precisely, the meter of its verse, which frazzled her internal circuitry. Despite such originality, the series fared poorly against ratings powerhouse *Bonanza*, and Cummings left the series after 21 episodes. A quick rewrite gave care of the robot to Peter, who learns about Rhoda's true nature in "Boy Gets Robot" (1965). The premature departure of a popular star never bodes well, of course, and the series was canceled after five more episodes.

But SF/fantasy TV wasn't done with Julie Newmar, who went on to achieve cult status as a recurring guest villain, the Catwoman, on *Batman*.

## *My Mother the Car* (1965–1966, 30 episodes, USA)
*Created by:* Allan Burns, Chris Hayward
*Production Co.:* Cottage Industries, Inc., United Artists Television
*Originally Aired:* NBC
*Main Cast:* Jerry Van Dyke, Maggie Pierce, Ann Sothern, Cindy Eilbacher, Randy Whipple, Avery Schreiber

Concepts don't get any higher (or lower) than this: a man's mother is reincarnated as a CAR. The man in question, attorney David Crabtree (Jerry Van Dyke), while shopping for an affordable used car, feels drawn to a shabby 1928 Porter. Before long the Porter is talking to Dave (through the radio), and he learns that the auto is the reincarnation of his deceased mother Gladys Crabtree (voiced by Ann Sothern). Various adventures ensue, especially at the hands of mustachioed villain Captain Manzini (Avery Schreiber), a car enthusiast who will stop at nothing to add the Porter/Mother to his collection. Mother also finds plenty of trouble on her own, as in "What Makes Auntie Freeze" (1965), when a trip to a mountaintop wedding gets Gladys drunk on anti-freeze. Dave's wife, Barbara (Maggie Pierce), finally learns Mother's secret, and in the aptly named "The Blabbermouth" (1966), isn't able to keep it to herself, causing a frenzy with the press and even more covetousness on the part of Manzini.

Considered by many to be the worst show of all time (or in the case of *TV Guide* in 2002, the second worst), *My Mother the Car* has managed to secure its place among television's most memorable shows, and with a one-season run at that, although perhaps not in the way originally intended.

### *Mysterious Ways* (2000–2002, 44 episodes, Canada/USA)
*Created by:* Peter O'Fallon
*Production Co.:* Lionsgate Television, Paxson Entertainment, et al.
*Originally Aired:* PAX/NBC
*Main Cast:* Adrian Pasdar, Rae Dawn Chong, Alisen Down

Declan Dunn (Adrian Pasdar), a professor of anthropology at Northern Oregon University, has expanded his research to non-traditional realms by searching for proof of miraculous phenomena. Professor Dunn had once survived an avalanche, and has been obsessed with the idea of miracles ever since, looking for an explanation of his personal deliverance. In "Amazing Grace" (2000), Declan meets Dr. Peggy Fowler (Rae Dawn Chong), a psychiatrist at a local hospital, when an 11-year-old boy survives drowning under a frozen lake, and ghostly help is intimated. Although skeptical about miracles, especially because her prayers to save her late husband's life weren't answered, Peggy begins to work with Declan on his research. Their views come into conflict at times, as in "Crazy" (2000), when one of Peggy's patients is hearing a voice, possibly God's, and Peggy prefers medication, while Declan wants further investigation.

Professor Dunn also receives help from Miranda Feigelsteen (Alisen Down), his black-clad, introverted research assistant. Miranda is glum and quiet, but she's still game for action, as in "Pure of Heart" (2001), when she accompanies Declan and Peggy to India in search of a "Holy Man" with healing powers.

*Mysterious Ways* was an *X-Files* wannabe, with its Mulder-like believer in Declan and its Scully-esque skeptic in Peggy (and even Miranda), not to mention the paranormal overtones of the series. But it didn't come close to the longevity of *The X-Files*, never quite fathoming the mysterious ways of television.

### *Nanny and the Professor* (1970–1971, 54 episodes, USA)
*Created by:* AJ Carothers, Thomas L. Miller
*Production Co.:* 20th Century–Fox Television
*Originally Aired:* ABC
*Main Cast:* Juliet Mills, Richard Long, David Doremus, Trent Lehman, Kim Richards

Mysteries surround Phoebe Figalilly (Juliet Mills). The British beauty turns up one day at the home of Professor Harold Everett (Richard Long), and in the nick of time too, as his three precocious children and their menagerie of pets have chased off yet another nanny. Everett hasn't summoned Figalilly—she's just THERE—but, as a widower, he needs the help, and hires her on a trial basis.

Nanny, as she prefers to be called, sets about bringing order to the chaos of the household, but oldest child Hal (David Doremus) thinks Nanny's a bit strange. She seems to know when the phone is going to ring and can communicate with animals, especially the family sheepdog, Waldo. Soon, however, Hal and his younger siblings, Butch (Trent Lehman) and Prudence (Kim Richards), are entranced by their enchanting nanny, although questions about her peculiar ways and hidden past remain. In "How Many Candles" (1971), Hal puzzles over Nanny's passport, which indicates she's over 100 years old, although she appears to be in her 30s. Then there's Nanny's 1930 Model A automobile, which does have a radio, but broadcasts only programs from the 1930s in "The Great Broadcast of 1936" (1970).

Needless to say, aloof Professor Everett eventually warms up to Nanny, although hints of mutual romantic interest remain just that, in the same way that Nanny's powers are suggested but never confirmed.

Subtlety can be magic.

## *The Neighbors* (2012–2014, 44 episodes, USA)
*Created by:* Dan Fogelman
*Production Co.:* 17–28 Black, Inc., Kapital Entertainment, ABC Studios
*Originally Aired:* ABC
*Main Cast:* Jami Gertz, Lenny Venito, Simon Templeman, Toks Olagundoye, Clara Mamet, Tim Jo, Ian Patrick, Max Charles, Isabella Cramp

Observant and surprisingly touching little comedy about the clash of cultures when humans move next door to extraterrestrials. The humans in question, Debbie and Marty Weaver (Jami Gertz and Lenny Venito), purchase their dream home in a gated New Jersey community, only to learn that all their neighbors are extraterrestrials of the human-appearing variety. Debbie and Marty soon meet next-door neighbor Larry Bird (Simon Templeman), the humorless leader of the alien group, all of whose members have taken the names of famous terran athletes. Larry is married to the stunning Jackie Joyner-Kersee (Toks Olagundoye), and she is his opposite in temperament, perpetually cheery and open to trying new Earth customs as explained by Debbie and Marty. The Bird-Kersees have two sons, weird, but brilliant Dick Butkus (Ian Patrick) and sweetly romantic Reggie Jackson (Tim Jo), who falls for the Weavers' oldest daughter, Amber (Clara Mamet), seeing through her perpetual façade of surly pessimism. The Weavers guide the Bird-Kersees through the rituals of American life, including shopping at the mall, birthday parties, holidays, school dances, and sporting events, while on occasion learning something about being human themselves.

A comedic gem that was canceled too soon.

## Nelson, Victoria "Vicki" (*Blood Ties*)

Toronto P.I. with failing eyesight, assisted in her investigations by a centuries-old vampire.

See: *Blood Ties* (2007–2008, 22 episodes, Canada)

### Neri (*Ocean Girl*)
Girl from an ocean planet who is on Earth to communicate with whales and save our environment.

See: ***Ocean Girl*** **(1994-1997, 78 episodes, Australia)**

### *The New Addams Family* (1998-1999, 65 episodes, Canada/USA)
*Based on:* The TV series *The Addams Family* created by David Levy
*Production Co.:* Film Incentive B.C., Fox Family Channel, Shavick Entertainment
*Originally Aired:* Fox Family
*Main Cast:* Glenn Taranto, Ellie Harvie, Brody Smith, Nicole Fugere, Betty Phillips, Michael Roberds, John DeSantis, Steven Fox

*The New Addams Family* is much like *The Addams Family* (down to the episode count, plus one), updating the 60s comedy for a 90s audience, thereby adding some (literal) color. Glenn Taranto portrays Gomez Addams here, patriarch of a bunch of creepy, but mostly harmless oddballs who think they're just like everyone else. Ellie Harvie dons the slinky black dress of Morticia Addams, Gomez's darkly seductive wife, who loves to tend her flowers, especially the ones that bite back, like carnivorous Cleopatra. The loving couple dotes on their children, peculiar Pugsley (Brody Smith) and weird Wednesday (Nicole Fugere), and the rest of the strange brood is back too, including looming Lurch (John DeSantis), frightful Fester (Michael Roberds), and ghastly Grandmama (Betty Phillips). John Astin, TV's original Gomez, even makes some appearances as Grandpapa Addams, and several episodes from the 60s series are reanimated, including "Morticia Joins the Ladies League" (1964/1998) and "The Addams Family Goes to School" (1964/1998).

The classics endure.

### *The New Adventures of Wonder Woman*
See: ***Wonder Woman*** **(1975-1979, 59 episodes, USA)**

### *The New Avengers* (1976-1977, 26 episodes, Canada/France/UK)
*Based on:* The TV series *The Avengers* created by Sydney Newman
*Created by:* Brian Clemens, Albert Fennell
*Production Co.:* The Avengers Enterprises, IDTV Production, TF1
*Originally Aired:* CBS
*Main Cast:* Patrick Macnee, Gareth Hunt, Joanna Lumley

Patrick Macnee reprises his role as John Steed in this sequel to the 60s spy-fi series ***The Avengers***, reimagined for 70s audiences. Joining Steed in stylish espionage are Gareth Hunt as Mike Gambit and Joanna Lumley as Purdey, two younger and more athletic agents who benefit from Steed's wisdom and starch. Ballet-trained, high-kicking Purdey and crack marksman Gambit assist their mentor on standard spy stuff, although bizarre cases still present themselves, such as "Gnaws" (1976), where the assignment is a giant rat. The pesky robots from the earlier series return in "The Last of the Cybernauts?" (1976), and the trio makes a valiant effort to pretend that no one is missing Mrs. **Emma Peel**.

### Nightingale, Cassie (*Good Witch*)
Mysterious, small-town beauty with keen intuition who may or may not be a witch.
See: *Good Witch* (2015- , 19 episodes, Canada/USA)

### Nika (*TekWar*)
Platinum-blonde operative with superior hacking skills at a private security firm in 2045.
See: *TekWar* (1994-1996, 18 episodes, Canada/USA)

### *The Nine Lives of Chloe King* (2011, 10 episodes, USA)
*Based on:* The book series by Liz Braswell
*Created by:* Dan Berendsen
*Production Co.:* Don't Borrow Trouble, Alloy Entertainment, ABC Family Original Productions
*Originally Aired:* ABC Family
*Main Cast:* Skyler Samuels, Amy Pietz, Grey Damon, Grace Phipps, Benjamin Stone, Alyssa Diaz, Ki Hong Lee

On her 16th birthday, Chloe King (Skyler Samuels) learns that she is a descendent of an ancient race called the Mai, supernatural folks with cat-like abilities, including heightened senses, increased speed, and retractable claws. (*Meow!*) Chloe finds out about her heritage the hard way, when she dies from a fall after being chased by a stalker and miraculously returns to life. She learns from high school jock Alek Petrov (Benjamin Stone) and his cousin Jasmine (Alyssa Diaz), both part of San Francisco's Mai community, that she is a special Mai called the "Uniter," who, legend has it, will end the war between human assassins and the Mai. They know this because the Uniter is the only Mai with nine lives.

Typical of the teen SF/fantasy genre, the series is equal parts emotional angst and intricate mythology. On the angst side, Chloe is caught in the requisite romantic triangle, attracted to both Brian Rezza (Grey Damon), a human whose father is trying to kill Chloe and wipe out the Mai, and the aforementioned Alek, who is Chloe's Mai protector. On the mythology end, there are loads of juicy morsels, such as the fact that humans become paralyzed or even die when kissed by Mai (something else that Chloe finds out the hard way). And, of course, there must be a secret society, in this case, "The Order," a group of assassins devoted to the destruction of the Mai.

This one was canceled after 10 episodes, leaving behind a slew of dead bodies in the incongruously named finale, "Beautiful Day" (2011).

Too bad TV series don't have nine lives.

### Number Six (*Battlestar Galactica*)
Android infiltrator who seduces a scientist as the opening salvo in a war against humans.
See: *Battlestar Galactica* (2004-2009, 75 episodes, USA)

### *Ocean Girl* (1994-1997, 78 episodes, Australia)
*Created by:* Jonathan M. Shiff

*Production Co.:* Jonathan M. Shiff Productions, Network Ten, Westbridge Productions
*Originally Aired:* Disney Channel
*Main Cast:* Marzena Godecki, David Hoflin, Jeffrey Walker, Kerry Armstrong, Liz Burch, Alex Pinder, Nina Landis, Brooke Anderson, Tony Briggs, Tharini Mudaliar, Lauren Hewett, Nicholas Bell

The ocean girl of the title is Neri, but a bikini-clad Malibu Barbie she isn't. Neri (Marzena Godecki) has grown up alone on an island off of Queensland, Australia, where she dives without a breathing apparatus, swims faster than most boats, and communicates directly with whales, especially one called Charley. Clearly Neri is no ordinary 13-year-old, as the Bates family soon discovers from its base aboard ORCA (Oceanic Research Centre of Australia), an underwater station. Mom Dianne Bates (Kerry Armstrong, later Liz Burch), studies whale song, while sons Jason (David Hoflin) and Brett (Jeffrey Walker) get into trouble, as sons do. Jason is the first to encounter Neri, while Brett later receives a natural antidote for poisonous berries from her. Neri eventually learns about her extraterrestrial origins and even discovers the existence of a sister, Mera (Lauren Hewett), who had also survived the crash of their spaceship (long story). The sisters stay one step ahead of Dr. Hellegren (Nicholas Bell), a sinister scientist out to capture them and exploit their downed spacecraft, which rests underwater. As the series progresses, Neri finds out more about her matriarchal home world, The Planet of the Oceans, and its politics, which begin to spill over to Earth.

*Ocean Girl* was geared towards children, but was more complex than most kiddie fare and emphasized ecological themes. Although it aired on the Disney Channel, it is still little-known in the U.S., but can be discovered on streaming services such as Amazon Prime.

## Octavia (*Star Maidens*)

Security chief on the planet Medusa, where women rule and men are treated as second-class citizens.

See: *Star Maidens* (1976, 13 episodes, UK/West Germany)

## Once Upon a Time (2011– , 111 episodes, USA)

*Created by:* Edward Kitsis, Adam Horowitz
*Production Co.:* ABC Studios, Kitsis/Horowitz
*Originally Aired:* ABC
*Main Cast:* Ginnifer Goodwin, Jennifer Morrison, Lana Parrilla, Josh Dallas, Jared S. Gilmore, Robert Carlyle, Emilie de Ravin, Colin O'Donoghue

In 1987, Snow White, Prince Charming, and a jealous, spellcasting queen came from the fairy-tale past into the modern world via a short-lived sitcom, *The Charmings*. In 2011, Snow White, Prince Charming, and a jealous, spellcasting queen came from the fairy-tale past into the modern world, but the new series, *Once Upon a Time*, wasn't *The Charmings*—not by a longshot.

On her 28th birthday, **Emma Swan** (Jennifer Morrison), a bail bond agent, meets Henry Mills (Jared S. Gilmore), a 10-year-old boy who turns out to be the son she once gave up for adoption. Henry has quite a tale to tell of his hometown, Storybrooke, where everyone is frozen in time due to a curse placed by the Evil Queen, who happens to be Henry's adoptive mother and the mayor of Storybrooke, Regina Mills (Lana Parrilla). While these might seem to be the imaginings of a troubled child, Henry is later shown to be telling the truth, as the citizens of Storybrooke are people known to us from fairytales and literature who have forgotten their true identities. Mary Margaret Blanchard (Ginnifer Goodwin), Henry's teacher, is Snow White, while David Nolan (Josh Dallas), a comatose patient at the hospital, is Prince Charming, whose happiness with Snow back in the Enchanted Forest had evoked the Queen's wrath. Snow and Charming had a daughter, none other than Emma Swan, who will ultimately break the Queen's curse by bringing Henry back from the dead with "true love's kiss," the most potent form of magic in this sentimental, but dark universe.

That's just the tip of the iceberg for this long-running series, which finds new curses and characters at every turn, including Rumplestiltskin/Mr. Gold (Robert Carlyle), Captain Hook/Killian Jones (Colin O'Donoghue), and even Belle (Emilie de Ravin) from *Beauty and the Beast*. At its core, though, *Once Upon a Time* is about three strong women, Emma, Snow, and Regina, who deal with issues of motherhood, romance, power, conquest, and loss, while facing every challenge head-on.

Each, in her own inimitable way, is searching for a happy ending.

See also: **Swan, Emma (*Once Upon a Time*)**

## 1-800-Missing
See: ***Missing* (2003–2006, 56 episodes, Canada/USA)**

## Original Cindy (*Dark Angel*)
Bicycle messenger in post-apocalyptic Seattle and coworker of a woman with genetically enhanced abilities.

See: ***Dark Angel* (2000–2002, 43 episodes, USA)**

## Orphan Black (2013– , 40 episodes, Canada)
*Created by:* Graeme Manson, John Fawcett
*Production Co.:* Temple Street Productions
*Originally Aired:* BBC America
*Main Cast:* Tatiana Maslany, Dylan Bruce, Jordan Gavaris, Kevin Hanchard, Michael Mando, Maria Doyle Kennedy, Kristian Bruun, Skyler Wexler, Josh Vokey, Évelyne Brochu, Ari Millen

Tatiana Maslany stars as Sarah Manning ... and Alison Hendrix ... and Cosima Niehaus ... and Rachel Duncan. Is this a distaff version of *The Fugitive*? Not exactly.

*Orphan Black* begins when Sarah, a con artist, witnesses the suicide of a woman who looks just like her. What Sarah doesn't know but eventually learns is that the dead woman, Beth Childs, was her clone, and that other of her clones exist, including Alison and Cosima. Even worse, someone is trying to kill all of them, and has already succeeded once, with a clone named Katja. As vast conspiracies swirl, the killer is revealed to be Helena, yet another clone, who is a member of an extremist religious group called the Proletheans. Sarah must work to protect her daughter Kira (Skyler Wexler) from both the Proletheans and the Neolutionists, the folks behind the cloning experiments, since Kira has inherited her mother's capacity for accelerated healing.

It will come as no surprise that more clones are revealed throughout the series, including a transgender clone named Tony, giving viewers an informal education in the science of epigenetics. Portraying so many roles within the same series afforded Tatiana Maslany a unique acting opportunity, and she rose to the occasion, with indelible portraits of a drug-addicted soccer mom in Alison, a lesbian grad student in Cosima, and a cold-hearted opportunist in Rachel. Maslany won a 2016 Emmy Award for her performances as Sarah, Alison, Cosima, Helena, Rachel, and … well, you get the idea.

"Just one. I'm a few. No family, too. Who am I?"

## Oswald, Clara (*Doctor Who*)

Woman who has a peculiar relationship with time thanks to her interaction with an extraterrestrial.

See: *Doctor Who* (1963–1989, 2005– , 821 episodes, UK)

## Out of This World (1987–1991, 96 episodes, USA)

*Created by:* John Boni, Bob Booker
*Production Co.:* Bob Booker Productions, MCA Television
*Originally Aired:* In Syndication
*Main Cast:* Maureen Flannigan, Donna Pescow, Doug McClure, Joe Alaskey, Steve Burton, Christina Nigra, Buzz Belmondo, Tom Nolan, Burt Reynolds

Maureen Flannigan is Evie Garland, a California girl who learns on her 13th birthday that her father is an extraterrestrial. When Evie begins to demonstrate strange powers, such as the ability to freeze time, her mother, Donna Garland (Donna Pescow), finally reveals a BIG secret about her husband. Evie's missing dad, Troy Garland, isn't really a secret agent, but is an alien from the planet Antareus. Troy had been called back to his home planet, after marrying Donna and merging "lifeforms" with her. (No living in sin for this alien!)

After the revelation, Evie is able to communicate with Troy (voiced by an uncredited Burt Reynolds) via the "cube," an interplanetary hotline, which allows Evie to receive paternal advice and information about her nascent powers. One of those abilities is "gleeping," which allows Evie to will things into existence. That power, however, is reliably unreliable, as in "Every Beano Has His Day" (1987), when Evie gleeps her Uncle Beano (Joe Alaskey) into a dog, and the mayor's dog at that.

Evie went from 13 to 18 in this cosmically broad series, which lasted four seasons, while managing not to become a critical darling. But you gotta love a show where the main character turns herself into a boy named Stevie so that her jilted best friend can have a date for the dance. That's *Out of This World*.

## Outlander (2014– , 29 episodes, UK/USA)

*Based on:* The novels of Diana Gabaldon

*Created by:* Ronald D. Moore
*Production Co.:* Sony Pictures Television, Left Bank Pictures, Tall Ship Productions, Story Mining and Supply Company
*Originally Aired:* Starz
*Main Cast:* Caitriona Balfe, Sam Heughan, Tobias Menzies, Gary Lewis, Graham McTavish, Lotte Verbeek, Duncan Lacroix, Grant O'Rourke, Stephen Walters, Gary Lewis

Claire Randall (Caitriona Balfe) is a combat nurse during World War II, newly returned from the battlefield horrors to rekindle her relationship with husband Frank Randall (Tobias Menzies). While visiting a Stonehenge-like formation near Inverness, Scotland, Claire is mysteriously transported to 1743, where she is promptly assaulted by her husband's look-alike ancestor, Captain "Black Jack" Randall (Menzies again). A passing Scotsman from the clan MacKenzie interrupts the assault, taking Claire back to his kinsmen, where she uses her medical knowledge to treat the dislocated shoulder of Jamie Fraser (Sam Heughan). As it dawns on Claire that she's "not in Kansas anymore," she becomes embroiled in the era's revolutionary politics, while serving as healer for the clan and prisoner of its laird, Colum MacKenzie (Gary Lewis).

Claire plots to escape, but is forced to marry Jamie, so she can stay out of the clutches of evil Captain Randall, who keeps turning up like a bad penny. She is ambivalent about the marriage, but is attracted to Jamie, who is strapping and handsome, while she still yearns to return to Frank. As time passes, she is accused of witchcraft, tells Jamie her secret, moves to France, and finds her way back to the future (with complications).

*Outlander's* production is lavish, its stories are well written (if sometimes sluggish), and its lead character is a strong and multidimensional woman. The series also has lots of pretty scenery and plenty of romance, but a Hallmark production it isn't. The occasional scenes of gore, torture, and rape may place this one out of bounds for more sensitive viewers.

## *Painkiller Jane* (2007, 22 episodes, Canada/USA)

*Based on:* The comic book series by Jimmy Palmiotti, Joe Quesada
*Created by:* Gil Grant
*Production Co.:* Insight Film Studios, IDT Entertainment, Indestructible Productions, Kickstart Productions
*Originally Aired:* Syfy
*Main Cast:* Kristanna Loken, Alaina Huffman, Rob Stewart, Stephen Lobo, Noah Danby, Sean O. Roberts

Kristanna Loken is Jane Vasco, a DEA agent recruited by a top-secret government agency to hunt "neuros," neurological aberrants who have superhuman mental abilities, but have trouble distinguishing right from wrong. During the course of her investigations, Jane discovers that she has a special power of her own, the ability to heal her injuries, even mortal ones, although she still feels the pain of her wounds until the regeneration is complete. While trying to learn more about her own background and miraculous gift, Jane and the team, led by Andre McBride (Rob Stewart), look into all manner of weird and mysterious circumstances, from rapid aging to group amnesia, from time loops to mythical beasts, in search of a "neuro" connection. Jane finds that her new world is dark, violent, and full of illusion.

### Palmer, Laura (*Twin Peaks*)

Laura Palmer (Sheryl Lee) is the all–American girl—high school homecoming queen, girlfriend to handsome football captain Bobby Briggs (Dana Ashbrook), and volunteer for Meals on Wheels. Laura seems to have a bright future, but when her body is found "wrapped in plastic" on a riverbank in Twin Peaks, FBI agent Dale Cooper (Kyle MacLachlan) begins to learn that pretty veneers, both Laura's and the town's, can't always be trusted.

It turns out that busy Laura was also having an affair with brooding biker James Hurley (James Marshall), as well as sexual relationships with sadistic trucker Leo Johnson (Eric Da Re), who supplied her with cocaine, and wealthy hotel owner Benjamin Horne (Richard Beymer), who employed her as a prostitute at his casino. While Laura was troubled, the dimensions of that trouble become clear only when Cooper discovers that Laura was touched by true evil in the form of BOB, a demonic spirit. Years earlier BOB had possessed Laura's tortured father, Leland Palmer (Ray Wise), leading him to rape and ultimately murder her. All is not complete darkness, however, as Leland sees a vision of Laura in the light just before he himself dies in "Arbitrary Law" (1990).

Neither the town of Twin Peaks nor the series bearing its name were ever the same after the identity of Laura's killer was revealed. Laura, ever the center of attention, is smiling somewhere.

See also: *Twin Peaks* (1990–1991, 30 episodes, USA)

### Parker, Audrey (*Haven*)

Former FBI agent, now a detective in a picturesque town with psychic and supernatural "troubles."

See: *Haven* (2010–2015, 78 episodes, Canada/USA)

### Parker, Liz (*Roswell*)

Waitress and student saved from a lethal gunshot wound by a boy from another planet.

See: *Roswell* (1999–2002, 61 episodes, USA)

### Parker, Sloan (*Prey*)

Bio-anthropologist who discovers a new hominid species of serial killers.

See: *Prey* (1998, 13 episodes, USA)

### Parrish, Juliet (*V*)

Biologist and founder of a resistance group which battles extraterrestrial "Visitors."

See: *V* (1984–1985, 19 episodes, USA)

**Peel, Emma (*The Avengers*)**

Leather-clad Emma Peel (Diana Rigg) fences her way into the fourth season of *The Avengers* in "The Town of No Return" (1965) and leaves an indelible imprint. Brilliant, witty, stylish, and accomplished in the martial arts, Mrs. Peel joins agent John Steed (Patrick Macnee) in pursuing spy-fi villains, such as "The Cybernauts" (1965), cybernetic assassins programmed to help a madman take over the world. Mrs. Peel has it all, and when judo chops won't do, her high IQ comes to the rescue, as in "The Master Minds" (1965), when she helps Steed pass a test to infiltrate a school for intellectuals. As busy as she is with her scientific pursuits, artistic hobbies, and, of course, her secret missions with Steed, Mrs. Peel somehow finds time for shopping, wearing the latest mod looks and a stunning array of catsuits. Emma Peel leaves behind the spy life, not to mention the repartee and innuendo with Steed, in "The Forget-Me-Knot" (1968), when her husband, presumed dead, returns to the living.

Although she may ride off into the sunset with her hubby, the appeal of Emma Peel, as portrayed by Diana Rigg, endures.

See also: ***The Avengers* (1961–1969, 161 episodes, UK)**

**Pendragon, Morgana (*Merlin*)**

Illegitimate daughter of a king who learns she is a seer and turns to the dark side.

See: ***Merlin* (2008–2012, 65 episodes, UK)**

**Petrelli, Angela (*Heroes*)**

Manipulative political guru and mother who is able to see the future via her dreams.

See: ***Heroes* (2006–2010, 77 episodes, USA)**

**Pezzini, Sara (*Witchblade*)**

New York City detective with an ancient, supernatural weapon and a hidden heritage.

See: ***Witchblade* (2001–2002, 23 episodes, USA)**

**Phillips, Fiona "Fi" (*So Weird*)**

Thirteen-year-old girl who encounters paranormal occurrences wherever she goes.

See: ***So Weird* (1999–2001, 65 episodes, Canada/USA)**

**Pierce, Lexa (*Mutant X*)**

Genetically enhanced woman who can make herself invisible, assisting a team of "New Mutants."

See: ***Mutant X* (2001–2004, 66 episodes, Canada/USA)**

**Pirzad, Rachel (*Alphas*)**

Defense Department consultant who can heighten any one of her five senses to help track criminals.

See: ***Alphas* (2011–2012, 24 episodes, USA)**

### *Poltergeist: The Legacy* (1996–1999, 88 episodes, Canada/USA)
*Created by:* Richard Barton Lewis
*Production Co.:* PMP Legacy Productions, Showtime Networks, Trilogy Entertainment Group
*Originally Aired:* Showtime (1996–1998), Syfy (1999)
*Main Cast:* Derek de Lint, Helen Shaver, Martin Cummins, Robbi Chong, Alexandra Purvis

"Since the beginning of time, mankind has existed between the world of light and the world of darkness. Our secret society has been here forever, protecting others from the creatures who inhabit the shadows and the night."

This series was less like the movie franchise of the same title and more like *The X-Files*, but with demons instead of extraterrestrials. The Legacy of the subtitle is an ancient society which investigates occult happenings around the world via its various branches, including the San Francisco house, where Dr. Derek Rayne (Derek de Lint) is "The Precept." Rayne invites Dr. Rachel Corrigan (Helen Shaver), a Scully-esque skeptic trained as a psychiatrist, to join his unconventional team. Science can take Corrigan only so far, however, as in "Revelations" (1996), when she encounters witches (not the good kind) at her former boarding school, and gets some help from the ghost of a white wolf. Rachel has an eight-year-old daughter named Kat (Alexandra Purvis), who possesses nascent psychic powers and is a magnet for malevolent spirits. In "Doppelgänger" (1996), Kat adopts an "imaginary friend," who turns out to be the spirit of an Egyptian princess searching for a new "home," i.e., body.

Ghostly troubles continue to beset the team, as in "The Devil's Lighthouse" (1997), when Alexandra "Alex" Moreau (Robbi Chong), the group's psychic and researcher, confronts a haunted spirit who literally traps her in a lighthouse beacon. Moreau is descended from a Creole family in New Orleans, so naturally she knows a vampire or two, even if she doesn't know she knows them. In "Darkness Falls" (1998), Alex is bitten by her former college roommate, and is on her way to being a bona fide bloodsucker unless The Legacy can stop the process.

In the series finale, The Legacy manages to close a portal to hell and save the world from the antichrist. They did it without any help from Buffy.

That's quite a Legacy.

### Pouran, Nasreen "Naz" (*Limitless*)

FBI agent supervising a man whose mental powers have been enhanced by a dangerous drug.

See: *Limitless* (2015–2016, 22 episodes, USA)

### Powers, Diana (*RoboCop*)

Woman murdered for her brain, which now runs a supercomputer and projects her as a hologram.

See: *RoboCop* (1994, 23 episodes, Canada)

### *Prey* (1998, 13 episodes, USA)
*Created by:* William Schmidt

*Production Co.*: Edelson Productions, Lars Thorwald Inc., Warner Bros. Television
*Originally Aired*: ABC
*Main Cast*: Debra Messing, Adam Storke, Larry Drake, Frankie Faison, Vincent Ventresca, Roger Howarth, Alexandra Hedison

"Forty thousand years ago, the most advanced species on Earth was wiped out by a powerful new life form ... us. Now another new species has evolved—stronger, smarter, and dedicated to our annihilation."

Short-lived series about *Homo dominant*, a new species of, um—serial killers. Dr. Sloan Parker (Debra Messing), a bio-anthropologist, building upon the work of her mentor, who was murdered, discovers that the killer's DNA is different from human DNA. Many serial killers share these same genetic markers, and Sloan postulates that the emergence of this new highly intelligent but sociopathic species might be due to global warming. (In for a pseudoscience penny, in for a pound.) Soon Dr. Sloan encounters Tom Daniels (Adam Storke), a federal agent who is a member of the new species, but not a big fan of serial killers. In addition to working with Daniels, Sloan develops a romantic attraction to him (the *Dominants* are uncommonly handsome), but Tom has a hard time reciprocating, as he lacks softer feelings, like others of his kind.

Scheduled opposite *Friends*, NBC's sitcom powerhouse, *Prey* was easy, er, prey for the terminally adorable series. That's an ironic ending for a show about bloodthirsty competition.

### *Primeval* (2007–2011, 36 episodes, UK)
*Created by*: Adrian Hodges, Tim Haines
*Production Co.*: ITV Studios, Impossible Pictures, Treasure Entertainment, et al.
*Originally Aired*: BBC America
*Main Cast*: Douglas Henshall, Hannah Spearritt, Andrew-Lee Potts, Lucy Brown, Juliet Aubrey, Ben Miller, Ben Mansfield, James Murray

What if creatures from the past, and even the future, were able to enter the here and now via doorways called "temporal anomalies"? That's the premise of this British series which had a revolving-door cast and experienced its own temporal anomaly with a two-year break between seasons due to cancellation ambivalence.

Professor Nick Cutter (Douglas Henshall) must deal with the misplaced beasties, assembling the requisite scientific team, including Abby Maitland (Hannah Spearritt), a zookeeper who loves lizards (handy) and hates spiders (not so handy). When Cutter returned a *Coelurosauravus* (winged reptile) to its era, the Permian, but it came back to the future, Abby adopted him as a pet. Nick is also searching for his wife, Helen Cutter (Juliet Aubrey), who disappeared eight years earlier, and has a mysterious connection to the anomalies. Helen becomes a major antagonist for Nick and his team, eventually killing her husband. (ANYONE can die in this series). She is even willing to wipe out humanity in the past to end war in the future, but she is later eaten by a raptor for her trouble. (That'll teach her.)

The series was canceled after season three in 2009, but rose from the dead in 2011. The same can't be said for many of its characters, who were long gone by the time the fourth season rolled around. By then, only three of the show's original characters were still alive, including Abby, who had been trapped in the Cretaceous Period, and Connor Temple (Andrew-Lee Potts), who had been stranded with her.

*Primeval* eked out one more season and generated a short-lived spin-off, *Primeval: New World*. Alas, there was no cancellation ambivalence about *Primeval*'s poorly rated progeny.

### Prince, Diana (*Wonder Woman*)

Operative for the Inter-Agency Defense Command and alter ego of Wonder Woman.

See: ***Wonder Woman*** (1975–1979, 59 episodes, USA)

### *Proof* (2015, 10 episodes, Canada/USA)

*Created by:* Rob Bragin
*Production Co.:* TNT Original Productions, Ipso Facto Productions, The Jacobson Company
*Originally Aired:* TNT
*Main Cast:* Jennifer Beals, David Sutcliffe, Edi Gathegi, Callum Blue, Caroline Kaplan, Annie Thurman, Joe Morton, Matthew Modine

Short-lived series starring Jennifer Beals as Dr. Carolyn Tyler, a brilliant surgeon who faces several personal crises, including the death of her teenage son. "Cat" is approached by a terminally ill billionaire, Ivan Turing (Matthew Modine), to find "proof," as per the show's title, that the afterlife exists. Turing offers his $10 billion estate to the hospital where Cat works and the charity she supports, but she is initially reluctant to agree. An encounter with a young coma patient changes her mind, however, and she begins investigating cases of ghosts, reincarnation, and near-death experiences, enlisting the help of an intern at the hospital, Dr. Zed Badawi (Edi Gathegi).

Although Cat's time as a psychic investigator was brief, her 10 cases live on in that weird afterlife we now call the online streaming service.

### Pryce-Jones, Adrian (*Space Academy*)

Pretty teen who studies human-simian communication at a school on a man-made planetoid in outer space.

See: ***Space Academy*** (1977, 15 episodes, USA)

### *Psi Factor: Chronicles of the Paranormal* (1996–2000, 88 episodes, Canada)

*Created by:* Peter Aykroyd, Christopher Chacon
*Production Co.:* Alliance Atlantis Communications, First Television, Paranormal Productions, Atlantis Films
*Originally Aired:* In Syndication
*Main Cast:* Paul Miller, Nancy Anne Sakovich, Barclay Hope, Colin Fox, Maurice Dean Wint, Matt Frewer, Nigel Bennett, Dan Aykroyd

Science fiction series documenting the cases of The Office of Scientific Investigation and Research, a covert organization which examines reports of paranormal activity. Dan Aykroyd introduces the episodes, explaining that they are based on "actual cases" of the OSIR, blurring the line between fact and fiction on this scripted show. Format changes and shifting plotlines pushed a lot of actors/characters in and out of this series (and back in again), but one mainstay was Nancy Anne Sakovich as data analyst Lindsay Donner. Lindsay and team members, like physicist Peter Axon (Barclay Hope), investigate mysterious phenomena, such as poltergeists, extraterrestrial encounters, psychic abilities, and demonic possessions, determining whether the weird occurrences have esoteric, but ultimately mundane explanations or are truly paranormal events. Hidden agendas and betrayals within OSIR complicate matters, as the group enters the realm of genetic engineering, alien DNA, and secret experiments.

**Purdey (*The New Avengers*)**

Ballet-trained secret agent who high-kicks her way through adventures with two male partners.

See: *The New Avengers* (1976–1977, 26 episodes, Canada/France/UK)

**Pushing Daisies (2007–2009, 22 episodes, USA)**

*Created by:* Bryan Fuller
*Production Co.:* The Jinks/Cohen Company, Living Dead Guy Productions, Warner Bros. Television
*Originally Aired:* ABC
*Main Cast:* Lee Pace, Anna Friel, Chi McBride, Field Cate, Ellen Greene, Swoosie Kurtz, Kristin Chenoweth

Inventive cross-genre series about a man who is able to bring the dead back to life, but finds there are a couple of CATCHES to his gift. Ned (Lee Pace) is a piemaker who learned as a child that his touch could resurrect the dead. Now an adult, Ned works with local private investigator Emerson Cod (Chi McBride) to solve murders with a unique investigative technique—Ned raises the dead, so Emerson can ask who killed them, then touches the victim a second time, laying them to rest forever. Things get complicated, however, when Ned's childhood sweetheart, Charlotte "Chuck" Charles (Anna Friel), is murdered on a cruise ship. Ned revives her at the local funeral home, but can't bring himself to let her go permanently. Chuck (or "Dead Girl," as the grumpy Cod likes to call her) joins the detective team, making the interrogations even more challenging, since they have only one minute to question the murder victims or someone in the vicinity will die (another rule of Ned's gift). In the meantime, Chuck begins a romance with glum Ned, no easy task, since they can't touch lest Chuck be returned to the dead permanently. Throw in a perky waitress who is lovesick for Ned (Kristin Chenoweth), a couple of eccentric, synchronized-swimming aunts (Ellen Greene, Swoosie Kurtz) who mourn Chuck's loss, stunning visuals, including a kitschy-noir restaurant called The Pie Hole, and you have the flaky goodness known as *Pushing Daisies*.

**Quark (1977–1978, 8 episodes, USA)**

*Created by:* Buck Henry

*Production Co.:* David Gerber Productions, Columbia Pictures Television
*Originally Aired:* NBC
*Main Cast:* Richard Benjamin, Tim Thomerson, Patricia Barnstable, Cyb Barnstable, Conrad Janis, Alan Caillou, Bobby Porter, Richard Kelton

A spicy spoof of space operas, such as *Star Wars* and especially *Star Trek*, *Quark* stars Richard Benjamin as Adam Quark, commander of an interstellar garbage scow, who yearns for more adventurous assignments à la Captain Kirk. If you're going to have a futuristic waste management crew, it might as well be a motley one, and Quark's fills the bill: Gene/Jean (Tim Thomerson), a "transmute" with both male and female chromosomes, who alternates between masculine and feminine personalities; the aptly named Ficus (Richard Kelton), a plant-man, who has the Spock/science officer gig; and Andy (Bobby Porter), a cowardly robot. On the distaff side (not including "Jean"), Quark's refuse patrol features Betty I and Betty II (Patricia and Cyb Barnstable, former "Doublemint" twins), the ship's identical pilots, who argue over which is the original and which is the clone. The scantily clad Bettys usually speak in eerie unison, and are equally passionate about Commander Quark, who loves one of them, but isn't sure which.

Space-faring adventures ensue, but not many, as *Quark* never struck ratings gold the way Buck Henry's prior spoofy creation, *Get Smart*, did. If only *Quark* had been allowed to "live long and prosper…."

## Queen Lillian (*The Charmings*)

Jealous ruler whose curse goes awry, transporting her to modern Los Angeles with her hated relatives.

See: *The Charmings* (1987–1988, 21 episodes, USA)

## Quinn, Alice (*The Magicians*)

Brilliant, but awkward and intense student at a grad school for magic.

See: *The Magicians* (2015– , 13 episodes, USA)

## Rachel (*The Starlost*)

Part of a love triangle searching for a way to save a generation ship from crashing.

See: *The Starlost* (1973–1974, 16 episodes, Canada)

## Randall, Claire (*Outlander*)

World War II combat nurse and wife mysteriously transported to 1743 where she must marry another man.

See: *Outlander* (2014– , 29 episodes, UK/USA)

## Ray, Vena (*Rocky Jones, Space Ranger*)

Navigator and translator on the Orbit Jet, helping to protect our solar system from evil interlopers.

See: *Rocky Jones, Space Ranger* (1954, 39 episodes, USA)

**Reed, Shannon** (*Mission: Impossible*)
: Former Secret Service agent, now a member of the Impossible Missions Force.
See: *Mission: Impossible* (1988–1990, 35 episodes, USA)

## *Relic Hunter* (1999–2002, 66 episodes, Canada/France)
*Created by:* Gil Grant
*Production Co.:* Fireworks Entertainment, Gaumont Télévision, et al.
*Originally Aired:* In Syndication
*Main Cast:* Tia Carrere, Christien Anholt, Lindy Booth, Tanja Reichert

"Welcome to ancient studies. I'm not a stickler for attendance. Sometimes I'm called away from the office myself."

Tia Carrere stars as Sydney Fox, professor and archaeologist, who drops her teaching responsibilities like a hot potato whenever evidence of a long-missing relic appears. Whether it's Elvis Presley's lost guitar or Buddha's alms bowl, Pandora's Box or even an extraterrestrial artifact, Sydney takes off in a flash to find the lost treasure. Nigel Bailey (Christien Anholt), Sydney's handsome, but awkward, teaching assistant, always accompanies his gorgeous boss on her adventures, but relies upon HER martial arts skills when confronted by their evil competitors. Claudia (Lindy Booth) minds the office back at Trinity College, when she's not doing her nails or buying clothes.

*Relic Hunter* was on trend for the 90s, with its female action hero who wasn't afraid to get (glamorously) dirty, and it even broke some new ground with an Asian-American female lead. The series is fun in small doses, with its distaff Indiana Jones and male "damsel in distress," but the episodes are otherwise so formula-bound that they quickly become interchangeable. One episode may be a kitschy treasure—the rest are just knockoffs.

**Reyes, Monica** (*The X-Files*)
: FBI agent assigned to investigate weird cases with paranormal overtones.
See: *The X-Files* (1993–2002, 2016– , 208 episodes, USA)

## *Roar* (1997, 13 episodes, Australia/USA)
*Created by:* Shaun Cassidy, Ron Koslow
*Production Co.:* Sea Change Productions, Universal Television
*Originally Aired:* Fox
*Main Cast:* Heath Ledger, Lisa Zane, Sebastian Roché, Vera Farmiga, John Saint Ryan, Alonzo Greer

Short-lived, but intriguing fantasy/adventure series set during the Roman conquest of ancient Ireland in AD 400. Heath Ledger stars as Conor, a young prince called to unite the Celtic tribes and expel the Roman invaders after his family is massacred. A ragtag band (is there any other kind?) coalesces around Conor, including Catlyn (Vera Farmiga), a former Roman slave turned bow-toting warrior, and Tully (Alonzo Greer), an apprentice magician. Conspiring on the Roman side are evil wizard Longinus (Sebastian Roché), a former Centurion cursed to walk the Earth forever because of his actions during Christ's crucifixion, and beautiful Diana (Lisa Zane), a Roman queen, who relishes conquest whether on the battlefield or in the boudoir. *Roar*, although sumptuously filmed and well-plotted, failed to capitalize on the popularity of contemporary sword and sorcery series such as *Xena: Warrior Princess* and *Hercules: The Legendary Journeys*, perhaps because its tone was more serious or maybe it was that ill-chosen title.

### Roberts, Vicky (*The Event*)

Former CIA operative turned private security contractor involved in a conspiracy regarding extraterrestrials.

See: *The Event* (2010–2011, 22 episodes, USA)

### Robinson, Maureen, Judy, and Penny (*Lost in Space*)

Mother and two daughters stranded with their family on an unknown planet.

See: *Lost in Space* (1965–1968, 83 episodes, USA)

### *RoboCop* (1994, 23 episodes, Canada)

*Based on:* The film directed by Paul Verhoeven
*Created by:* Michael Miner, Edward Neumeier
*Production Co.:* Rysher Entertainment, Skyvision Entertainment, Robocop Productions Ltd.
*Originally Aired:* In Syndication
*Main Cast:* Richard Eden, Yvette Nipar, Blu Mankuma, Andrea Roth, David Gardner, Sarah Campbell, Ed Sahely, Dan Duran, Erica Ehm

After the *RoboCop* franchise brought mayhem to the big screen in several movies, it set its sights on television with a family-friendlier version. Richard Eden is Alex Murphy, a police officer shot and resurrected as RoboCop, a cyborg with Murphy's brain and an indestructible body. RoboCop keeps the peace both in shiny Delta City and in grimy, crime-ridden Old Detroit. Robo/Murphy is re-partnered with Lisa Madigan (Yvette Nipar), and she deduces the secret hidden under his steely visor: "Murphy, it IS you." Madigan does most of the brain work for the duo, which makes sense, since brawn is what the cyber-cop is all about.

It's hard for RoboCop to find love for obvious reasons, but he has a kindred—er, spirit in Diana Powers (Andrea Roth), whose mind becomes NeuroBrain, the supercomputer which runs Delta City. Diana had been murdered by bad guys at OCP (Omni Consumer Products) so they could use her brain to power their new system, but her personality persisted, and she can now project herself as a hologram. (Don't try this at home.)

Despite its lighter tone and the addition of child characters, including Gadget (Sarah Campbell), *RoboCop* lasted just one season. But it's hard to kill a cyber-cop, and *RoboCop* was re-resurrected for a miniseries in 2001 and a film remake in 2014.

Everything old is new again. And again. And again. And again.

### *Rocky Jones, Space Ranger* (1954, 39 episodes, USA)

*Created by:* Roland D. Reed
*Production Co.:* Roland Reed Productions, Space Ranger Enterprises

*Originally Aired:* In Syndication
*Main Cast:* Richard Crane, Sally Mansfield, Scotty Beckett, Robert Lyden, Patsy Parsons

Rocky Jones (Richard Crane) is a Space Ranger, a defender of our solar system against evil, extraterrestrial interlopers, who somehow look just like us. Handsome, heroic Rocky rides into space in his rocket, the Orbit Jet, accompanied by the requisite motley crew, including his co-pilot Winky (Scotty Beckett), 10-year-old Bobby (Robert Lyden), and Vena Ray (Sally Mansfield), who serves as the ship's navigator and translator. Pretty Vena brings the short skirt to space opera well ahead of Lt. Uhura of *Star Trek*, but is more involved in the action. Crashing the gate at the Office of Space Affairs to deliver vital information in "Beyond the Curtain of Space" (1954), Vena pushes her way into the mission, whether Rocky wants her there or not. As it turns out, she's just in time to meet another spacefaring female, arch villainess Cleolanthe (Patsy Parsons), Suzerain of the planet Ophiuchus. Cleo looks like a beautiful, bejeweled movie star—she is the queen of a planet after all. Further exciting exploits ensue, all of which were captured on film rather than broadcast live, allowing modern audiences to cheer with or laugh at the wholesome adventures, now preserved on DVD.

## Roget, Jacqueline (*Young Blades*)

17th century French woman who masquerades as a male musketeer to hide from an evil Cardinal.

See: *Young Blades* (2005, 13 episodes, Canada/USA)

## Rommie (*Andromeda*)

Beautiful android who is the avatar for the artificial intelligence system of a starship.

See: *Andromeda* (2000–2005, 110 episodes, Canada/USA)

## Rosenberg, Willow (*Buffy the Vampire Slayer*)

Alyson Hannigan stars as Willow Rosenberg, a shy sophomore at Sunnydale High School, whose life changes forever when she meets transfer student Buffy Summers (Sarah Michelle Gellar). Buffy is the Slayer, a girl chosen by fate to protect humans against vampires and other forces of darkness. Willow soon becomes Buffy's BFF as well as a prominent member of the Slayer's informal army known as the Scooby Gang. Willow is highly intelligent, and at first uses her computer and hacking skills to research the occult. Later she becomes a supernatural being in her own right, a witch with extensive magical powers.

Willow's empowerment, both as a woman and as a witch, is mirrored in her romantic relationships. At first, she is mostly a bystander, performing her library research and giving emotional support to Buffy, while pining for Xander Harris (Nicholas Brendon), who has eyes only for Buffy. As Willow develops a romantic relationship with Oz (Seth Green), a rock musician and werewolf, she becomes more confident and begins to study magic. After a setback when Oz leaves her, Willow meets fellow witch Tara Maclay (Amber Benson), and what begins as a relationship of friendship and magic blossoms into love, as their spells together become more and more powerful. In "The Body" (2001), the two share a watershed on-screen kiss, when Willow is inconsolable at the death of Buffy's mother. Their relationship progresses into true and tender affection, but ends in tragedy, when Tara is fatally shot in "Seeing Red" (2002).

Willow Rosenberg became a role model for teens and adults who were searching for realistic depictions of lesbians on television. It is both ironic and rich that this authenticity occurred not in mainstream drama, but in teen horror, a genre normally considered banal and inferior.

Willow Rosenberg, slaying preconceived notions since 1997.

See also: ***Buffy the Vampire Slayer*** (1997–2003, 144 episodes, USA)

## Roslin, Laura (*Battlestar Galactica*)

Secretary of Education promoted to President after war wipes out a federation of planets.

See: ***Battlestar Galactica*** (2004–2009, 75 episodes, USA)

## *Roswell* (1999–2002, 61 episodes, USA)

*Based on:* The book series *Roswell High* by Melinda Metz
*Created by:* Jason Katims
*Production Co.:* Jason Katims Productions, Regency Television, 20th Century–Fox Television
*Originally Aired:* WB (1999–2001), UPN (2001–2002)
*Main Cast:* Shiri Appleby, Jason Behr, Katherine Heigl, Brendan Fehr, Majandra Delfino, Nick Wechsler, Colin Hanks, William Sadler, Emilie de Ravin

Teen angst meets alien mythology in this series which proposes that the alleged Roswell UFO incident deposited three extraterrestrial kids on Earth who were later adopted by local families. When high school student Liz Parker (Shiri Appleby) is accidentally shot while working at the Crashdown Café, fellow student Max Evans (Jason Behr) heals her gunshot wound, saving her life, but leaving a glowing hand print on her abdomen. Curious and grateful Liz pursues this medical mystery and soon gets Max to admit that he isn't from these parts or this world, for that matter. Even more surprising, Max isn't the only alien teen in Roswell. His sister Isabel Evans (Katherine Heigl) and best friend Michael Guerin (Brendan Fehr) are also from up above, and all three are searching for their origins, while trying to figure out their purpose in our world.

Girl-next-door Liz and boy-from-space Max are drawn to each other, and a forbidden romance ensues. Michael has a love/hate relationship with Liz's best friend and fellow waitress Maria DeLuca (Majandra Delfino), and the two are more physical and less moony than the Liz/Max pairing. Liz's buddy Alex Whitman (Colin Hanks) is obsessed with aloof Isabel, and tries to date her at every turn, with short-lived success. These nascent human/alien romances and a few love triangles play themselves out, while the town's relentless sheriff, Jim Valenti (William Sadler), tries to prove that Max and company are really ETs.

The second season saw less emphasis on smooching and more on science fiction in an attempt to improve the show's ratings, but the WB canceled the series when the change didn't help, and UPN picked it up for a final season. Finding the right balance between teen soap and SF thriller was always a cosmic challenge for *Roswell*.

## Rothschild, Emilia (*Jack of All Trades*)

British spy and inventor working with a cheeky American on a South Pacific island in the early 1800s.

See: *Jack of All Trades* (2000, 22 episodes, USA/New Zealand)

## Russell, Grace (*Good Witch*)

Small-town teen with intuitive gifts who may be the daughter of a witch.

See: *Good Witch* (2015– , 19 episodes, Canada/USA)

## Russell, Helena (*Space: 1999*)

Chief medical officer for a moon base propelled into deep space after a nuclear blast.

See: *Space: 1999* (1975–1977, 48 episodes, Italy/UK)

## Russo, Alex (*Wizards of Waverly Place*)

Greenwich Village teen competing with her brothers to see who will become the Family Wizard.

See: *Wizards of Waverly Place* (2007–2012, 106 episodes, USA)

## Ruth (*Ark II*)

Well-coiffed medic and scientist, part of a team bringing new civilization to the world after an environmental apocalypse.

See: *Ark II* (1976, 15 episodes, USA)

## Rutledge, Maia (*The 4400*)

Once missing child who returns with the ability to predict the future.

See: *The 4400* (2004–2007, 44 episodes, USA)

## *Sabrina the Teenage Witch* (1996–2003, 163 episodes, USA)

*Based on:* The comic book series by Dan DeCarlo, George Gladir
*Created by:* Jonathan Schmok, Nell Scovell
*Production Co.:* Hartbreak Films, Viacom Productions
*Originally Aired:* ABC (1996–2000), WB (2000–2003)
*Main Cast:* Melissa Joan Hart, Caroline Rhea, Beth Broderick, Nate Richert, Nick Bakay, Jenna Leigh Green, Martin Mull, Soleil Moon Frye

**Sabrina Spellman's** 16th birthday is more shocking than sweet when she learns that she's a witch. Starting at a new high school is challenging enough for most teens, but Sabrina (Melissa Joan Hart) must also learn how to control her nascent powers lest she accidentally turn someone into a pineapple. Luckily she has help in the form of her aunts and guardians, Zelda Spellman (Beth Broderick), a witch who specializes in quantum physics, and Hilda Spellman (Caroline Rhea), whose forte is ditzy, witchy fun. Also offering advice (most of it bad) and rounding out the Spellman household is Salem Saberhagen (voiced by Nick Bakay), a witch sentenced to spend 100 years as a talking cat for trying to take over the world (as often happens).

Many trials ensue for Sabrina in both the mortal and magical realms. In our world, Sabrina has the usual teenage problems: boys, especially high school hunk Harvey Kinkle (Nate Richert), jealous rivals, like mean-girl cheerleader Libby Chessler (Jenna Leigh Green), and school administrators, such as ever watchful and suspicious Willard Kraft (Martin Mull). Those issues pale, however, in comparison to what Sabrina must face in the magical or "Other Realm," where she must obtain her witch's license or lose her magic, solve her family's secret, which involves an evil twin (don't they all), and put Aunt Hilda back together again when she literally falls to pieces. And let's not forget those obstreperous pirates!

Suddenly the SATs don't seem so daunting.

See also: **Spellman, Sabrina (*Sabrina the Teenage Witch*)**

## *Salem* (2014– , 26 episodes, USA)

*Created by:* Brannon Braga, Adam Simon
*Production Co.:* Beetlecod Productions, Prospect Park, Fox 21
*Originally Aired:* WGN America
*Main Cast:* Janet Montgomery, Shane West, Seth Gabel, Tamzin Merchant, Ashley Madekwe, Elise Eberle, Iddo Goldberg, Xander Berkeley, Oliver Bell, Michael Mulheren

What if real witches existed in 17th century Salem during the time of the infamous trials? *Salem* poses this question, but it's a far cry from the perky, earlier interpretations of *Bewitched*.

In this dark, sex-obsessed telling, the trouble all started when Mary Walcott (Janet Montgomery) became pregnant by her lover John Alden (Shane West). The lovers weren't married—a definite Puritan no-no—and John was soon sent to the Indian wars, where he perished, or so everyone thought. Mary faced some nasty punishments if she revealed her out-of-wedlock pregnancy, so her slave, Tituba (Ashley Madekwe), a bona fide witch, suggested that a deal with the devil might be a better, er—deal. Mary gave up her unborn child (via an abortion/sacrifice) in exchange for great powers, and Tituba convinced her to begin preparations for the complicated Grand Rite, which would pave the way for the devil's return to Earth.

So far, so good (or bad, depending on your viewpoint), but complications ensue when Alden, alive and surprisingly strapping, returns to Salem seven years later. Mary, now married to George Sibley (Michael Mulheren), is working with Tituba to turn the Puritans against each other by means of the witch trials. If all goes according to plan, the Puritans will execute 13 innocent souls, the exact number needed for the Grand Rite. Mary begins to lose her resolve, however, when her love for John is rekindled, placing her at odds with Tituba and members of their "hive."

It will come as no surprise to anyone that LOTS more complicated mythology is revealed (including a surprise about Mary's sacrificed offspring), as lots of complicated mythology is de rigueur for modern speculative shows. From Mary's viewpoint, though, that's business as usual: "This is Salem. I think that there are no limits to what is possible."

### *Sanctuary* (2008–2011, 59 episodes, Canada)
*Created by:* Damian Kindler
*Production Co.:* Sanctuary 1 Productions, Stage 3 Media
*Originally Aired:* Syfy
*Main Cast:* Amanda Tapping, Robin Dunne, Emilie Ullerup, Christopher Heyerdahl, Ryan Robbins, Agam Darshi

Dr. Helen Magnus (Amanda Tapping) heads the Sanctuary Network, a group of laboratories/residences which provide safe haven for intelligent non-humans. Some of the "Abnormals," as they are called, are creatures of our myths (or so we thought), such as mermaids or werewolves, but others have never been cataloged by our legends, such as Nubbins (Tribble-like furballs with the power of invisibility), Folding Men (self-explanatory), and Peridax (koala-like beings who release a toxic gas).

Dr. Magnus herself is an Abnormal. Born in 1850s Victorian England, Magnus ages slowly due to a serum she developed from vampire blood. In addition to studying and housing Abnormals, Dr. Magnus fights against the aptly named Cabal, a secret (of course) society which wants to wipe out Abnormals, but uses them for their own ends when convenient. Helen is assisted by her daughter, Ashley Magnus (Emilie Ullerup), also an Abnormal, who has the ability to teleport around the world, which she inherited from her father, Jack the Ripper (long story). Eventually Ashley is captured by the Cabal, brainwashed, and turned into a vampire, but she ultimately sacrifices herself to save her mother. Her replacement is Kate Freelander (Agam Darshi), a human (yay!) con artist who switches sides to team Sanctuary after the Cabal tries to terminate her employment by using something a little stronger than a pink slip.

As with most modern SF/fantasy shows, there's lots of complicated mythology here, including a vampire Nikola Tesla, a pandemic supervirus, and that when-all-else-fails SF trope, the alternate timeline. The hearty stuck it out for four seasons and 59 episodes, but viewership began to decline, especially late in the third season. Still, that's an impressive tenure for a series which started out on the web with eight low-budget episodes.

### Sanders, Niki (*Heroes*)
Woman with superhuman strength exhibited through a violent alter ego named Jessica.
See: ***Heroes*** (2006–2010, 77 episodes, USA)

### Sarge (*Cleopatra 2525*)
One of a team of scantily clad warriors who battle flying robots in the year 2525.
See: ***Cleopatra 2525*** (2000–2001, 28 episodes, USA)

### Sato, Hoshi (*Star Trek: Enterprise*)
Communications Officer and brilliant linguist aboard a prototype starship.
See: ***Star Trek: Enterprise*** (2001–2005, 98 episodes, USA)

### Saving Grace (2007–2010, 46 episodes, USA)
*Created by:* Nancy Miller
*Production Co.:* Fox Television Studios, Grand Productions, Paid My Dues Productions
*Originally Aired:* TNT
*Main Cast:* Holly Hunter, Leon Rippy, Kenny Johnson, Laura San Giacomo, Bailey Chase, Gregory Norman Cruz, Lorraine Toussaint, Dylan Minnette

Grace Hanadarko (Holly Hunter) is a police detective in Oklahoma City's Major Crimes division. Grace isn't exactly a paragon of virtue—she drinks too much, sleeps around, tells lots of lies, and her language would make a sailor blush. One night while intoxicated, Grace runs down and kills a pedestrian, and an angel appears in answer to her plea for God's help. The angel, a tobacco-chewing charmer named Earl (Leon Rippy), is a "last chance angel," who tells Grace it's time she found the Lord and that "God is using you for great things." Angel Earl cleans up (almost) all signs of the accident, but that doesn't mean Grace cleans up her act. She continues her wanton ways, including an affair with her married partner on the squad, Hamilton "Ham" Dewey (Kenny Johnson). In between bouts of bad behavior, Grace does get some police work done, but darkness always surrounds her, as in "Have a Seat, Earl" (2008), when she kidnaps the priest who molested her in her youth. She endures more trials, including accidentally killing a child, and in series finale, "I'm Gonna Need a Big Night Light" (2010), she finally accepts God, but whether she finds redemption in battling an evil entity is open to interpretation.

### Schade, Adalind (*Grimm*)
Young lawyer who can turn into a witchlike creature resembling a decaying corpse.
See: *Grimm* (2011– , 110 episodes, USA)

### Scott, Nicole (*Missing*)
Sassy FBI agent whose partner has psychic visions that lead them to missing people.
See: *Missing* (2003–2006, 56 episodes, Canada/USA)

### Scott, Valerie (*Land of the Giants*)
Glamorous jet-setter on a doomed flight which crash-lands on a planet full of giants.
See: *Land of the Giants* (1968–1970, 51 episodes, USA)

### Scully, Dana (*The X-Files*)
Dana Scully (Gillian Anderson) is an FBI agent assigned to investigate weird, unsolved cases from the bureau's "X-Files," while keeping an eye on her partner, Fox "Spooky" Mulder (David Duchovny), who is obsessed with the paranormal. A medical doctor, Scully looks to science and rationality for explanations to strange phenomena, but is forced to become a believer, like Mulder, when she finds direct evidence of UFOs, alien abductions, and a global conspiracy. Although a skeptic when it comes to her otherworldly cases, Scully draws comfort from her Catholic

faith and wears an iconic crucifix around her neck. Scully's involvement with the X-Files leads to major personal ramifications, including terminal cancer when an implanted microchip is removed from her neck, and a return to full health when a new chip is inserted. After a later diagnosis of infertility, Scully becomes pregnant under mysterious circumstances, giving birth to a son in "Existence" (2001). She later puts the boy up for adoption in "William" (2002), when it becomes clear that his life is in danger due to the alien conspiracy.

Dana Scully's intelligence, resilience, and sex appeal (in a business suit no less) made her an iconic character in science fiction. She inspired young women to seek careers in science and law enforcement, a phenomenon known as "The Scully Effect."

Gillian Anderson received multiple awards, including an Emmy, a Golden Globe, and a Saturn Award, for her nuanced portrayal of this complex character. She reprises her role in Fox's revival of the series, which began in 2016.

See also: *The X-Files* (1993–2002, 2016– , 208 episodes, USA)

## *seaQuest DSV* (1993–1996, 57 episodes, USA)

*Created by:* Rockne S. O'Bannon
*Production Co.:* Amblin Television, Universal Television
*Originally Aired:* NBC
*Main Cast:* Roy Scheider, Jonathan Brandis, Stephanie Beacham, Stacy Haiduk, Don Franklin, Ted Raimi, Marco Sanchez, Kathy Evison, Michael Ironside

"The twenty-first century—mankind has colonized the last unexplored region on earth, the ocean. As captain of the SeaQuest and its crew, we are its guardians, for beneath the surface lies the future."

As TV fans, we like to think that there's "one big happy family" behind our favorite show, but then a trouble-filled series comes along to tell a different story. *seaQuest DSV* is one such show, where the disputes between network executives, producers, and actors ultimately crippled a promising series.

Captain Nathan Bridger (Roy Scheider) is designer and commander of *seaQuest DSV 4600*, a "Deep Submergence Vehicle" which conducts both military and scientific missions for the United Earth Oceans Organization. Bridger works closely with chief medical officer Dr. Kristin Westphalen (Stephanie Beacham), a pacifist and environmentalist sometimes at odds with the submarine's naval personnel. Westphalen also serves as a mother figure for Lucas Wolenczak (Jonathan Brandis), a teen techo-genius who is the Wesley Crusher to her Beverly Crusher for this *Star Trek* under the sea.

The original *seaQuest* vessel blew up at the end of season one (a metaphor for the entire series), allowing the producers to retool the show for season two, which included relocation of the production from Los Angeles to Orlando. Beacham did not return for the second season due to the move as well as the contentious nature of work on the series. Scheider subsequently became unhappy with the new, juvenile (in his opinion) direction of the series, and departed after season two. At that juncture the series was fast-forwarded 10 years to become *seaQuest 2032*, after aliens had abducted the vessel and its crew. Adding aliens and Michael Ironside as the replacement captain didn't help with the ratings, however, and the network finally placed seaQuest in dry dock after 13 episodes had been completed.

Some vehicles just can't be repaired.

### The Secret Adventures of Jules Verne (2000, 22 episodes, Canada/UK)
Created by: Gavin Scott
Production Co.: Filmline International, Talisman Crest
Originally Aired: Syfy
Main Cast: Michael Praed, Francesca Hunt, Michel Courtemanche, Chris Demetral

Steampunk adventure based on the premise that the novels of SF pioneer Jules Verne were taken from actual incidents in the author's life and not his imagination. Jules (Chris Demetral) sketches strange, futuristic contraptions while he should be paying attention to his law professor, but the evil League of Darkness wants to capture him and pick his brain (almost literally) for ideas that they might make a reality. Rebecca Fogg (Francesca Hunt) works as an undercover operative for the British Secret Service, a beautiful, intelligent young woman with well-honed fighting skills, a Victorian Emma Peel who sometimes plays the demure country lady to keep up appearances. Rebecca's second cousin Phileas Fogg (Michael Praed), who has resigned from the Secret Service, wins the dirigible airship Aurora in a poker game rigged by Queen Victoria and her ministers. The paths of these three exceptional individuals cross, leading them on a wild ride to do battle with extraordinary menaces, from rocket-propelled vampires to animated relics of the saints. Assisting them is Passepartout (Michel Courtemanche), also "won" by Phileas in the card game, but much more than a manservant, an accomplished inventor and navigator. The empire is in good hands.

### The Secret Circle (2011–2012, 22 episodes, Canada/USA)
Based on: The book series by L.J. Smith
Created by: Andrew Miller
Production Co.: Outerbanks Entertainment, Alloy Entertainment, CBS Television Studios, Warner Bros. Television
Originally Aired: The CW
Main Cast: Britt Robertson, Thomas Dekker, Gale Harold, Phoebe Tonkin, Shelley Hennig, Jessica Parker Kennedy, Ashley Crow, Natasha Henstridge, Chris Zylka, Joe Lando

After the death of her mother, Cassie Blake (Britt Robertson) moves to Chance Harbor, Washington to live with her maternal grandmother Jane (Ashley Crow). Cassie soon learns she is descended from a long line of witches (where have we heard that before?) and is the final member of a teenage coven. It turns out that the leader of the six-member circle, Diana Meade (Shelley Hennig), is Cassie's half-sister by John Blackwell (Joe Lando), a witch with dark magic and even darker intentions. Diana's boyfriend, Adam Conant (Thomas Dekker), is immediately attracted to Cassie, helping her to unlock both hidden powers and the requisite love triangle.

As we have learned from the Halliwell sisters in Charmed and other practitioners of fictional magic, the unlocking of magical powers tends to attract DARK forces, which are a definite buzzkill in the leading-a-normal-life department. In "Prom"

(2012), the sentimental high-school tradition turns into a life-and-death struggle for the circle, when a powerful magical crystal ends up in the hands of a witch hunter.

The CW canceled the series after one season due to low ratings and high costs. *The Secret Circle*'s small, but loyal following launched several letter-writing campaigns to save or revive the series, but to no avail.

If only they'd had one of those magic crystals.

### *The Secret World of Alex Mack* (1994–1998, 78 episodes, USA)
*Created by:* Thomas W. Lynch, Ken Lipman
*Production Co.:* Lynch Entertainment, RHI Entertainment, Hallmark Entertainment, Nickelodeon Productions
*Originally Aired:* Nickelodeon
*Main Cast:* Larisa Oleynik, Darris Love, Meredith Bishop, Michael Blakley, Dorian Lopinto

"I was just another average kid until my first day of junior high. One minute I'm walking home, the next there's a crash and I'm drenched in some weird chemical. And since then ... nothing's been the same."

"Girl power" was a prevalent theme in the 90s, taken literally on SF/fantasy shows like *Buffy the Vampire Slayer* and *The Secret World of Alex Mack*. Alexandra "Alex" Mack (Larisa Oleynik) suddenly acquires strange powers after she's accidentally doused with a top-secret chemical by an out-of-control truck. Alex soon discovers that she can levitate objects, shoot electricity from her fingertips, and, most peculiarly, morph into a silver puddle of goo. Controlling those powers is another matter, especially when she finds that extreme emotions make her GLOW. In addition to coping with her new gifts and attending junior high, Alex must stay one step ahead of Danielle Atron (Louan Gideon), owner of the Paradise Valley Chemical Plant, who has secrets she doesn't want revealed, including the existence of the chemical known as GC-161. Since Alex's father, George Mack (Michael Blakley), works for villainous Atron as a chemist, Alex decides to hide her abilities from her parents.

Alex confides in two people about her transformation, best friend Ray Alvarado (Darris Love) and older sister Annie (Meredith Bishop). Annie isn't the kindest big sister, but she uses her prodigious brain to conduct tests on Alex, ensuring that her little sister remains healthy.

*The Secret World of Alex Mack* ran in primetime on Saturday nights as part of Nickelodeon's SNICK lineup geared towards preteens and teens. The show generated a tie-in book series of over 30 titles, demonstrating the popularity of the glowing girl with the HUGE collection of hats.

### *The Secrets of Isis*
See: *Isis* (1975–1976, 22 episodes, USA)

### SELMA (*Time Trax*)
Pocket-sized computer with a prim appearance and maternal attitude when in holographic mode.
See: *Time Trax* (1993–1994, 44 episodes, USA)

### Serra, Inara (*Firefly*)
High-class courtesan whose presence confers prestige on a small spaceship and its ragtag crew.
See: *Firefly* (2002, 14 episodes, USA)

### Seven Days (1998–2001, 66 episodes, USA)
*Created by:* Christopher Crowe, Zachary Crowe
*Production Co.:* Crowe Entertainment, Paramount Television
*Originally Aired:* UPN
*Main Cast:* Jonathan LaPaglia, Don Franklin, Justina Vail, Nick Searcy, Alan Scarfe, Sam Whipple, Norman Lloyd, Kevin Christy

The NSA recruits Frank Parker (Jonathan LaPaglia), a former CIA agent and current psychiatric hospital resident, to pilot its time machine. The "Chronosphere," as they call it, uses extraterrestrial technology extracted from the secret/not-very-secret Roswell crash. Frank's job, which requires a high pain threshold, will be to "backstep" into the past, with a limit of seven days, to prevent national security disasters before they happen. Recognizing a good opportunity for improved mental health when he sees it, Frank joins the Backstep team, which includes Dr. Olga Vukavitch (Justina Vail), a scientist who had worked on an unsuccessful Russian time-travel project.

Vukavitch and Parker have one of TV's more unusual "will they or won't they" relationships. Although sometimes succumbing to Parker's questionable charms, Olga has no memory of the incidents, as Parker's "backsteps" change history, and he is afterwards unable to replicate the circumstances which brought them together in the first place. In another departure from series norms, anyone on *Seven Days*, even series regulars, can die, although Frank's Chronosphere travels usually save them from death in the revised timeline. In "Olga's Excellent Vacation" (2000), Vukavitch dies in a not-so-excellent explosion at an Alaskan pipeline, and Parker must backstep to avert both the loss of Olga and the pipeline.

Justina Vail won a Saturn Award in 2000 for her portrayal of Olga Vukavitch. As far as we know, backsteps played no part in determining the outcome of the Saturn Award that year.

### Seven of Nine (*Star Trek: Voyager*)
Human turned cybernetic organism turned human again, now trying to adjust to a new life.
See: *Star Trek: Voyager* (1995–2001, 172 episodes, USA)

### Shad (*It's About Time*)
Prehistoric woman who meets some misplaced astronauts and is whisked with her family to the 20th century.
See: *It's About Time* (1966–1967, 26 episodes, USA)

### Sheena (*Sheena*)
Orphaned girl who grows up to be a shape-shifting jungle queen.
See: *Sheena* (2000–2002, 35 episodes, USA)

## *Sheena* (2000–2002, 35 episodes, USA)
*Based on:* The comic book series *Sheena, Queen of the Jungle* by Jerry Iger
*Created by:* Douglas Schwartz, Steven L. Sears
*Production Co.:* Douglas Schwartz/Steven L. Sears Productions, Sony Pictures Entertainment
*Originally Aired:* In Syndication
*Main Cast:* Gena Lee Nolin, John Allen Nelson, Margo Moorer, Kevin Quigley

The 2000 edition of *Sheena* updates the 1955 Irish McCalla series by adding supernatural powers (and a better vocabulary) to the heroine's jungle queen shtick. Little Cheryl Hamilton had been left to fend for herself in the African jungle when her archaeologist parents were killed. Enter Kali (Margo Moorer), a local shaman, who adopted Cheryl and taught her to love the jungle animals and protect their habitat. Now fully grown, Cheryl, rechristened Sheena (Gena Lee Nolin), looks more like a Playboy bunny than a woman living in a cave, and has learned from Kali how to morph into animals simply by gazing into their eyes. Her shape-shifting talent comes in handy when, as a GORILLA, she saves the life of Matt Cutter (John Allen Nelson) by chasing off his pursuers and pulling him from quicksand. Sheena and Cutter, who runs a local air safari business, become allies in fighting off interlopers to this natural paradise, including terrorists, smugglers, treasure hunters, slavers, CIA operatives and killer ants.

That's one crowded jungle.

### Sibley, Mary Walcott (*Salem*)
17th century woman who sacrifices her unborn child to the devil in exchange for vast powers.
See: *Salem* (2014– , 26 episodes, USA)

### Silverton, Juliette (*Grimm*)
Veterinarian paying a high price for having a cop boyfriend who fights supernatural creatures.
See: *Grimm* (2011– , 110 episodes, USA)

### Simmons, Jemma (*Agents of S.H.I.E.L.D.*)
Life sciences expert on a team that investigates threats to the U.S. and the world.
See: *Agents of S.H.I.E.L.D.* (2013– , 66 episodes, USA)

### Sister Bertrille (*The Flying Nun*)
Novice nun at a Puerto Rican convent who finds she can fly due to an aerodynamic anomaly.
See: *The Flying Nun* (1967–1970, 82 episodes, USA)

### Skouris, Diana (*The 4400*)
Jacqueline McKenzie portrays Diana Skouris, an agent with The National Threat Assessment Command (NTAC), who investigates the sudden reappearance of 4400 people abducted under mysterious circumstances. Diana partners with Tom

Baldwin (Joel Gretsch) to interview and track the returnees, who have begun to exhibit special abilities, such as telekinesis, enhanced strength, and healing powers. Diana quickly forms a bond with one young abductee, Maia Rutledge (Conchita Campbell), who can accurately predict future events, and in "The New and Improved Carl Morrissey" (2004), Diana brings Maia home, later adopting her. Diana's loyalties are continually tested, as in "Mommy's Bosses" (2005), when she and Tom learn that NTAC is responsible for a plague affecting some of the returnees, including Maia.

See also: ***The 4400* (2004–2007, 44 episodes, USA)**

## Skye (*Agents of S.H.I.E.L.D.*)

Former computer hacker investigating threats to the world, while seeking clues to her own mysterious past.

See: *Agents of S.H.I.E.L.D.* (2013– , 66 episodes, USA)

## Sleepy Hollow (2013– , 49 episodes, USA)

*Based on:* The short story *The Legend of Sleepy Hollow* by Washington Irving
*Created by:* Alex Kurtzman, Roberto Orci
*Production Co.:* 20th Century–Fox Television, Sketch Films, K/O Paper Products
*Originally Aired:* Fox
*Main Cast:* Tom Mison, Nicole Beharie, Orlando Jones, Katia Winter, Lyndie Greenwood, John Noble, Nikki Reed, Shannyn Sossamon, Zach Appelman

Ichabod Crane (Tom Mison) rises from the dead (literally) in this reimagining of Washington Irving's famous story. Handsome Crane, a former spy for General George Washington, is resurrected in modern-day Sleepy Hollow at the same time as the Headless Horseman, soon revealed to be one of the Four Horsemen of the Apocalypse. When Sheriff August Corbin (Clancy Brown) is beheaded by the Horseman, Lt. **Abbie Mills** (Nicole Beharie), Corbin's protégé and surrogate daughter, begins to investigate, learning that Sleepy Hollow will be ground zero for the coming apocalypse, and that she and Crane, the prophesied witnesses, are the only two people who can stop it. Helping, but sometimes complicating, matters is Katrina Crane (Katia Winter), Ichabod's wife, a witch stuck in purgatory, who can communicate with Ichabod through dreams. Captain Frank Irving (Orlando Jones), Abbie's boss, is also an ally, but pays a high price when the evil touches his own daughter. Family connections, in fact, are pivotal in the haunted Hollow. Abbie's sister, Jenny Mills (Lyndie Greenwood), has been institutionalized for being honest about the weird things she's seen, and Ichabod's son, Jeremy Crane/Henry Parrish (John Noble), is actually another of the Four Horsemen of the Apocalypse (don't ask).

More complex mythology is revealed, as Crane and Abbie avert the Apocalypse, but not without releasing demons trapped in purgatory, including Pandora (Shannyn Sossamon). In defeating Pandora's master, the Hidden One, Abbie sacrifices herself to save the world once again. Not to worry, though, as Ichabod immediately sets off to find Abbie's replacement witness in Washington, D.C.

This Hollow is anything but sleepy.

See also: **Mills, Abbie (*Sleepy Hollow*)**

## Small Wonder (1985–1989, 96 episodes, USA)
*Created by:* Howard Leeds
*Production Co.:* Metromedia Video Productions, 20th Century–Fox Television
*Originally Aired:* In Syndication
*Main Cast:* Tiffany Brissette, Dick Christie, Marla Pennington, Jerry Supiran, Emily Schulman

The small wonder in question is Vicki, also known as V.I.C.I. or Voice Input Child Identicant, which gives you a hint that Vicki is a special 10-year-old girl. Vicki/V.I.C.I. (Tiffany Brissette) is the creation of Ted Lawson (Dick Christie), who brings the adorable android home in hopes of improving her programming. Lawson and his wife Joan (Marla Pennington) try to pass Vicki off as a family member, a difficult task since the little robot tends to speak in a monotone and interpret what she hears literally. The task is made even more difficult because the Lawsons have buttinskies for neighbors, the Brindles, especially young Harriet (Emily Schulman), who has a crush on Vicki's "brother" Jamie (Jerry Supiran). Jamie tries to exploit his android sister's special talents at every turn, as in "Victor/Vicki-toria" (1987), when he disguises her as a boy to help out his baseball team.

Creator Howard Leeds was a producer on *My Living Doll* and apparently couldn't get the idea of a female android out of his head, although this one was 20 years younger than Julie Newmar and wore a pinafore. Kid sitcoms were big during the 80s, so a show about a kid robot made perfect sense. But not the pinafore. Never the pinafore.

## Smallville (2001–2011, 217 episodes, USA)
*Based on:* The DC Comics character Superman created by Jerry Siegel, Joe Shuster
*Created by:* Alfred Gough, Miles Millar
*Production Co.:* Tollin/Robbins Productions, Millar Gough Ink, DC Comics, Warner Bros. Television, et al.
*Originally Aired:* WB (2001–2006), The CW (2006–2011)
*Main Cast:* Tom Welling, Kristin Kreuk, Michael Rosenbaum, Allison Mack, Annette O'Toole, John Schneider, Erica Durance, John Glover

*Smallville* took the premise of its predecessor, *Superboy*, but went even further back in Superman's life to his high school days. In the process, it doubled the earlier show's staying power, lasting a full 10 seasons in an impressive display of super-longevity.

Tom Welling is Clark Kent, a Kansas teen who begins to exhibit strange powers and learns that he is from another planet. The usual suspects from the Superman canon soon fall into Clark's orbit, including Lex Luthor (Michael Rosenbaum), who is saved from drowning by the superteen and becomes his friend, but heads into darkness as his obsession with Clark's secrets intensifies.

On the distaff side of the "L.L." ledger, Lana Lang (Kristin Kreuk) is here as a pretty cheerleader who becomes Clark's love interest, but also has problems with his super-sized secrets. As Lana and Clark ride the relationship roller coaster into adulthood, their future together looks bright, especially when Lana gains her own superpowers thanks to LuthorCorp's Prometheus technology. But the prospect of a happily-ever-after for the couple is short-lived when Lana absorbs the radiation from a kryptonite bomb, saving Metropolis, but killing her relationship with Clark, when she becomes his human kryptonite. Exit Lana Lang in season eight.

Enter a more famous L.L., Lois Lane (Erica Durance), who had come into Clark's life a few years earlier, when she was investigating the apparent death of her cousin Chloe Sullivan (Allison Mack) in Smallville. Lois later moves on to work as a reporter for the *Daily Planet* alongside very-much-alive Chloe and later Clark himself, who arrives as an intern and finds a mentor in the formidable Ms. Lane. Lois and Clark develop a romantic relationship in this pre–Superman period, when Clark comes to be known as "The Blur" for his speedy superheroics. It is Lois who suggests to Clark that he develop an alter ego so he won't be recognized, and she works with him on his "mild-mannered" persona. Their wedding day finally arrives, but it is interrupted (what a surprise) by a planetary invasion in "Finale" (parts one and two, 2011). A flash forward reveals that Lois and Clark are still talking about getting married seven years later.

Durance was the fourth actress to portray Lois Lane on television, following in the footsteps of Phyllis Coates, Noel Neill, and Teri Hatcher, icons to a one. Each actress placed her individual stamp on the role, but the character's fierce independence and dedication to her work were a common thread running through every incarnation.

Lois Lane was never JUST Superman's girlfriend.

### Smith, Sarah Jane (*Doctor Who*)

While working undercover at a secret research facility, Sarah Jane Smith (Elizabeth Sladen), a young journalist, meets a time traveler who is searching for missing scientists. Thus begins her association with "The Doctor" (Jon Pertwee), an alien Time Lord, who travels in a craft resembling a British police box, while regenerating into a different body from time to time. Smith signs on for the Doctor's many adventures, hanging around long enough to see his regeneration from the Third to the Fourth Doctor (Tom Baker) in "Robot" (parts one to four, 1974–1975). While Sladen later observed that her character Sarah Jane had been a bit of a "cardboard cut-out," Sarah Jane was braver and more determined than the Doctor's prior female companions, providing a template for the women who followed her.

After the revival of *Doctor Who* in 2005, an older Sarah Jane returned to assist the Tenth Doctor (David Tennant) in "School Reunion" (2006). From her success there, Sarah Jane went on to become the protagonist of her own show in *The Sarah Jane Adventures* (2007–2011), a more youth-oriented series than *Doctor Who*. Smith investigates alien activity from her own home in England with the help of her genetically engineered son and an extraterrestrial computer. The series ended with the untimely death of Elizabeth Sladen, after three episodes had been filmed for the fifth season.

With appearances in both the classic and revived series of *Doctor Who*, her own spinoff, and a lasting appeal across the generations, Sarah Jane Smith stands out among the Doctor's outstanding companions.

See also: ***Doctor Who* (1963–1989, 2005– , 821 episodes, UK)**

### Snow, Caitlin (*The Flash*)

Bio-engineer working at a high-tech laboratory with a superhero who has lightning speed.

See: ***The Flash* (2014– , 46 episodes, USA)**

### Snow White (*The Charmings*)

Los Angeles woman with a princely husband and great kids, but an unusual stepmother problem.

See: ***The Charmings* (1987–1988, 21 episodes, USA)**

### Snow White (*Once Upon a Time*)

Teacher in a Maine town unaware of her enchanted past due to an evil queen's curse.

See: ***Once Upon a Time* (2011– , 111 episodes, USA)**

## *So Weird* (1999–2001, 65 episodes, Canada/USA)

*Created by:* Tom J. Astle
*Production Co.:* Disney Channel Original Productions, Fair Dinkum Productions, So Weird Productions, et al.
*Originally Aired:* Disney Channel
*Main Cast:* Cara DeLizia, Alexz Johnson, Mackenzie Phillips, Patrick Levis, Erik von Detten, Eric Lively, Belinda Metz, Dave "Squatch" Ward

Cara DeLizia is Fiona "Fi" Phillips, a 13-year-old girl who tours the country with her rock-star mom, Molly Phillips (Mackenzie Phillips), and an entourage of family and friends. As if that lifestyle isn't unique enough for a young teen, Fi encounters paranormal occurrences wherever she goes, writing about them on a website called *So Weird*. It turns out that Fi is a supernatural lightning rod, as was her father, whose mysterious death she investigates throughout the first two seasons. Fi also possesses powers of her own, as in "Strangeling" (1999), when she finds a family book of Celtic spells and inadvertently conjures a dragon-like creature while visiting her maternal aunt. Family ties become magical ties again in "Will o' the Wisp" (1999), when Fi's brother Jack (Patrick Levis) is possessed by a will o' the wisp, and Fi must guess the Scottish spirit's true name or lose Jack forever.

After two years of pursuing her own X-Files, Fi decides the quiet life would be more, well, quiet, and goes to live with an aunt. Annie Thelen (Alexz Johnson), a family friend and musician, joins the tour, and learns she has a panther spirit guide. (Doesn't everyone?) Annie has her own paranormal adventures, as in "Detention" (2000), when she and Jack are time-warped back to a 1970s detention class.

DeLizia's departure to pursue less Disney-esque acting opportunities forced an end to the spookier story arcs and gave the show a lighter and more musical ambience with the addition of Johnson. Disney Press released five *So Weird* novels in the summer of 2000, featuring Fi Phillips, always the heart of this atypical Disney series.

### Solomon, Sally (*3rd Rock from the Sun*)

Sally Solomon (Kristen Johnston) is pursuing the usual goals of a twentysomething woman in a Midwestern town—looking for love, seeking a good job, and attempting to understand her place in the universe. Oh, and she's also trying to hide the fact that she's an extraterrestrial researcher sent to Earth to learn about humans. Sally isn't exactly a girly girl. As security officer for the expedition of four, she is combat-tough and her Amazonian frame is imposing. It's not surprising, then, that her imperious ways are problematic for boyfriend "Mr. Randell" (John D'Aquino), and her attempts to be more demure backfire in "Big Angry Virgin from Outer Space" (1996). Soon Sally sets her cap for Don Orville (Wayne Knight), attracted to the power represented by his police uniform, and unaware that he's a sniveling coward. Blonde bombshell Sally and faux tough guy Don often banter like a cop and his dame from a 40s detective movie. Sally finally sees Don's true colors before she and the crew must beam back home in series finale "The Thing That Wouldn't Die" (parts one and two, 2001).

Kristen Johnston won two Supporting Actress Emmy Awards for her portrayal of Sally Solomon in one of television's premier examples of perfect casting.

See also: ***3rd Rock from the Sun*** **(1996–2001, 139 episodes, USA)**

### *Something Is Out There* (1988, 8 episodes, USA)

*Created by:* Frank Lupo
*Production Co.:* Columbia Pictures Television
*Originally Aired:* NBC
*Main Cast:* Joseph Cortese, Maryam d'Abo, Gregory Sierra

*Something Is Out There* wrote the book on how to turn a highly successful miniseries into a short-lived, weekly flop. The miniseries, which had aired in May 1988, paired maverick police detective Jack Breslin (Joseph Cortese) with extraterrestrial medical doctor Ta'Ra (Maryam d'Abo), who together hunted a murderous, shapeshifting monster called a xenomorph. Cortese and d'Abo returned for the weekly series, but the show's emphasis shifted from pulpy SF to paranormal themes and *Moonlighting*-esque banter, mostly due to budget constraints.

In the bargain-basement edition, Ta'Ra, now stranded on our planet, poses as Breslin's cousin and informally helps him with his unusual cases by using her telepathic abilities. The deception is reasonably convincing, since Ta'Ra looks like a human, a beautiful, blonde human, with shapely legs, as emphasized in the opening titles of the series. Her "10" status on Earth notwithstanding, Ta'Ra wants to return home, and in "Night of the Visitors" (1988), she thinks the author of a book about alien abduction might lead the way back.

Up against tough competition from *Dallas* and experiencing viewer defections over the thematic changes, *Something Is Out There* was canceled after only six episodes had aired.

A leggy alien with a gun can only distract us for so long.

### Sommers, Jaime (*The Bionic Woman*)

Lindsay Wagner stars as Jaime Sommers, a former tennis star who suffers critical injuries during a skydiving accident and is saved by the addition of some computerized body parts. Jaime becomes a schoolteacher by day, but moonlights as an operative for the Office of Scientific Investigations under the watchful eye of Oscar Goldman (Richard Anderson). She uses her exceptional abilities, such as massive strength and lightning speed, for the cause of good around the globe, as in "Angel of Mercy" (1976), when she must rescue a U.S. ambassador and his wife from a collapsed building in Costa Brava. In the three-part "Kill Oscar" (1976), the bionic woman must fight other cyborgs, called Fembots, to save Oscar and the world from a weather-control device. The series concludes with the *Prisoner*-esque "On the Run" (1978), where Jaime learns it's not easy to retire from secret government work, but staying on the job may finally give her what she needs.

See also: ***The Bionic Woman*** **(1976–1978, 58 episodes, USA)**

### Sommers, Jaime (*Bionic Woman*)

Bionic woman for the new millennium, this time using her enhanced abilities for a private intelligence firm.

See: ***Bionic Woman*** **(2007, 8 episodes, USA)**

### *Space Academy* (1977, 15 episodes, USA)

*Created by:* Allen Ducovny
*Production Co.:* Filmation
*Originally Aired:* CBS
*Main Cast:* Jonathan Harris, Pamelyn Ferdin, Ric Carrott, Maggie Cooper, Brian Tochi, Ty Henderson, Eric Greene

"Welcome to Man's most magnificent achievement in the conquest of space, the man-made planetoid Space Academy, founded in the Star Year 3732. Here we have gathered young people from the farthest reaches of all the known worlds."

Teenagers make the best adventurers, at least according to Saturday-morning science fiction shows like *Ark II* and *Space Academy*.

Commander Isaac Gampu (Jonathan Harris) oversees his teen charges at the Space Academy, drawing upon his 300-some-odd years of experience in exploration. (Space travel does funny things to a person apparently.) Handsome Chris Gentry (Ric Carrott) leads the Academy's Blue Team into action, while his sister Laura Gentry (Pamelyn Ferdin) is the second in command. Students are chosen for their unique abilities, and the Gentry siblings have psychic powers. In "Castaways in Time and Space" (1977), Gampu and Laura are pulled into a black hole (actor Harris knew something about being lost in space), and Chris must use his psychic link with Laura to locate them. Chris has a love interest in pretty Adrian Pryce-Jones (Maggie Cooper), who studies human-simian communication in the aptly named "Monkey Business." Laura and Adrian wear hyper-short, 70s versions of the space-opera miniskirt, but also have jumpsuits, in a nod to practicality. (Practicality? A word not often used in regard to women's SF costuming.)

Pamelyn Ferdin was a prolific young actress in the 60s and 70s, with many guest-starring roles, including a memorable *Star Trek* turn in "And the Children Shall

Lead" (1968). She had psychic powers in that one too and a jumpsuit, proving that in space, no one can escape the dreaded SF trope.

## *Space: 1999* (1975–1977, 48 episodes, Italy/UK)
*Created by:* Gerry Anderson, Sylvia Anderson
*Production Co.:* Group 3 Productions, Incorporated Television Company (ITC), et al.
*Originally Aired:* In Syndication
*Main Cast:* Martin Landau, Barbara Bain, Nick Tate, Zienia Merton, Barry Morse, Catherine Schell, Tony Anholt

When it comes to the accuracy of its near-future predictions, science fiction would be better served using a cloudy crystal ball. Artificial intelligence was not advanced enough to take over the world in 1997 à la *Terminator 2: Judgment Day*, and space exploration had not progressed to the point of moon colonization by 1999, as prophesied by this expensively made series. As for real-world predictions, 1999's Y2K scare was also a bust. Tarot cards, anyone?

In 1999, a nuclear blast on the moon's surface propels the earth's satellite, along with a resident research colony, into deep space. The 311 inhabitants of Moonbase Alpha, led by Commander John Koenig (Martin Landau), search for a new home, while encountering new life and new civilizations à la *Star Trek*. Dr. Helena Russell (Barbara Bain) is the chief medical officer for the base, attending to the crew's health needs in a detached, robotic fashion. She does display flashes of humanity, however, as in "Missing Link" (1976), when she must decide whether or not to turn off Koenig's life support system.

Although the series was filmed and produced in the UK, lots of attention was paid to the American market, where the show had failed to interest any networks and had run in syndication. After a mediocre performance in season one, the series was revamped for the next season, with an emphasis on action, comedy, and passion, instead of intellectual conversation. The costumes became more colorful, the visuals were brighter, and the relationship between John and Helena heated up. The producers also added an extraterrestrial character, Maya (Catherine Schell), who was to be the Spock of the piece, the alien science officer. Maya, a "metamorph," had a power that Spock didn't have, however, the ability to change into any lifeform. But her sideburns (yes, sideburns) were longer than Spock's, and she wore miniskirts and revealing gowns to amp up the show's sex appeal.

Ultimately the changes didn't matter, as ITC canceled the series after two seasons due to financial issues.

In space, 1999 or otherwise, no one can hear you scream when you're cancelled.

## *Space Patrol* (1950–1955, 210 episodes, USA)
*Created by:* Mike Moser
*Production Co.:* Mike Moser Productions, American Broadcasting Company
*Originally Aired:* ABC
*Main Cast:* Ed Kemmer, Lyn Osborn, Ken Mayer, Virginia Hewitt, Nina Bara, Bela Kovacs

More than 15 years before Captain Kirk and company brought their galactic exploits to television on *Star Trek*, Commander Buzz Corry and his crew were lighting up the small screen with their futuristic adventures on *Space Patrol*. The series began as a 15-minute local show on KECA-TV in Los Angeles, but proved so popular that ABC added a half-hour version, which was eventually broadcast live from coast to coast.

In the 30th century, Commander Corry (Ed Kemmer) of the United Planets patrols the space lanes in his ship, the *Terra V*. Assisting the square-jawed officer in keeping the peace is youthful Cadet Happy (Lyn Osborn), who has an exuberant knack for getting himself into cosmic trouble. Carol Carlisle (Virginia Hewitt), daughter of the UP's Secretary-General, provides some blonde cheesecake appeal, while working as a daring secret operative. Her sister in short-skirted adventure is Tonga (Nina Bara), who was once a criminal known as The Lady of Diamonds, but now serves as assistant security chief to Major "Robbie" Robertson (Ken Mayer). Often the women find themselves in the damsel in distress role, but they are portrayed as strong and resourceful officers, and when not in distress, make scientific contributions and even pilot the *Terra*. Close quarters on the ship notwithstanding, there's no time for romance on the frontier, but Carol shows extra concern for Buzz, while Robbie keeps an eye on Tonga.

Carol Carlisle (Virginia Hewitt) and Commander Buzz Corry (Ed Kemmer) work in close quarters on *Space Patrol* (ABC Television).

The crew battled their share of space villains, including Prince Baccarratti (Bela Kovacs), Agent X (Norman Jolley), and Mr. Proteus (Marvin Miller)—so many evildoers, in fact, that they accumulated 210 half-hour adventures and 900 15-minute vignettes.

As Cadet Happy would say, "Smokin' rockets!"

## *Space Precinct* (1994–1995, 24 episodes, UK)
*Created by:* Gerry Anderson
*Production Co.:* Gerry Anderson Productions, Grove Television Enterprises, Mentorn Films
*Originally Aired:* In Syndication

Main Cast: Ted Shackelford, Rob Youngblood, Simone Bendix, Mary Woodvine, Jerome Willis

In 2040, the place to be if you're a cop who enjoys a challenge is Demeter City, "the crime capital of the galaxy," located on the planet Altor. Former NYPD detective Patrick Brogan (Ted Shackelford) moves his wife and kids to the distant solar system, and tackles cases where humans or one of several alien races may be the perpetrators. Assisting Brogan is his partner from the old days back on Earth, Jack Haldane (Rob Youngblood), and another human officer, Jane Castle (Simone Bendix), who later becomes Haldane's love interest. Other police at the precinct are from alien races, including Aurelia Took (Mary Woodvine), a Tarn, who possesses telepathic and telekinetic abilities. Together, this motley crew investigates murders, counterfeiting, jewelry heists, and illicit drugs, because there is nothing new under the sun (or any sun) when it comes to crime.

## *Space Rangers* (1993, 6 episodes, USA)
Created by: Pen Densham
Production Co.: RHI Entertainment, Trilogy Entertainment Group, Ranger Productions Inc.
Originally Aired: CBS
Main Cast: Jeff Kaake, Marjorie Monaghan, Cary-Hiroyuki Tagawa, Jack McGee, Clint Howard, Danny Quinn, Gottfried John, Linda Hunt

This space opera lasted only four episodes as a midseason replacement, despite the presence of Oscar-winning actress Linda Hunt as part of its ensemble cast. Hunt portrays Commander Chennault, the leader of an Earth colony called Fort Hope on the far-off planet Avalon. Chennault is diminutive in size, but high in rank, martial in her training, yet maternal in her concern for the colonists.

Keeping the peace on and around this frontier outpost are the Space Rangers, epitomized by Captain John Boon (Jeff Kaake), a tough guy who commands Ranger Slingship #377. Boon has a motley crew, of course, and members include Jojo Thorsen (Marjorie Monaghan), a pilot who hails from the women-only planet of New Venus, Doc Kreuger (Jack McGee), a flight engineer who's been wounded so many times he's made up mostly of artificial parts, and Zylyn (Cary-Hiroyuki Tagawa), a member of a warrior race which has embraced peace and controls its emotions. (How very Spock.) The Rangers confront some exotic problems, including Banshees, who teleport aboard spaceships at will to murder their crews. Like the banshees of legend, they emit a high-pitched scream, which was also heard after this series was canceled with two of its six episodes still unaired.

## *Special Unit 2* (2001–2002, 19 episodes, USA)
Created by: Evan Katz
Production Co.: Paramount Television, Rego Park Productions
Originally Aired: UPN
Main Cast: Michael Landes, Alexondra Lee, Danny Woodburn, Richard Gant

Special Unit 2 is a secret division within the Chicago Police Department, tasked with handling cases which involve "Links," missing links between apes and humans, traditionally thought of as the monsters of mythology, but in actuality quite real and living in Chicago. Nick O'Malley (Michael Landes) is the unit's maverick, tortured by guilt over the loss of his partner to a Link called The Chameleon. Alexandra Lee portrays Detective Kate Benson, Nick's new partner, who has known since childhood about the things that go bump in the night, so is the perfect recruit for SU2. Nick and Kate battle gargoyles, werewolves, spider-women, the Sandman, and Medusa, while relying upon a kleptomaniac gnome named Carl (Danny Woodburn) to feed them information about the Link community. These detectives surely have their hands full, especially when Links can form even from the discarded fat of liposuction patients ("The Waste," 2001).

### Spellman, Hilda and Zelda (*Sabrina the Teenage Witch*)

Aunts and guardians who provide magical training and motherly guidance to their niece, a novice witch.

See: ***Sabrina the Teenage Witch* (1996–2003, 163 episodes, USA)**

### Spellman, Sabrina (*Sabrina the Teenage Witch*)

The title of this series states the high concept—Sabrina Spellman is a teenage witch. Pretty Sabrina (Melissa Joan Hart) lives with her eccentric aunts Zelda (Beth Broderick) and Hilda (Caroline Rhea), also witches, and tries to learn how to wield her powers while coping with the mundane problems of the mortal adolescent world. Boys are first and foremost, of course, and attracting the right one has more than the usual degree of difficulty in "First Kiss" (1997), when Sabrina's innocent smooch turns her love interest, Harvey Kinkle (Nate Richert), into a frog. Dealing with a mean girl is the high school norm, but not when you accidentally transform her into puzzle pieces, as Sabrina does to arch enemy Libby Chessler (Jenna Leigh Green) in "Five Easy Pieces of Libby" (1998).

Sabrina eventually moves on to college and away from high school sweetheart Harvey, but supernatural problems still beset her, as in "You Can't Twin" (2000), when her evil twin Katrina escapes the "Other Realm" and attempts to sabotage Sabrina's life (as evil twins do). While juggling classes, work, and more magical challenges, Sabrina auditions various boyfriends, finally becoming engaged to Aaron Jacobs (Dylan Neal). But Aaron's and Sabrina's "soul stones" aren't a good fit, and Sabrina learns in series finale "Soul Mates" (2003) that her true love has been in front of her all along.

Sabrina Spellman was a wholesome role model for kids and teens, managing to be just cool enough, especially with her witchy ways, to keep them (and even some adults) interested in her madcap, magical adventures for seven seasons.

See also: ***Sabrina the Teenage Witch* (1996–2003, 163 episodes, USA)**

### Stackhouse, Sookie (*True Blood*)

Louisiana waitress, a human-fairy hybrid with telepathic powers, who falls in love with a vampire.

See: ***True Blood* (2008–2014, 80 episodes, USA)**

### Star Maidens (1976, 13 episodes, UK/West Germany)
*Production Co.:* Portman Productions, Scottish Television Enterprises, Werbung im Rundfunk GmbH, Jost Graf von Hardenberg & Co.
*Originally Aired:* In Syndication
*Main Cast:* Judy Geeson, Lisa Harrow, Christiane Krüger, Pierre Brice, Christian Quadflieg, Gareth Thomas, Dawn Addams

Imagine a 70s planet where one sex is dominant and one is submissive. Now think again, because we're not talking about Earth, but Medusa, where females rule, and males do menial tasks and are prized as sex objects.

Things are humming along nicely on Medusa, until the planet, kicked out of orbit by a comet, enters Earth's solar system. Two males, Adam (Pierre Brice) and Shem (Gareth Thomas), steal a spaceship to escape their female overlords (or is it overladies?) and head to Earth, where things may be more to their liking. Supreme Councillor Fulvia (Judy Geeson) and security chief Octavia (Christiane Krüger) set off to recapture the renegades, but end up taking two Earth hostages, Dr. Liz Becker (Lisa Harrow) and Dr. Rudi Schmidt (Christian Quadflieg). Various battles of the sexes ensue, as the principles experience culture shock and pursue their own agendas. Fulvia and Adam continue to lock horns, as Adam is both her servant and her lover, but his plot to coax her into "normal" coupledom on Earth backfires in "The Perfect Couple" (1976).

The rest is 70s camp with low-budget special effects, pretty faces in "futuristic" makeup, and outrageous costumes, such as midriff-baring police uniforms.

Given the brief exposure, the Medusan wave of feminism never made it into our history books.

### Star Trek (1966–1969, 79 episodes, USA)
*Created by:* Gene Roddenberry
*Production Co.:* Desilu Productions, Paramount Television, Norway Corporation
*Originally Aired:* NBC
*Main Cast:* William Shatner, Leonard Nimoy, DeForest Kelley, Nichelle Nichols, James Doohan, George Takei, Walter Koenig

"Space, the final frontier. These are the voyages of the starship *Enterprise*. Its five-year mission: to explore strange new worlds, to seek out new life and new civilizations, to boldly go where no man has gone before."

It's hard to overestimate the influence and popularity of *Star Trek*, a show that in its time never rose above 52 in the yearly Nielsen rankings, and survived cancellation in its second season because of a letter-writing campaign. *Star Trek* lived on, however, in syndication, bringing new fans and new life, and later spawning an entire franchise, including movie sequels, TV series spin-offs, novels, and a galaxy of merchandise.

But before there was a franchise, there was a 60s series called *Star Trek*, conceived by creator Gene Roddenberry as a "*Wagon Train* to the stars." William Shatner heads the celestial wagon train as Captain James T. Kirk, handsome, brave, athletic, and in love with his lady, the majestic USS *Enterprise*. Commander Spock (Leonard

Nimoy) serves as Kirk's second in command and science officer, a half-human, half-Vulcan, guided by his logical alien side, but sometimes in conflict with his emotional human half. Rounding out *Star Trek*'s command trinity is Dr. Leonard "Bones" McCoy (DeForest Kelley), the ship's chief medical officer, an irascible humanist, who often takes Spock to task for his cold calculations.

Women also made the trip to the stars, but mostly in occupations considered acceptable for contemporary 60s women. **Lieutenant Uhura** (Nichelle Nichols) is the ship's communications officer, a "glorified telephone operator" to use Nichols's own words, whose main dialog often consists of the now iconic line, "hailing frequencies open." Nichols, who is African American, had planned to leave the show during the first season because of her limited screen time, but was convinced by Dr. Martin Luther King to remain due to her character's example of racial equality in the future.

Nurse Christine Chapel (Majel Barrett) assists Dr. McCoy in the ship's sick bay, but also harbors some romantic feelings for Mr. Spock, who cannot reciprocate them. Barrett had played the more forward-looking role of Number One, second in command on the *Enterprise*, in the original series pilot "The Cage" (1965), a pilot rejected by NBC for being too cerebral.

Kirk, Spock, McCoy, and company battle (and sometimes befriend) aliens, travel back in time, encounter androids, and meet their alternate selves, while tackling 60s issues such as race relations, utopian communities, and global warfare. While the settings and costumes are exotic (and sometimes cheesy), the formula for each episode is mostly the same: Courageous Captain Kirk, balancing his two sides personified by logical Mr. Spock and humanistic Dr. McCoy, saves us from evil, foolishness, or even our own shortsightedness. That's the appeal.

Live long and prosper.

See also: **Uhura, Lieutenant (*Star Trek*)**

## *Star Trek: Deep Space Nine* (1993–1999, 176 episodes, USA)

*Based on:* The TV series *Star Trek* created by Gene Roddenberry
*Created by:* Rick Berman, Michael Piller
*Production Co.:* Paramount Domestic Television
*Originally Aired:* In Syndication
*Main Cast:* Avery Brooks, René Auberjonois, Terry Farrell, Cirroc Lofton, Colm Meaney, Armin Shimerman, Alexander Siddig, Nana Visitor, Michael Dorn, Nicole de Boer

In a break from *Trek* tradition, the characters of *Star Trek: Deep Space Nine* boldly stay put in this series set on a space station rather than a voyaging starship. There's lots of political and military backstory surrounding this station, which guards a wormhole to the far side of the galaxy and protects it from Federation enemies such as the Cardassians (not to be confused with the Kardashians) and the Klingons. The United Federation of Planets assigns Benjamin Sisko (Avery Brooks) to be commander of the station, which orbits the planet Bajor, once occupied by the Cardassians.

Major Kira Nerys (Nana Visitor) is Sisko's Bajoran liaison and First Officer, initially resentful of the Federation presence on *DS9* and in the lives of the Bajoran people. Kira, a former resistance fighter who had been raised in a labor camp, carries lots of emotional baggage from her harrowing past, but persists in trying to surmount it. She grows to become an ally of Sisko and the UFP, refusing to give up security secrets when tortured by Bajoran extremists in "The Circle" (1993).

Kira's closest friend on *DS9* is Jadzia Dax (Terry Farrell), the station's chief science officer. Jadzia Dax combines two species in one body, a humanoid Trill named Jadzia and a symbiotic, slug-like creature called Dax. Dax had been hosted by seven prior Trill, both male and female, and Jadzia retains the memories and skills from all of Dax's prior incarnations, making her wise, complex, and sometimes conflicted. Jadzia is heterosexual, eventually marrying Lt. Commander Worf (Michael Dorn), a Klingon, but sexual orientation can be a muddy business for joined Trills. In "Rejoined" (1995), one of Dax's prior spouses, herself a joined Trill, visits *DS9*, and pursues an ostensibly same-sex relationship with Jadzia Dax, although the two had been male and female when they were married. (Got that?) Jadzia is killed in the sixth season finale, "Tears of the Prophets"(1998), a plot development which happened to coincide with Farrell's desire for a reduced role in season seven (although she hadn't been thinking along the lines of a 100 percent reduction). While Jadzia does die, the Dax symbiont survives to be implanted in another Trill host, the two becoming Ezri Dax (Nicole de Boer), a new (half-new?) character in the final season.

Televised science fiction is all about miracles, mostly wrought by writers and FX people, but occasionally performed by wizards in the casting department.

### Star Trek: Enterprise (2001–2005, 98 episodes, USA)

*Based on:* The TV series *Star Trek* created by Gene Roddenberry
*Created by:* Rick Berman, Brannon Braga
*Production Co.:* Paramount Network Television, Braga Productions, Rick Berman Productions
*Originally Aired:* UPN
*Main Cast:* Scott Bakula, John Billingsley, Jolene Blalock, Dominic Keating, Anthony Montgomery, Linda Park, Connor Trinneer

Thirty-five years after Captain Kirk jump-kicked his way into our hearts on *Star Trek*, Jonathan Archer (Scott Bakula) commands the *Enterprise*, a starship prototype which launches 100 years before Kirk's five-year mission. In 2151, interstellar travel is new, and *Enterprise*, here numbered NX-01, is exploring strange new worlds with a crew which cannot call upon Starfleet's wisdom and experience about deep space travel, since it has neither.

Enter our pointy-eared friends, the Vulcans, who have been overseeing humanity's use of warp-drive technology with some concern that our emotional species is not ready to meet the neighbors, so to speak. The Vulcan High Command assigns Sub-Commander T'Pol (Jolene Blalock) as their liaison for *Enterprise*'s first mission, and her presence initially engenders suspicion and resentment among the crew. T'Pol's continued loyalty to Captain Archer, however, as well as her extensive scientific knowledge and command experience eventually land her a Starfleet commission and the formal assignment of First Officer aboard the *Enterprise*.

Despite her logical Vulcan heritage, T'Pol continues in a long line of *Star Trek* women from Lieutenant Uhura to Seven of Nine, who wear sexy clothing that bears no resemblance to a military uniform. In T'Pol's case that means a body-hugging catsuit, with a neckline that plunges in direct proportion to the drop in series ratings. And once she wears no clothing at all, in "Harbinger" (2004), during a scene with Chief Engineer "Trip" Tucker (Connor Trinneer), which caused U.S. TV stations to do some creative trimming.

Communications Officer Hoshi Sato (Linda Park) is more conservatively attired, usually wearing the standard duty jumpsuit of *Enterprise* crew members. Sato is a brilliant linguist, speaking more than 40 languages, including Klingon, a necessary skill since the Universal Translator was in its infancy when NX-01 launched.

*Star Trek: Enterprise* lasted one season longer than the original series, but didn't have the longevity of the intervening Treks, such as *Voyager*, which ran for seven seasons each. Did it suffer a premature death because it was Trek dreck? Or was it simply a case of franchise fatigue?

The Vulcans have a saying. Roughly translated, it means, "To each their own Trek."

### *Star Trek: The Next Generation* (1987–1994, 178 episodes, USA)
*Based on:* The TV series *Star Trek* created by Gene Roddenberry
*Created by:* Gene Roddenberry
*Production Co.:* Paramount Domestic Television
*Originally Aired:* In Syndication
*Main Cast:* Patrick Stewart, Jonathan Frakes, LeVar Burton, Marina Sirtis, Brent Spiner, Michael Dorn, Gates McFadden, Wil Wheaton, Denise Crosby, Colm Meaney, Michelle Forbes, Majel Barrett, Whoopi Goldberg

"Space, the final frontier. These are the voyages of the starship *Enterprise*. Its continuing mission: to explore strange new worlds, to seek out new life and new civilizations, to boldly go where no one has gone before."

In this first live-action sequel to *Star Trek*, the USS *Enterprise*, now the souped-up *Enterprise-D*, roams the galaxy almost a century after its predecessor, with a similar, but gender-neutral mission statement for its 80s TV audience. Captain Jean-Luc Picard (Patrick Stewart) steps in for James T. Kirk as commanding officer of the new *Enterprise*, more the intellectual diplomat and less the man of action than Captain Kirk. (What, no jump kicks?)

Dr. Beverly Crusher (Gates McFadden) is the Bones McCoy of the piece, chief medical officer for the *Enterprise*, but also a mother, with another nod to changing gender roles since the original *Star Trek* took flight. Crusher, a widow, brings her teenaged prodigy of a son, Wesley (Wil Wheaton), on board with her, and frets over giving him a well-balanced life, while attending to the medical needs of the crew. After one season, she leaves to become Head of Starfleet Medical, a development which just happened to coincide with McFadden's firing from the series. Crusher returns to the *Enterprise* in season three after the departure of the show's head writer, Maurice Hurley, who hadn't been McFadden's biggest fan. She resumes her duties as chief medical officer and renews her attraction to Picard, which he reciprocates, *Star Trek*–style, in "Attached" (1993), where Beverly and Jean-Luc become telepathically linked, and reveal their true feelings for one another.

Lieutenant Commander Deanna Troi (Marina Sirtis) sits next to Captain Picard on the bridge. Troi is the ship's counselor, a psychologist who looks after the crew's emotional health during the *Enterprise*'s long, and often stressful voyages. Her Betazoid heritage (on her mother's side) has given her the ability to sense people's emotions, even to the point of knowing when they are lying, which makes her a valuable advisor to Picard. Although a military officer, Troi doesn't wear the Starfleet uniform, but rather a series of slinky, low-cut bodysuits, because of a rule apparently established in television's infancy that every space opera must have a woman who wears a sexy costume. It wasn't until season six with the two-part episode "Chain of Command" (1992) that Troi finally adopted the standard Starfleet uniform, much to the delight of Marina Sirtis, who felt her character became smarter and was given more to do once her cleavage was covered. (In Hollywood, cleavage is a no-brainer.)

The adventures of Captain Picard, Dr. Crusher, Counselor Troi, et al. continued in four feature films, piles of video games, and a library of novels. So many *Star Treks*, so many formats—aren't they all the same after a while? The wisdom of Guinan (Whoopi Goldberg), *Enterprise-D*'s bartender and sage, may be appropriate to the matter:

"Some may argue that a diamond is still a diamond, even if it is one amongst millions. It still shines as brightly."

### *Star Trek: Voyager* (1995–2001, 172 episodes, USA)

*Based on:* The TV series *Star Trek* created by Gene Roddenberry
*Created by:* Rick Berman, Michael Piller, Jeri Taylor
*Production Co.:* Paramount Television, United Paramount Network (UPN)
*Originally Aired:* UPN
*Main Cast:* Kate Mulgrew, Robert Beltran, Roxann Dawson, Jennifer Lien, Robert Duncan McNeill, Ethan Phillips, Robert Picardo, Tim Russ, Jeri Ryan, Garrett Wang

In this fourth live-action entry in *Star Trek*'s TV franchise, and the first with a female captain as lead character, Kate Mulgrew portrays **Kathryn Janeway**, commanding officer of USS *Voyager*, a small Federation vessel. As the series opens, *Voyager* is chasing a ship of rebels known as the Maquis, when a freak plasma storm interrupts pursuit, stranding *Voyager* about 75 years' travel from home and destroying the Maquis ship. Janeway forges an alliance with the Maquis leader, Chakotay (Robert Beltran), once of Starfleet, and merges his crew with hers after experiencing heavy losses on *Voyager*.

B'Elanna Torres (Roxann Dawson), also of the Maquis ship, takes a position in engineering, later becoming Chief Engineer. Torres is half-human and half–Klingon, possessing some of the combative instincts of her Klingon forbears, a moody disposition, and difficulty in expressing her feelings. In "Day of Honor" (1997), Torres finally tells shipmate Tom Paris (Robert Duncan McNeill) she loves him, but only when their deaths appear imminent while stranded in space. *Voyager* arrives in the nick of time (naturally) to save the couple, and Torres later marries Paris, giving birth to a daughter.

Sometimes Janeway works with traditional enemies of the Federation to fight a greater threat, as in "Scorpion" (parts one and two, 1997), when she collaborates with the Borg, cybernetic organisms linked together in a hive mind. In the course of the operation, Seven of Nine (Jeri Ryan), a human assimilated by the Borg 20 years earlier, is rescued by the crew, even if Seven doesn't see it as a rescue at the time. She has difficulty adjusting to human ways, and tries to return to the Borg in "The Raven" (1997). Seven initially wears a skin-tight, silver bodysuit, emphasizing her human beauty and sex appeal, a sharp contrast to her impassive face and monotone voice, relics of her cybernetic past.

*Voyager* returns home after 23 years in series finale "Endgame" (parts one and two, 2001), but Janeway, then an admiral, isn't happy about the deaths and suffering caused by the long journey home. In true *Star Trek* fashion, she goes back in time to fix it, meeting her younger self and taking out the Borg Queen (Alice Krige), while sacrificing her older self in the process. Shaving 16 years off the trip the second time around, Janeway ends the series as she began it...

"Set a course ... for home."

See also: **Janeway, Kathryn (*Star Trek: Voyager*)**

## *Star-Crossed* (2014, 13 episodes, USA)

*Created by:* Meredith Averill
*Production Co.:* Space Floor Television, Olé Productions, CBS Television Studios
*Originally Aired:* The CW
*Main Cast:* Aimee Teegarden, Matt Lanter, Grey Damon, Malese Jow, Titus Makin, Jr., Natalie Hall, Chelsea Gilligan, Greg Finley, Brina Palencia

This short-lived series takes the term "star-crossed lovers" more literally than Shakespeare did, as the Juliet of the piece is human, while the Romeo is from another planet. Emery Whitehill (Aimee Teegarden) returns to school after a four-year, health-related absence on the same day that seven students from the planet Atria will become her classmates. Emery meets Roman (Matt Lanter), a 16-year-old Atrian student, and there's an immediate attraction, fueled by a chance encounter 10 years earlier, when Emery had protected Roman from alien-hunting authorities. The Atrians are no longer outlaws, but they are segregated and heavily guarded in an area known as The Sector. Although Roman's alien heritage would probably be enough to seal their fate as forbidden lovers, Emery's father accidentally kills Roman's father, adding an extraterrestrial Montagues and Capulets dimension.

Emery and Roman have friends, both human and Atrian, including Julia Yeung (Malese Jow), who has a terminal illness, and Taylor Beecham (Natalie Hall), the requisite popular girl. Throw in terrorist groups, love triangles, teen pregnancy, and Shakespearean episode titles ("These Violent Delights Have Violent Ends"), and you have *Star-Crossed*, a star-crossed SF/romance that couldn't find an audience.

## Stargate SG-1 (1997–2007, 214 episodes, Canada/USA)

*Based on:* The film *Stargate* directed by Roland Emmerich
*Created by:* Brad Wright, Jonathan Glassner
*Production Co.:* Double Secret Productions, Gekko Film Corp., et al.
*Originally Aired:* Showtime (1997–2002), Syfy (2002–2007)
*Main Cast:* Richard Dean Anderson, Michael Shanks, Amanda Tapping, Christopher Judge, Don S. Davis, Gary Jones, Teryl Rothery, Dan Shea, Claudia Black, Morena Baccarin

What if you could open a door, walk through it, and step out onto another planet? That's the premise of this series, which follows the events of the 1994 theatrical film *Stargate*, starring Kurt Russell and James Spader. Richard Dean Anderson takes over Russell's role as Colonel Jack O'Neill, called back to active duty when the alien Goa'uld use an interplanetary portal known as a "Stargate" to enter a secret military installation in Colorado. O'Neill investigates the incursion, leading a team through the Stargate to Abydos, a planet where his associate Dr. Daniel Jackson (Michael Shanks) resides, having married a local woman. Jackson has discovered that the Stargates are part of a vast interplanetary network. When his wife is kidnapped by the Goa'uld and their nasty leader Apophis, Jackson hopes to use the Stargate system to find her.

The Stargate program ramps up again, this time to search for advanced alien technology that might be used to defend Earth against the Goa'uld. O'Neill takes charge of the first Air Force special ops team, SG-1, which includes Dr. Jackson, Teal'c (Christopher Judge), an alien who had defected from service to Apophis, and **Samantha Carter** (Amanda Tapping), an Air Force Captain and theoretical astrophysicist. Carter, a brilliant scientist and compassionate soldier, appears in all ten seasons of *SG-1*, and is a prominent presence in the spin-off series *Stargate Atlantis*.

General George Hammond (Don S. Davis) sends SG-1 on its missions to explore the Milky Way and Pegasus galaxies, while Dr. Janet Fraiser (Teryl Rothery), Chief Medical Officer of Stargate Command (SGC), patches everyone up on their return. Fraiser serves for seven years and dies off-world while saving an airman on the field of battle in "Heroes" (parts one and two, 2004). At her memorial service, Carter reads the names of those still alive today thanks to Fraiser's acumen, including Carter herself, O'Neill, Jackson, and Teal'c.

Vala Mal Doran (Claudia Black), a sassy con artist and thief, joins the team late in the series, assisting SGC after she gives birth to the new leader of another threatening race called the Ori. Events move quickly, culminating in a final confrontation with her daughter, Adria (Morena Baccarin), who had grown to adulthood in a mere few days. In the end, they are sealed together inside an infirmary, and Adria ascends to a higher plane of existence in "Dominion" (2007).

While never a critical darling, *SG-1* was a ratings winner for Showtime and later Syfy (Sci-Fi at the time). The series also gained a sizable international following, especially in the UK and Australia. Interest in the Stargate mythos was high enough to sustain the series for 10 seasons and to spur production of two spin-offs, *Stargate*

*Atlantis* and *Stargate Universe*. Novels, comics, games, action figures, and amusement rides fed the fan appetite for ever more *Stargate* and demonstrated that not all television space travel needs to occur on a starship.

See also: **Carter, Samantha (*Stargate SG-1*)**

## *The Starlost* (1973–1974, 16 episodes, Canada)

*Created by:* Harlan Ellison (as Cordwainer Bird)
*Production Co.:* 20th Century–Fox Television, CTV Television Network, Glen Warren Productions
*Originally Aired:* In Syndication
*Main Cast:* Keir Dullea, Gay Rowan, Robin Ward

Short-lived science fiction series with lots of backstory, both on and off the screen.

A generation ship called Earthship Ark launched when our planet faced a cataclysmic event in the 23rd century. The ship later faced its own cataclysmic event, which killed the pilots and sent the Ark on a deadly trajectory toward a distant star. After 500 years, the inhabitants have lost the knowledge that they're on a spaceship, aware only of their local communities, which are actually biospheres, now sealed off from each other.

Enter Devon (Keir Dullea), a member of the agrarian community/biosphere called Cyprus Corners. Devon is an independent thinker who questions authority and tradition, especially when they appear to be leading to the arranged marriage of his love Rachel (Gay Rowan) to another man, Garth (Robin Ward). During the course of his mini-rebellion, Devon discovers the secrets of the ship and asks Rachel to run away with him. Garth follows, and their love triangle turns into a salvation brigade, as they search for the backup bridge to the ship and someone to pilot it. Their adventures take them to various biospheres, such as one populated only by men, who worship a deity resembling Rachel in "The Goddess Calabra" (1973).

Off screen, production problems led creator Harlan Ellison to end his association with the series and change his credit to "Cordwainer Bird," his protest byline. It was an omen of bad things to come for a series now known mostly for said production problems and its place on many "worst of" SF television lists.

Starlost, indeed.

## **Starr, Krista** (*Blade: The Series*)

Iraqi war veteran looking for revenge against the vampire who killed her brother.
See: ***Blade: The Series*** (2006, 13 episodes, USA)

## **Stephens, Samantha** (*Bewitched*)

Samantha Stephens is a witch! Her mortal husband, Darrin Stephens (Dick York and later Dick Sargent), learns this fact on their wedding night, but Samantha (Elizabeth Montgomery) promises to become a model suburban wife in true early–60s, pre-women's liberation style—no witchcraft allowed. That promise doesn't last long, however, when Sam uses her powers to get revenge against a haughty ex-girlfriend of Darrin's in "I, Darrin, Take This Witch, Samantha" (1964), the pilot episode for the series.

Like others of her kind, Samantha ages slowly over the centuries. Her strong-willed mother Endora (Agnes Morehead), who doesn't approve of the marriage, taunts Darrin with an antique portrait of Samantha from 1690 Salem in "Eye of the Beholder"(1965). Samantha deals with the constant tug-of-war between Darrin and Endora, each trying to keep Samantha firmly rooted in their world, and neither willing to admit that Samantha is part of both worlds. In "Be It Ever So Mortgaged" (1964), Endora explains why domestic bliss isn't right for a witch like Samantha. "Our home has no boundaries beyond which we cannot pass. We live in music, in a flash of color. We live on the wind, in the sparkle of a star."

The link between the supernatural and mortal realms is more firmly established when Samantha and Darrin receive a little bundle of joy, a baby witch named Tabitha (Erin Murphy), in "And Then There Were Three" (1966). Despite the good news, the battle for Sam's loyalty rages on, and the unnatural withholding of her witchcraft causes problems, as in "Okay, Who's the Wise Witch?" (1970), when a supernatural vapor lock traps the family inside the Stephens home. Samantha must also try to control Tabitha's witchcraft for Darrin's sake, as in "TV or Not TV" (1971), when Tabitha zaps herself into the TV puppet show "Punch and Judy" to take a stand for "women's lib" and nonviolence. (Go, Tabitha!) The mother-and-daughter witches make another progressive statement, this time against racism, in "Sisters at Heart" (1970), based on a story written by an inner-city, 10th grade English class and reportedly Montgomery's favorite.

It was always hard to see what beautiful, gifted Samantha saw in that awkward, wet blanket Darrin, but as sitcom premises go, it was magic.

See also: ***Bewitched* (1964–1972, 254 episodes, USA)**

### Stephens, Tabitha (*Bewitched*)

Daughter of a witch, who takes after her mother's side of the family to the consternation of her mortal father.

See: ***Bewitched* (1964–1972, 254 episodes, USA)**

### Stephens, Tabitha (*Tabitha*)

Twenty-something witch, working at a television station in Los Angeles.

See: ***Tabitha* (1977–1978, 12 episodes, USA)**

### *Stitchers* (2015– , 21 episodes, USA)

*Created by:* Jeffrey Alan Schechter
*Production Co.:* StoryBy Productions, Like The Wind Productions, Freeform Original Productions, ProdCo, et al.
*Originally Aired:* Freeform
*Main Cast:* Emma Ishta, Kyle Harris, Ritesh Rajan, Salli Richardson-Whitfield, Allison Scagliotti, Damon Dayoub

Kirsten Clark (Emma Ishta) is a grad student in computer science at Caltech.

That's exceptional, but even more unusual is the fact that she is unable to perceive the passage of time, an affliction known as temporal dysplasia. But, good news—Kirsten's condition makes her an ideal candidate for the top-secret "Stitchers" program, which inserts ("stitches") an agent's consciousness into the mind of a recently dead person to solve crimes. (Handy!) While investigating the suicide of her father, Kirsten is recruited into Stitchers by Maggie Baptiste (Salli Richardson-Whitfield), a former CIA assassin. (You can't have a covert program without one of those.) Soon Kirsten is stitching away, with the help of Cameron Goodkin (Kyle Harris), a brilliant neuroscientist, Linus Ahluwalia (Ritesh Rajan), a bioelectrical engineer, and Camille Engelson (Allison Scagliotti), Kirsten's roommate and fellow grad student. Camille had initially betrayed Kirsten for 30 pieces of silver (or the modern equivalent in tuition and housing from Stitchers), but Kirsten soon discovers her secret, and the two learn to work together on the team.

Secrets, of course, are a big part of shows about covert agencies, and *Stitchers* has plenty, even family secrets, involving Kirsten's foster father, biological father, and mother, all of whom have a connection to the Stitchers program.

As Linus would say, "Stitch happens."

### Stoddard, Elizabeth Collins (*Dark Shadows*)
Matriarch of a wealthy family cursed by supernatural afflictions.
See: *Dark Shadows* (1966–1971, 1225 episodes, USA)

### Strauss, Tracy (*Heroes*)
Political adviser who runs into trouble when she discovers the ability to freeze whatever she touches.
See: *Heroes* (2006–2010, 77 episodes, USA)

### Summers, Buffy (*Buffy the Vampire Slayer*)
Despite her lighter-than-air name, Buffy Summers is one of the greatest SF/fantasy characters ever to grace the small screen. In another era, petite, blonde Buffy would have been the stereotypical victim in a horror movie, but as portrayed by Sarah Michelle Gellar starting in 1997, Buffy became a modern horror savior, turning an out-of-date trope on its ear. More than that, the character of Buffy and her story examined the deep and sometimes terrifying issues of young adulthood, transcending the "monster of the week" subgenre to become something rich and meaningful.

As the series begins, Buffy arrives in Sunnydale, CA to start her sophomore year in high school. Buffy has a secret, though—she is the "Slayer," a girl endowed with special powers by fate to battle vampires, demons, and other supernatural horrors. While that sounds like kick-ass stuff, and it is, thanks to Gellar's martial arts training, creator Joss Whedon's "high school as hell" concept kept the action in its place, never forgetting that people and even demons might have feelings. In "Out of Mind, Out of Sight" (1997), Buffy discovers that attacks by an invisible force at school are coming from a classmate who was so figuratively invisible to teachers and students that her body literally disappeared.

Buffy eventually moves on to college, but has to drop out of school to take care of her sister, Dawn (Michelle Trachtenberg), in "Tough Love" (2001). The Slayer's life gets increasingly dark and complicated thereafter, when she sacrifices herself to save Dawn and the world in "The Gift" (2001), but later rises from the dead in "Bargaining" (parts one and two, 2001), thanks to a magic spell performed by her friend Willow Rosenberg (Alyson Hannigan). Buffy and all the members of her informal army, the "Scooby Gang," experience the devastating loss of loved ones, belying the lighthearted fun that their name suggests. All is not darkness, however, as the series finale, "Chosen" (2003), suggests that Buffy's unique burden will be lighter going forward.

By the light of the silvery moon Buffy Summers (Sarah Michelle Gellar) fights the forces of darkness on *Buffy the Vampire Slayer* (WB/Photofest).

Sarah Michelle Gellar won a 1999 Saturn Award in the Best Actress category for her portrayal of Buffy Summers. Buffy frequently appears on "greatest TV characters" lists, and is the subject, along with her show, of an informal academic discipline known as "Buffy Studies."

Her youth, fluffy name, and delicate looks notwithstanding, Buffy was completely convincing as the most powerful and important woman in the world, making her a truly groundbreaking character in television history.

See also: *Buffy the Vampire Slayer* (1997–2003, 144 episodes, USA)

## Sun, Aeryn (*Farscape*)

Emotionless military officer who warms up to her alien crewmates aboard a biomechanical ship.

See: *Farscape* (1999–2003, 88 episodes, Australia/USA)

## Superboy (1988–1992, 100 episodes, USA)

*Based on:* The DC Comics character Superman created by Jerry Siegel, Joe Shuster
*Production Co.:* Cantharus Productions, Lowry Productions
*Originally Aired:* In Syndication
*Main Cast:* John Haymes Newton, Gerard Christopher, Stacy Haiduk, Peter Jay Fernandez, Robert Levine, Zevi Wolmark, Jim Calvert, Sherman Howard, Scott Wells

*Superboy* chronicles the adventures of the Man of Steel when he was a boy, or, more correctly, a young man, but *Superyoungman* doesn't have the same ring to it. John Haymes Newton portrays Clark Kent, a journalism student at Shuster University who also writes for the college newspaper. Not much noteworthy there, but Kent is also Superboy, who can leap tall buildings in a single bound and is impervious to all weapons (except kryptonite). Clark attends college with T.J. White (Jim Calvert), nephew of Kent's future boss Perry White, and Lex Luthor (Scott Wells), who will go on to become Superboy's bitter and bald nemesis after a lab explosion at school.

The second season brought cast changes, including a new Superboy (Gerard Christopher), but the one constant throughout the show's four seasons is Stacy Haiduk as Lana Lang, Clark's high-school girlfriend and classmate at Shuster. Lana is a frequent hostage/kidnap victim, all the better to be saved by Superboy, as in "The Invisible People" (1989), when she runs afoul of a club owner trying to clear his beach of a homeless group. Lana is more independent and less the damsel in distress in the last two seasons of the series, after she and Clark join the Bureau for Extra-Normal Matters, a government group which investigates strange occurrences and extraterrestrial creatures (pre–*X-Files*). In "Know Thine Enemy: Part 2" (1991), Lana turns the tables, rescuing Superboy from a virtual reality program where Lex Luthor has trapped him. Lana begins to fall in love with Superboy, unaware that he is Clark, causing literal nightmares for the Boy of Steel in "Mindscape" (1990).

*Superboy* endured more changes, including a new title, *The Adventures of Superboy*, cast departures, and a legal dispute with Warner Bros., which ended the series before it's time.

Definitely not Super.

## *Supergirl* (2015– , 20 episodes, USA)

*Based on:* The DC Comics character created by Otto Binder, Al Plastino
*Created by:* Greg Berlanti, Ali Adler, Andrew Kreisberg
*Production Co.:* Berlanti Productions, DC Entertainment, Warner Bros. Television
*Originally Aired:* CBS (2015–2016), The CW (2016– )
*Main Cast:* Melissa Benoist, Mehcad Brooks, Chyler Leigh, Jeremy Jordan, David Harewood, Calista Flockhart

Everyone knows the story of Superman, sent to Earth from the doomed planet Krypton by his loving parents just before their world exploded. Fewer know the story of his cousin, Supergirl, who shares a similar backstory, but has traditionally suffered in the PR department. This series rectifies that oversight.

Supergirl, born Kara Zor-El and now known as Kara Danvers (Melissa Benoist), works as a mild-mannered assistant for condescending media magnate Cat Grant (Calista Flockhart). Kara does not embrace her "super" side the way her cousin does, but an airplane emergency forces her to reveal her powers, if not her true identity, to the citizens of National City. Grant christens the new hero "Supergirl," recognizing the story of the decade when she sees it and hoping for a scoop as to Supergirl's who/what/when. Kara's adoptive sister Alex Danvers (Chyler Leigh) isn't as thrilled at this super-development, even though her own life was saved on the almost doomed flight. Eventually Kara/Supergirl joins Alex at the Department of Extra-Normal Operations (DEO), which searches for suspicious extraterrestrial activity on Earth, a seeming hotbed of former Kryptonian criminals, including Kara's aunt Astra In-Ze (Laura Benanti), her mother's evil twin. Said suspicious extraterrestrial activity even extends to Kara's boss at the DEO, Hank Henshaw (David Harewood), who turns out to be a shape-shifting Martian, but a NICE one.

Since Kara is sweet and pretty and SUPERGIRL, she does attract some hunky male attention. James Olsen (Mehcad Brooks), the art director at CatCo Worldwide Media, is keeping an eye on Kara for Superman, and apparently likes what he sees, but there are complications with his former fiancée. Winn Schott (Jeremy Jordan), CatCo's tech guru, becomes Kara's confidant and wants to be more, although he notices how Kara lights up when James is around.

Kara juggles a full-time job with a demanding, snarky boss, not to mention her self-appointed gig as protector of National City, and, of course, her love triangle with James and Winn.

She truly is a Supergirl.

### Swan, Emma (*Once Upon a Time*)

Emma Swan (Jennifer Morrison) is a bail bond agent who grew up in foster care and spent some time in prison. While that doesn't sound like the traditional backstory of a fairytale character, Emma is actually the daughter of Snow White (Ginnifer Goodwin) and Prince Charming (Josh Dallas), who have been stripped of their memories and trapped in the modern world by the Evil Queen, Regina (Lana Parrilla).

Emma is no shrinking violet. She confronts a fire-breathing dragon to save her son's life, but slaying the dragon isn't the magic that Henry (Jared S. Gilmore) needs. Emma brings him back from the dead with "true love's kiss," which also reverses the Queen's curse, restoring the memories of Snow, Charming, and all the people of Storybrooke, Maine.

The happy ending is short-lived, however, as Emma and Snow are sucked into a portal to the Enchanted Forest, while trying to protect Regina for Henry's sake, since she is his adoptive mother. Further curses ensue, and for a time Emma even takes "The Darkness" into herself to keep it from destroying the world.

Emma's tough girl turned savior was a feminist breath of fresh air for the fairy tale genre. Although she had spent most of her life relying only on herself, she led the charge when required, sacrificed to save others, and became an instant mother when the son she gave up for adoption needed her.

All, of course, in a leather jacket. No ball gowns allowed.

See also: *Once Upon a Time* (2011– , 111 episodes, USA)

### Szalinski, Diane and Amy (*Honey, I Shrunk the Kids*)

Wife and daughter of a wacky inventor, who sometimes use his unpredictable creations for their own purposes.

See: *Honey, I Shrunk the Kids* (1997–2000, 66 episodes, USA)

## *Tabitha* (1977–1978, 12 episodes, USA)
*Based on:* Characters from the TV series *Bewitched*
*Created by:* Jerry Mayer
*Production Co.:* Columbia Pictures Television
*Originally Aired:* ABC
*Main Cast:* Lisa Hartman, David Ankrum, Robert Urich, Mel Stewart, Karen Morrow

Spin-off from the long-running series *Bewitched* that was unable to capitalize on its predecessor's immense popularity. Lisa Hartman stars as Tabitha Stephens, a 20-something witch, and daughter of Samantha from the earlier series. Tabitha works as a production assistant at a Los Angeles television station alongside her brother Adam (David Ankrum), who is mortal, and without magical powers just like their father Darrin. Adam tries to keep Tabitha from using witchcraft, much as Darrin had tried to restrain Samantha in *Bewitched*. Pulling Tabitha in the supernatural direction, however, is Aunt Minerva (Karen Morrow), who encourages Tabitha's use of magic and stands in for *Bewitched*'s Endora as the interloping mother-figure. Rounding out the cast are Robert Urich as Paul Thurston, an egotistical TV host and sometimes love interest for Tabitha, and Mel Stewart as Marvin Decker, her irascible boss.

Except for the witchy/twitchy action, *Tabitha* was a lot like another earlier series, *Mary Tyler Moore*, with its TV station setting, single woman in a traditionally man's world, self-centered TV personality, etc. But all of that made it less like *Bewitched*, to the consternation of the parent show's fans, especially with so many changes to the characters, such as fast-forwarding Tabitha's age and taking away Adam's warlock powers in favor of mortality.

No matter what they did, however, Elizabeth Montgomery's Samantha was always going to be a hard act to follow.

## Tam, River (*Firefly*)
Escapee from a sinister program whose experiments have left her with emotional problems and special abilities.
See: ***Firefly*** **(2002, 14 episodes, USA)**

## Tanner, Kate and Lynn (*ALF*)
Suburban mother and daughter whose family's domestic bliss is shattered by a furry, sarcastic extraterrestrial.
See: ***ALF*** **(1986–1990, 102 episodes, USA)**

## Ta'Ra (*Something Is Out There*)
Extraterrestrial M.D. who helps a cop with his weird cases while searching for a way back to her world.
See: ***Something Is Out There*** **(1988, 8 episodes, USA)**

## *TekWar* (1994–1996, 18 episodes, Canada/USA)
*Based on:* The *TekWar* novels by William Shatner
*Created by:* Stephen Roloff
*Production Co.:* Atlantis Films Ltd., USA Network, Universal Television, et al.

*Originally Aired:* USA Network
*Main Cast:* Greg Evigan, Eugene Clark, William Shatner, Natalie Radford, Maria del Mar, Maurice Dean Wint, Torri Higginson, Dana Brooks, Lexa Doig, Ernie Grunwald

William Shatner, an actor who likes to keep busy, wrote the novel *TekWar* (with ghostwriting help from Ron Goulart) in 1989. The novel went on to become a franchise, with eight more books, a comic book series, four TV movies, and this one-season TV series.

It's 2045, and "Tek" is all the rage, a highly addictive "drug," which in reality is virtual reality, an interface which can make your fantasies come true if it doesn't burn out your brain in the process. Enter Jake Cardigan (Greg Evigan), a disgraced former cop, now an investigator working for Cosmos, a private security firm owned by wealthy and mysterious Walter Bascom (William Shatner). Bascom, for reasons that are not entirely clear, wants Jake to pursue the "Tek lords," bad guys who make a lucrative business out of selling the stuff around the world. Tek/tech troubles require tech solutions, and Bascom's platinum-blonde assistant Nika (Natalie Radford), provides cyber-support via her superior hacking skills at Cosmos. When Nika is off limits or in trouble, as in "Cyberhunt" (1995), Jake turns to freelance hackers, including "Cowgirl" (Lexa Doig), a cyberpunk queen with braids, glove, and headset, who penetrates computer networks with a wave of her hand, while pretty virtual screens swirl around her. On the actual rather than virtual streets, Jake works with Sid Gomez (Eugene Clark) and later Sam Houston (Maria del Mar), a former police lieutenant, who is now Jake's partner at Cosmos. In "Deep Cover" (1995), Sam takes the "deep" in deep cover seriously, when a mind-sculpting technique sublimates her real personality so she can infiltrate a crime family.

*TekWar*'s premiere had a high viewership (by cable TV standards), but its ratings tanked over time, leading to cancellation after 14 episodes had aired. The series still lives on DVD and maybe, just maybe, on a Tek headset somewhere.

### *Terminator: The Sarah Connor Chronicles* (2008–2009, 31 episodes, USA)

*Based on:* The film *The Terminator* directed by James Cameron
*Created by:* Josh Friedman
*Production Co.:* Sarah Connor Pictures, Bartleby Company, Warner Bros. Television, et al.
*Originally Aired:* Fox
*Main Cast:* Lena Headey, Thomas Dekker, Summer Glau, Brian Austin Green, Richard T. Jones, Garret Dillahunt, Shirley Manson

"In the future, my son will lead mankind in a war against Skynet, the computer system programmed to destroy the world. It has sent machines back through time, some to kill him, one to protect him."

In 1984, a low-budget film called *The Terminator* was released to critical acclaim and big box-office, both wildly exceeding expectations. In the movie, a young woman named Sarah Connor (Linda Hamilton) learns that she will give birth to a son who will one day lead the resistance against an artificial intelligence out to kill every human on earth. Hamilton reprised her role as Sarah in the 1991 blockbuster sequel

*Terminator 2: Judgment Day* (*T2*), which ends as the bleak, machine-ruled future appears to have been averted.

*Terminator: The Sarah Connor Chronicles* (*TSCC*) picks up after the events of *T2*, when (surprise, surprise!) the dystopian future is shown not to have been averted, but merely delayed. Lena Headey now portrays **Sarah Connor**, a woman who walks the impossible line between being mother and military commander to her teenaged son, the future savior, John Connor (Thomas Dekker). When a "Terminator," who looks something like the one from the movies (but turns out to be Owain Yeoman rather than Arnold Schwarzenegger), shows up to kill John, future John once again sends his younger self a protector, Cameron (Summer Glau), a Terminator who has been reprogrammed to defend him. In the course of making their escape, Sarah, John, and Cameron jump forward in time to 2007, where they focus their efforts on preventing Skynet from being built.

Many of the episodes in *TSCC* deal with the question of what it means to be human. For Sarah, John, and John's uncle, Derek Reese (Brian Austin Green), the issue is often how much of their humanity they are willing to sacrifice for their own safety and the future of the world. For Cameron, it is the continual challenge of understanding human behavior, a need which seems to go beyond her programming as efficient bodyguard.

For a show about metal, *TSCC* has a lot of heart.

See also: **Connor, Sarah** (*Terminator: The Sarah Connor Chronicles*)

## Tess (*Touched by an Angel*)

Sassy, supervisory angel who travels from town to town in an Eldorado convertible.

See: *Touched by an Angel* (1994–2003, 212 episodes, USA)

## That's So Raven (2003–2007, 100 episodes, USA)

*Created by:* Michael Poryes, Susan Sherman
*Production Co.:* Disney Channel, Brookwell McNamara Entertainment, et al.
*Originally Aired:* Disney Channel
*Main Cast:* Raven-Symoné, Orlando Brown, Kyle Massey, Anneliese van der Pol, T'Keyah Crystal Keymáh, Rondell Sheridan, Anne-Marie Johnson

Raven Baxter (Raven-Symoné, credited simply as "Raven") is a teenager with a BIG personality, made even BIGGER by the fact that she has psychic visions. Scripted television's psychics tend to be an inconsistent lot, and Raven is no exception, usually misinterpreting the snippets of future events she sees, thereby causing problems for her family and friends. Raven loves fashion design, an interest which comes in handy when she disguises herself on outlandish escapades. In "Mother Dearest" (2003), she impersonates her mother, Tanya Baxter (T'Keyah Crystal Keymáh), at a parent-teacher conference to cover up for questionable behavior at school. She cares for her friends, including Chelsea Daniels (Anneliese van der Pol), but sometimes helps too much, as in "Campaign in the Neck" (2003), when Raven has a vision that Chelsea will lose her student election.

In later years, Raven accepts an internship with superstar designer Donna Cabonna (Anne-Marie Johnson), and runs afoul of Donna's personal assistant, Tiffany (Jodi Shilling). When the psychic teen has a vision that she's going to get her own glamorous, executive-style office, her cloudy clairvoyance leads to embarrassment in front of her entire class in "Dues and Don'ts" (2006).

Raven-Symoné won five NAACP Image Awards for her exuberant portrayal of sassy psychic Raven Baxter. Her show, in typical Disney Channel fashion, generated lots of tie-in merchandise, including video games, soundtrack albums, and a whopping 20 novels.

"Oh, snap!" That's what Raven would say.

### Thelen, Annie (*So Weird*)

Teen musician protected from supernatural forces by a panther spirit guide.
See: *So Weird* (1999–2001, 65 episodes, Canada/USA)

### Theroux, Nina (*Alphas*)

Defense Department consultant with the enhanced ability to "push" people into doing her bidding.
See: *Alphas* (2011–2012, 24 episodes, USA)

### 3rd Rock from the Sun (1996–2001, 139 episodes, USA)

*Created by:* Bonnie Turner, Terry Turner
*Production Co.:* The Carsey-Werner Company, YBYL Productions
*Originally Aired:* NBC
*Main Cast:* John Lithgow, Kristen Johnston, French Stewart, Joseph Gordon-Levitt, Jane Curtin, Simbi Khali, Elmarie Wendel, Wayne Knight

The Solomons appear to be a normal American family living in Rutherford, Ohio, but appearances can be deceiving. In actuality, the "Solomons" are extraterrestrial researchers who have taken human form to study the behavior of Earth natives. The group is led by the High Commander, who morphs into a middle-aged man named Dick Solomon (John Lithgow), patriarch of the family, but actually the youngest and most immature of the aliens. Second in command is the security officer, now known as **Sally Solomon** (Kristen Johnston), a blonde Amazon who doesn't enjoy being a girl. The expedition's information officer, the oldest and smartest of the visitors, has taken on the challenging role of a teenager, Tommy Solomon (Joseph Gordon-Levitt). Finally, serving as the group's transmitter for instructions from home is Harry Solomon (French Stewart), who poses as Tommy's uncle, and is the craziest of this decidedly wacky bunch.

The Solomons try to blend in with the locals by pursuing traditional human occupations and interests, but often end up sticking out like a sore thumb. Dick works as a physics professor at Pendleton State University, where he shares an office with Dr. Mary Albright (Jane Curtin), a professor of anthropology. Dick gets a crush on Mary, which she eventually reciprocates despite his boorish ways, leading to many ups and downs on the relationship roller coaster. Human relationships, in fact, are a continual source of confusion for the aliens, as when statuesque Sally takes up with portly police officer Don Orville (Wayne Knight), attracted to the power of his uniform and blinded to his cowardice and professional incompetence.

The aliens pursue their comic antics for six years before beaming back home, taking with them profound insights into the human condition and a galaxy full of Emmy Awards.

See also: **Solomon, Sally** (*3rd Rock from the Sun*)

## Thomas, Andrea (*Isis*)

High school science teacher who can transform herself into the goddess Isis via an Egyptian amulet.

See: *Isis* (**1975–1976, 22 episodes, USA**)

## Thorsen, Jojo (*Space Rangers*)

Slingship pilot and Space Ranger who hails from the women-only planet of New Venus.

See: *Space Rangers* (**1993, 6 episodes, USA**)

## Thrace, Kara "Starbuck" (*Battlestar Galactica*)

Ace fighter pilot and occasional troublemaker in a fleet of war survivors searching for Earth.

See: *Battlestar Galactica* (**2004–2009, 75 episodes, USA**)

## *Three Moons Over Milford* (2006, 8 episodes, USA)

*Created by:* Howard Chesley, Jon Boorstin
*Production Co.:* Three Moons Film, Touchstone Television
*Originally Aired:* ABC Family
*Main Cast:* Elizabeth McGovern, Sam Murphy, Teresa Celentano, Nora Dunn, Samantha Quan, Rob Boltin, Donavon Stinson

What would you do if the moon broke into three pieces, threatening to plummet at any moment, ending life as we know it? That question is explored in this series through the eyes of the Davis family, a seemingly normal Vermont household—normal, that is, until suddenly three moons appear over Milford. Mom Laura Davis (Elizabeth McGovern) must hold the family unit together after husband Carl (Henry Czerny) absconds with some of his company's money, leaving her and the kids in the poor house. Daughter Lydia (Teresa Celentano) thinks the best plan is to save the world through a Wiccan ritual, which doesn't save the world, but accidentally burns down her high school. Son Alex (Sam Murphy), a 16-year-old math prodigy, finds comfort in the arms of a woman almost twice his age, Claire Ling (Samantha Quan), a computer analyst who becomes the family's next-door neighbor.

You get the idea—everyone is living as if it's the end of days, except for real estate agent Michelle Graybar (Nora Dunn), who is snapping up property around town just in case the moons DON'T fall.

The end of days did come, and quickly, for this quirky series, thanks to the cosmic catastrophe known as low ratings.

## *Threshold* (2005–2006, 13 episodes, UK/USA)
*Created by:* Bragi F. Schut
*Production Co.:* Braga Productions, Heyday Films, Phantom Four Films, Paramount Television, Sky Television
*Originally Aired:* CBS
*Main Cast:* Carla Gugino, Brian Van Holt, Brent Spiner, Rob Benedict, Peter Dinklage, Charles S. Dutton

"My name is Molly Caffrey, and I work for the Federal Government. I deal in worst-case scenarios, the unthinkable. On September 16th, 2005, the unthinkable happened...."

Short-lived science fiction series starring Carla Gugino as Dr. Molly Anne Caffrey, a contingency analyst who has developed response plans for catastrophes ranging from nuclear war to alien invasion. It's her latter plan, code-named Threshold, that the U.S. government activates when an extraterrestrial object attacks a U.S. Navy vessel by releasing a high-frequency signal. Deaths ensue, DNA changes, fractals appear, and people have linked dreams of "trees made of glass." Molly and the usual motley crew, including Dr. Nigel Fenway (Brent Spiner), a cynical microbiologist, and Arthur Ramsey (Peter Dinklage), a dissolute mathematician/linguist, fight the alien onslaught, while Molly herself suffers from hallucinations due to brief exposure to the alien signal.

This series had some off-key potential, but didn't find an audience fast enough for CBS, which stopped transmitting it on any frequency after nine of its 13 episodes had run.

## Thunderman, Phoebe (*The Thundermans*)
Honors student with special abilities who tries to lead a normal life along with her superhero family.

See: ***The Thundermans*** (2013– , 68 episodes, USA)

## *The Thundermans* (2013– , 68 episodes, USA)
*Created by:* Jed Spingarn
*Production Co.:* Nickelodeon Productions, et al.
*Originally Aired:* Nickelodeon
*Main Cast:* Kira Kosarin, Jack Griffo, Addison Riecke, Diego Velazquez, Chris Tallman, Rosa Blasi, Maya Le Clark

Phoebe Thunderman (Kira Kosarin) is a 14-year-old honors student whose parents move her and her siblings to Hiddenville, which sounds like a good place to hide your secrets. The entire family possesses superpowers, and Phoebe is no exception, exhibiting telekinesis as well as the ability to freeze and burn with her breath. (Ouch!) Since double trouble is better than just plain trouble in sitcomville, Phoebe has a twin, Max Thunderman (Jack Griffo), who has the same superpowers as she does, but wants to use them for evil (albeit family-friendly evil).

Although parents Hank (Chris Tallman) and Barb (Rosa Blasi) want the kids to have a normal childhood, Phoebe isn't the best at keeping secrets, as in "Adventures in Supersitting" (2013), when she invites a "non-supe" friend to the house against parental wishes, and superpowers are revealed. Then, too, sometimes secrets announce themselves, as in "Thundersense" (2014), when Phoebe develops the ability to sense danger and becomes a hero at school.

The Thundermans tried to do Pixar's acclaimed The Incredibles (2004) one better by adding live action to the superhero family formula, but it didn't succeed, at least with the critics. Its sophomoric humor did make it a hit with juveniles, however, which was just fine by kiddie channel Nickelodeon.

### *Time Trax* (1993–1994, 44 episodes, USA)

*Created by:* Harve Bennett, Jeffrey M. Hayes, Grant Rosenberg
*Production Co.:* Gary Nardino Productions, Lorimar Television, Warner Bros. Television
*Originally Aired:* PTEN
*Main Cast:* Dale Midkiff, Elizabeth Alexander, Peter Donat

"It began in the future. A scientist turning to evil, a time machine called TRAX, criminals who vanish and a lawman with a mission. He has one weapon and a computer named SELMA."

In the year 2193, Darien Lambert (Dale Midkiff), a cop who specializes in retrieving fugitives, has to take a BIG trip, one that will transport him back to 1993 in search of 100 criminals who have escaped into the past. The machine used by the outlaws, called TRAX, was invented by an evil genius, Dr. Mordecai Sahmbi (Peter Donat), who himself sets the dial for 1993 to avoid apprehension by the authorities. Lambert tracks the fugitives with the help of SELMA (Specified Encapsulated Limitless Memory Archive), a powerful computer about the size of a credit card that Lambert carries with him. SELMA (Elizabeth Alexander) has audio-only and visual modes, and in the latter appears to Lambert as a hologram, a pleasant-looking, but prim woman who wears a high collar and her hair in a bun. SELMA resembles Lambert's mother (calling Dr. Freud), whom he knows only from a single photograph he's had in his possession since his days at an orphanage. In addition to her prodigious database, SELMA can hack government computers to give Lambert needed credentials, project sounds to create diversions, and do more mundane things like making travel reservations. She and Lambert have a "personal," almost mother/son relationship, which shows that navigating the treacherous byways of the past is always easier if you have a maternal GPS as your guide.

### *The Time Tunnel* (1966–1967, 30 episodes, USA)

*Created by:* Irwin Allen
*Production Co.:* Irwin Allen Productions, Kent Productions, 20th Century–Fox Television
*Originally Aired:* ABC
*Main Cast:* James Darren, Robert Colbert, Lee Meriwether, Whit Bissell, John Zaremba

"Two American scientists are lost in the swirling maze of past and future ages, during the first experiments on America's greatest and most secret project, the Time Tunnel."

Tony Newman (James Darren) and Doug Phillips (Robert Colbert) are scientists working for Project Tic Toc in a massive complex underneath the Arizona desert. When government funding for the project is threatened, Tony tries to prove its worth by sending himself through the tunnel, and Doug follows, only to find themselves adrift "along the infinite corridors of time." Although the men are lost, they have an unerring knack for finding history's most noteworthy moments, such as the sinking of the Titanic, the attack on Pearl Harbor, and the siege at the Alamo, not to mention important future events like a mission to Mars.

Back in the underground lab, concerned scientists Dr. Ann MacGregor (Lee Meriwether) and Dr. Raymond Swain (John Zaremba), along with Lt. Gen. Heywood Kirk (Whit Bissell), monitor the control panels and do every-

Dr. Ann MacGregor (Lee Meriwether) works with two scientists (James Darren, left, and Robert Colbert), who are soon lost "along the infinite corridors of time" via *The Time Tunnel* (ABC Television).

thing in their power to bring the boys back. Ann and company are able to observe the time travelers at their current destination, as though watching them on television, and sometimes can communicate with them, occasionally sending some form of help when Tony and Doug are in danger. Even the lives of the lab team members are placed in jeopardy at times, as in "End of the World" (1966), when the link between the tunnel and the time travelers allows the gravitation of Halley's Comet to pull one of the technicians (Sam Groom) into the tunnel. Ann's quick thinking saves his life, when she uses severed power cables to jumpstart his heart after he goes into cardiac arrest.

*The Time Tunnel* is one of the most memorable series of the mid–60s, despite its one-season tenure, due to its imaginative premise and the evocative image of the swirling, surrealistic time tunnel itself.

### Tituba (*Salem*)

Seventeenth-century slave who practices witchcraft to pave the way for the devil's return to Earth.

See: *Salem* (**2014– , 26 episodes, USA**)

## Tom Corbett, Space Cadet (1950–1955, 58 episodes, USA)
Created by: Joseph Greene
Based on: The novel *Space Cadet* by Robert A. Heinlein
Production Co.: Rockhill Productions
Originally Aired: CBS (1950), ABC (1951–1952), NBC (1951, 1954–1955), DuMont (1953–1954)
Main Cast: Frankie Thomas, Al Markim, Jan Merlin, Jack Grimes, Edward Bryce, Margaret Garland, Carter Blake

"Space Academy, USA, in the world beyond tomorrow. Here the Space Cadets train for duty on distant planets...."

Tom Corbett (Frankie Thomas) is a handsome, teenage cadet at the Space Academy, training to become a member of the Solar Guard, which protects "the liberties of the planets." Tom studies alongside Roger Manning (Jan Merlin), an egotistical wiseguy, and Astro (Al Markim), an introvert who was born on the planet Venus. Dr. Joan Dale (Margaret Garland and later Pat Ferris), a professor at the Academy, serves as a mother figure for the boys, but also contributes brilliant technological innovations to the Solar Guard, such as a pre–*Star Trek* "hyperdrive." Sometimes she even accompanies the lads on missions along with Captain Steve Strong (Edward Bryce), as in "Graveyard of the Rockets" (1951), where the adults and teens search for a missing Academy scientist on an uncharted planet. There are hints of a romance between Captain Strong and Dr. Dale, but nothing more than hints, so as not to offend the sensibilities of the young boys in the television audience at the time. Dr. Dale wears a sensible, below-the-knee dress and heavy boots, as opposed to the futuristic short skirt so popular for women in early space operas.

*Tom Corbett, Space Cadet* had tremendous reach, not just "through the millions of miles from Earth to far-flung stars," but also through the media of the decade, spending time on all four TV networks and radio, as well as in novels, comic books, and tie-in products. Like Tom's rocket cruiser, *Polaris*, it burned brightly while it lasted.

## Tonga (*Space Patrol*)
Former criminal known as The Lady of Diamonds, now an assistant security chief on a spaceship.
See: *Space Patrol* (1950–1955, 210 episodes, USA)

## Took, Aurelia (*Space Precinct*)
Telepathic alien on the planet Altor, using her skills as a member of Demeter City's police force.
See: *Space Precinct* (1994–1995, 24 episodes, UK)

## Topper (1953–1955, 78 episodes, USA)
Based on: The novel by Thorne Smith
Production Co.: Columbia Broadcasting System
Originally Aired: CBS
Main Cast: Anne Jeffreys, Robert Sterling, Leo G. Carroll, Lee Patrick

**The Kerbys (Anne Jeffreys and Robert Sterling, top), along with a St. Bernard named Neil, haunt poor Cosmo Topper (Leo G. Carroll) and his unknowing wife (Lee Patrick) in** *Topper* **(Saul Krieg Associates, New York).**

George and Marion Kerby perished in an avalanche. That doesn't sound like much of a sitcom premise, but the comic potential becomes clearer when you realize that the fun-loving Kerbys are haunting their former home along with the ghost of a brandy-swilling St. Bernard.

The spirits of George and Marion (real-life marrieds Robert Sterling and Anne

Jeffreys) reestablish residence in their Los Angeles house, now owned by staid banker Cosmo Topper (Leo G. Carroll). Cosmo lives with his wife Henrietta (Lee Patrick), but only Mr. Topper can see and hear the ghosts. The Kerbys think Topper should loosen up a bit, and they help when they can, as in "Topper Goes to Las Vegas" (1954), where their assistance at the gambling tables causes trouble for Cosmo with a suspicious casino detective. In general, their supernatural "help" is not very helpful, but in "Second Honeymoon" (1954), Cosmo must call upon George and Marion to chase away *other* ghosts from his vacation suite. Would that make them ghost-ghostbusters?

### Torcoletti, Roxie (*Eastwick*)

Sculptor and widow who wishes for a change in her life and finds that she can see the future.

See: *Eastwick* (2009, 13 episodes, USA)

### Torres, B'Elanna (*Star Trek: Voyager*)

Human/Klingon hybrid working as Chief Engineer aboard a Federation starship.

See: *Star Trek: Voyager* (1995–2001, 172 episodes, USA)

### Touched by an Angel (1994–2003, 212 episodes, USA)

*Created by:* John Masius
*Production Co.:* Moon Water Productions, CBS Productions, et al.
*Originally Aired:* CBS
*Main Cast:* Roma Downey, Della Reese, John Dye, Valerie Bertinelli

Long-running drama series about angels who appear in human form to help people at pivotal points in their lives. Roma Downey portrays Monica, an angel on her way up, so to speak, who has just been promoted from unseen "search and rescue" angel to earthly caseworker. Monica travels around the country with her supervisor, Tess (Della Reese), who drives an Eldorado convertible and dispenses sassy wisdom while calling everyone "baby." Their cases involve undercover work, as in "Last Dance" (1998), where Monica takes on the role of high school teacher and Tess becomes a flower shop clerk to help a teenage couple whose relationship is endangered by their feuding mothers. Sometimes their cases have life and death consequences, as in "Monica's Bad Day" (2000), when Monica prevents a woman from jumping off a bridge, while Tess gives her apprentice some lessons in anger management. (Angels need anger management?)

Later angelic regulars include Andrew (John Dye), the angel of death, and Gloria (Valerie Bertinelli), a trainee caseworker.

Della Reese, who began her career as a singer, performed the show's opening theme song, "Walk with You." Ms. Reese, a groundbreaker all her life, continued the trailblazing trend on *Touched by an Angel*. A woman over the age of 60 was rare enough in the main cast of a network series, but such a woman of African American/Native American descent was truly unique.

No doubt she was heaven sent.

### T'Pol (*Star Trek: Enterprise*)
Vulcan liaison and later First Officer aboard a prototype starship.
See: ***Star Trek: Enterprise* (2001–2005, 98 episodes, USA)**

### Troi, Deanna (*Star Trek: The Next Generation*)
Starship counselor whose alien heritage allows her to sense people's emotions.
See: ***Star Trek: The Next Generation* (1987–1994, 178 episodes, USA)**

### *Tru Calling* (2003–2005, 27 episodes, Canada/USA)
*Created by:* Jon Harmon Feldman
*Production Co.:* Original Film, Oh That Gus!, Inc., 20th Century–Fox Television, Millennium Canadian Productions Ltd.
*Originally Aired:* Fox
*Main Cast:* Eliza Dushku, Zach Galifianakis, Shawn Reaves, A.J. Cook, Matt Bomer, Jessica Collins, Benjamín Benítez, Jason Priestley

Tru Davies (Eliza Dushku) accepts a job on the city morgue's graveyard shift prior to enrolling in medical school. On Tru's first night, the corpse of a woman appears to wake up, saying, "Help me." Tru suddenly finds herself reliving the same day, which gives her the opportunity to alter events and stop the woman's murder. This scenario repeats itself on other nights with different corpses, as Tru goes on to prevent their deaths, but also begins to change the circumstances of her personal life.

While Tru pursues her new calling, she learns from Davis (Zach Galifianakis), her supervisor at the morgue, that her late mother also possessed the gift. She continues to rewind her days, as she copes with family secrets and maintains a love life, but a further complication arises in the form of a new coworker, Jack Harper (Jason Priestley). Jack possesses the same ability as Tru, but he believes that fate should be allowed to take its course. In "Two Weddings and a Funeral" (2004), Tru's brother Harrison (Shawn Reaves) is murdered, and she must fight for his life, while Jack vows to see Harrison dead at the end of the rewind (or else).

*Tru Calling* ended with multiple cliffhangers due to an abrupt cancellation. If only Tru had been able to rewind the day that Fox canceled her series.

### Trubel (*Grimm*)
Street-smart young woman who has inherited special powers to hunt and kill supernatural creatures.
See: ***Grimm* (2011– , 110 episodes, USA)**

### *True Blood* (2008–2014, 80 episodes, USA)
*Based on:* The Sookie Stackhouse Novels by Charlaine Harris
*Created by:* Alan Ball
*Production Co.:* Your Face Goes Here Entertainment, HBO
*Originally Aired:* HBO
*Main Cast:* Anna Paquin, Stephen Moyer, Sam Trammell, Ryan Kwanten, Rutina Wesley, Chris Bauer, Nelsan Ellis, Carrie Preston, Alexander Skarsgard, Deborah Ann Woll

Sookie Stackhouse (Anna Paquin) has a colorful name, reflective of her colorful life. Sookie is a waitress at Merlotte's Bar and Grill in Bon Temps, Louisiana, where the times they are a-changin' thanks to the invention of something called "Tru Blood," a synthetic formula which has allowed vampires to "come out of the coffin." When a couple visiting Merlotte's tries to drain the blood of a vampire named Bill Compton (Stephen Moyer), because "V" (vampire blood) is a strong narcotic, Sookie rescues him, and an unusual love affair is born. One of Bill's particular appeals is that his mind is unreadable by Sookie, who is a telepath, giving her a respite from all the human thoughts constantly bombarding her. Sookie sometimes uses her telepathic powers to solve crimes, as in season one, when a serial killer targets women called "fangbangers," who have sex with vampires.

Other types of supernatural creatures appear in later seasons to help pump new—er, blood into the series. Sam Merlotte (Sam Trammell), owner of the bar where Sookie works, is revealed to be a shapeshifter, while Sookie herself is a human-fairy hybrid called a "halfling." Cue the ghosts, witches, and assorted werecreatures.

Paquin won a Golden Globe Award for her performance as Sookie in 2009. While the caliber of the acting and writing in the series is generally high, especially in the earlier seasons, *True Blood* may not be everyone's cup of ruby-red tea. Graphic violence, profanity, and explicit sex are commonplace here, so if you're looking for the sparkly, teen-friendly vampires of *Twilight*, you've come to the wrong bloody town.

### Tucker, Amanda (*Tucker's Witch*)
Half of a married sleuthing couple, the half that also happens to be a witch.
See: *Tucker's Witch* (1982–1983, 12 episodes, USA)

### Tucker's Witch (1982–1983, 12 episodes, USA)
*Created by:* William Bast, Paul Huson
*Production Co.:* Hill/Mandelker Films
*Originally Aired:* CBS
*Main Cast:* Tim Matheson, Catherine Hicks, Bill Morey, Alfre Woodard, Barbara Barrie

Rick and Amanda Tucker are a pair of married sleuths with a twist—Amanda is a bona fide witch. With a detective agency in the Laurel Canyon area of Los Angeles, Rick (Tim Matheson) and Amanda (Catherine Hicks) solve cases, often with the help of Amanda's special gifts, and sometimes in spite of them, since Amanda is still learning how to control her powers. In "Abra Cadaver" (1982), the Tuckers investigate when a conductor's dead body disappears from a funeral home and leads to smuggled diamonds. Other only-in-La-La-Land cases involve a rockstar's missing girlfriend and a celebrity hairdresser targeted by an international assassin. The Tuckers are assisted by Amanda's cat Dickens, who has a Lassie-esque ability to help out in times of trouble.

### Turnabout (1979, 7 episodes, USA)
*Based on:* The novel by Thorne Smith
*Production Co.:* Sam Denoff Productions, Universal Television

*Originally Aired:* NBC
*Main Cast:* John Schuck, Sharon Gless, Richard Stahl, Bobbi Jordan, Bruce Kirby

Short-lived series about a married couple whose minds switch bodies à la *Freaky Friday*. Sam Alston (John Schuck), a sportswriter, and Penny Alston (Sharon Gless), a cosmetics executive, run afoul of a gypsy's wish-granting statue when each fleetingly thinks the other has the easier life. The soul-switching takes place overnight, and once Sam and Penny realize what has happened, they try to keep up appearances until they can find a way to reverse the curse. Each gets an up-close view of gender roles during the 70s, as when Sam (in the body of beautiful Penny) must play the eager cheerleader to Penny's jock quarterback at a charity football game in "Cry Me a Touchdown" (1979). Off the gridiron, Sam must field inappropriate passes from male acquaintances, while Penny (as schlubby Sam) must forgo her duties as sister of the bride in "Till Dad Do Us Part" (1979). The situation led to some amusingly incongruous images, such as scenes of Penny, with her soft blond curls, chomping on an ugly cigar.

This promising series wasn't allowed to prosper due to an unfortunate time slot after failed comedy *Hello Larry* and opposite ratings blockbuster *Dallas*. They should have used that gypsy's statue to wish for a better time slot.

### Turner, Beth (*Moonlight*)

Sophia Myles stars as Beth Turner, investigative reporter for *Buzzwire*, an Internet tabloid with a taste for sensational stories. Beth hits the jackpot in "No Such Thing as Vampires" (2007), when a college coed turns up dead with two puncture marks on her neck, and a brooding Los Angeles detective may hold the key to solving the crime. Soon Beth and the P.I., Mick St. John (Alex O'Loughlin), are teaming up to solve cases, and Beth learns that they share a past that she doesn't quite remember, a past in which vampire Mick saved her life. As Beth is introduced to the world of undead L.A., she and Mick fight their romantic longings, while the murder of Beth's fiancé (Jordan Belfi) causes a rift in "Love Lasts Forever" (2008). But Beth's fate is intertwined with Mick's, at least for the duration of this short-lived series.

See also: **Moonlight (2007–2008, 16 episodes, USA)**

### *Twin Peaks* (1990–1991, 30 episodes, USA)

*Created by:* Mark Frost, David Lynch
*Production Co.:* Lynch/Frost Productions, Propaganda Films, Spelling Television
*Originally Aired:* ABC
*Main Cast:* Kyle MacLachlan, Michael Ontkean, Mädchen Amick, Dana Ashbrook, Richard Beymer, Lara Flynn Boyle, Joan Chen, Sherilyn Fenn, Warren Frost, Michael Horse, Piper Laurie, Sheryl Lee, Peggy Lipton, James Marshall, Everett McGill, Jack Nance, Kimmy Robertson, Ray Wise, Catherine E. Coulson

*Twin Peaks* is a genre unto itself, both an homage to and parody of soap operas, if those soap operas inhabited a macabre, surrealistic and supernatural world.

FBI Agent Dale Cooper (Kyle MacLachlan) is called to the picturesque Northwestern town of Twin Peaks, when the body of a young woman is found "wrapped in plastic" on a riverbank. The unfortunate victim is **Laura Palmer** (Sheryl Lee), a local high school student and homecoming queen, who seemed to be the all-American girl, but concealed dark secrets, including cocaine addiction and prostitution. Cooper begins to investigate the crime and becomes immersed in the life of the town, which is plagued by sinister forces, but also possesses great charm, albeit in an off-kilter way. On the charm end, Twin Peaks has been blessed with more than its share of beautiful people, especially young women, including the aforementioned Laura Palmer. Other stunners include Audrey Horne (Sherilyn Fenn), a sultry Liz Taylor–esque teen whose crush on Agent Cooper puts her life in danger, Shelly Johnson (Mädchen Amick), a waitress at the local diner, who's married to a sadistic trucker with a sexual link to Laura (like most of the men in town), and Norma Jennings (Peggy Lipton), diner owner and organizer of the Meals on Wheels program, where ever-busy Laura had volunteered.

Cooper receives many of his clues via dreams featuring either a dwarf or a giant, and eventually learns that an evil supernatural entity with the incongruously common name of BOB is inhabiting Laura's killer. This knowledge comes too late to save Maddy Ferguson (Sheryl Lee in a dual role), Laura's look-alike cousin, who has come to town to console the family. Eventually the killer is revealed to be Leland Palmer (Ray Wise), Laura's tortured father, who had been possessed by BOB years before.

Fans were obsessed with the mystery of who killed Laura Palmer, sparking frequent "water cooler" discussions at work. Pressure built on the show's producers Mark Frost and David Lynch to reveal the killer of Laura Palmer, and they yielded to it, hoping to keep viewers coming back with new (and weirder) plot lines. Alas, in the end, it was always about Laura, and the show was canceled after its second season. As the "Log Lady" (Catherine E. Coulson) once said, "Laura is the one."

See also: **Palmer, Laura** (*Twin Peaks*)

### Tyler, Alice (*Whiz Kids*)

Amateur detective who solves crimes with three boys and a computer named Ralf.

See: *Whiz Kids* (**1983–1984, 18 episodes, USA**)

### Tyler, Carolyn "Cat" (*Proof*)

Brilliant surgeon enticed by a terminally ill billionaire to search for proof that the afterlife exists.

See: *Proof* (**2015, 10 episodes, Canada/USA**)

### Tyler, Jaye (*Wonderfalls*)

Clerk at a Niagara Falls souvenir shop who begins to hear messages from toy animals.

See: *Wonderfalls* (**2004, 13 episodes, Canada/USA**)

### Tyler, Rose (*Doctor Who*)

Working-class London teen who accompanies a Time Lord on his adventures.

See: *Doctor Who* (**1963–1989, 2005– , 821 episodes, UK**)

## Uhura, Lieutenant (*Star Trek*)

Lieutenant Uhura (Nichelle Nichols) is Chief Communications Officer on the starship *Enterprise*, whose five-year mission is "to boldly go where no man has gone before." *Star Trek* itself boldly went where no television series had gone before, particularly with the inclusion of Lieutenant Uhura, who, as a prominent member of the *Enterprise*'s bridge crew, was one of the first African American characters to be featured in a non-stereotypical role on U.S. television. Prior roles had often depicted blacks as domestics, such as the title character in *Beulah* (1950–1953).

Although her character was groundbreaking, Uhura herself often didn't have much to do in each episode beyond reciting the now iconic phrase "hailing frequencies open." As a result, Nichols had planned to leave the series for a Broadway career after the first season. But an unlikely source, none other than Dr. Martin Luther King, Jr., convinced Nichols to stay, emphasizing that her character sent a positive message of racial equality in the future.

Uhura travels the galaxy with Captain Kirk (William Shatner), Mr. Spock (Leonard Nimoy), and company, seeking out "new life and new civilizations." Often they get more than they bargained for, as in "Charlie X" (1966), when the *Enterprise* beams aboard a seemingly human young man who quickly demonstrates dangerous telekinetic powers. Nichols gets to show off her singing talent in this episode, as Uhura performs a space song to the accompaniment of Spock's Vulcan lyre, until her teasing lyrics prompt Charlie to silence her voice.

Psychic beings again cause problems for the *Enterprise* in "Plato's Stepchildren" (1968), when an alien society resembling Earth's ancient Greece holds the command crew hostage. The Platonians use telekinesis to humiliate the officers, forcing Kirk and Uhura to kiss, one of the earliest interracial kisses on American television. Nichols and Shatner had intentionally flubbed all the non-kissing takes of the scene, using some power of their own to compel the now-famous kiss into existence.

Nichelle Nichols appears as her *Star Trek* character Lieutenant Uhura on a recruiting poster for NASA.

Uhura's name was based upon the Swahili word for freedom, *uhuru*, a perfect name for a character who represented freedom from the past and hope for the future.

See also: **Star Trek (1966–1969, 79 episodes, USA)**

**Underlay, Mariel (*Invasion*)**

Medical doctor in Homestead, Florida, who may have morphed into an alien hybrid after a strange hurricane.

See: *Invasion* **(2005–2006, 22 episodes, USA)**

**V (1984–1985, 19 episodes, USA)**
*Created by:* Kenneth Johnson
*Production Co.:* Warner Bros. Television
*Originally Aired:* NBC
*Main Cast:* Jane Badler, June Chadwick, Jennifer Cooke, Robert Englund, Faye Grant, Michael Ironside, Marc Singer, Lane Smith, Blair Tefkin, Michael Wright, Jeff Yagher

"They arrived in 50 motherships offering their friendship and advanced technology to Earth. Skeptical of the Visitors, Mike Donovan and Juliet Parrish infiltrated their ranks and soon discovered some startling secrets."

Two highly successful miniseries, *V* (1983) and *V: The Final Battle* (1984), had revealed some of the startling secrets alluded to in the opening narration of this sequel. The biggie: the beautiful, human-appearing extraterrestrials known as the Visitors were actually lizard folk planning to conquer Earth! At the end of the second miniseries, the Visitors had been vanquished by a bacterium called Red Dust. As the weekly series opens, Diana (Jane Badler), Supreme Commander of the Visitors, faces a Nuremburg-style trial for committing wartime atrocities. Since there's no such thing as a FINAL battle in sequel-land, Diana soon escapes captivity to launch a new invasion. What's a new invasion without a new resistance movement, so some of the folks from the old one reappear, including Mike Donovan (Marc Singer) and Juliet Parrish (Faye Grant), a biologist and original founder of the Los Angeles group. New recruits enlist as well, including Elizabeth (Jennifer Cooke), a Human/Visitor hybrid (ick!), who uses her extraordinary powers to help the resistance.

Alas, the popularity of the two miniseries did not transfer to the weekly series, and incessant tinkering by the network didn't help. But the character of Diana remained popular—she was ranked number five in *TV Guide*'s "25 Greatest Sci-Fi Legends" in 2004, and she went on to appear in the 2009 *V* reboot, again portrayed by Jane Badler. That kind of staying power is simply out of this world.

**V (2009–2011, 22 episodes, USA)**
*Based on:* The TV mini-series *V* created by Kenneth Johnson
*Created by:* Scott Peters
*Production Co.:* The Scott Peters Company, HDFilms, Warner Bros. Television
*Originally Aired:* ABC
*Main Cast:* Elizabeth Mitchell, Morris Chestnut, Joel Gretsch, Logan Huffman, Laura Vandervoort, Morena Baccarin, Scott Wolf, Jane Badler

A reimagining of the 1983 miniseries of the same title, *V* again brings us

"Visitors," the extraterrestrial type, who seemingly come in peace, but actually have planetary conquest on their (reptilian) minds. Led by the luscious Anna (Morena Baccarin), the visitors look like humans, incredibly beautiful humans, and offer their technological and medical advances to the people of our planet. But FBI agent **Erica Evans** (Elizabeth Mitchell) quickly learns that extraterrestrial beauty is only skin deep (literally), and that the aliens' intentions aren't very pretty either. While keeping her day job and ostensibly protecting the aliens against terrorist attacks, Evans secretly joins a resistance movement, sabotaging Anna's plans at every turn.

In the meantime, Erica's teenaged son Tyler (Logan Huffman) finds himself attracted to the visitors and their message, as Anna's lovely daughter Lisa (Laura Vandervoort) encourages his interest. Lisa finds herself conflicted by her growing human emotions, but, not to worry, as her evil twin (also played by Vandervoort) will succeed in carrying out Anna's nefarious plan in regard to Tyler.

The series was canceled at this point, so keep your eye out for beautiful people, as the Visitors may still be among us.

See also: **Evans, Erica (*V*)**

### Valentine, Rebecca "Beka" (*Andromeda*)

Con artist who gives up her salvage ship to become first officer for an idealistic starship captain.

See: *Andromeda* (2000–2005, 110 episodes, Canada/USA)

### Valerii, Sharon "Boomer" (*Battlestar Galactica*)

Android who doesn't know she is a sleeper agent in the war against humans.

See: *Battlestar Galactica* (2004–2009, 75 episodes, USA)

### *The Vampire Diaries* (2009– , 155 episodes, USA)

*Based on:* The book series by L.J. Smith
*Created by:* Kevin Williamson, Julie Plec
*Production Co.:* Alloy Entertainment, Warner Bros. Television, et al.
*Originally Aired:* The CW
*Main Cast:* Nina Dobrev, Paul Wesley, Ian Somerhalder, Kat Graham, Candice King, Steven R. McQueen, Zach Roerig, Michael Trevino, Matt Davis

This teen vampire series appeared a year after the film *Twilight* had taken the world by storm, but it wasn't a rip-off of the sparkly movie sensation. The source novels for *The Vampire Diaries*, published in 1991 and thereafter, had preceded *Twilight* and its own parent book series by more than a decade.

Elena Gilbert (Nina Dobrev) returns to Mystic Falls High School in Virginia after mourning the death of her parents, who had died in a car accident. Elena soon meets Stefan Salvatore (Paul Wesley), a 162-year-old new kid at school, who turns out to be a vampire, but a nice one—no human blood allowed. Stefan has a brother, Damon Salvatore (Ian Somerhalder), who is also a gorgeous vamp, but not nearly as nice, and there's no doubt that the two brothers will form the requisite love triangle with Elena. As if the trio's relationship isn't complicated enough, Elena has a doppelgänger named Katherine Pierce, known as Katerina Petrova when she was born in the 15th century, who was in love with the two brothers and became their vampire sire. (There are enough triangles here for a geometry class.) Katherine pursues Elena for nefarious supernatural reasons throughout most of the series.

Blood-letting, torture, and evil aside, it's still high school, and you need best friends, so Elena has two. Bonnie Bennett (Kat Graham), a powerful witch with a compassionate nature, has the bad habit of dying and returning from the dead, given her tendency toward self-sacrifice. Caroline Forbes (Candice King), an overachieving cheerleader and honors student, becomes a vampire when Damon's blood heals her severe injuries after a car accident.

As the young women move on to college, swap loves, and fight supernatural threats from the past and present, Elena continues to record the sometimes gory, sometimes glorious details in her "vampire diaries." Her stories were popular enough with TV audiences that a new series, *The Originals*, premiered in 2013 to expand the mythology of the first-ever vampires to exist, as introduced in *The Vampire Diaries*.

The mythology may have changed since Bram Stoker's *Dracula* was published in 1897, but the allure of these immortal creatures endures.

### Van Pelt, Maddie (*Every Witch Way*)

High school popularity queen threatened by the presence of a new girl, who is a fellow witch.

See: *Every Witch Way* (2014–2015, 85 episodes, USA)

### Vargas, Tess (*Beauty & the Beast*)

New York homicide detective and keeper of "beastly" secrets.

See: *Beauty & the Beast* (2012– , 68 episodes, Canada/USA)

### Vasco, Jane (*Painkiller Jane*)

Operative for a top-secret agency which hunts aberrants with superhuman mental abilities.

See: *Painkiller Jane* (2007, 22 episodes, Canada/USA)

### Vetter, Tracy (*Forever Knight*)

Tracy Vetter (Lisa Ryder) is a detective for the Toronto police department, newly assigned to work with Nicholas Knight (Geraint Wyn Davies) after the death of Knight's previous partner. Unbeknownst to Tracy, Nick is a vampire, but she quickly learns about the existence of fanged immortals from Javier Vachon (Ben Bass), a vampire who survives the plane bombing she is investigating. Nick places Tracy under Vachon's protection, because her new knowledge makes her a threat to vampires, and she is a "resistor," someone who is not susceptible to mesmerizing by vampires. In the meantime, Tracy must work with Nick in the mortal world to solve crimes, even though the human and supernatural realms often overlap, as in "Blind Faith" (1995), when a vampiric dog may be a vigilante killer. As a police commissioner's daughter, Tracy wants to prove she deserves the job of detective on her own merits, and takes a risky undercover assignment in "My Boyfriend Is a Vampire"

(1995). Tracy continues to resist her growing attraction to Vachon, while keeping her secret from Nicholas, still unaware that Nick is hiding an ironic truth of his own.

See also: *Forever Knight* (1992–1996, 70 episodes, Canada/West Germany)

## Vicki/V.I.C.I. (*Small Wonder*)

Ten-year-old girl who is actually an android living with her creator and his nuclear family.

See: *Small Wonder* (1985–1989, 96 episodes, USA)

## VR.5 (1995, 13 episodes, USA)

*Created by:* Jeannine Renshaw
*Production Co.:* Samoset Productions, Rysher Entertainment
*Originally Aired:* Fox
*Main Cast:* Lori Singer, Michael Easton, Will Patton, Anthony Head, David McCallum, Louise Fletcher, Tracey Needham

If impressive casts were enough to ensure the survival of a series, this show would have had a long life. Alas, that's not how TV works.

Lori Singer portrays Sydney Bloom, a telephone lineworker and computer enthusiast with a tragic past. Sydney's father, Dr. Joseph Bloom (David McCallum), a computer scientist, and her twin sister, Samantha (Tracey Needham), had died in a car accident, which Sydney had survived. As if losing her father and sister weren't enough, Sydney can no longer communicate with her mother, Nora Bloom (Academy Award winner Louise Fletcher), a neurochemist, who is now in a catatonic state due to the emotional trauma of the incident. No wonder Sydney likes to escape the real world by entering a computer-generated virtual reality (VR) with the help of her homemade gear.

Things get complicated, however, when Sydney accidentally discovers the fifth level of virtual reality, VR.5, where she can bring other people with her simply by calling them and connecting the phone to her computer's modem. (Modems!) In VR.5, Sydney can access the memories of others and affect events in the real world, a talent which quickly brings her to the attention of a shadowy organization known as The Committee. Sydney begins to work with the clandestine group through its representatives, Frank Morgan (Will Patton), and later Oliver Sampson (Anthony Head, pre–*Buffy The Vampire Slayer*). It's not hard to guess that Sydney's pop and sis are not really dead, and The Committee, or at least part of it, is responsible for the deception.

Fox aired only 10 of the show's 13 episodes in its original run, after which cancellation occurred in the real world. But the characters went on to lead happy lives in a virtual reality of their own making. Or so we hope.

## Vukavitch, Olga (*Seven Days*)

Scientist for a time-travel project who dies frequently and is saved by corrections to the timeline.

See: *Seven Days* (1998–2001, 66 episodes, USA)

## Walker, Darcy (*Black Scorpion*)
A police detective in Angel City, who turns into a vigilante superhero at night. See: **Black Scorpion (2001, 22 episodes, USA)**

## Walker, Sarah (*Chuck*)
Sarah Walker (Yvonne Strahovski) is a CIA agent with a unique assignment. Dispatched to Burbank, California, Sarah must guard Chuck Bartkowski (Zachary Levi), a computer nerd at an electronics superstore, who has accidentally downloaded "The Intersect"—the CIA/NSA's complete database—into his BRAIN. Sarah adopts the cover of Chuck's girlfriend, a fish-out-of-water fast food jockey first at Weinerlicious and later at Orange Orange, an always empty yogurt emporium. Protecting Chuck from evil spies who want to access the information in his head is hard work, especially when Sarah starts to develop romantic feelings for her asset and vice versa. In "Chuck Versus the Broken Heart" (2009), Sarah is reassigned when it appears that her budding relationship with Chuck is impeding her effectiveness, but is reinstated once she rescues Chuck from kidnappers. Their relationship experiences twists and turns as old lovers reappear and disappear, and especially when Chuck decides to train as a full-fledged operative, raising questions of how they could remain spies and share a normal domestic life. Eventually Sarah and Chuck come to believe they can have it all, and are married in "Chuck Versus the Cliffhanger" (2011), deciding to set up shop as freelance operatives. But this is the spy game, so complications ensue, when Sarah loses her memory and can't remember her feelings for Chuck. In series finale "Chuck Versus the Goodbye" (2012), there is a hint that a single kiss may set things to rights.

See also: **Chuck (2007–2012, 91 episodes, USA)**

## War of the Worlds (1988–1990, 43 episodes, Canada/USA)
*Based on:* The novel *The War of the Worlds* by H.G. Wells
*Created by:* Greg Strangis
*Production Co.:* Hometown Films, Paramount Domestic Television, Ten Four, Triumph Entertainment
*Originally Aired:* In Syndication
*Main Cast:* Jared Martin, Lynda Mason Green, Rachel Blanchard, Philip Akin, Richard Chaves, Adrian Paul, Catherine Disher, Denis Forest, Keram Malicki-Sanchez

"In 1953, Earth experienced a War of the Worlds. Common bacteria stopped the aliens, but it didn't kill them. Instead, the aliens lapsed into a state of deep hibernation. Now the aliens have been resurrected, more terrifying than ever before."

Sometimes you have to wait a LONG time for a sequel. In the case of *War of the Worlds*, George Pal's 1953 film classic about invaders from Mars, it took 35 years and a switch to the small screen for a follow-up to appear. Since Martian invaders were now dated in science fiction, the aliens were from Mor-Tax, a planet with a dying sun.

As the series opens, some terrorists accidentally awaken the extraterrestrials from their bacteria-induced comas (as you do). The Mor-taxans take over the terrorists' human bodies, evoking another 50s SF classic, *Invasion of the Body Snatchers*. A small team is formed (as they are), led by Harrison Blackwood (Jared Martin), an astrophysicist with a new-age outlook—he's a pacifist, vegetarian, and yogi. The eccentric professor works with Dr. Suzanne McCullough (Lynda Mason Green), a microbiologist who's a bit more grounded, especially since she's a single mother to Debi (Rachel Blanchard). In "The Good Samaritan" (1988), Suzanne and the team investigate a billionaire industrialist whose plans to feed the world may be co-opted by the aliens via deadly spores.

A major reboot occurs in season two of the rechristened *War of the Worlds: The Second Invasion*, with the introduction of aliens called the Morthren, who exterminate the Mor-taxans for their incompetence. (And we thought the Martians were bad.) The scene shifts to the near future, when the team's headquarters has changed from a pastoral military facility to an urban, er, sewer. In "Loving the Alien" (1989), young Debi sneaks out from the underground hideout (who could blame her), and befriends an alien boy named Ceeto (Keram Malicki-Sanchez).

Early cancellation allowed the producers to provide closure in series finale "The Obelisk" (1990), but Ceeto dies, and little Debi avenges his death, as per this show's excessive violence. At least the human race survives.

## *Warehouse 13* (2009–2014, 64 episodes, USA)

*Created by:* Jane Espenson, D. Brent Mote
*Production Co.:* Universal Cable Productions
*Originally Aired:* Syfy
*Main Cast:* Eddie McClintock, Joanne Kelly, Saul Rubinek, Allison Scagliotti, Genelle Williams, Aaron Ashmore, CCH Pounder

Warehouse 13 is in South Dakota, but it isn't a wheat storage facility. Located miles from anyone, the warehouse protects the world's supernatural artifacts, which have been collected for thousands of years since the time of Warehouse 1 during the reign of Alexander the Great. Secret Service Agents Pete Lattimer (Eddie McClintock) and **Myka Bering** (Joanne Kelly) are assigned to the warehouse's latest incarnation, number 13, and their task is to acquire new artifacts, which usually come to light after reports of bizarre and unexplained deaths or illnesses. Pete and Myka work under the supervision of the Warehouse's irascible Agent in Charge, Artie Nielsen (Saul Rubinek), and receive tech support from young **Claudia Donovan** (Allison Scagliotti), who later becomes a field agent in her own right. Almost as weird as the warehouse and the wonders it possesses is Mrs. Irene Frederic (CCH Pounder), the warehouse's caretaker, who seems to appear and disappear at will, ages slowly (or not at all), and has a mental link to the warehouse itself. The agents collect seemingly harmless items, such as Catherine O'Leary's Cowbell or Lewis Carroll's Looking Glass, but the quaint appeal of these historical curiosities belies their power as spontaneous firestarters or mysterious soul-swappers. The artifacts are so dangerous, in fact, that sometimes they threaten the very existence of the world. But Pete, Myka, Claudia, and Artie are always on hand with purple goo, neutralizing bags, and sometimes even artifacts themselves to save the world and set things right. We can all rest easy.

See also: **Bering, Myka** (*Warehouse 13*); **Donovan, Claudia** (*Warehouse 13*)

## Washburne, Zoe (*Firefly*)

Second-in-command on a spaceship full of renegades on the frontiers of space in 2517.

See: *Firefly* (2002, 14 episodes, USA)

## Weaver, Debbie (*The Neighbors*)

New Jersey housewife living in a gated community full of extraterrestrials.

See: *The Neighbors* (2012–2014, 44 episodes, USA)

## Webster, Shelly (*The Crow: Stairway to Heaven*)

Murdered photographer who can't move on to the afterlife until her undead fiancé finds redemption.

See: *The Crow: Stairway to Heaven* (1998–1999, 22 episodes, Canada)

## *Weird Science* (1994–1998, 88 episodes, USA)

*Based on:* The film *Weird Science* directed by John Hughes
*Created by:* Tom Spezialy, Alan Cross
*Production Co.:* St. Clare Entertainment, Universal Television
*Originally Aired:* USA Network
*Main Cast:* John Mallory Asher, Michael Manasseri, Vanessa Angel, Lee Tergesen, Bruce Jarchow, Andrew Prine, Joyce Bulifant

What are two nerdy students to do when they have trouble communicating with the opposite sex? Why, create the perfect woman, of course, one who can give them the scoop on what women really want. Gary Wallace (John Mallory Asher) and Wyatt Donnelly (Michael Manasseri) set out to program a computer simulation of such a lady, but things go awry when lightning strikes during their work, bringing Lisa (Vanessa Angel) to life. (It's alive!) Unlike Frankenstein's monster, however, Lisa is sexy and wears low-cut dresses (she is the boys' fantasy, after all), but she is also highly intelligent and can even grant their wishes. Needless to say, this genius genie causes some problems, sometimes through willfulness and other times by accident, although she is not bound by the traditional master/genie arrangement as in *I Dream of Jeannie*. In fact, when Gary "commands" her to speed up their lessons on the opposite sex, Lisa transforms both boys into teenage girls, where they learn firsthand about catcalls and ogling in "The Feminine Mistake" (1994). Lisa has a few things of her own to learn, as when she makes Wyatt President of the United States, when all he'd wanted was to be president of the chess club in "Mr. President" (1994).

By the time they were done, Lisa, the boys, and Wyatt's brother Chett (Lee Tergesen) had dealt with vampires, zombies, ghosts and extraterrestrials. When your premise is a simulation-generated genie, "over the top" just doesn't compute.

### West, Iris (*The Flash*)
Blogger and later newspaper reporter who writes about a superhero with lightning speed.
See: *The Flash* (2014– , 46 episodes, USA)

### Westphalen, Kristin (*seaQuest DSV*)
Chief medical officer on a submarine after the colonization of Earth's oceans.
See: *seaQuest DSV* (1993–1996, 57 episodes, USA)

### *The Whispers* (2015, 13 episodes, USA)
*Based on:* The short story "Zero Hour" by Ray Bradbury
*Created by:* Soo Hugh
*Production Co.:* Clickety-Clack Productions, Amblin Television, ABC Studios
*Originally Aired:* ABC
*Main Cast:* Lily Rabe, Barry Sloane, Milo Ventimiglia, Kristen Connolly, Derek Webster, Catalina Denis, Kylie Rogers, Kyle Harrison Breitkopf

In this complex sf thriller, several children in the Washington, D.C., area begin playing games with an "imaginary" friend named "Drill," leading to cosmic consequences. FBI Agent Claire Bennigan (Lily Rabe), an expert in child psychology, is called to investigate the strange circumstances, working with her former lover, Wes Lawrence (Barry Sloane) of the Department of Defense. It turns out that both Claire's son Henry (Kyle Harrison Breitkopf) and Wes's daughter Minx (Kylie Rogers) are playing the game with Drill, who gives big rewards, such as restoring Henry's hearing, when the kids do things like hacking into government databases and breaking into nuclear power plants. It further turns out that Claire's husband, Capt. Sean Bennigan (Milo Ventimiglia), presumed dead in a plane crash, is also connected to Drill, who (gasp!) may not be of this world. Drill travels through the power lines in a very small D.C., where everyone seems to be connected, including the first family, either by their occupations or their kids. Drill appears to be victorious in the aptly named "Game Over" (2015), when the extraterrestrials "beam up" Minx and the other kids, except for Henry, who has been pushed out of the beam by Claire, his accidental replacement. Any possible way back to Earth for the abductees was blocked at this point by cancellation of the series.

Those network executives are even more ruthless than Drill.

### Whitehill, Emery (*Star-Crossed*)
High-school Juliet in love with a Romeo from another planet.
See: *Star-Crossed* (2014, 13 episodes, USA)

### *Whiz Kids* (1983–1984, 18 episodes, USA)
*Created by:* Philip DeGuere, Bob Shayne
*Production Co.:* Universal TV
*Originally Aired:* CBS
*Main Cast:* Matthew Laborteaux, Todd Porter, Jeffrey Jacquet, Andrea Elson, Melanie Gaffin, Max Gail, A Martinez

SF/adventure series about four teenagers who use their computer (a.k.a. "hacking") skills to solve crimes as amateur detectives. Richie Adler (Matthew Laborteaux) is the leader of the group, who assembles obsolete computer equipment into an advanced system he calls, "Ralf." Assisting Richie and Ralf are friends Ham Parker (Todd Porter), Alice Tyler (Andrea Elson), and Jeremy Saldino (Jeffrey Jacquet), and together this group of whiz kids takes on L.A.'s bad guys, especially corrupt officials in business or government. They even get involved with the KGB, when they learn that Alice's new boyfriend is being sought by Russian agents in "Father's Day" (1984). Making sure that the kids stay out of danger is local reporter Llewellen Farley (Max Gail) and police lieutenant Neal Quinn (A Martinez).

Never has so much been accomplished with floppy disks.

### Wicker, Julia (*The Magicians*)

New Yorker who gets involved in illicit spellcasting when she is refused admission to a grad school for magic.

See: ***The Magicians*** (2015– , 13 episodes, USA)

### Wingate, Laura (*Beyond Reality*)

University parapsychologist who investigates telekinesis, astral projection, and other strange phenomena.

See: ***Beyond Reality*** (1991–1993, 44 episodes, Canada/USA)

### Winters, Talia (*Babylon 5*)

Telepath whose true identity is obliterated by a sleeper personality during her service aboard a space station.

See: ***Babylon 5*** (1994–1998, 110 episodes, USA)

### Winters, Victoria (*Dark Shadows*)

Unsuspecting governess whose job description will include time travel back to 1795.

See: ***Dark Shadows*** (1966–1971, 1225 episodes, USA)

### *Witchblade* (2001–2002, 23 episodes, USA)

*Based on:* The comic book series by Marc Silvestri, David Wohl, Brian Haberlin, Christina Z, Michael Turner
*Created by:* Ralph Hemecker
*Production Co.:* Blade TV Productions, Halsted Pictures, Top Cow Productions
*Originally Aired:* TNT
*Main Cast:* Yancy Butler, David Chokachi, Anthony Cistaro, Will Yun Lee, John Hensley, Eric Etebari

Yancy Butler stars as Sara Pezzini, just another New York City detective on the job until she runs into an ancient, supernatural weapon called the Witchblade, a device which attaches to her hand like a gauntlet, but seems to have a will of its own. "Pez," as she is known, sets out to learn more about the blade, running into wealthy and mysterious Kenneth Irons (Anthony Cistaro), who seems to have a dark connection to the blade and Sara's past. In "Legion" (2001), the Witchblade allows Sara to speak with the dead, both the murder victim in her current case and her deceased partner Danny Woo (Will Yun Lee), who has been giving her cryptic hints about her warrior bloodline since his passing. She must prove she is worthy to wield the Witchblade in "Periculum" (2001), a test of her mettle, where she meets those who have worn the gauntlet before her, such as Joan of Arc. The Witchblade can manipulate time, and in "Emergence" (2002), Pez uses it to undo the circumstances which led to Danny's death.

Although tantalizing tidbits about the blade's history were sprinkled throughout the series, such as a Vatican connection, many fascinating questions went unanswered when the series was prematurely canceled. Although *Witchblade* was highly rated, especially for a cable show at the time, star Yancy Butler reportedly faced continuing problems with alcohol abuse, including a stint in rehab during series production.

It was a shame to see *Witchblade* go, as Butler was mesmerizing in her role as tough (with a capital T), but damaged Pez, a woman struggling with a hidden heritage, dirty cops, and even plain old misogyny. In 2002, Butler won a Saturn Award for her portrayal of Sara Pezzini, giving a glint of the bright future that wasn't to be for *Witchblade*.

## *Witches of East End* (2013–2014, 23 episodes, USA)
*Based on:* The novel by Melissa de la Cruz
*Created by:* Maggie Friedman
*Production Co.:* 3 Arts Entertainment, Curly Girly Productions, Fox 21
*Originally Aired:* Lifetime
*Main Cast:* Julia Ormond, Mädchen Amick, Jenna Dewan Tatum, Rachel Boston, Daniel Di Tomasso, Eric Winter, Christian Cooke, Virginia Madsen

The witches of East End are the powerful, but benighted Beauchamp women, Joanna, Wendy, Ingrid, and Freya. Soft-spoken Joanna (Julia Ormond) is the matriarch of the family, an immortal witch who has been cursed to watch her daughters die young, usually in their early 30s. Once her daughters die, Joanna becomes immediately pregnant with the SAME daughters again, one right after the other. (That's one humdinger of a curse.) In their current life/iteration, Joanna has decided to withhold the information about their origins and powers from her daughters in hopes that leading normal lives will help the girls to live longer.

Older daughter Ingrid (Rachel Boston) is a librarian, who has written a dissertation on the historical practice of witchcraft and the occult, but doesn't believe in magic herself. Younger sister Freya (Jenna Dewan Tatum) works as a local bartender, a pedestrian job for a powerful witch, but she was given professional counseling early in life to convince her there was no such thing as witchcraft.

Into their idyllic lives enters a black cat (omen!), who turns out to be Wendy Beauchamp (Mädchen Amick), Joanna's estranged sister, who has come to warn Joanna that her life is in danger. Wendy is quickly proven correct when an evil shapeshifter, Penelope Gardiner (Virginia Madsen), begins to wreak havoc in Joanna's life, payback for the death of Penelope's father in 1906. (Supernatural grudges last a long time!) Penelope just happens to be Freya's prospective mother-in-law, and she is playing nice (for the moment) as son Dash (Eric Winter) prepares to be wed. Needless to say, the wedding will not take place, especially since Freya actually loves Dash's brother Killian (Daniel Di Tomasso), her soulmate from previous lives.

If this sounds like a supernatural soap opera, it is, but it has its charms, not the least of which is the spirited performance of Mädchen Amick as wild witch Wendy. And then there's the fact that this is an amazingly good-looking group of witches and warlocks.

No crones allowed in East End.

### *Wizards of Waverly Place* (2007–2012, 106 episodes, USA)

*Created by:* Todd J. Greenwald
*Production Co.:* It's a Laugh Productions
*Originally Aired:* Disney Channel
*Main Cast:* Selena Gomez, David Henrie, Jake T. Austin, Jennifer Stone, Maria Canals Barrera, David DeLuise

Alex Russo (Selena Gomez) is a pretty teen living in Greenwich Village. She goes to school, flirts with boys, fights with her brothers, fusses over her wardrobe, and tries to avoid hard work whenever possible. Oh, and she's a wizard. Or she will be a wizard, the official Family Wizard, if she wins a competition with her two brothers, Justin (David Henrie) and Max (Jake T. Austin). So the Russo kids pursue their magical studies, while keeping (or trying to keep) their secret from the mortal world, especially their friends at Tribeca Preparatory School. But that's a BIG secret, and when chaos ensues after Alex enchants a superhero costume at a comic book convention, she spills the (magic) beans to best friend Harper Finkle (Jennifer Stone) in "Harper Knows" (2008).

Alex follows in the footsteps of Samantha Stephens, Sabrina Spellman, and other sitcom spellcasters, who use magic to solve problems, only to create more problems. (When will they ever learn?) In "Baby Cupid" (2008), Alex summons Cupid to Earth when her mortal mom (Maria Canals Barrera) and ex-wizard dad (David DeLuise) argue about magic on their anniversary, but Cupid's arrow ends up hitting Justin instead, complicating his relationship with Harper. The Russo children's sibling rivalry on steroids finally comes to a head in series finale "Who Will Be the Family Wizard" (2012). A multi-round wizarding competition leads to the happiest of endings, when Alex becomes the Family Wizard, Justin becomes Headmaster of WizTech, and Max, now mortal, inherits the family sub shop.

The *Wizards of Waverly Place* led an enchanted life on television, achieving both high ratings and scads of awards, including two Emmy Awards for Outstanding Children's Program in 2009 and 2012. Selena Gomez, who is of Mexican and Italian descent (just like her character Alex Russo) won the ALMA (American Latino Media Arts Award) in 2009 for her positive portrayal of a Latina in a television comedy.

Wizards, indeed.

### *Wonder Woman* (1975–1979, 59 episodes, USA)

*Based on:* The comic book series by William Moulton Marston

**Diana Prince (Lynda Carter) puts "all her might on the side of right" as her alter-ego *Wonder Woman* (ABC/Photofest).**

*Created by:* Douglas S. Cramer, Stanley Ralph Ross
*Production Co.:* Warner Bros. Television, Bruce Lansbury Productions, Douglas S. Cramer Company
*Originally Aired:* ABC (1975–1977), CBS (1977–1979)
*Main Cast:* Lynda Carter, Lyle Waggoner, Norman Burton, Richard Eastham, Beatrice Colen

The adventures of the classic superhero move from comic books to the small screen in this campy series, starring Lynda Carter as Wonder Woman and her alter ego, Diana Prince. The action begins in World War II, as Wonder Woman battles the Nazis and defends America with the help of Major Steve Trevor (Lyle Waggoner) and her magic bracelets, tiara, and lasso. Wonder Woman always knows when dashing Steve is in trouble and shows up in the nick of time to rescue him, thereby reversing the "damsel in distress" trope so popular at the time. In these early episodes, Wonder Woman is supportive of the women around her, even her adversaries, summing up her philosophy in the pilot movie: "Women are the wave of the future and sisterhood is stronger than anything."

The scene shifts to the 70s in season two, where the camp quotient rises even higher while the feminist aphorisms diminish. The ageless Amazon princess leaves her island sanctuary once again to help Steve Trevor, Jr., the Major's son (Waggoner again), and the U.S., this time via the Inter-Agency Defense Command. The IADC fights contemporary blights such as crime and terrorism, and in "Mind Stealers from Outer Space" (parts one and two, 1977), deals with the ultimate threat, planetary invasion! Ghosts of the Third Reich surface in "Anschluss '77" (1977), when Diana/Wonder Woman must thwart an attempt to clone Hitler!

Season three shifts again, in tone, if not setting, with more of a youth orientation. Wonder Woman rescues lots of teenage boys in trouble and even gets to wear a special skateboarding costume. (Cool!)

But our superhero would never let a little thing like a show's identity crisis get in her way. Wonder Woman, one of television's first female action heroes, is now and forever "putting all her might on the side of right!"

## *Wonderfalls* (2004, 13 episodes, Canada/USA)

*Created by:* Bryan Fuller, Todd Holland
*Production Co.:* Living Dead Guy Productions, Walking Bud Productions, Regency Television, 20th Century–Fox Television, Millennium Canadian Productions
*Originally Aired:* Fox
*Main Cast:* Caroline Dhavernas, Katie Finneran, Tyron Leitso, Lee Pace, William Sadler, Diana Scarwid, Tracie Thoms

One-season wonder about a young woman who talks to the animals—or, more precisely, is talked to by animals, in the form of figurines and toys. Jaye Tyler (Caroline Dhavernas) is an Ivy League graduate, currently underachieving as a retail clerk at a Niagara Falls souvenir shop, Wonderfalls Gift Emporium. Slacker Jaye is moving through life in her usual sarcastic way, when she starts receiving instructions from wax lions and pink flamingos. If the messengers aren't weird enough, the messages they send are strange and cryptic: "See a penny, pick it up." She begins to realize that the orders are meant to help people—not her usual stock in trade. Jaye tries to resist, but the animals have their ways of making a point, such as keeping her awake all night with their singing. Her behavior begins to appear bizarre to those around her, including her grad-student brother Aaron (Lee Pace) and waitress best friend Mahandra McGinty (Tracie Thoms). In "Wound-Up Penguin"(2004), a nun even thinks that Jaye's problem might be demonic possession and attempts an exorcism.

Fox yanked this quirky, but critically acclaimed series after four episodes, but pressure from the show's devoted fans helped bring about the DVD release of all 13 episodes produced. Just one more wonder for *Wonderfalls*.

## Woods, Molly (*Extant*)

Astronaut on a solo mission in outer space, who returns home after 13 months to find herself inexplicably pregnant.

See: *Extant* (2014–2015, 26 episodes, USA)

## *Wynonna Earp* (2016– , 13 episodes, Canada/USA)

*Based on:* The comic book series by Beau Smith
*Created by:* Emily Andras
*Production Co.:* Seven24 Films, IDW Entertainment
*Originally Aired:* Syfy
*Main Cast:* Melanie Scrofano, Shamier Anderson, Tim Rozon, Dominique Provost-Chalkley, Katherine Barrell

Wynonna Earp (Melanie Scrofano) is the great-great-granddaughter of famed lawman Wyatt Earp. So far, so simple. But Wynonna has been tasked with killing Revenants—outlaws originally dispatched by her great-great-grandpappy, but now resurrected as demons due to the Earp Curse (long story). To accomplish her mission, Wynonna must shoot each Revenant in the head, using Wyatt's "Peacemaker," an antique pistol with a barrel 12 inches long. Since there are 77 Revenants, Wyatt's lucky heir has her work cut out for her.

But Wynonna has help—a weird, western Scooby gang. Waverly Earp (Dominique Provost-Chalkley), Wynonna's youngest sister, has made a lifelong study of the Earp Curse, and uses her research skills to help Wynonna track down Revenants. Waverly is in love with Officer Nicole Haught (Katherine Barrell), a deputy sheriff in their aptly named town of Purgatory, who also works with Wynonna. Other members of the posse include Xavier Dolls (Shamier Anderson), a U.S. Marshal of the Black Badge Division (don't ask), who has lizard—yes, lizard—DNA. Also along for the ride is Doc Holliday (Tim Rozon)—THE Doc Holliday—who was cursed by a witch to endure good health and immortality at the bottom of a well 130 years earlier, and is now Wynonna's love interest.

If all of this sounds campy, it is, but it harks back to another irreverent horror show with strong female characters, *Buffy The Vampire Slayer*. That there is some *Deadwood* thrown in, well, as Wynonna would say, "Make your peace."

## *The X-Files* (1993–2002, 2016– , 208 episodes, USA)

*Created by:* Chris Carter
*Production Co.:* Ten Thirteen Productions, 20th Century–Fox Television, X-F Productions
*Originally Aired:* Fox
*Main Cast:* David Duchovny, Gillian Anderson, Robert Patrick, Annabeth Gish, Mitch Pileggi

"THE TRUTH IS OUT THERE"

Iconic SF/horror/mystery series about a pair of FBI agents who are assigned weird cases with paranormal overtones. Special Agent Fox "Spooky" Mulder (David Duchovny) is the true believer, expecting extraterrestrials around every corner, and suspecting conspiracies and coverups at each turn. **Dana Scully** (Gillian Anderson) is the skeptic, a medical doctor who applies scientific analyses to the evidence and whose initial assignment is to debunk Mulder's outlandish theories. As evidence mounts, however, of UFOs, alien abductions, and a global conspiracy, Scully is forced to re-examine her views, and the partners come to trust only each other. In the meantime, they confront all manner of strangeness, including golems, shape-shifters, time travelers, demonic babies, brain-eating mutants, and even genies.

Gillian Anderson celebrates the 20th Anniversary of *The X-Files* at San Diego Comic Con International in 2013 (from a color photograph by Gage Skidmore, CC BY-SA 2.0).

In later years, when Agent Mulder goes missing, John Doggett (Robert Patrick) becomes Scully's new partner, and after Scully is assigned to the FBI Academy, Monica Reyes (Annabeth Gish) replaces her on the X-Files project. A resolution of sorts for Mulder and Scully occurs in the series finale, "The Truth" (parts one and two, 2002), including a reunion with series villain "Cigarette Smoking Man" (William B. Davis).

Nowadays, however, even series finales aren't final, and *The X-Files* emerged in 2016 after a 14-year hiatus with new cases for Mulder and Scully, new alien mythology, new conspiracies, but the same old Cigarette Smoking Man.

The search for the truth goes on…

See also: **Scully, Dana** (*The X-Files*)

## *Xena: Warrior Princess* (1995–2001, 134 episodes, USA)

*Created by:* John Schulian, Robert Tapert, Sam Raimi, R.J. Stewart
*Production Co.:* Renaissance Pictures, MCA Television, Studios USA Television
*Originally Aired:* In Syndication
*Main Cast:* Lucy Lawless, Renée O'Connor, Ted Raimi, Kevin Smith

"In a time of ancient gods, warlords, and kings, a land in turmoil cried out for a hero. She was Xena, a mighty princess forged in the heat of battle."

This spinoff from *Hercules: The Legendary Journeys* surpassed its progenitor in both popularity and cultural impact. Xena (Lucy Lawless), once an evil warrior who had killed thousands, undergoes a sudden conversion, seeking redemption for her sins by using those same fighting skills to help the helpless. During her first adventure, the aptly named "Sins of the Past" (1995), Xena meets a peasant girl named **Gabrielle** (Renée O'Connor), who follows Xena on her amazingly far-flung travels throughout the ancient world, eventually becoming an Amazon warrior in her own right. Xena is more than a match for any man on the battlefield, both in strength and cunning, but she also possesses a couple of unusual weapons to drive home the point, including her Chakram, a razor-sharp, metal hoop that returns to her like a boomerang, and "the pinch," a pressure-point technique that can kill her adversaries in 30 seconds.

Xena is equal opportunity in her choice of opponents, battling mortals and gods alike, when the need arises. In "The Reckoning" (1995), her antagonist is Ares (Kevin Smith), the god of war, who tries to force Xena back to the dark side, but their battle is waged with mind games rather than war games. In "The Furies" (1997), however, Xena and Ares go toe-to-toe in a duel which Xena wins, and their relationship becomes increasingly complicated thereafter.

Xena (Lucy Lawless) battles "ancient gods, warlords, and kings" in her quest for redemption on *Xena: Warrior Princess* (Universal TV/Photofest).

The warrior princess has several male lovers throughout the series, all of the brawny sort, including Marcus (Bobby Hosea), Borias (Marton Csokas), with whom she later has a son, and Ares, that lovable bad boy, who finally earns a single kiss from the object of his obsession. Xena's greatest love, however, may be her constant companion over the six seasons, Gabrielle, although an explicit relationship is never depicted. Some fans saw a lesbian subtext, however, especially in the series finale, "A Friend in Need, Part 2" (2001), when

Gabrielle tries to revive Xena with water from the Fountain of Strength, and administers it with mouth-to-mouth transfers that look suspiciously like kisses.

Xena was something never before seen on television. While *Wonder Woman* and *The Bionic Woman* had paved the way in the 70s for women in action roles, their action was more genteel, with the sense that the villains weren't really getting hurt at the hands of those sweet-as-apple-pie female heroes. Xena, on the other hand, was fierce, if not savage, reveling in her strength and power, taking on the full mantle of the action hero right down to the "I'm-not-afraid-of-you" sneer.

Not easy to do in a bustier, but Lucy Lawless had the soul of a warrior.

See also: **Gabrielle (*Xena: Warrior Princess*)**

### Yardeen, Yalena "Dutch" (*Killjoys*)

Bounty hunter who pursues warrants in outer space while sorting out issues from her mysterious past.

See: *Killjoys* (2015– , 19 episodes, Canada)

### *You Wish* (1997–1998, 13 episodes, USA)

*Created by:* Michael Jacobs
*Production Co.:* Michael Jacobs Productions, Touchstone Television
*Originally Aired:* ABC
*Main Cast:* John Ales, Harley Jane Kozak, Jerry Van Dyke, Alex McKenna, Nathan Lawrence, John Rhys-Davies

There are good genies and bad genies. Some, such as Jeannie in *I Dream of Jeannie*, have successful series that last five seasons. Others, such as Genie in *You Wish*, disappear in seven episodes, the TV equivalent of a puff of smoke.

Genie (John Ales) has been imprisoned in a rug for 2000 years. His captivity ends when Gillian Apple (Harley Jane Kozak), a single mother of two, buys a rug from Mustafa (John Rhys-Davies) and unrolls it, releasing Genie. (Clearly that rug hadn't been cleaned in a very long time.) Gillian thinks Genie looks like curly-haired trouble, but the kids, teen daughter Mickey (Alex McKenna) and younger brother Travis (Nathan Lawrence), believe every family should have its own genie. Genie joins the Apple household, and hijinks ensue, as when Genie creates a clone of Gillian to help her balance home and work in "Jillions of Gillians" (1997).

ABC had been hoping for another Friday-night fantasy hit à la *Sabrina the Teenage Witch*, but this one seemed forced and the audience fled. Yanked in November, the series returned in May and June, running four more of the 13 episodes produced. After that ABC rolled up the carpet for at least 2000 more years.

### *Young Blades* (2005, 13 episodes, Canada/USA)

*Based on:* The novel *The Three Musketeers* by Alexandre Dumas
*Created by:* Dan Angel, Billy Brown
*Production Co.:* Shavick Entertainment, Insight Film Studios
*Originally Aired:* PAX
*Main Cast:* Tobias Mehler, Karen Cliche, Mark Hildreth, Zak Santiago, Robert Sheehan, Bruce Boxleitner, Michael Ironside, Sheena Easton

This one could have been called *Musketeers: The Next Generation*. D'Artagnan (Tobias Mehler), son of the hero of Dumas's classic novel, swashes his buckle(r) at the Bastille with fellow Musketeers Siroc (Mark Hildreth), an inventor, Ramon (Zak Santiago), a poet, and Captain Duvall (Bruce Boxleitner), their commander. Into this 17th century bastion of male bravery enters Jacqueline Roget (Karen Cliche), a woman who has run afoul of the law and especially the French Prime Minister, evil Cardinal Mazarin (Michael Ironside). Jacqueline masquerades as a male, Jacques LePonte, to escape capture, and proves herself worthy to be one of the Musketeers. Adventures ensue, as well they should, when the dashing lady and gents set out to rescue Jacqueline's brother from Mazarin and his murderous secret society in "Wanted" (2005). Jacqueline later finds herself under the power of a legendary sword, which makes her an invincible fighter, but one in danger of losing her soul in "The Invincible Sword."

Anachronistic inventions, modern attitudes, and plenty of broad humor round out this short-lived action-adventure.

## Zhaan (*Farscape*)

Blue-skinned priestess on the run with other alien fugitives aboard a biomechanical ship.

See: ***Farscape* (1999–2003, 88 episodes, Australia/USA)**

# Appendix: Honorable Mentions

This appendix lists honorable mentions: series considered for the main body of the book, but ultimately excluded. Information on the inclusion criteria for *Women of Science Fiction and Fantasy Television* can be found in the Preface.

Each series in this Appendix has a brief entry under title, including the range of years in production, number of episodes, country of origin, main cast, and a brief description.

### *The Adventures of Sinbad* (1996–1998, 44 episodes, Canada)
*Main Cast:* Zen Gesner, George Buza, Tim Progosh, Oris Erhuero, Jacqueline Collen, Mariah Shirley, Julianne Morris

Maritime exploits of a well-known character from the *Arabian Nights*.

### *All Souls* (2001, 6 episodes, USA)
*Main Cast:* Grayson McCouch, Serena Scott Thomas, Reiko Aylesworth, Daniel Cosgrove, Irma P. Hall, Adam Rodriguez, Christian Tessier

Medical staff deal with haunted happenings at a Boston hospital.

### *American Gothic* (1995–1996, 22 episodes, USA)
*Main Cast:* Gary Cole, Lucas Black, Paige Turco, Brenda Bakke, Sarah Paulson, Jake Weber, Nick Searcy

An evil sheriff with supernatural powers tries to corrupt a young boy.

### *Animorphs* (1998–1999, 26 episodes, Canada/USA)
*Main Cast:* Shawn Ashmore, Boris Cabrera, Nadia-Leigh Nascimento, Brooke Nevin, Christopher Ralph

Five teens who can morph into animals fight a secret alien invasion.

### *Arrow* (2012– , 92 episodes, USA)
*Main Cast:* Stephen Amell, Katie Cassidy, Colin Donnell, David Ramsey, Willa Holland, Susanna Thompson, Paul Blackthorne, Emily Bett Rickards

After he is stranded on an uncharted island for five years, a billionaire returns home to fight crime with a bow and arrow.

### *Atlantis* (2013–2015, 25 episodes, UK)
*Main Cast:* Jack Donnelly, Mark Addy, Robert Emms, Aiysha Hart, Sarah Parish, Juliet Stevenson, Jemima Rooper, Amy Manson

A modern man discovers the lost city of Atlantis and characters from Greek mythology.

### *Beastmaster* (1999–2002, 66 episodes, Australia/Canada/USA)
*Main Cast:* Daniel Goddard, Jackson Raine, Marjean Holden, Monika Schnarre, Dylan Bierk, Grahame Bond, Steven Grives

The last survivor of a doomed tribe searches for his lost love, while commanding the beasts and fighting sorcerers.

### *Being Erica* (2009–2011, 49 episodes, Canada)
*Main Cast:* Erin Karpluk, Michael Riley, Tyron Leitso, Vinessa Antoine, Reagan Pasternak, Morgan Kelly, John Boylan, Kathleen Laskey, Joanna Douglas, Adam MacDonald, Paula Brancati

A woman finds a therapist who can send her back in time to undo her bad decisions.

### *Bitten* (2014–2016, 33 episodes, Canada)
*Main Cast:* Laura Vandervoort, Greyston Holt, Greg Bryk, Steve Lund, Michael Xavier, Genelle Williams, Tommie-Amber Pirie

A werewolf is torn between her city life as a photographer and her traditional obligations back home.

### *Blake's 7* (1978–1981, 52 episodes, UK)
*Main Cast:* Gareth Thomas, Michael Keating, Sally Knyvette, Paul Darrow, David Jackson, Peter Tuddenham, Jan Chappell, Jacqueline Pearce, Stephen Greif, Brian Croucher, Josette Simon, Steven Pacey, Glynis Barber

Revolving-door space opera about convicts and dissidents who battle a totalitarian regime.

### *Camelot* (2011, 10 episodes, Canada/Ireland/UK/USA)
*Main Cast:* Joseph Fiennes, Jamie Campbell Bower, Tamsin Egerton, Claire Forlani, Peter Mooney, Clive Standen, Philip Winchester, Eva Green, Chipo Chung, Sinéad Cusack

Merlin, Arthur, and the usual suspects fight dark forces to bring 5th-century Britain into the future.

### *The Chronicle* (2001–2002, 22 episodes, USA)
*Main Cast:* Chad Willett, Rena Sofer, Reno Wilson, Jon Polito, Curtis Armstrong, Sharon Sachs

A reporter takes a job at a tabloid newspaper and finds that aliens and ghosts are real.

### Honorable Mentions 221

***Code Name: Eternity*** **(2000, 26 episodes, Canada/France/Germany/ USA)**
*Main Cast:* Cameron Bancroft, Ingrid Kavelaars, Andrew Gillies, Joseph Baldwin, Gordon Currie, Olivier Gruner
    An alien takes on human form to pursue a rogue scientist out to destroy humanity.

***Colony*** **(2016– , 10 episodes, USA)**
*Main Cast:* Josh Holloway, Sarah Wayne Callies, Peter Jacobson, Amanda Righetti, Tory Kittles, Alex Neustaedter, Isabella Crovetti-Cramp, Jacob Buster
    Extraterrestrials take over Los Angeles and a family fights back.

***Commando Cody: Sky Marshal of the Universe*** **(1955, 12 episodes, USA)**
*Main Cast:* Judd Holdren, Aline Towne, Gregory Gaye, Craig Kelly
    A masked scientist and his team battle an evil alien out to take over the Earth.

***Damien*** **(2016, 10 episodes, USA)**
*Main Cast:* Bradley James, Megalyn Echikunwoke, Omid Abtahi, David Meunier, Barbara Hershey
    After his appearance as a child in *The Omen*, the Antichrist is back, now a 30-year-old war photographer.

***Dark Matter*** **(2015– , 22 episodes, Canada)**
*Main Cast:* Melissa O'Neil, Anthony Lemke, Alex Mallari, Jr., Zoie Palmer, Jodelle Ferland, Roger Cross, Marc Bendavid
    Six people awaken aboard a derelict spaceship with no memory of who they are or what their mission is.

***Dark Skies*** **(1996–1997, 20 episodes, USA)**
*Main Cast:* Eric Close, Megan Ward, J.T. Walsh, Tim Kelleher, Conor O'Farrell, Charley Lang, Jeri Ryan
    Two people try to thwart the plans of extraterrestrials who have been on Earth since the 1940s.

***The Dead Zone*** **(2002–2007, 80 episodes, Canada/USA)**
*Main Cast:* Anthony Michael Hall, Nicole de Boer, Chris Bruno, John L. Adams
    A man awakens from a six-year coma to find he has psychic abilities, which he uses to solve crimes.

***Defiance*** **(2013–2015, 38 episodes, USA)**
*Main Cast:* Grant Bowler, Julie Benz, Stephanie Leonidas, Tony Curran, Jaime Murray, Jesse Rath, Trenna Keating, Graham Greene
    Humans and extraterrestrials battle for control of Earth, endangering the fragile peace in Defiance, once known as St. Louis.

***Dominion*** **(2014–2015, 21 episodes, USA)**
*Main Cast:* Christopher Egan, Tom Wisdom, Roxanne McKee, Luke Allen-Gale, Anthony Head, Shivani Ghai, Alan Dale, Carl Beukes, Kim Engelbrecht

Archangels Gabriel and Michael take sides in a war between the lower angels and the human race.

### *Dracula* (2013–2014, 10 episodes, UK/USA)
*Main Cast:* Jonathan Rhys Meyers, Jessica De Gouw, Thomas Kretschmann, Victoria Smurfit, Oliver Jackson-Cohen, Nonso Anozie, Katie McGrath, Ben Miles

Bram Stoker's vampire returns from the dead once again, this time in Victorian London.

### *Dracula: The Series* (1990–1991, 21 episodes, Canada/USA)
*Main Cast:* Bernard Behrens, Geordie Johnson, Joe Roncetti, Jacob Tierney, Mia Kirshner

American teens are sent to live with their vampire-hunting uncle, who is after the usual suspect.

### *Earth: Final Conflict* (1997–2002, 110 episodes, Canada/Germany/USA)
*Main Cast:* Kevin Kilner, Lisa Howard, Von Flores, Richard Chevolleau, Leni Parker, David Hemblen, Anita La Selva, Robert Leeshock, Jayne Heitmeyer

Extraterrestrials come bearing gifts, but some humans are skeptical in this revolving-door series.

### *The Expanse* (2015– , 10 episodes, Canada/USA)
*Main Cast:* Thomas Jane, Steven Strait, Shohreh Aghdashloo, Cas Anvar, Dominique Tipper, Wes Chatham, Florence Faivre, Shawn Doyle, Frankie Adams

A police detective, a freighter officer, and a U.N. diplomat work to keep peace in our colonized solar system.

### *Falling Skies* (2011–2015, 52 episodes, USA)
*Main Cast:* Noah Wyle, Moon Bloodgood, Drew Roy, Maxim Knight, Seychelle Gabriel, Peter Shinkoda, Mpho Koaho, Connor Jessup, Will Patton, Sarah Carter, Colin Cunningham

Extraterrestrials invade, wiping out most of humanity and leaving only a ragtag group (surprise) to fight back.

### *First Wave* (1998–2001, 66 episodes, Canada)
*Main Cast:* Sebastian Spence, Rob LaBelle, Roger Cross, Traci Lords

A reformed thief and a computer hacker use some lost prophecies of Nostradamus to combat an alien invasion.

### *FreakyLinks* (2000–2001, 13 episodes, USA)
*Main Cast:* Ethan Embry, Lisa Sheridan, Karim Prince, Lizette Carrion, Dennis Christopher

A man investigates weird phenomena with his friends, while searching for clues about his brother's death.

### *Game of Thrones* (2011– , 60 episodes, USA)
*Main Cast:* Peter Dinklage, Lena Headey, Emilia Clarke, Kit Harington, Sophie Turner,

Maisie Williams, Nikolaj Coster-Waldau, Iain Glen, Alfie Allen, John Bradley, Aidan Gillen, Conleth Hill, Gwendoline Christie, Sean Bean, Michelle Fairley

The largest ensemble cast on television tackles fictional and fantastical dynastic wars during the Middle Ages. Based on the works of George R.R. Martin.

### *Gemini Man* (1976, 12 episodes, USA)
*Main Cast:* Ben Murphy, Katherine Crawford, William Sylvester

A secret agent becomes invisible after an underwater explosion, using a special wristwatch to control his power.

### *Homeboys in Outer Space* (1996–1997, 21 episodes, USA)
*Main Cast:* Flex Alexander, Darryl M. Bell, Rhona Bennett, Kevin Michael Richardson, Paulette Braxton

Two astronauts roam the galaxy in a winged car guided by a sassy female computer.

### *The Immortal* (2000–2001, 22 episodes, Canada)
*Main Cast:* Lorenzo Lamas, Steve Braun, April Telek

A man whose daughter was kidnapped by demons in the 16th century pursues them into the current day.

### *iZombie* (2015– , 32 episodes, USA)
*Main Cast:* Rose McIver, Malcolm Goodwin, Rahul Kohli, Robert Buckley, David Anders, Aly Michalka

A medical student finds purpose as a zombie, when eating the brains of dead people helps to solve their murders.

### *Jake 2.0* (2003–2004, 16 episodes, Canada/USA)
*Main Cast:* Christopher Gorham, Philip Anthony-Rodriguez, Judith Scott, Marina Black, Keegan Connor Tracy, Miranda Frigon

A computer technician becomes an agent for the NSA after he is infected with nanobots and gains special powers.

### *The Journey of Allen Strange* (1997–2000, 57 episodes, USA)
*Main Cast:* Arjay Smith, Erin J. Dean, Shane Sweet, Jack Tate

A young extraterrestrial is stranded on Earth and takes human form, befriending two kids and their dad.

### *The Last Ship* (2014– , 34 episodes, USA)
*Main Cast:* Eric Dane, Rhona Mitra, Adam Baldwin, Charles Parnell, Travis Van Winkle, Marissa Neitling, Christina Elmore, John Pyper-Ferguson, Jocko Sims, Kevin Michael Martin, Fay Masterson

The crew of a naval destroyer must deal with the aftermath of a global pandemic and save the remnants of humanity.

### *The Leftovers* (2014– , 20 episodes, USA)
*Main Cast:* Justin Theroux, Amy Brenneman, Christopher Eccleston, Liv Tyler, Chris Zylka, Margaret Qualley, Carrie Coon, Emily Meade, Amanda Warren, Ann Dowd

Three years after the "Sudden Departure" of two percent of the world's population, survivors struggle to cope.

### Legends of Tomorrow (2016– , 16 episodes, USA)
Main Cast: Brandon Routh, Arthur Darvill, Caity Lotz, Franz Drameh, Victor Garber, Ciara Renée, Falk Hentschel, Amy Pemberton, Dominic Purcell, Wentworth Miller, Matt Letscher, Maisie Richardson-Sellers, Nick Zano

LOTS of superheroes team up to save the world and preserve our timeline.

### Lexx (1997–2002, 61 episodes, Canada/Germany/UK/USA)
Main Cast: Brian Downey, Michael McManus, Xenia Seeberg, Jeffrey Hirschfield, Tom Gallant

Another motley crew aboard a spacecraft, this time an organic starship.

### Life on Mars (2008–2009, 17 episodes, USA)
Main Cast: Jason O'Mara, Harvey Keitel, Jonathan Murphy, Michael Imperioli, Gretchen Mol

A police detective wakes up in 1973 after being hit by a car in 2008. Based on the UK series of the same title.

### The Listener (2009–2014, 65 episodes, Canada)
Main Cast: Craig Olejnik, Ennis Esmer, Mylène Dinh-Robic, Lisa Marcos, Lauren Lee Smith, Rainbow Sun Francks, Peter Stebbings, Tara Spencer-Nairn

A telepathic paramedic uses his abilities to help people in trouble and assist the police in crime-solving.

### Logan's Run (1977–1978, 14 episodes, USA)
Main Cast: Gregory Harrison, Heather Menzies, Donald Moffat, Randy Powell

A man and woman escape a futuristic city, where people are exterminated when they reach the age of 30.

### Lucifer (2016– , 13 episodes, USA)
Main Cast: Tom Ellis, Lauren German, Kevin Alejandro, D.B. Woodside, Lesley-Ann Brandt, Scarlett Estevez, Rachael Harris

Lucifer grows weary of Hell and moves to Los Angeles, where he opens a club and consults for the LAPD.

### Man from Atlantis (1977–1978, 13 episodes, USA)
Main Cast: Patrick Duffy, Belinda Montgomery, Alan Fudge

The lone survivor of Atlantis uses his native undersea abilities to assist humans at a research institute.

### The Man in the High Castle (2015– , 10 episodes, USA)
Main Cast: Alexa Davalos, Rupert Evans, Luke Kleintank, DJ Qualls, Joel de la Fuente, Cary-Hiroyuki Tagawa, Rufus Sewell, Brennan Brown, Bella Heathcote

In an alternate 1962, Germany and Japan won World War II, and have divided the United States between them.

### Max Headroom (1987–1988, 14 episodes, USA)
*Main Cast:* Matt Frewer, Amanda Pays, W. Morgan Sheppard, Chris Young, Charles Rocket, Jeffrey Tambor, George Coe

A crusading TV reporter battles corruption with the help of his computer-generated alter ego in a dystopian future.

### Millennium (1996–1999, 67 episodes, USA)
*Main Cast:* Lance Henriksen, Megan Gallagher, Terry O'Quinn, Brittany Tiplady, Klea Scott

A former FBI agent with the ability to read the minds of murderers begins to work for a mysterious organization.

### Mister Ed (1961–1966, 143 episodes, USA)
*Main Cast:* Alan Young, Connie Hines, Allan Lane, Edna Skinner, Larry Keating, Leon Ames, Florence MacMichael

The comic misadventures of an architect who owns a talking horse, and a troublemaking one at that.

### My Favorite Martian (1963–1966, 107 episodes, USA)
*Main Cast:* Ray Walston, Bill Bixby, Pamela Britton, Alan Hewitt

An anthropologist from Mars crash-lands on Earth and becomes the roommate of a newspaper reporter.

### No Ordinary Family (2010–2011, 20 episodes, USA)
*Main Cast:* Michael Chiklis, Julie Benz, Kay Panabaker, Jimmy Bennett, Autumn Reeser, Romany Malco, Stephen Collins, Josh Stewart

An ordinary American family becomes extraordinary after gaining superpowers in the Amazon.

### Odyssey 5 (2002–2004, 19 episodes, Canada)
*Main Cast:* Peter Weller, Christopher Gorham, Sebastian Roché, Leslie Silva, Tamara Craig Thomas

When the earth suddenly implodes, five astronauts go back in time to prevent the cataclysm.

### The Others (2000, 13 episodes, USA)
*Main Cast:* Julianne Nicholson, Gabriel Macht, Melissa Crider, Bill Cobbs, John Billingsley, Kevin J. O'Connor

A college student with psychic abilities joins with others of her kind to investigate paranormal phenomena.

### Otherworld (1985, 8 episodes, USA)
*Main Cast:* Sam Groom, Gretchen Corbett, Tony O'Dell, Jonna Lee, Chris Hebert, Jonathan Banks

A family is transported to an alternate dimension while visiting an Egyptian pyramid.

### *Out of the Blue* (1979, 12 episodes, USA)
*Main Cast:* Jimmy Brogan, Dixie Carter, Clark Brandon, Olivia Barash, Tammy Lauren, Jason Keller, Shane Keller, Hannah Dean, Eileen Heckart

A novice angel is assigned to assist a Chicago family of newly orphaned siblings and their aunt.

### *Phil of the Future* (2004–2006, 43 episodes, USA)
*Main Cast:* Raviv Ullman, Aly Michalka, Amy Bruckner, Craig Anton, Lise Simms

A teen and his unusual family try to adapt to life in the 21st century after their time machine malfunctions.

### *Point Pleasant* (2005, 13 episodes, USA)
*Main Cast:* Elisabeth Harnois, Grant Show, Samuel Page, Aubrey Dollar, Dina Meyer, Cameron Richardson, Clare Carey, Brent Weber, Susan Walters, Richard Burgi

After Satan's teenage daughter is saved by a lifeguard in New Jersey, strange things happen around town.

### *The Pretender* (1996–2000, 86 episodes, USA)
*Main Cast:* Michael T. Weiss, Andrea Parker, Patrick Bauchau, Jon Gries

A talented imposter assumes new identities while staying one step ahead of his former kidnappers.

### *Ravenswood* (2013–2014, 10 episodes, USA)
*Main Cast:* Nicole Gale Anderson, Tyler Blackburn, Steven Cabral, Brett Dier, Britne Oldford, Merritt Patterson

Five teens, one of them a ghost, are connected by a town's deadly curse.

### *Resurrection* (2014–2015, 21 episodes, USA)
*Main Cast:* Omar Epps, Frances Fisher, Matt Craven, Devin Kelley, Mark Hildreth, Samaire Armstrong, Landon Gimenez, Kurtwood Smith

Deceased loved ones return to the world of the living in a small Missouri town.

### *Revolution* (2012–2014, 42 episodes, USA)
*Main Cast:* Billy Burke, Tracy Spiridakos, Giancarlo Esposito, Zak Orth, David Lyons, Elizabeth Mitchell, J.D. Pardo, Daniella Alonso, Stephen Collins

A family struggles to survive after a permanent electrical blackout changes life in the America they once knew.

### *Shadowhunters: The Mortal Instruments* (2016– , 13 episodes, USA)
*Main Cast:* Katherine McNamara, Dominic Sherwood, Alberto Rosende, Matthew Daddario, Emeraude Toubia, Isaiah Mustafa, Harry Shum, Jr.

On her 18th birthday, a woman learns that she is descended from angels and must fight demons.

### *The Shannara Chronicles* (2016– , 10 episodes, New Zealand/USA)
*Main Cast:* Austin Butler, Poppy Drayton, Ivana Baquero, Manu Bennett, Aaron Jakubenko, Marcus Vanco

Elves and their human allies undertake a quest to save a tree which protects their lands from demons.

### *666 Park Avenue* (2012–2013, 13 episodes, USA)
*Main Cast:* Rachael Taylor, Dave Annable, Robert Buckley, Mercedes Masohn, Erik Palladino, Helena Mattsson, Samantha Logan, Vanessa Williams, Terry O'Quinn
    A couple arrives to manage a posh Manhattan apartment building, but finds that darkness resides within.

### *The Sixth Sense* (1972, 25 episodes, USA)
*Main Cast:* Gary Collins, Catherine Ferrar, Percy Rodriguez
    A college professor investigates mysteries with paranormal overtones.

### *Sleepwalkers* (1997–1998, 9 episodes, USA)
*Main Cast:* Bruce Greenwood, Naomi Watts, Abraham Benrubi, Jeffrey D. Sams
    Researchers use computer technology to enter the dreams of patients and diagnose their psychological problems.

### *Sliders* (1995–2000, 88 episodes, USA)
*Main Cast:* Jerry O'Connell, Cleavant Derricks, Sabrina Lloyd, John Rhys-Davies, Kari Wuhrer, Charlie O'Connell
    A group slides helplessly from parallel universe to universe, losing original cast members along the way.

### *Space: Above and Beyond* (1995–1996, 23 episodes, USA)
*Main Cast:* Lanei Chapman, Kristen Cloke, Joel de la Fuente, James Morrison, Rodney Rowland, Morgan Weisser
    U.S. Marines stationed on a carrier in outer space battle an alien invasion of our solar system.

### *Space Cases* (1996–1997, 27 episodes, Canada)
*Main Cast:* Walter Emanuel Jones, Jewel Staite, Rebecca Herbst, Kristian Ayre, Rahi Azizi, Paige Christina, Anik Matern, Cary Lawrence, Paul Boretski
    Five students and two of their teachers are trapped aboard an alien spaceship and must find their way home.

### *Starhunter* (2000–2004, 44 episodes, Canada)
*Main Cast:* Michael Paré, Tanya Allen, Claudette Roche, Stephen Marcus, Murray Melvin, Clive Robertson, Dawn Stern, Paul Fox
    Bounty hunters search for criminals in outer space.

### *Stranger Things* (2016– , 8 episodes, USA)
*Main Cast:* Winona Ryder, David Harbour, Finn Wolfhard, Millie Bobby Brown, Gaten Matarazzo, Caleb McLaughlin, Natalia Dyer, Charlie Heaton, Cara Buono, Joe Keery, Noah Schnapp
    In 1983 a boy is taken from an Indiana town to an alternate dimension.

### Surface (2005–2006, 15 episodes, USA)
*Main Cast:* Lake Bell, Jay R. Ferguson, Carter Jenkins, Ian Anthony Dale, Leighton Meester, Lou Anne Cooper, Ric Reitz

People around the world encounter a new form of sea life, while government agents act suspiciously.

### The Tick (2001–2002, 9 episodes, USA)
*Main Cast:* Patrick Warburton, David Burke, Nestor Carbonell, Liz Vassey

Superhero parody about a big blue bug of justice and his sidekicks.

### The Tomorrow People (2013–2014, 22 episodes, USA)
*Main Cast:* Robbie Amell, Luke Mitchell, Peyton List, Aaron Yoo, Madeleine Mantock, Mark Pellegrino

A group of young telepaths must hide their gifts from a fearful public. Based on the 70s British series.

### Torchwood (2006–2011, 41 episodes, UK)
*Main Cast:* John Barrowman, Gareth David-Lloyd, Eve Myles, Burn Gorman, Naoko Mori, Kai Owen

Members of a secret institute in Wales battle extraterrestrial threats in this spin-off from *Doctor Who*.

### Total Recall 2070 (1999, 22 episodes, Canada/Germany)
*Main Cast:* Michael Easton, Karl Pruner, Cynthia Preston, Michael Rawlins, Judith Krant, Matthew Bennett

Two detectives, one human and one android, solve techno-crimes in a future ruled by corporations.

### Tracker (2001–2002, 22 episodes, Canada)
*Main Cast:* Adrian Paul, Amy Price-Francis, Leanne Wilson, Geraint Wyn Davies

An extraterrestrial comes to earth to recapture escaped prisoners and receives help from a Chicago bar owner.

### Tremors (2003, 13 episodes, USA)
*Main Cast:* Victor Browne, Gladise Jimenez, Marcia Strassman, Lela Lee, Dean Norris, Michael Gross

Residents of a small Nevada town try to coexist with a giant sandworm.

### 12 Monkeys (2015– , 26 episodes, USA)
*Main Cast:* Aaron Stanford, Amanda Schull, Kirk Acevedo, Todd Stashwick, Emily Hampshire, Barbara Sukowa, Andrew Gillies

A man travels back in time to prevent the release of a deadly virus that will kill billions of people.

### UFO (1970–1973, 26 episodes, UK)
*Main Cast:* Ed Bishop, Keith Alexander, Michael Billington, Ayshea Brough, Antonia Ellis, Dolores Mantez, George Sewell

A secret military agency is established in 1980 to combat aliens who kill humans for body parts.

### *Under the Dome* (2013–2015, 39 episodes, USA)
*Main Cast:* Mike Vogel, Rachelle Lefevre, Natalie Martinez, Alexander Koch, Nicholas Strong, Colin Ford, Aisha Hinds, Dean Norris, Mackenzie Lintz, Eddie Cahill

A massive dome suddenly seals off a small town, and its residents scramble to survive while searching for answers.

### *The Walking Dead* (2010– , 83 episodes, USA)
*Main Cast:* Andrew Lincoln, Jon Bernthal, Sarah Wayne Callies, Laurie Holden, Jeffrey DeMunn, Steven Yeun, Chandler Riggs, Norman Reedus, Lauren Cohan, Danai Gurira, Michael Rooker, David Morrissey, Melissa McBride, Scott Wilson, Alanna Masterson, Josh McDermitt, Christian Serratos, Sonequa Martin-Green

Survivors tackle a zombie apocalypse, with frequent casualties and cast changes.

### *Wolfblood* (2012– , 51 episodes, UK)
*Main Cast:* Aimee Kelly, Shorelle Hepkin, Kedar Williams-Stirling, Louisa Connolly-Burnham, Leona Vaughan, Gabrielle Green, Rachel Teate

A werewolf family in England tries to hide its secret, but new arrivals in town cause trouble.

### *Woops!* (1992, 13 episodes, USA)
*Main Cast:* Evan Handler, Fred Applegate, Meagen Fay, Cleavant Derricks, Marita Geraghty, Lane Davies

The end of the world is played for laughs when six survivors of a nuclear holocaust join forces.

### *Z Nation* (2014– , 28 episodes, USA)
*Main Cast:* Kellita Smith, DJ Qualls, Keith Allan, Russell Hodgkinson, Anastasia Baranova, Nat Zang, Pisay Pao

Survivors of a zombie apocalypse must transport a special patient from New York to a lab in California.

# A Note on Sources

Information contained in this volume comes from a variety of sources, an individual listing of which might comprise a book on its own.

The most important sources, of course, were the TV shows themselves, viewed over the decades via broadcast TV, cable, VHS tapes, satellite, DVR, and streaming services. DVDs were pivotal to the research for this book, providing the opportunity both to revisit old programs and to discover new shows that can be easily missed in an increasingly crowded TV environment. Series descriptions and episode blurbs included on DVD menus and packaging provided additional information.

Two comprehensive guides to TV programming were invaluable in compiling the list of series to be included in this work: *The Complete Directory to Prime Time Network and Cable TV Shows: 1946–Present* by Tim Brooks and Earle Marsh (Ballantine Books, 2007) and *The Complete Encyclopedia of Television Programs: 1947–1979* by Vincent Terrace (A.S. Barnes, 1979).

Two SF–focused guides, *Science Fiction Television Series: Episode Guides, Histories, and Casts and Credits for 62 Prime Time Shows, 1959 Through 1989* (McFarland, 1996) and *Science Fiction Television Series, 1990–2004: Histories, Casts and Credits for 58 Shows* (McFarland, 2009) both by Mark Phillips and Frank Garcia, helped to solidify the list of science fiction shows to be covered and made it easier to see thematic links between shows for the book's introduction. *Fantasy Girls: Gender in the New Universe of Science Fiction and Fantasy Television* (Rowman & Littlefield, 2000), a collection of essays edited by Elyce Rae Helford, provided scholarly and feminist perspective on 1990s SF/fantasy series with female leads.

It's the information age and this book would not have been completed without the extensive reach of the Internet. Valuable Internet resources, particularly for more recent series, include *Wikipedia* (en.wikipedia.org), *IMDb* (imdb.com), and *TV.com*, all of which contain articles on individual series, including cast lists, production credits and episode summaries. Also helpful were product descriptions and professional reviews for DVDs at *Amazon.com*, wikis for individual TV shows at *Fandom.com*, series descriptions and thematic analyses at *TV Tropes* (tvtropes.org), and official websites for the series, where available.

Specialized sites, such as *The Classic TV Archive* (ctva.biz) and *TV Acres* (www.tvacres.com) were useful in tracking down information about older series, as was *The Encyclopedia of Science Fiction: Third Edition* edited by John Clute, David Langford, Peter Nicholls and Graham Sleight (www.sf-encyclopedia.com). The *BFI/British Film Institute* website (bfi.org.uk) was a good source for esoteric production credits. *YouTube* (youtube.com) and *dailymotion* (dailymotion.com) were helpful repositories of clips for verifying cast/production credits, opening narrations, and plot details.

At least four sources were consulted for each entry, and inconsistencies between sources were resolved wherever possible.

# Index

Abercrombie, Ian 40
Abtahi, Omid 221
Acevedo, Kirk 81, 228
Acker, Amy 25
Acovone, Jay 33
Adams, Don 5, 19, 83
Adams, Frankie 222
Adams, John L. 221
Adams, Rahart 70–71
Addams, Dawn 172
Addy, Mark 220
Aghdashloo, Shohreh 222
Agyeman, Freema 60–61
Akin, Philip 205
Alaskey, Joe 140
Alba, Jessica 10, 56–57
Alden, Norman 68
Alejandro, Kevin 224
Ales, John 217
Aletter, Frank 100
Alexander, Elizabeth 191
Alexander, Flex 223
Alexander, Jaimie 107
Alexander, Keith 228
Ali, Mahershalalhashbaz 79
Allan, Keith 229
Allen, Alfie 223
Allen, Laura 79
Allen, Tanya 227
Allen-Gale, Luke 221
Alonso, Daniella 226
Alvarez, Tyler 70
Amell, Robbie 228
Amell, Stephen 219
Ames, Leon 225
Amick, Mädchen 198–199, 210
Anders, David 223
Anderson, Brooke 138

Anderson, Gillian 9, 57, 156–157, 214–215
Anderson, Jo 33
Anderson, Melody 120
Anderson, Nicole Gale 34, 226
Anderson, Richard 39, 167
Anderson, Richard Dean 47, 178
Anderson, Shamier 214
Andino, Paola 70
Andrews, David 121
Andrews, Naveen 113
Angel, Vanessa 207
Anholt, Christien 10, 149
Anholt, Tony 168
Ankrum, David 185
Annable, Dave 227
Anozie, Nonso 222
Anthony-Rodriguez, Philip 223
Antoine, Vinessa 220
Anton, Craig 226
Anvar, Cas 222
Appelman, Zach 162
Appleby, Shiri 152
Applegate, Fred 229
Appleman, Hale 118
Armstrong, Curtis 220
Armstrong, Kerry 138
Armstrong, Samaire 226
Arngrim, Stefan 108
Arquette, Patricia 65, 85, 122
Ashbrook, Dana 142, 198
Asher, John Mallory 207
Ashmore, Aaron 62, 106, 206
Ashmore, Shawn 219
Astin, John 15–16
Atwell, Hayley 12, 18–19

Auberjonois, René 173
Aubrey, Juliet 145
Austin, Jake T. 211
Austin, Reggie 18
Avgeropoulos, Marie 96–97
Aykroyd, Dan 146–147
Aylesworth, Reiko 219
Ayre, Kristian 227
Azizi, Rahi 227

Baccarin, Morena 69, 74–75, 178, 201–202
Badler, Jane 8, 126–127, 201
Bain, Barbara 5, 7, 46, 126–127, 168
Baird, Jenni 79
Bakay, Nick 153–154
Baker, Tom 60–61, 164
Bakke, Brenda 219
Bakula, Scott 174
Baldwin, Adam 52, 74, 223
Baldwin, Joseph 221
Balfe, Caitriona 141
Balfour, Eric 91–92
Bamber, Jamie 31
Bancroft, Cameron 221
Banks, Jonathan 225
Baquero, Ivana 226
Bara, Nina 4, 168–169
Baranova, Anastasia 229
Barash, Olivia 226
Barber, Glynis 220
Barnstable, Cyb 148
Barnstable, Patricia 148
Barrell, Katherine 214
Barrera, Maria Canals 211
Barrett, Majel 3, 173, 175
Barrett, Nancy 57
Barrie, Barbara 197

# 234  Index

Barrowman, John  228
Basis, Austin  34
Bass, Ben  78, 203
Bastedo, Alexandra  47–48
Bauchau, Patrick  226
Bauer, Chris  196
Beacham, Stephanie  157
Beals, Jennifer  146
Bean, Sean  223
Beattie, Joseph  93
Beckett, Scotty  151
Beharie, Nicole  10, 124, 162
Behr, Jason  152
Behrens, Bernard  222
Belafonte, Shari  10, 38
Belfi, Jordan  198
Bell, Catherine  87
Bell, Darryl M.  223
Bell, Lake  228
Bell, Nicholas  138
Bell, Oliver  154
Belmondo, Buzz  140
Beltran, Robert  176
Benanti, Laura  184
Bendavid, Marc  221
Bendix, Simone  170
Benedict, Dirk  31
Benedict, Rob  190
Benítez, Benjamín  196
Benjamin, Richard  148
Bennet, Chloe  20–21
Bennett, Cle  114
Bennett, Jimmy  225
Bennett, Joan  12, 57–58
Bennett, Manu  226
Bennett, Matthew  228
Bennett, Nigel  78–79, 146
Bennett, Rhona  223
Benoist, Melissa  183
Benrubi, Abraham  227
Benson, Amber  11, 44, 151
Benson, Ashley  67
Ben-Victor, Paul  99
Benymon, Chico  91
Benz, Julie  221, 225
Berkeley, Xander  154
Bernthal, Jon  67, 229
Berry, Halle  10, 71
Bertinelli, Valerie  195
Bertram, Laura  24
Beukes, Carl  221
Beymer, Richard  142, 198
Bhaneja, Raoul  63
Bickart, Sanford  43
Bierk, Dylan  220
Biggs, Richard  28

Billingsley, John  174, 225
Billington, Michael  228
Bilodeau, Jean-Luc  107
Bishil, Summer  118
Bishop, Ed  228
Bishop, Meredith  159
Bissell, Whit  191–192
Bixby, Bill  225
Black, Claudia  73, 178
Black, Lucas  219
Black, Marina  223
Blackburn, Tyler  226
Blackman, Honor  5, 27, 83
Blackthorne, Paul  63, 219
Blake, Carter  193
Blake, Madge  30
Blakely, Rachel  117
Blakley, Michael  159
Blalock, Jolene  174
Blanc, Mel  43
Blanchard, Rachel  205–206
Blanche, Robert  89
Blasi, Rosa  190
Bloodgood, Moon  222
Blucas, Marc  44
Blue, Callum  59, 146
Boltin, Rob  189
Bomer, Matt  196
Bond, Grahame  220
Bond, Rhys Matthew  87
Booth, Lindy  111, 149
Boreanaz, David  25, 44–45, 51
Boretski, Paul  227
Bostick, Devon  96
Boston, Rachel  210
Bower, Jamie Campbell  220
Bowers, Chris  39–40
Bowlby, April  64
Bowler, Grant  221
Boxleitner, Bruce  28, 217–218
Boyd, Guy  40
Boylan, John  220
Boyle, Lara Flynn  198
Bradley, John  223
Brancati, Paula  220
Brandis, Jonathan  157
Brandon, Clark  226
Brandt, Lesley-Ann  224
Braun, Steve  223
Braxton, Paulette  223
Breitkopf, Kyle Harrison  208
Brendon, Nicholas  44–45, 51, 151
Brenneman, Amy  223
Brenner, Dori  50

Brice, Pierre  172
Briggs, Tony  138
Brissette, Tiffany  7, 163
Britton, Pamela  225
Brochu, Évelyne  139
Broderick, Beth  153, 171
Brogan, Jimmy  226
Brooks, Avery  173
Brooks, Dana  186
Brooks, Martin E.  39
Brooks, Mehcad  183–184
Brough, Ayshea  228
Browder, Ben  73
Brown, Blair  81
Brown, Brennan  224
Brown, Clancy  66, 162
Brown, Lucy  145
Brown, Max  34
Brown, Millie Bobby  227
Brown, Orlando  187
Browne, Victor  228
Bruce, Dylan  139
Bruckner, Amy  226
Bruno, Chris  221
Bruun, Kristian  139
Bryant, Lucas  91–92
Bryce, Edward  193
Bryk, Greg  220
B.T.  40
Buckley, Robert  223, 227
Bulifant, Joyce  207
Buono, Cara  227
Burch, Liz  138
Burger, Zoey  70
Burgi, Richard  226
Burke, Billy  226
Burke, David  228
Burton, LeVar  175
Burton, Norman  212
Burton, Steve  140
Buster, Jacob  221
Butler, Austin  226
Butler, Yancy  121, 209–210
Buza, George  95, 120, 219
Buzzi, Ruth  116

Cabral, Steven  226
Cabrera, Boris  219
Cahill, Eddie  229
Caillou, Alan  148
Cain, Dean  112–113
Call, Brandon  50
Callan, K  112
Callies, Sarah Wayne  221, 229
Callis, James  31–32
Calvert, Jim  182–183

Index   235

Cameron, JoAnna  6, 100
Campbell, Bill  79
Campbell, Bruce  101
Campbell, Conchita  79, 162
Campbell, Nicholas  91
Campbell, Sarah  150
Capaldi, Peter  60
Carbonell, Nestor  228
Cardi, Pat  100
Carey, Clare  226
Carlyle, Robert  138–139
Carpenter, Charisma  25, 44–45, 51
Carpenter, Jennifer  111
Carraher, Harlen  84
Carrere, Tia  10, 149
Carrion, Lizette  222
Carroll, Leo G.  86, 193–195
Carrott, Ric  167
Carter, Dixie  226
Carter, Jason  28–29
Carter, Lynda  6, 212–213
Carter, Sarah  222
Cartwright, Angela  115–116
Cartwright, Ryan  23
Cartwright, Veronica  67
Cassidy, Katie  219
Cassidy, Ted  15–16
Cate, Field  147
Caulfield, Emma  44
Cavanagh, Tom  75
Celentano, Teresa  189
Cerra, Erica  69, 117
Chadwick, June  201
Champlin, Irene  4, 76
Chandler, Kyle  65
Chapman, Lanei  227
Chappell, Jan  220
Charles, Max  135
Chase, Bailey  156
Chatham, Wes  222
Chaves, Richard  205
Chen, Joan  198
Chenoweth, Kristin  147
Chestnut, Morris  201
Chevolleau, Richard  222
Chiklis, Michael  225
Cho, John  77
Cho, Margaret  64
Chokachi, David  209
Chong, Rae Dawn  134
Chong, Robbi  144
Christian, Claudia  11, 28–29
Christie, Dick  163
Christie, Gwendoline  223
Christie, Warren  23

Christina, Paige  227
Christopher, Dennis  222
Christopher, Gerard  182–183
Christopher, Thom  43–44
Christy, Kevin  160
Chung, Chipo  220
Chung, Jamie  35
Cibrian, Eddie  32, 99
Cistaro, Anthony  209
Clark, Eugene  186
Clarke, Emilia  222
Cliche, Karen  132, 217–218
Cloke, Kristen  227
Close, Eric  221
Coates, Conrad  63
Coates, Phyllis  4, 17–18, 109–110, 164
Cobb, Keith Hamilton  24
Cobbs, Bill  225
Coca, Imogene  100
Coe, George  225
Coffee, Claire  89
Cohan, Lauren  229
Colbert, Robert  191–192
Cole, Christina  11, 93
Cole, Gary  219
Cole, Taylor  70
Coleman, Jack  36, 92–93
Coleman, Jenna  60–61
Coleman, Kathy  109
Colen, Beatrice  212
Collen, Jacqueline  219
Collins, Clifton, Jr.  70
Collins, Gary  227
Collins, Jessica  196
Collins, K.C.  114
Collins, Stephen  225–226
Colter, Mike  104
Combs, Holly Marie  9, 49
Conaway, Jeff  28
Condon, Kerry  35
Connolly, Kristen  208
Connolly-Burnham, Louisa  229
Conrad, David  85
Consuelos, Mark  125
Conway, Gary  108
Coogan, Jackie  15–16
Cook, A.J.  196
Cooke, Christian  210
Cooke, Jennifer  201
Coon, Carrie  223
Cooper, Bradley  111
Cooper, Dominic  13, 18
Cooper, Lou Anne  228
Cooper, Maggie  167

Copeland, Adam  91
Corbett, Gretchen  225
Cortese, Joseph  166
Cosgrove, Daniel  219
Cosnett, Rick  75
Coster-Waldau, Nikolaj  223
Coulby, Angel  123–124
Coulson, Catherine E.  198–199
Courtemanche, Michel  158
Coutts, Christopher  68
Cox, Christina  42
Cox, Courteney  125
Coyne, Jonny  21
Coyote, Peter  79
Crabbe, Buster  76
Craig, Yvonne  30–31
Cramp, Isabella  135
Crane, Richard  151
Craven, Matt  226
Crawford, Katherine  223
Crider, Melissa  225
Criss, Darren  67
Crosby, Denise  175
Cross, Roger  54, 221–222
Croucher, Brian  220
Crovetti-Cramp, Isabella  221
Crow, Ashley  92, 158
Cruz, Gregory Norman  156
Cruz, Valerie  63
Csokas, Marton  216
Cubitt, David  122
Culp, Robert  88
Cummings, Bob  133
Cummins, Martin  144
Cunningham, Colin  222
Curran, Tony  221
Currie, Gordon  221
Curtin, Jane  188
Cusack, Sinéad  220
Cusick, Henry Ian  96, 113
Cutler, Brian  100
Czerny, Henry  189

d'Abo, Maryam  166
Dacascos, Mark  55
Daddario, Matthew  226
Daily, Bill  97–98
Dale, Alan  221
Dale, Ian Anthony  70, 228
Dallas, Josh  138–139, 184
Dallas, Matt  67, 107
Dalton, Brett  20–21
Damon, Grey  137, 177
Damon, Stuart  47–48
Danby, Noah  141

# 236 Index

Dane, Eric 223
Dangcil, Linda 77
D'Aquino, John 166
D'Arcy, James 18
Da Re, Eric 142
Darren, James 191–192
Darrow, Paul 220
Darshi, Agam 155
Darvill, Arthur 224
Darville, Eka 104
Davalos, Alexa 224
Davenport, Jack 77
David, Thayer 57
David-Lloyd, Gareth 228
Davidson, John 86–87
Davies, Geraint Wyn 78, 203, 228
Davies, Lane 229
Davis, Don S. 178
Davis, Jamie 93
Davis, Matt 202
Davis, William B. 215
Davis-Williams, Shanésia 65
Dawber, Pam 128–129
Dawson, Roxann 176
Dayoub, Damon 180
Dean, Erin J. 223
Dean, Hannah 226
Dean, Ron 65
Debnam-Carey, Alycia 96–97
de Boer, Nicole 38, 173–174, 221
De Caestecker, Iain 20–21
De Carlo, Yvonne 5, 130–131
De Gouw, Jessica 222
Dekker, Thomas 53, 95, 158, 186–187
de la Fuente, Joel 224, 227
DeLancie, John 111
Delano, Michael 63
Delfino, Majandra 152
de Lint, Derek 144
DeLizia, Cara 9, 165
del Mar, Maria 123, 186
DeLuise, David 47, 211
Demetral, Chris 158
DeMunn, Jeffrey 229
Denis, Catalina 208
Denisof, Alexis 25
Denton, James 87
de Ravin, Emilie 113–114, 138–139, 152
Derricks, Cleavant 227, 229
D'Errico, Donna 32
DeSantis, John 136
Devenie, Stuart 101

Dhavernas, Caroline 213
Diaz, Alyssa 137
Dibbs, Kem 43
Dier, Brett 226
Dillahunt, Garret 186
Dinh-Robic, Mylène 224
Dinklage, Peter 190, 222
Disher, Catherine 78–79, 87, 205
Di Tomasso, Daniel 210
Dobrev, Nina 202
Doherty, Shannen 9, 49–50
Dohring, Jason 128
Doig, Lexa 24, 54, 186
Dollar, Aubrey 226
Donat, Peter 191
Donat, Richard 91
Donnell, Colin 219
Donnelly, Jack 220
Doohan, James 172
Doremus, David 134–135
Dorn, Michael 173–175
D'Orsay, Brooke 64
Dotchin, Angela 101
Dotrice, Roy 33
Douglas, Aaron 31
Douglas, Joanna 220
Dowd, Ann 223
Dowling, Doris 133
Down, Alisen 134
Downey, Brian 224
Downey, Roma 195
Doyle, Jerry 28
Doyle, Shawn 222
Drake, Larry 145
Drameh, Franz 224
Drayton, Poppy 226
Duchene, Deborah 78
Duchovny, David 156, 214–215
Dudley, Olivia Taylor 118
Duffy, Patrick 224
Dullea, Keir 179
Dunn, Nora 189
Dunne, Robin 155
Dunsworth, John 91
Duran, Dan 150
Durance, Erica 163–164
Dushku, Eliza 61, 196
Dutton, Charles S. 190
Dye, John 195
Dyer, Natalia 227
Dyke, Jerry Van 217
Dziena, Alexis 99

Eastham, Richard 212

Easton, Michael 204, 228
Easton, Sheena 217
Eberle, Elise 154
Eccleston, Christopher 223
Echikunwoke, Megalyn 79, 221
Eden, Barbara 5, 97–98, 102
Eden, Richard 150
Edgley, Gigi 73
Edmonds, Louis 57–58
Egan, Christopher 221
Egerton, Tamsin 220
Ehm, Erica 150
Eiding, Paul 50
Eilbacher, Cindy 133
Eisenmann, Ike 72
Elliott, Brooke 64
Ellis, Antonia 228
Ellis, Nelsan 196
Ellis, Tom 224
Elmore, Christina 223
Elson, Andrea 21–22, 208–209
Embry, Ethan 222
Emerson, Michael 113
Emms, Robert 220
Engel, Georgia 103
Engelbrecht, Kim 221
Englund, Robert 201
Epps, Omar 226
Erhuero, Oris 219
Eriksen, Kaj-Erik 79
Esmer, Ennis 224
Esposito, Giancarlo 226
Estevez, Scarlett 224
Etebari, Eric 209
Eure, Wesley 109
Evans, Chris 12, 18
Evans, Kylee 87
Evans, Maurice 38
Evans, Rupert 224
Everett, Wynn 18
Evigan, Greg 186
Evison, Kathy 157

Fabares, Shelley 94
Fairley, Michelle 223
Faison, Frankie 145
Faivre, Florence 222
Farentino, Debrah 66
Farmer, Gary 78
Farmiga, Vera 149
Farrell, Terry 11, 173–174
Fassbender, Michael 93
Fassler, Ron 22
Faust, Chad 79

Fay, Meagen 229
Fedor, Matreya 68
Fehr, Brendan 152
Feldman, Ben 64
Feldon, Barbara 5, 19, 83–84
Fenn, Sherilyn 198–199
Ferdin, Pamelyn 167
Ferguson, Colin 42, 69, 117
Ferguson, Jay R. 228
Ferland, Jodelle 221
Fernandez, Peter Jay 182
Ferrar, Catherine 227
Ferrer, Miguel 39
Ferris, Pat 193
Ferris, Samantha 79
Fichtner, William 99
Field, Sally 5, 77, 86
Fiennes, Joseph 77, 220
Fillion, Nathan 74
Finley, Greg 177
Finneran, Katie 213
Fisher, Frances 226
Flack, Enya 40
Flaherty, Joe 120
Flanagan, Kellie 84
Flanery, Sean Patrick 47
Flannigan, Maureen 7, 140
Fletcher, Lester 63
Fletcher, Louise 204
Flockhart, Calista 183
Flores, Benjamin "Lil' P-Nut," Jr. 91
Flores, Jose 26
Flores, Von 222
Flueger, Patrick 79
Forbes, Michelle 175
Ford, Colin 229
Forest, Denis 205
Forlani, Claire 220
Forster, Robert 21
Fox, Colin 146
Fox, Matthew 27, 113–114
Fox, Paul 227
Fox, Steven 136
Fox, Vivica A. 125
Frakes, Jonathan 175
Francks, Rainbow Sun 224
Franklin, Carl 72
Franklin, Don 157, 160
Frewer, Matt 146, 225
Frid, Jonathan 57–58
Friedericy, Bonita 52
Friel, Anna 147
Frigon, Miranda 223
Frost, Warren 198
Frye, Soleil Moon 153

Fudge, Alan 224
Fugere, Nicole 136
Furlan, Mira 28–29
Furst, Stephen 28
Fusco, Paul 21–22

Gabel, Seth 81, 154
Gabriel, Seychelle 222
Gade, Ariel 99
Gaffin, Melanie 208
Gagnon, Pierce 71
Gail, Max 208–209
Galifianakis, Zach 196
Gallagher, Megan 225
Gallant, Tom 224
Gant, Richard 170
Garber, Victor 224
Garcia, Jorge 21, 113
Gardner, David 150
Garland, Margaret 4, 193
Garner, Jay 43
Garr, Teri 86
Garrison, Scott 82
Gathegi, Edi 146
Gaunt, William 47–48
Gautier, Richard 84
Gavaris, Jordan 139
Gaye, Gregory 221
Gayheart, Rebecca 66
Geeson, Judy 172
Gegenhuber, John 66
Gellar, Sarah Michelle 9, 44, 51, 57, 151, 181–182
George, Lynda Day 126
Geraghty, Marita 229
Gerard, Gil 7, 43
German, Lauren 224
Gertz, Jami 135
Gesner, Zen 219
Ghai, Shivani 221
Ghanizada, Azita 23
Gibbs, Connor 85
Gideon, Louan 159
Gillan, Karen 60
Gillen, Aidan 223
Gillies, Andrew 221, 228
Gilligan, Chelsea 177
Gilmore, Jared S. 138, 184
Gimenez, Landon 226
Gish, Annabeth 214–215
Giuntoli, David 89
Gjokaj, Enver 18–19, 61
Glass, Ron 74
Glau, Summer 53, 74–75, 186–187
Glen, Iain 223

Gless, Sharon 198
Glover, John 163
Goddard, Daniel 220
Goddard, Mark 115–116
Goddard, Paul 73
Godecki, Marzena 138
Goglia, Juliette 105
Goldberg, Iddo 154
Goldberg, Whoopi 175–176
Gomes, Marc 55
Gomez, Joshua 52
Gomez, Selena 11, 211
Goodwin, Ginnifer 138–139, 184
Goodwin, Malcolm 223
Gordon, Gerald 94
Gordon-Levitt, Joseph 188
Gorham, Christopher 223, 225
Gorman, Burn 228
Gorshin, Frank 30
Gower, Jessica 41
Grace, Mary 100
Gracen, Elizabeth 94
Graham, Gary 22
Graham, Kat 202–203
Grant, Faye 88, 201
Graves, Peter 46, 126
Gray, Erin 7, 43
Grayston, Neil 69
Green, Brian Austin 186–187
Green, Eva 220
Green, Gabrielle 229
Green, Jenna Leigh 153–154, 171
Green, Lorne 31
Green, Lynda Mason 205–206
Green, Seth 44, 151
Greene, Ellen 147
Greene, Eric 167
Greene, Graham 221
Greenwood, Bruce 227
Greenwood, Lyndie 124, 162
Greer, Alonzo 149
Gregg, Clark 12, 20
Gregory, Benji 21
Gregory, Dorian 32, 49
Greif, Stephen 220
Gretsch, Joel 79, 162, 201
Gries, Jon 226
Griffo, Jack 190
Grimes, Jack 193
Grives, Steven 220
Groom, Sam 192, 225
Gross, Michael 228

## Index

Gross, Paul 67
Grunberg, Greg 92
Gruner, Olivier 221
Grunwald, Ernie 186
Gugino, Carla 190
Gummer, Grace 71
Gunn, Richard 56–57
Gupta, Arjun 118
Gurira, Danai 229
Gustin, Grant 75
Guy, Jasmine 59
Gwynne, Fred 130–131

Hager, Kristen 34
Hagman, Larry 5, 97–98, 102
Haiduk, Stacy 7, 157, 182–183
Hale, Lucy 39–40
Hall, Anthony Michael 221
Hall, Diedre 6, 68
Hall, Grayson 57–58
Hall, Irma P. 219
Hall, Kevin Peter 125
Hall, Natalie 177
Hallett, Andy 25
Hamilton, John 17–18
Hamilton, Linda 33, 48, 53–54, 186
Hamilton, Neil 30
Hamilton, Tony 126
Hampshire, Emily 228
Hanchard, Kevin 139
Handler, Evan 229
Hankin, Larry 105
Hanks, Colin 152
Hannigan, Alyson 9, 44, 151, 182
Harbour, David 227
Hardy, Jonathan 73
Harewood, David 183–184
Harington, Kit 222
Harmon, Angie 32
Harmon, Richard 96
Harner, Jason Butler 21
Harnois, Elisabeth 226
Harold, Gale 158
Harper, Hill 111
Harper, Ron 109
Harris, Curtis 91
Harris, Jonathan 115, 167
Harris, Kyle 180–181
Harris, Laura 59
Harris, Rachael 224
Harrison, Gregory 224
Harrison, Noel 5, 86
Harrow, Lisa 172
Hart, Aiysha 220

Hart, Hannah 68
Hart, Melissa Joan 9, 153, 171
Hartman, Lisa 185
Hartnell, William 60
Harvie, Ellie 136
Hasselhoff, David 32
Hatch, Richard 31
Hatcher, Teri 112–113, 164
Hawthorne, Elizabeth 53
Hayes, Mia 67
Head, Anthony 123, 204, 221
Head, Anthony Stewart 44
Headey, Lena 53–54, 186–187, 222
Heathcote, Bella 224
Heaton, Charlie 227
Hebert, Chris 225
Hecht, Gina 128
Heckart, Eileen 226
Hedison, Alexandra 145
Heigl, Katherine 152
Heitmeyer, Jayne 222
Helbig, Grace 68
Helfer, Tricia 31–32
Hemblen, David 222
Hemphill, John 120
Henderson, Ty 167
Hendry, Ian 27
Henesy, David 57–58
Hennig, Shelley 158
Henrie, David 211
Henriksen, Lance 225
Henry, Emmaline 97
Henshall, Douglas 145
Hensley, John 209
Hensley, Pamela 43–44
Henson, Garette Ratliff 50
Henstridge, Elizabeth 20–21
Henstridge, Natasha 158
Hentschel, Falk 224
Hepkin, Shorelle 229
Herbst, Rebecca 227
Hershey, Barbara 221
Heughan, Sam 141
Hewett, Lauren 138
Hewitt, Alan 225
Hewitt, Jennifer Love 85
Hewitt, Virginia 4, 168–169
Hey, Virginia 73
Heyerdahl, Christopher 155
Hicks, Catherine 197
Higginson, Torri 186
Hildreth, Mark 217–218, 226
Hill, Conleth 223
Hill, Jacqueline 60
Hill, Steven 126–127

Hilton, Tyler 71
Hinds, Aisha 99, 229
Hines, Connie 225
Hinson, Jordan 69
Hirschfield, Jeffrey 224
Hodgkinson, Russell 229
Hoflin, David 138
Hogan, Michael 31
Holden, Gina 42, 76
Holden, Laurie 229
Holden, Marjean 220
Holden-Ried, Kris 114–115
Holdren, Judd 221
Holland, Steve 4, 76
Holland, Willa 219
Holloway, Josh 27, 113–114, 221
Holmes, Jennifer 125
Holt, Greyston 220
Hon, Jean Marie 26
Hope, Barclay 146–147
Hornsby, Russell 89
Horse, Michael 198
Hosea, Bobby 216
Howard, Clint 170
Howard, Lisa 222
Howard, Sherman 182
Howarth, Roger 145
Howland, Rick 114
Hubbert, Cork 50
Hudson, Ernie 94
Huffman, Alaina 141
Huffman, Logan 69, 201–202
Hunt, Francesca 158
Hunt, Gareth 136
Hunt, Linda 170
Hunter, Holly 156
Huntington, Sam 34
Hurst, Jackson 64
Hurst, Michael 82
Hurt, John 123–124
Huston, Carol 50
Hyde-White, Wilfrid 43

Imperioli, Michael 224
Innes, Laura 70
Ironside, Michael 157, 201, 217–218
Ishta, Emma 180
Ivanek, eljko 70

Jackson, David 220
Jackson, Joshua 81
Jackson, Neil 41
Jackson-Cohen, Oliver 222
Jacobson, Peter 221

Index 239

Jacquet, Jeffrey 208–209
Jakubenko, Aaron 226
James, Bradley 123, 221
James, Ralph 128
Jane, Thomas 222
Janis, Conrad 128–129, 148
Jarchow, Bruce 207
Jeannotte, Dan 87
Jefferson, Herb, Jr. 31
Jeffrey, Myles 65
Jeffreys, Anne 193–195
Jenkins, Carter 228
Jessup, Connor 222
Jillian, Ann 8, 103
Jimenez, Gladise 228
Jo, Tim 135
Johansson, Paul 94
John, Gottfried 170
John-Kamen, Hannah 106
Johnson, Alexz 165
Johnson, Anne-Marie 187–188
Johnson, Bob 126
Johnson, Eric 76
Johnson, Geordie 222
Johnson, Jarrod 116
Johnson, Kenny 156
Johnson, Stephen 63
Johnston, Kristen 166, 188
Jolley, Norman 169
Jones, Carolyn 4, 15–16
Jones, Eddie 99, 112
Jones, Gary 178
Jones, Henry 86
Jones, Kirk "Sticky" 41
Jones, Mickey 125
Jones, Orlando 162
Jones, Richard T. 186
Jones, Sarah 21
Jones, Walter Emanuel 227
Joosten, Kathryn 105
Jordan, Bobbi 198
Jordan, Jeremy 183–184
Josselyn, Randy 8, 63
Jow, Malese 177
Judge, Christopher 178
Juliani, Alessandro 31
Jurasik, Peter 28

Kaake, Jeff 170
Kake, Patrick 53
Kane, Christian 111
Kapelos, John 78
Kaplan, Caroline 146
Kariti, Eddy 34
Karloff, Boris 86

Karpluk, Erin 220
Karsenti, Sabine 55
Kartheiser, Vincent 25
Karvelas, Robert 83
Kasznar, Kurt 108
Katsulas, Andreas 28
Katt, William 7, 88
Kaufman, David 63
Kavelaars, Ingrid 221
Keating, Dominic 174
Keating, Larry 225
Keating, Michael 220
Keating, Trenna 221
Keery, Joe 227
Keitel, Harvey 224
Kelleher, Tim 221
Keller, Jason 226
Keller, Shane 226
Kelley, DeForest 172–173
Kelley, Devin 226
Kelly, Aimee 229
Kelly, Craig 221
Kelly, Joanne 36, 206
Kelly, Morgan 220
Kelton, Richard 148
Kemmer, Ed 4, 168–169
Kennedy, Jamie 85
Kennedy, Jessica Parker 158
Kennedy, Maria Doyle 139
Kenny, Shannon 99–100
Kerr, Elizabeth 128
Keymáh, T'Keyah Crystal 187
Khali, Simbi 188
Kiel, Richard 98
Kilner, Kevin 222
Kim, Daniel Dae 113–114
Kim, John Harlan 111
Kim, Yunjin 113–114
King, Candice 202–203
King, Ginifer 91
King, T.W. 49
Kingston, Harry 43
Kirby, Bruce 198
Kirshner, Mia 222
Kitt, Eartha 30
Kittles, Tory 221
Kleintank, Luke 224
Knight, Maxim 222
Knight, Wayne 166, 188–189
Knighton, Zachary 77
Knudsen, Erik 54
Knyvette, Sally 220
Koaho, Mpho 222
Koch, Alexander 229
Koenig, Walter 172
Kohli, Rahul 223

Kopell, Bernie 84
Kosarin, Kira 190
Kovacs, Bela 168–169
Kozak, Harley Jane 217
Krant, Judith 228
Kranz, Fran 61
Krause, Brian 49
Kravitz, Steven 40
Kretschmann, Thomas 222
Kreuk, Kristin 34, 163
Krige, Alice 177
Krinsky, Scott 52
Kristen, Marta 5, 115–116
Krüger, Christiane 172
Kurtz, Swoosie 147
Kwanten, Ryan 196

LaBelle, Rob 222
Labine, Tyler 99
Laborteaux, Matthew 208–209
Lachman, Dichen 61
Lacroix, Duncan 141
Lamarr, Hedy 18
Lamas, Lorenzo 223
Lampert, Zohra 86
Lancaster, Sarah 52
Landau, Martin 7, 46, 126–127, 168
Landers, Audrey 94
Landes, Michael 112, 170–171
Landis, Nina 138
Lando, Joe 158
Lane, Allan 225
Lang, Charley 221
Lange, Hope 84–85
Lanter, Matt 177
LaPaglia, Jonathan 160
Lark, Maria 122
Larkin, Christopher 96
Larroquette, John 111
Larsen, Larry 116
Larson, Jack 17–18
Larter, Ali 92–93
La Selva, Anita 222
Laskey, Kathleen 220
Lauren, Tammy 226
Laurie, Piper 198
Lawless, Lucy 8, 82, 215–217
Lawrence, Cary 227
Lawrence, Mark Christopher 52
Lawrence, Nathan 217
Le Clark, Maya 190
Ledford, Brandy 24–25, 99–100

## 240 Index

Ledger, Heath 149
Lee, Alexondra 170–171
Lee, James Kyson 92
Lee, Jonna 225
Lee, Ki Hong 137
Lee, Lela 228
Lee, Nelson 41
Lee, Reggie 89
Lee, Sheryl 142, 198–199
Lee, Will Yun 39, 209–210
Leeshock, Robert 222
Lefevre, Rachelle 229
Lehman, Trent 134–135
Leick, Hudson 82
Leigh, Chyler 183
Leitso, Tyron 213, 220
LeMay, John D. 80–81
Lemke, Anthony 87, 221
Lennix, Harry 61
Leonidas, Stephanie 221
Lester, Terry 26
Letscher, Matt 224
Levering, Kate 64
Levi, Zachary 52, 205
Levine, Robert 182
Levis, Patrick 165
Lewis, Al 130
Lewis, Gary 141
Lien, Jennifer 176
Lilly, Evangeline 27, 113–114
Lincoln, Andrew 229
Lindo, Delroy 35
Lintel, Michelle 40
Lintz, Mackenzie 229
Lipton, Peggy 198–199
Lisandrello, Nina 34
List, Peyton 77, 228
Lithgow, John 188
Lively, Eric 165
Lloyd, Norman 160
Lloyd, Sabrina 227
Lobo, Stephen 54, 141
Lockhart, June 5, 115–116
Lofton, Cirroc 173
Logan, Samantha 227
Loken, Kristanna 141
Lombard, Karina 79
Long, Richard 134
Lonsdale, Keiynan 75
Lopinto, Dorian 159
Lords, Traci 222
Loring, Lisa 15–16
Lorne, Marion 38
Lotz, Caity 224
Louis, Justin 125–126
Love, Darris 159

Lumley, Joanna 136
Lund, Deanna 108
Lund, Jordan 123
Lund, Steve 220
Lupus, Peter 126
Lyden, Robert 151
Lyons, David 226

MacCorkindale, Simon 120
MacDonald, Adam 220
Macfarlane, Luke 106
Machado, Justina 125
Macht, Gabriel 225
MacIntosh, Tammy 73
MacIntyre, Marguerite 107
Mack, Allison 163–164
MacKenzie, J.C. 56–57
MacLachlan, Kyle 35, 142, 198
MacLane, Barton 97–98
MacMichael, Florence 225
Macnee, Patrick 27, 83, 136, 143
MacNeill, Peter 87
Madekwe, Ashley 154
Madison, Bailee 87
Madsen, Virginia 210
Maeve, Stella 118
Maggart, Brandon 103
Maher, Sean 74–75
Majors, Lee 39
Makin, Titus, Jr. 177
Malco, Romany 225
Malicki-Sanchez, Keram 205–206
Mallari, Alex, Jr. 221
Mamet, Clara 135
Manasseri, Michael 207
Mando, Michael 139
Manheim, Camryn 71, 85
Mankuma, Blu 78, 150
Mann, Terrence 63
Mansell, Carol 8, 63
Mansfield, Ben 145
Mansfield, Sally 4, 151
Manson, Amy 220
Manson, Shirley 186
Mantegna, Joe 104
Mantez, Dolores 228
Mantock, Madeleine 228
March, Forbes 132
Marcos, Lisa 224
Marcus, Jeff 22–23
Marcus, Stephen 227
Markim, Al 193
Markinson, Brian 54

Marlowe, Chris 94
Marotte, Carl 10, 38
Marquette, Chris 104
Marsden, Jason 130
Marshall, Don 108
Marshall, James 142, 198
Marsters, James 44
Martin, Dean Paul 125
Martin, Jared 72, 205–206
Martin, Jesse L. 75
Martin, Kevin Michael 223
Martin-Green, Sonequa 229
Martinez, A. 208–209
Martinez, Natalie 229
Maslany, Tatiana 139
Masohn, Mercedes 227
Massey, Kyle 187
Masterson, Alanna 229
Masterson, Fay 223
Mastrantonio, Mary Elizabeth 111
Matarazzo, Gaten 227
Matchett, Kari 99
Matern, Anik 227
Matheson, Don 108
Matheson, Tim 197
Matson, April 107
Matter, Niall 69, 117
Mattsson, Helena 227
Mayer, Ken 168–169
Mazurki, Mike 100
McBride, Chi 147
McBride, Melissa 229
McCafferty, Mike 99
McCalla, Irish 161
McCallum, David 99, 204
McCamus, Tom 132
McCauley, Peter 117
McClellan, Katie 35
McClintock, Eddie 36, 206
McClure, Doug 140
McClure, Kandyse 31
McCouch, Grayson 219
McDermitt, Josh 229
McDermott, Dean 125
McDonnell, Mary 12, 31
McDonough, Tamsen 106
McDorman, Jake 111–112
McDowall, Roddy 72–73
McFadden, Gates 175–176
McGee, Jack 170
McGill, Everett 198
McGovern, Elizabeth 189
McGowan, Rose 49–50
McGrath, Katie 123–124, 222

# Index 241

McHattie, Stephen 33, 94
McIver, Rose 223
McKee, Roxanne 221
McKenna, Alex 217
McKenzie, Jacqueline 79, 161
McKillip, Britt 59
McLaughlin, Caleb 227
McLaughlin, Jake 35
McMahon, Julian 49
McManus, Michael 224
McNamara, Brian 123
McNamara, Katherine 226
McNeill, Robert Duncan 176–177
McQueen, Steven R. 202
McPartlin, Ryan 52
McTavish, Graham 141
Meade, Emily 223
Meaney, Colm 173, 175
Meara, Anne 22
Medlin, Lex 64
Meester, Leighton 228
Mehler, Tobias 31, 217–218
Melvin, Murray 227
Mennell, Laura 23
Menzies, Heather 224
Menzies, Tobias 141
Merchant, Tamzin 154
Meredith, Burgess 30
Merico, Nick 70
Meriwether, Lee 130–131, 191–192
Merkerson, S. Epatha 121
Merlin, Jan 193
Merton, Zienia 168
Messing, Debra 145
Metz, Belinda 165
Meunier, David 221
Meyer, Dina 40, 226
Meyers, Jonathan Rhys 222
Michalka, Aly 223, 226
Midkiff, Dale 191
Milano, Alyssa 9, 49–50
Miles, Ben 222
Millen, Ari 139
Miller, Ben 145
Miller, Mark Thomas 125
Miller, Marvin 169
Miller, Paul 146
Miller, Valarie Rae 56–57
Miller, Wentworth 104–105, 224
Milligan, Spencer 109
Mills, Juliet 134
Minnette, Dylan 156
Mison, Tom 10, 124, 162

Mitchell, Elizabeth 69, 113, 201–202, 226
Mitchell, Luke 228
Mitchell, Silas Weir 89
Mitra, Rhona 223
Modine, Matthew 146
Moffat, Donald 224
Mohr, Jay 85
Mol, Gretchen 224
Moltke, Alexandra 57–58
Monaghan, Dominic 77, 113
Monaghan, Marjorie 170
Monarque, Steve 80
Montana, Amber 91
Montgomery, Anthony 174
Montgomery, Belinda 224
Montgomery, Elizabeth 4, 37–38, 179–180, 185
Montgomery, Janet 154
Mooney, Peter 220
Moore, Shemar 40
Moorehead, Agnes 5, 12, 37–38, 180
Moorer, Margo 161
Morey, Bill 197
Morgan, Colin 123
Morgan, Jeffrey Dean 71
Morgan, Lindsey 96
Mori, Naoko 228
Moriarty, Erin 104
Morley, Bob 96
Morris, Greg 126
Morris, Julianne 219
Morris, Phil 126
Morrison, James 227
Morrison, Jennifer 138, 184
Morrison, Shelley 77–78
Morrissey, David 229
Morrow, Karen 185
Morse, Barry 168
Morton, Howard 130
Morton, Joe 69, 123, 146
Moss, Carrie-Anne 104
Moyer, Stephen 196–197
Mudaliar, Tharini 138
Mulgrew, Kate 3, 57, 101–102, 176
Mulhare, Edward 84
Mulheren, Michael 154
Mull, Martin 153–154
Mullaney, Jack 100, 133
Mumy, Bill 28
Mumy, Billy 115
Murphy, Ben 223
Murphy, Erin 5, 37–38, 180
Murphy, Jonathan 224

Murphy, Sam 189
Murray, Chad Michael 18–19
Murray, Jaime 221
Murray, James 145
Muscat, Olivia Williams 61–62
Mustafa, Isaiah 226
Muth, Ellen 59
Myles, Eve 228
Myles, Sophia 128, 198

Nabors, Jim 116
Nagra, Parminder 21
Nance, Jack 198
Napier, Alan 30
Nascimento, Nadia-Leigh 219
Nash, Joseph 76
Navin, John P., Jr. 8, 103
Neal, Dylan 42, 171
Needham, Tracey 204
Neill, Noel 4, 17–18, 110, 164
Neill, Sam 21
Neitling, Marissa 223
Nelson, John Allen 161
Neustaedter, Alex 221
Nevin, Brooke 79, 219
Newman, Jaime Ray 67
Newmar, Julie 30, 133, 163
Newton, John Haymes 7, 182–183
Newton, Omari 54
Nicholls, Anthony 47
Nichols, Nichelle 3, 172–173, 200
Nichols, Rachel 54
Nicholson, Julianne 225
Nicole, Jasika 81
Nieves, Daniela 70–71
Nigra, Christina 140
Nimoy, Leonard 126, 172–173, 200
Nipar, Yvette 150
Noble, John 81, 162
Nolan, Tom 140
Nolin, Gena Lee 161
Norris, Dean 228–229
Norton, Cliff 100

O'Byrne, Brian F. 77
O'Connell, Charlie 227
O'Connell, Jerry 227
O'Connor, Kevin J. 225
O'Connor, Renée 8, 82, 215–216
O'Connor, Tim 43

## 242 Index

O'Dell, Jennifer 117
O'Dell, Tony 225
O'Donoghue, Colin 138–139
O'Farrell, Conor 221
Ohama, Natsuko 78–79
O'Hara, Jenny 94
O'Hare, Michael 28
O'Heaney, Caitlin 8, 50
Oka, Masi 92
Olagundoye, Toks 135
Oldford, Britne 226
Olejnik, Craig 224
Oleynik, Larisa 9, 159
Olivero, Chris 107
Olmos, Edward James 31
O'Loughlin, Alex 128, 198
O'Mara, Jason 224
O'Neil, Melissa 221
O'Neill, Michael 71
Ontkean, Michael 198
O'Quinn, Terry 113, 225, 227
Ormond, Julia 210
O'Rourke, Grant 141
Orth, David 117
Orth, Zak 226
Osborn, Lyn 168–169
Osment, Haley Joel 85
O'Toole, Annette 163
Owen, Beverly 130
Owen, Kai 228

Pace, Lee 147, 213
Pacey, Steven 220
Page, Samuel 226
Palencia, Brina 177
Paley, Phillip 109
Palladino, Erik 227
Palmer, Zoie 11, 114–115, 221
Panabaker, Danielle 75–76
Panabaker, Kay 225
Panettiere, Hayden 35–36, 92
Pao, Pisay 229
Paquin, Anna 196–197
Pardo, J.D. 226
Paré, Michael 88, 227
Parfitt, Judy 8, 50
Parish, Sarah 220
Park, Grace 31
Park, Linda 174–175
Parker, Andrea 226
Parker, Lara 57–58
Parker, Leni 222
Parnell, Charles 223
Parrilla, Lana 138–139, 184
Parsons, Patsy 4, 151
Pasdar, Adrian 36, 92–93, 134

Pastene, Robert 43
Pasternak, Reagan 220
Patinkin, Mandy 59
Patrick, Butch 130
Patrick, Ian 135
Patrick, Lee 193–195
Patrick, Robert 214–215
Patterson, Merritt 226
Patterson, Scott 70
Patton, Candice 75
Patton, Will 204, 222
Paul, Adrian 205, 228
Paulson, Sarah 219
Pays, Amanda 225
Pearce, Jacqueline 220
Pellegrino, Mark 228
Pemberton, Amy 224
Penghlis, Thaao 126
Penikett, Tahmoh 31, 61–62
Pennington, Julia 123
Pennington, Marla 163
Perlman, Ron 33, 48
Perrineau, Harold 113
Pertwee, Jon 60, 164
Pescow, Donna 140
Peters, Evan 99
Petersen, Luvia 54
Petersen, Paul 77
Phillips, Avi 120
Phillips, Betty 136
Phillips, Ethan 176
Phillips, Mackenzie 165
Phipps, Grace 137
Picardo, Robert 176
Pierce, Maggie 133–134
Pierpoint, Eric 22
Pietz, Amy 137
Pileggi, Mitch 214
Pinder, Alex 138
Piper, Billie 60–61
Pirie, Tommie-Amber 220
Platt, Edward 83
Playten, Alice 116
Polito, Jon 220
Porter, Bobby 148
Porter, Todd 208–209
Poston, Tom 128
Potts, Andrew-Lee 145–146
Pounder, CCH 12, 63, 206
Powell, Randy 224
Powers, Stefanie 5, 86
Praed, Michael 158
Pratt, Victoria 53, 132
Prentis, Lou 43
Preston, Carrie 196
Preston, Cynthia 228

Price, Lindsay 67
Price, Molly 39
Price, Vincent 30
Price-Francis, Amy 228
Priest, Pat 130
Priestley, Jason 196
Prince, Karim 222
Prine, Andrew 207
Progosh, Tim 219
Prout, Kirsten 107
Provost-Chalkley, Dominique 214
Pruner, Karl 228
Puckler, Damien 89
Purcell, Dominic 224
Purvis, Alexandra 144
Pygram, Wayne 73
Pyper, Laura 93–94
Pyper-Ferguson, John 223

Quadflieg, Christian 172
Qualley, Margaret 223
Qualls, DJ 224, 229
Quan, Samantha 189
Quigley, Kevin 161
Quinn, Danny 170
Quinn, Ed 42, 69
Quinn, Glenn 25
Quinto, Zachary 92

Rabe, Lily 208
Radford, Natalie 186
Raimi, Ted 157, 215
Raine, Jackson 220
Rajan, Ritesh 180–181
Ralph, Christopher 219
Ralph, Jason 118
Ramamurthy, Sendhil 34, 92
Ramsey, David 219
Rath, Jesse 221
Rath, Meaghan 34–35
Raven-Symoné 10–11, 187–188
Rawlins, Michael 228
Rawls, Lou 32
Reaves, Shawn 196
Reddick, Lance 81
Redmond, Marge 77–78
Reed, Nikki 162
Reedus, Norman 229
Reese, Della 12, 195
Reeser, Autumn 225
Reeves, George 4, 17–18, 109, 113
Reeves, Scott 132
Regan, Bridget 18

Index 243

Reichert, Tanja 149
Reilly, Charles Nelson 84
Reitz, Ric 228
Renée, Ciara 224
Repp, Stafford 30
Reuben, Gloria 125
Rey, Alejandro 77–78
Reynolds, Burt 140
Reynolds, Debbie 103
Rhea, Caroline 153, 171
Rhys-Davies, John 217, 227
Rich, Christopher 50
Richards, J. August 25
Richards, Kim 134–135
Richards, Kyle 63
Richardson, Cameron 226
Richardson, Kevin Michael 223
Richardson, Salli 123
Richardson-Sellers, Maisie 224
Richardson-Whitfield, Salli 41, 69, 180–181
Richert, Nate 153–154, 171
Rickards, Emily Bett 219
Riecke, Addison 190
Rigg, Diana 5, 27, 143
Riggs, Chandler 229
Righetti, Amanda 221
Riley, Michael 220
Rippy, Leon 156
Ritter, Jason 70, 104
Ritter, Krysten 104
Robbins, Ryan 155
Roberds, Michael 136
Roberts, Michael D. 120
Roberts, Sean O. 141
Robertson, Britt 158
Robertson, Clive 227
Robertson, Kathleen 120
Robertson, Kimmy 198
Robey, Louise 80
Roche, Claudette 227
Roché, Sebastian 149, 225
Rock, Blossom 12, 15–16
Rocket, Charles 225
Rodriguez, Adam 219
Rodriguez, Percy 227
Roemer, Sarah 70
Roerig, Zach 202
Rogers, Kylie 208
Roiz, Sasha 89
Romero, Cesar 30
Romijn, Rebecca 67, 111
Roncetti, Joe 222
Rooker, Michael 229

Rooper, Jemima 11, 93–94, 220
Rorke, Hayden 97–98
Rose, Cristine 92–93
Rose, Emily 91
Rosenbaum, Michael 163
Rosende, Alberto 226
Ross, Joe E. 100
Ross-Leming, Eugenie 94
Roth, Andrea 150
Rothery, Teryl 178
Routh, Brandon 224
Rowan, Gay 179
Rowland, Rodney 227
Roy, Drew 222
Rozon, Tim 214
Rubinek, Saul 63, 206
Rubinoff, Marla 63
Rue, Sara 67
Russ, Tim 176
Russell, Kurt 178
Ryan, Jay 34
Ryan, Jeri 10, 102, 176–177, 221
Ryan, Michelle 39
Ryder, Lisa 24, 78, 203
Ryder, Winona 227

Sabàto, Antonio, Jr. 66
Sachs, Sharon 220
Sackhoff, Katee 31
Sadler, William 152, 213
Sahay, Vik 52
Sahely, Ed 150
Sainsbury, Amber 93
Saint, Eva Marie 43
Saint Ryan, John 149
Sakovich, Nancy Anne 146–147
Salmon, Colin 93
Sams, Jeffrey D. 227
Samuels, Skyler 137
Sanada, Hiroyuki 71
Sanchez, Marco 157
Sanders, Christoph 85
Sandoval, Miguel 122
San Giacomo, Laura 156
Santiago, Zak 217–218
Santoni, Reni 120
Sara, Mia 40
Sargent, Dick 37–38, 63, 179
Savage, John 56–57
Saylor, Katie 72
Scagliotti, Allison 62, 180–181, 206
Scarabelli, Michele 22

Scarfe, Alan 160
Scarpelli, Glenn 103
Scarwid, Diana 213
Schedeen, Anne 21–22
Scheider, Roy 157
Schell, Catherine 168
Schell, Ronnie 63
Schmid, Kyle 42
Schnapp, Noah 227
Schnarre, Monika 220
Schneider, John 163
Schreiber, Avery 133
Schuck, John 130–131, 198
Schull, Amanda 228
Schulman, Emily 163
Schwarzenegger, Arnold 54, 187
Scoggins, Tracy 28, 112
Scolari, Peter 95
Scorsone, Caterina 125
Scott, Ashley 40
Scott, Judith 223
Scott, Kathryn Leigh 57
Scott, Klea 225
Scotti, Vito 77
Scrofano, Melanie 214
Searcy, Nick 160, 219
Seeberg, Xenia 224
Selby, David 57–58
Sellecca, Connie 7, 88
Sequoyah, Johnny 35
Serratos, Christian 229
Server, Eric 43
Sewell, George 228
Sewell, Rufus 224
Shackelford, Ted 170
Shanks, Michael 178
Shatner, William 101, 172, 186, 200
Shaver, Helen 144
Shaw, Reta 84
Shayne, Robert 17–18
Shea, Dan 178
Shea, John 112–113, 132
Sheehan, Robert 217
Sheldon, Jack 87
Shepherd, Cybill 67
Sheppard, W. Morgan 225
Sheridan, Lisa 99, 222
Sheridan, Rondell 187
Sherwood, Dominic 226
Sherwood, Madeleine 5, 77–78
Shilling, Jodi 188
Shimerman, Armin 173
Shinkoda, Peter 222

## 244 Index

Shirley, Mariah 219
Show, Grant 226
Shum, Harry, Jr. 226
Siddig, Alexander 173
Sierra, Gregory 166
Silk, Anna 11, 114
Silla, Felix 43
Silva, Leslie 225
Simcoe, Anthony 73
Simmons, Henry 20
Simms, Lise 226
Simon, Josette 220
Sims, Jocko 223
Sinelnikoff, Michael 117
Singer, Lori 204
Singer, Marc 201
Sirtis, Marina 8, 175–176
Six, Sean 22–23
Skarsgard, Alexander 196
Skarsten, Rachel 40
Skinner, Edna 225
Sky, Jennifer 53
Sladen, Elizabeth 60–61, 164
Sloane, Barry 208
Smith, Arjay 223
Smith, Brody 136
Smith, Kellita 229
Smith, Kevin 215–216
Smith, Kurtwood 226
Smith, Lane 112, 201
Smith, Lauren Lee 132, 224
Smith, Matt 60
Smith, Paris 70
Smitrovich, Bill 70
Smurfit, Victoria 222
Snow, William 117
Sofer, Rena 220
Solo, Ksenia 114–115
Somerhalder, Ian 202
Sorbo, Kevin 24
Sossamon, Shannyn 124, 128, 162
Sothern, Ann 133
Sothern, Harry 43
Spader, James 178
Spano, Joe 123
Spearritt, Hannah 145
Spence, Jennifer 54
Spence, Sebastian 222
Spencer-Nairn, Tara 224
Spiner, Brent 175, 190
Spiridakos, Tracy 226
Stahl, Lisa 32
Stahl, Richard 198
Staite, Jewel 74–75, 227
Stamberg, Josh 64

Standen, Clive 220
Stanford, Aaron 228
Stark, Mya 103
Stashwick, Todd 228
Stebbings, Peter 224
Steen, Jessica 66
Steenburgen, Mary 104
Sterling, Robert 193–194
Stern, Dawn 227
Stevens, Fisher 65
Stevenson, Cynthia 59
Stevenson, Juliet 220
Stewart, French 188
Stewart, Josh 225
Stewart, Mel 185
Stewart, Patrick 175
Stewart, Rob 106, 141–142
Stinson, Donavon 189
Stone, Benjamin 137
Stone, Jennifer 211
Storke, Adam 145
Strahovski, Yvonne 52, 205
Strait, Steven 222
Strangis, Judy 6, 68
Strassman, Marcia 228
Strathairn, David 23
Stratten, Dorothy 43
Strong, Nicholas 229
Stuart, Katie 55
Sukowa, Barbara 228
Sullivan, Susan 105
Supiran, Jerry 163
Sutcliffe, David 146
Sutherland, Kristine 44–45
Swanson, Kristy 65
Sweet, Shane 223
Sylvester, William 223

Tagawa, Cary-Hiroyuki 170, 224
Tailor, Jade 118
Takei, George 172
Tallman, Chris 190
Tallman, Patricia 20
Tamblyn, Amber 104
Tamblyn, Russ 105
Tambor, Jeffrey 225
Tapping, Amanda 46–47, 155, 178
Taranto, Glenn 136
Tate, Jack 223
Tate, Nick 168
Tatum, Jenna Dewan 210
Taylor, Eliza 12, 96–97
Taylor, Rachael 104, 227
Taylor, Rip 63

Teate, Rachel 229
Teegarden, Aimee 177
Tefkin, Blair 201
Telek, April 223
Templeman, Simon 135
Tennant, David 60–61, 104, 164
Tergesen, Lee 207
Tessier, Christian 219
Theaker, Deborah 120
Theroux, Justin 223
Thomas, Bruce 107
Thomas, Frankie 193
Thomas, Gareth 172, 220
Thomas, Gay 123
Thomas, Jay 128
Thomas, Serena Scott 219
Thomas, Tamara Craig 225
Thomerson, Tim 148
Thompson, Andrea 11, 28–29
Thompson, Susanna 11, 219
Thoms, Tracie 213
Thorson, Linda 27
Thurman, Annie 146
Tierney, Jacob 222
Tiplady, Brittany 225
Tipper, Dominique 222
Tobeck, Joel 53
Toboni, Jacqueline 89
Tochi, Brian 167
Tonkin, Phoebe 158
Torres, Gina 53, 74–75
Torv, Anna 81
Toubia, Emeraude 226
Toussaint, Lorraine 156
Towne, Aline 221
Trachtenberg, Michelle 44, 182
Tracy, Keegan Connor 223
Trammell, Sam 196–197
Traval, Wil 104
Treas, Terri 22–23
Trevino, Michael 202
Trinneer, Connor 174–175
Troughton, Patrick 60
Tuck, Hillary 95
Tuddenham, Peter 220
Tudyk, Alan 74–75
Tulloch, Bitsie 89
Tupu, Lani 73
Turco, Paige 12, 96, 219
Turner, Bree 89
Turner, Sophie 222
Tyler, Aisha 85
Tyler, Liv 223

# Index 245

Ullerup, Emilie 155
Ullman, Raviv 226
Underwood, Blair 70
Urb, Johann 67
Urich, Robert 185

Vail, Justina 160
Valdes, Carlos 75
Valentine, Scott 40–41
Valley, Mark 81
Vance, Courtney B. 77
Vanco, Marcus 226
van der Pol, Anneliese 187
Vandervoort, Laura 69, 201–202, 220
Van Dyke, Hilary 130, 132
Van Dyke, Jerry 133
Van Holt, Brian 190
Van Winkle, Travis 223
Vassey, Liz 228
Vassilieva, Sofia 65, 122
Vaughan, Leona 229
Vaughn, Robert 86
Velazquez, Diego 190
Venito, Lenny 135
Ventimiglia, Milo 36, 92–93, 208
Ventresca, Vincent 99, 145
Verbeek, Lotte 141
Verdi, Michele 70–71
Vidal, Lisa 70
Visitor, Nana 173
Visnjic, Goran 71
Vogel, Mike 229
Vokey, Josh 139
von Detten, Erik 165

Wade, Henderson 71–72
Waggoner, Lyle 6, 212–213
Wagner, Jill 41
Wagner, Lindsay 6, 39, 166
Wahlstrom, Becky 104
Walger, Sonya 77
Walker, Jeffrey 138
Walker, Sullivan 66
Walsh, J.T. 221
Walston, Ray 225
Walters, Stephen 141
Walters, Susan 226
Wang, Garrett 176
Warburton, Patrick 228
Ward, Burt 30

Ward, Dave "Squatch" 165
Ward, Megan 221
Ward, Robin 179
Warren, Amanda 223
Washington, Isaiah 96
Watts, Naomi 227
Weatherly, Michael 56–57
Weatherwax, Ken 15–16
Weber, Brent 226
Weber, Jake 65, 122, 219
Webster, Derek 208
Webster, Victor 54, 132
Wechsler, Nick 152
Weiss, Michael T. 226
Weisser, Morgan 227
Welch, Michael 104
Weller, Peter 225
Welling, Tom 163
Wells, Scott 182–183
Wen, Ming-Na 12, 20
Wendel, Autumn 70
Wendel, Elmarie 188
Wesley, Paul 202
Wesley, Rutina 196
West, Adam 30
West, Shane 154
Wexler, Skyler 139–140
Whalin, Justin 112
Wheaton, Wil 175
Whigham, Shea 18–19
Whipple, Randy 133
Whipple, Sam 160
White, Brian 34
White, David 37–38
Whittle, Ricky 96–97
Wiggins, Chris 80–81
Wilcox, Mary Charlotte 120
Willes, Christine 59
Willett, Chad 220
Williams, Genelle 206, 220
Williams, Gregory Alan 32
Williams, Guy 115–116
Williams, Maisie 223
Williams, Robin 128–129
Williams, Vanessa 227
Williams-Stirling, Kedar 229
Willis, Jerome 170
Wilson, Alexandra 123
Wilson, Denisea 70
Wilson, Leanne 228
Wilson, Reno 220
Wilson, Richard 123

Wilson, Scott 229
Winchester, Philip 220
Winfield, Paul 50
Wint, Maurice Dean 146, 186
Winter, Eric 210
Winter, Katia 162
Winters, Dean 54
Winters, Jonathan 128–129
Wisdom, Tom 221
Wise, Ray 142, 198–199
Witwer, Sam 34
Wolf, Scott 201
Wolfhard, Finn 227
Woll, Deborah Ann 196
Wolmark, Zevi 182
Woodard, Alfre 197
Woodburn, Danny 170–171
Woodland, Lauren 22
Woods, Barbara Alyn 95
Woods, Christine 77
Woods, Ren 33
Woodside, D.B. 224
Woodvine, Mary 170
Woolvett, Gordon Michael 24
Worley, Billie 65
Worthy, Rick 118
Wright, J. Madison 66
Wright, Max 21–22, 125
Wright, Michael 201
Wuhrer, Kari 227
Wyle, Noah 111, 222

Xavier, Michael 220

Yagher, Jeff 201
Yde, Breanna 91
Yeoman, Owain 187
Yeun, Steven 229
Yoba, Malik 23
Yoo, Aaron 228
York, Dick 4, 37–38, 179
Young, Alan 225
Young, Chris 225
Young, Heather 108
Youngblood, Rob 170

Zane, Lisa 149
Zang, Nat 229
Zano, Nick 224
Zaremba, John 191–192
Zimmerman, Joey 66
Zylka, Chris 158, 223

www.ingramcontent.com/pod-product-compliance
Ingram Content Group UK Ltd.
Pitfield, Milton Keynes, MK11 3LW, UK
UKHW041938140426
5217IPUK00014B/551